BARRON'S

CHSPE

HOW TO PREPARE FOR THE CALIFORNIA HIGH SCHOOL PROFICIENCY EXAMINATION

5TH EDITION

Sharon Weiner Green
Formerly English Department
Merritt College, California

Michael Siemon
Consultant
CGA

Lexy Green
English Department
Pinole Valley High School, California

BARRON'S

All inquiries should be addressed to:
Barron's Educational Series, Inc.
250 Wireless Boulevard
Hauppauge, New York 11788

Library of Congress Catalog Card No. 92-36238

International Standard Book No. 0-7641-0128-5

International Standard Serial No. 1095-0176

PRINTED IN THE UNITED STATES OF AMERICA

9876

Contents

Preface

We have prepared this book to help those students who wish to take advantage of California's special opportunity—the California High School Proficiency Examination (CHSPE). In addition to providing three chapters reviewing essential basic skills, we have included three practice tests in this book. However, tests change and from time to time the testing authorities will include new types of questions to see how well they work as indicators of student ability. Newly developed tests are even more likely than the older, established ones to change, both in content and in format.

In its twenty years of administration, the California High School Proficiency Examination has changed visibly: in Part One of the test, the written part, students were originally asked to show their ability to fill out forms (statements of employee grievances, gift order forms, etc.); currently they are asked to show their ability to write a brief essay.

We have had a lot of help in putting together this book, and we would like to thank the people who assisted and/or put up with us. In particular, we thank our fellow Barron's authors who allowed us to use review materials from their books *Barron's How to Prepare for the Test of Standard Written English* and *Barron's How to Prepare for the New High School Equivalency Examination (GED)*. In addition, we thank Deborah Abramovitz, Nathan Oliver, and Chris Waters, who passed the test; Bob Valentine of California Proficiency Testing, who answered our questions about the appropriateness of our model tests; and David Green and the two John Seals, who coped.

Introduction

WHAT THE TEST IS LIKE AND HOW TO STUDY FOR IT

Who May Take the Test?

High school students who are 16 or older may take the California High School Proficiency Examination. Students younger than 16 may also take the test if they have already finished the tenth grade or will finish the tenth grade at the end of the semester in which they plan to take the test. If you are 16 or older on the date the test is given, or if you have already completed or are just about to complete the tenth grade, you may take the test. You do not need your parents' permission to take the test. You do need your high school guidance counselor's signature on your registration form to do so.

What Happens Once You Pass the Test?

Once you pass the test, you will receive a Certificate of Proficiency from the State Board of Education. The Certificate of Proficiency is legally equivalent to a high school diploma, but it is not a diploma. Even if you have received your Certificate of Proficiency, you may still have to continue to attend high school: California state law provides that students younger than 18 who do not have a regular high school diploma may not leave high school until they

1) have turned 16 years of age, *and*
2) have received their Certificate of Proficiency, *and*
3) have presented their school with signed parental permission forms allowing them to leave school.

To be excused from attending high school, you need to have your parents' permission.

What Happens Once You Leave High School?

Once you leave high school with a Certificate of Proficiency, you have many options facing you. Your Certificate of Proficiency will qualify you for admission to a California community college: it is recognized as the equivalent of the high school diploma and is accepted by community colleges throughout the state. Outside California, community colleges differ from state to state in accepting the Certificate of Proficiency for admission; however, more and more states are developing proficiency examinations of their own, and the proficiency certificates are becoming more widely accepted each year.

Your Certificate of Proficiency also will prove useful to you should you wish to enlist in the Armed Services: it is recognized as the equivalent of the high school diploma by most branches of the service (you must nevertheless meet service age requirements before you enlist). Your Certificate of Proficiency also will show potential employers and college admission committees that you have mastered those basic skills taught in California public schools. Both potential employers and four-year colleges may ask you to take additional aptitude and achievement tests; they may also ask you to provide them with a transcript of your high school record. Your options are those of a regular high school graduate: college, work, travel, military service. You also have one additional option: if you leave high school with a Certificate of Proficiency, at any time before you turn 18 years of age you may re-enter high school and resume your course work there.

How Do You Sign Up for the CHSPE?

You need to fill out the registration form at the back of the *Information Bulletin*. Send the completed form and a check or money order for $47 (made out to CHSPE) to the address at the top of the form. You may also pay by credit card by filling out the information at the bottom of the form. An envelope is included for mailing the registration form. Your high school counselor should have copies of the *Information Bulletin* or you can ask for one at any public library. If you have trouble finding a copy, California Proficiency Testing can be reached at (916) 383-9506.

Do You Need Permission to Take the CHSPE?

No. You don't need permission from your parents or from your school to take the test. You do need to have your counselor fill out the verification of eligibility at the bottom of the registration form. The verification isn't necessary if you are over 18, but it's a good idea anyway. You can omit the verification if you are not currently enrolled in high school.

When Is the Test Given?

The CHSPE is generally given twice each year, in November and April. Your registration must be received at least ten days prior to the date of the test (do it earlier if possible) in order for California Proficiency Testing to send you an admission ticket for the test. Dates for the test and the deadlines for registration are printed in the *Information Bulletin*. If you miss the deadline, you may still be able to register for the test. Call California Proficiency Testing at (916) 383-9506 for information on "walk-in" registration.

If you need to make special arrangements because of religious observance, you must contact California Proficiency Testing at least four weeks before the test date. You must provide evidence of your need, such as a letter from an appropriate authority attesting to your religious conviction.

Where Is the Test Given?

There are over 60 test centers in high schools and colleges throughout California. The locations are listed in the *Information Bulletin,* and you should select the one that is most convenient for you. If you would have to travel over 100 miles to get to the nearest test center, you can ask California Proficiency Testing to arrange for a special test center. This request must accompany your registration form. It must be received by California Proficiency Testing at least four weeks before the test date. Please note that this deadline is significantly earlier than the normal registration deadline.

If you need to make special arrangements because of a physical disability, you must contact California Proficiency Testing at least four weeks before the test date. You must provide evidence of your need, such as a letter from a physician verifying your disability.

What Should You Bring to the Test?

You must bring the admission ticket and a photo ID. Acceptable identification includes a school ID card with your photograph, a permanent driver's license or a DMV ID. The *Information Bulletin* lists a few more possibilities, and you can call the testing service at the phone number given in the bulletin if you have questions about your ID. This is important. If you don't have acceptable ID, you will not be permitted to take the test. The admission ticket is also important. If you don't receive this by the Tuesday eight days after the registration deadline, you must call the testing service to confirm whether you are registered for the test.

You should also bring a No. 2 pencil and an eraser with you. (There should be pencils at the test center, but play it safe.) Do not bring anything like paper, rulers, calculators, or books. These aids are prohibited, and if you use them, you can be dismissed from the test.

How Do You Find Out the Test Results?

All examinees will receive a report of "Pass" or "Not Pass" in the mail from the testing service. If you are enrolled in high school and pass the test, your name and the names of the other students who pass will be reported to your school and to the district and county superintendents.

How Is the Test Organized?

The High School Proficiency Examination is divided into two parts. Part One, the essay section, is 30 minutes long. In Part One you will be asked to write a short essay on your choice of two topics. Part Two, the multiple-choice section, is two hours and thirty minutes long. In Part Two you must select the best answer to 100 questions. Part Two is made up of 56 math questions and 44 English questions. There is a short break between sections one and two. If you complete Part Two before the time has elapsed, you may leave the test site early.

How Is the Test Scored?

The maximum possible score on the High School Proficiency Exam is 112 points. Part One, the essay, is scored on a scale from 0–6 points. That score is then doubled. In other words, an essay score of 3 is worth 6 points. A score of 5 earns the test taker 10 points. In Part Two, the multiple-choice section, each of the 100 questions answered correctly is worth one point. There are more math than English questions in Part Two, so when the two scores are added together, the English and math portions of the test have equal weight.

There is no set passing score for the High School Proficiency Exam. Each test is different, and the passing score varies from test to test. The required passing score is established by the state by piloting the test on thousands of high school seniors throughout California. In order to pass the exam you must equal the average score earned by the students in the pilot administration. Though the minimum score required to pass the test does vary, it tends to fall in the 65 to 75 percent correct range. This is a score of from 73 to 84 points. If you can score in the high end of this range, you will most likely pass.

What Part One Is Like

Part One requires you to write a short (one to two page) essay. You will be given two topics from which to choose. Topics vary, but they generally deal with questions that concern young people in your age group. They frequently include more than one element that should be included in your essay. Consider, for example, the following sample essay question:

> All of us have a favorite style of music. Describe your favorite musical style in detail, explaining why you like it. Under what circumstances did you first hear this style of music? What role does it play in your life? The heading for this essay should be "Favorite Music."

In the following section, we shall describe what Part Two is like. We shall then go on to give you some hints on studying for both parts of the test, and some hints on taking the test as well.

What Part Two Is Like

Part Two is made up of approximately 100 multiple-choice questions designed to test basic academic and life skills. The English questions test your ability to read a variety of material, from newspaper articles to poetry. They also test your mastery of basic English grammar and vocabulary. You will be asked to identify and repair errors in grammar and punctuation in sample sentences. You will also be asked to choose words that match given definitions. Some questions even require you to identify the connotations of words. For example, you may be asked which word among the choices has the most positive meaning.

The mathematics questions in Part Two range from simple computation to basic algebra and geometry problems. Some require you to read graphs or tables. Others require you to calculate the area or volume of a given shape. You will be asked to determine averages and calculate percentages.

Most of the questions test practical skills or knowledge. As a citizen you need to be able to interpret the ballot and voting materials you receive in the mail. You need to be able to read the newspaper in order to assess the performance of the public officials you elect. You need to be able to fill out common legal forms, such as requests for absentee ballots, and to interpret legal ordinances and rules. You need to be able to read the graphs and charts published by government agencies. As an employee or job seeker, you need to be able to read help wanted advertisements and fill out job applications. You may be required to prepare a resume and write cover letters to potential employers. You need to be able to compare pay scales and to figure out your take-home pay. As a consumer, you need to be able to calculate which product is your best buy. You need to be able to interpret advertisements, product labels, and instructions. You also need to be able to read warranty information and credit contracts. These are your basic skills, skills stressed in the multiple-choice section of the test.

Hints on Studying for the Test

You may not realize it, but you are already actively studying for the High School Proficiency Examination. Every time you go to the supermarket and compare the prices of the items on sale, you are practicing for the test. Every time you fill out a form or follow a written direction, you are practicing for the test. As you go through the model tests in this book, pay attention to the sorts of questions you come across. Then, when you come across a similar question in your daily life, think about it the way you would think about a question on the test. Read the label on the package and ask yourself questions about what it says. Compare costs of similar items at a store to figure out the best buys. Read the help wanted advertisements in the newspaper and figure out which job is best for you. Use odd moments: while you wait for your bus, read the bus schedule; while you stand in line at the post office, read the official notices. Above all else, *read*. The more you read, the better you will be able to understand what you read. Nothing improves reading comprehension as much as practice. Read anything you like, but READ.

Similarly, the more you write, the better able you will be to express your ideas in writing. As you go through the model tests, pay attention to the sorts of essay questions you come across. Then try to think up essay questions of your own. Here are some sample essay questions:

EXPOSITORY ESSAY QUESTIONS

1) We all remember special characters in books we have read. Describe your favorite fictional hero. What happened to this character in the course of the story? Why does he or she have special significance for you? Title your essay "Favorite Literary Hero."

2) Most of us know just what we want for our birthdays. Describe the birthday present that would delight you most. What made you realize how much you wanted this particular present? How would you react if you actually were to receive this gift? Title your essay "My Ideal Gift."

3) What was your most memorable family vacation? Describe where you went and why you remember the trip. If you were planning a vacation today, would you go back to the same place? Why, or why not? Title your essay "A Vacation to Remember."

ARGUMENTATIVE ESSAY QUESTIONS

1) Should school athletics receive financial support?
2) Should high school students be allowed to elect their own courses?
3) Should children be allowed to choose their own religion?
4) Should cities have a curfew for teenagers?
5) Should the drinking age be lowered in California?
6) Should high schools be coeducational?

You can think up questions as good as these. Try answering them. The writing practice will help. If you come up with an essay question you think is particularly good, send us a copy. We'll try to include it in future editions of the text. In that way you'll be able to help other students prepare for the High School Proficiency Examination.

Don't try to cram for the test. The only thing a study session lasting several hours will do for you is tire you out. If, in the course of taking the model tests, you find out you have trouble reading and interpreting graphs, spend a half hour or hour each day studying graphs. Don't try to do everything all at once. Set up a study schedule, one you can keep, and follow it. Regular practice handling particular problem areas will pay off.

In the review sections that follow the diagnostic test, you will find all the practice materials you need to review the basic skills covered on the test. Even if you feel you have done well on the diagnostic test, go over the review sections as well. Concentrate on the sorts of problems that slowed you down on the diagnostic test. If you know you have difficulty dealing with certain questions—word problems, fractions, graphs—concentrate on these problems as well. Again, don't cram, but pace yourself and allow yourself sufficient time for review.

Hints on Handling Essay Questions

The essay questions on the test call for simple expository or persuasive writing: you are asked to explain something to somebody. Where do you begin? Obviously, begin with the question. Consider once more the following sample essay question:

> All of us have a favorite style of music. Describe your favorite musical style in detail, explaining why you like it. Under what circumstances did you first hear this style of music? What role does it play in your life? The heading for this essay should be "Favorite Music."

The first step in answering this question is identifying all of its elements. Underline or number each of the elements in the question. This topic has four elements: (1) a description of your favorite musical style, (2) an explanation of your reasons for enjoying it, (3) a description of your first experience of this style of music, and (4) an explanation of the role this music plays in your life. You must be sure to include each of these four elements in your essay.

This type of essay should be simple for you to write. First, there is no wrong or right answer. You are the expert on your own life, opinions, and tastes. Second, you need not develop any complicated organization for your essay. The order in which the elements are presented in the question will generally serve as an excellent outline for your essay. Plan to devote one paragraph to each element of the topic.

Your essay will receive a score from 0 to 6. That score will then be doubled and added to the points you earn on Part Two. The following list of criteria used in scoring essays for the High School Proficiency Exam will give you a good idea of what the readers are looking for.

Score

0   Blank paper.

1   The essay contains only a few sentences that do not address the topic, or it is unreadable.

2   The essay does not address the topic. It reveals serious errors in mechanics, usage, sentence structure, or word choice.

3   The essay responds to the topic and is adequately organized, but it contains errors in mechanics, usage, sentence structure, or word choice.

4   The essay responds to the topic, is organized, and explains key ideas. It contains some errors in spelling, punctuation, and grammar.

5   The essay responds to all points of the topic, is well organized, and contains few errors in spelling, punctuation, or grammar.

6   The essay responds to all points of the topic, is well organized, and contains no errors in spelling, punctuation, or grammar. It displays outstanding writing skills.

Here is an essay on the sample topic:

Favorite Music

Melodic punk rock is my favorite style of music. While most assume that punk is always aggressive and abrasive, this is not the case. Many punk groups, from California's Screeching Weasel to Great Britain's China Drum, play music that is very similar to the melodic pop music of the 1960s. Their songs are short and catchy, following the traditional structure of verse/chorus/verse. The instruments are also the same, the basic combination of drums, electric bass, and a guitar or two. Today's melodic punk groups even sing harmony, much like the Beatles and earlier pop groups. The biggest difference between melodic punk rock and its earlier counterparts is that it is played with more energy and at far greater speed.

The high energy and blazing speed of melodic punk rock are its major attractions to me. While I enjoy their catchy melodies, I find the high energy of these groups even more infectious. When I hear a good, fast song on my car radio, I cannot avoid tapping the steering wheel in time to the manic music. It makes me feel happy and alive, even before I have had my morning cup of coffee!

I first heard this style of music on the local college radio station when I was a freshman in high school. It sounded okay, but I cannot say that I rushed out to buy it. Later that year, however, I attended my first punk rock concert at a warehouse in West Oakland. While the sound was terrible because of poor equipment, the performances were fantastic. Before I left the show, I bought the debut single of Green Day, one of the bands whom I had just heard perform.

Though I did not know it at the time, that concert would mark a turning point in my life. Until that night, I had never been really passionate about anything. I did not have a strong interest in school. I did not have any hobbies or participate in any activities. Suddenly, after seeing that concert, I loved music. I started taking guitar lessons. I even wrote a few record reviews for the school newspaper. Though I am no longer in high school, I plan to attend a local junior college that offers courses in recording engineering so that I can work with the bands that I admire.

Here are some additional writing hints for you:
1) Never use a long word where a short one will do.
2) Keep your sentences short.
3) If you can cut out a word, do so.
4) Use the active voice, not the passive. (Write "I bought Green Day's debut single," not "Green Day's debut single was bought by me.")
5) Be sure to cover each of the required elements in your essay, and do not forget to include the title (if one is requested).

Again, if you feel underprepared in writing skills, be sure to work your way through Chapter 2. Its sections on grammar, punctuation, and usage are sure to be helpful to you.

Hints on Handling Reading Comprehension Questions

Although you will find reading comprehension questions throughout the actual test, for convenience in our model tests we have placed an extended group of such questions at the beginning of each short-answer section. (Additional reading passages occur throughout the test.) In reading these questions and the reading passages on which the questions are based, try asking yourself the following questions:

1) What is the *main idea* of the passage?
2) What *key phrases and ideas* are there in the passage?
3) Are there any words or phrases in a question that change or qualify its meaning? Watch out for the following words: *no, some, many, all; sometimes, never, always; not at all, partly, completely,* etc.

Some of the passages will be several paragraphs long. Don't expect to find all the answers to all the questions in the first paragraph you read. Read *all* the paragraphs belonging to the passage. When hunting for the answer to a particular question, hunt through the entire passage. Don't expect the questions to follow the order in which the material in the passage is organized: your first question may ask you for information found in the passage's fourth paragraph, whereas your second question may ask you for information found in the first paragraph.

Remember that the sort of reading involved in many of the comprehension passages is practical reading, reading to locate specific factual information. You will find additional practice in both practical and general reading in Chapter 3.

Hints on Handling Mathematics Questions

There are special skills needed for the different kinds of math problems. You will find a basic math review in Chapter 4, covering these skills. Whenever you do a calculation, or read an answer from a graph, or solve a word problem, think about the question *before* you start to do calculations. Many times, you can find an easy way if you look for it; we will point out some ways in the answers to the model test questions. When you are done with your work, *always* ask yourself "Does the answer make sense?" If the answer doesn't seem reasonable, you have probably made a mistake.

Even though different types of questions require different techniques, you can follow some general rules:

1) Check your work. Everyone makes errors in arithmetic, but you can catch yours if you try. If you arrived at the answer by subtracting, add the answer and the number you subtracted to check it out. If you divided to get the answer, check it by multiplying.
2) When a problem involves fractions or other complicated numbers, it helps to get an approximate answer by simplifying the numbers. For example, $\frac{9}{16} \times 30$ has to be a bit more than half ($\frac{8}{16}$) of 30, that is, it has to be more than 15. By finding an approximate answer, you can be confident that the more difficult calculation is correct.
3) For word problems, you have to translate sentences into numbers and equations. Read *all* the sentences of the question; then go back and write down any numbers or relationships mentioned in the question. Stop and think about the question. Many times you are expected to fill in some more information from your own experience, maybe a formula like "distance = rate × time." The arithmetic will usually be straightforward once you know *what number* the question is asking for.

Remember that most of the questions on the test deal with everyday situations and the sort of mathematics you can use and practice anywhere—at the store, reading the newspaper, balancing your checkbook, or any time you encounter numbers. Some require you to apply what you learned in your basic algebra and geometry classes in high school. You can find additional study materials in Chapter 4.

General Test-Taking Tips

1. Answer every question. There is no penalty for guessing on the High School Proficiency Exam. You get one point for each correct answer in the multiple-choice section. No points will be subtracted for incorrect answers. It is therefore to your benefit to guess whenever you do not know the answer to a question. Blind guessing should give you correct answers and earn you points roughly 25 percent of the time.

2. Make educated guesses. You can improve the odds of getting the right answer when you guess by eliminating answers you know to be incorrect. If you do not know the correct answer, but you can eliminate two of the possibilities, your guesses should be correct approximately 50 percent of the time.

3. Skip difficult problems and return to them later. If you find that you have trouble answering all of the questions on the test in the alloted time, you should skip the difficult test questions and return to them later. Mark the skipped questions in your test booklet (not on the answer form) so that you will see them easily. Move on to the questions that you can answer with ease. When you have completed all of the easy questions, return to the more difficult ones. Each question is worth just one point, whether it is easy or difficult. You do not want to miss an easy point at the end of the test because you got bogged down on a tough one early on. Remember to go ahead and guess on any answers that remain blank in the last few minutes of the test.

4. Take care of yourself. Be sure to get enough sleep the night before the test. This is far more valuable than any last minute review that you can do. Wake up early enough to eat breakfast before the test. Studies show that people perform better on tests when they have had something to eat recently. Bring a snack to eat during the break. This is a long and grueling test. Your body will require fuel if your brain is to continue functioning at its most effective level.

CHAPTER 1
Diagnostic Test

ANSWER SHEET

Part One: Essay

Use the space allowed following the test question to write your answers to each of the essay questions.

Part Two: Short-Answer Questions

1. Ⓐ Ⓑ Ⓒ Ⓓ	26. Ⓐ Ⓑ Ⓒ Ⓓ	51. Ⓐ Ⓑ Ⓒ Ⓓ	76. Ⓐ Ⓑ Ⓒ Ⓓ
2. Ⓐ Ⓑ Ⓒ Ⓓ	27. Ⓐ Ⓑ Ⓒ Ⓓ	52. Ⓐ Ⓑ Ⓒ Ⓓ	77. Ⓐ Ⓑ Ⓒ Ⓓ
3. Ⓐ Ⓑ Ⓒ Ⓓ	28. Ⓐ Ⓑ Ⓒ Ⓓ	53. Ⓐ Ⓑ Ⓒ Ⓓ	78. Ⓐ Ⓑ Ⓒ Ⓓ
4. Ⓐ Ⓑ Ⓒ Ⓓ	29. Ⓐ Ⓑ Ⓒ Ⓓ	54. Ⓐ Ⓑ Ⓒ Ⓓ	79. Ⓐ Ⓑ Ⓒ Ⓓ
5. Ⓐ Ⓑ Ⓒ Ⓓ	30. Ⓐ Ⓑ Ⓒ Ⓓ	55. Ⓐ Ⓑ Ⓒ Ⓓ	80. Ⓐ Ⓑ Ⓒ Ⓓ
6. Ⓐ Ⓑ Ⓒ Ⓓ	31. Ⓐ Ⓑ Ⓒ Ⓓ	56. Ⓐ Ⓑ Ⓒ Ⓓ	81. Ⓐ Ⓑ Ⓒ Ⓓ
7. Ⓐ Ⓑ Ⓒ Ⓓ	32. Ⓐ Ⓑ Ⓒ Ⓓ	57. Ⓐ Ⓑ Ⓒ Ⓓ	82. Ⓐ Ⓑ Ⓒ Ⓓ
8. Ⓐ Ⓑ Ⓒ Ⓓ	33. Ⓐ Ⓑ Ⓒ Ⓓ	58. Ⓐ Ⓑ Ⓒ Ⓓ	83. Ⓐ Ⓑ Ⓒ Ⓓ
9. Ⓐ Ⓑ Ⓒ Ⓓ	34. Ⓐ Ⓑ Ⓒ Ⓓ	59. Ⓐ Ⓑ Ⓒ Ⓓ	84. Ⓐ Ⓑ Ⓒ Ⓓ
10. Ⓐ Ⓑ Ⓒ Ⓓ	35. Ⓐ Ⓑ Ⓒ Ⓓ	60. Ⓐ Ⓑ Ⓒ Ⓓ	85. Ⓐ Ⓑ Ⓒ Ⓓ
11. Ⓐ Ⓑ Ⓒ Ⓓ	36. Ⓐ Ⓑ Ⓒ Ⓓ	61. Ⓐ Ⓑ Ⓒ Ⓓ	86. Ⓐ Ⓑ Ⓒ Ⓓ
12. Ⓐ Ⓑ Ⓒ Ⓓ	37. Ⓐ Ⓑ Ⓒ Ⓓ	62. Ⓐ Ⓑ Ⓒ Ⓓ	87. Ⓐ Ⓑ Ⓒ Ⓓ
13. Ⓐ Ⓑ Ⓒ Ⓓ	38. Ⓐ Ⓑ Ⓒ Ⓓ	63. Ⓐ Ⓑ Ⓒ Ⓓ	88. Ⓐ Ⓑ Ⓒ Ⓓ
14. Ⓐ Ⓑ Ⓒ Ⓓ	39. Ⓐ Ⓑ Ⓒ Ⓓ	64. Ⓐ Ⓑ Ⓒ Ⓓ	89. Ⓐ Ⓑ Ⓒ Ⓓ
15. Ⓐ Ⓑ Ⓒ Ⓓ	40. Ⓐ Ⓑ Ⓒ Ⓓ	65. Ⓐ Ⓑ Ⓒ Ⓓ	90. Ⓐ Ⓑ Ⓒ Ⓓ
16. Ⓐ Ⓑ Ⓒ Ⓓ	41. Ⓐ Ⓑ Ⓒ Ⓓ	66. Ⓐ Ⓑ Ⓒ Ⓓ	91. Ⓐ Ⓑ Ⓒ Ⓓ
17. Ⓐ Ⓑ Ⓒ Ⓓ	42. Ⓐ Ⓑ Ⓒ Ⓓ	67. Ⓐ Ⓑ Ⓒ Ⓓ	92. Ⓐ Ⓑ Ⓒ Ⓓ
18. Ⓐ Ⓑ Ⓒ Ⓓ	43. Ⓐ Ⓑ Ⓒ Ⓓ	68. Ⓐ Ⓑ Ⓒ Ⓓ	93. Ⓐ Ⓑ Ⓒ Ⓓ
19. Ⓐ Ⓑ Ⓒ Ⓓ	44. Ⓐ Ⓑ Ⓒ Ⓓ	69. Ⓐ Ⓑ Ⓒ Ⓓ	94. Ⓐ Ⓑ Ⓒ Ⓓ
20. Ⓐ Ⓑ Ⓒ Ⓓ	45. Ⓐ Ⓑ Ⓒ Ⓓ	70. Ⓐ Ⓑ Ⓒ Ⓓ	95. Ⓐ Ⓑ Ⓒ Ⓓ
21. Ⓐ Ⓑ Ⓒ Ⓓ	46. Ⓐ Ⓑ Ⓒ Ⓓ	71. Ⓐ Ⓑ Ⓒ Ⓓ	96. Ⓐ Ⓑ Ⓒ Ⓓ
22. Ⓐ Ⓑ Ⓒ Ⓓ	47. Ⓐ Ⓑ Ⓒ Ⓓ	72. Ⓐ Ⓑ Ⓒ Ⓓ	97. Ⓐ Ⓑ Ⓒ Ⓓ
23. Ⓐ Ⓑ Ⓒ Ⓓ	48. Ⓐ Ⓑ Ⓒ Ⓓ	73. Ⓐ Ⓑ Ⓒ Ⓓ	98. Ⓐ Ⓑ Ⓒ Ⓓ
24. Ⓐ Ⓑ Ⓒ Ⓓ	49. Ⓐ Ⓑ Ⓒ Ⓓ	74. Ⓐ Ⓑ Ⓒ Ⓓ	99. Ⓐ Ⓑ Ⓒ Ⓓ
25. Ⓐ Ⓑ Ⓒ Ⓓ	50. Ⓐ Ⓑ Ⓒ Ⓓ	75. Ⓐ Ⓑ Ⓒ Ⓓ	100. Ⓐ Ⓑ Ⓒ Ⓓ

DIAGNOSTIC TEST

Part One: Essay

30 MINUTES

Directions: The following two essay questions are designed to test your knowledge of written English. Read each question carefully, and then select one as your essay topic. You have 30 minutes to write a short essay on the topic you choose.

ESSAY TOPICS

Topic A

Most people have a favorite hobby or activity. Describe your favorite hobby or activity. Explain what you like best about it. How were you introduced to this hobby or activity? Title your essay "Favorite Hobby."

Topic B

What person has had the greatest influence on your life? What is your relationship to this person? Describe his or her most outstanding characteristics. Explain how he or she has influenced you. Title your essay "My Greatest Influence."

_____

_____

_____

_____

_____

_____

_____

_____

_____

_____

_____

_____

_____

_____

_____

_____

Part Two: Short-Answer Questions

2 HOURS, 30 MINUTES

The kinds of questions used on this part of the test are varied. Be sure you read the directions carefully before beginning to answer the questions that follow.

Directions: Refer to the following passage to answer the next five questions. You are to choose the *one* best answer, marked A, B, C, or D, to each question. Then, on your answer sheet, find the number of the problem and mark your answer clearly. Answer all the questions following a passage on the basis of what is *stated* or *implied* in that passage.

FUEL RESOURCES

California's mineral fuel resources are primarily oil and gas. The few bituminous and subbituminous coal seams in the state have not been mined for many years. Output from the one remaining lignite mine near Ione, in Amador County, is now processed not as fuel but for its content of montan wax, used as an additive in making phonograph records, shoe polish, and rubber products. Peat from four counties is used only for soil conditioning or other agricultural purposes.

Despite its huge output, California's liquid fuels industry cannot meet the demands of the consumers within the state. Crude petroleum and gasoline and other refinery products must be imported each year in constantly increasing quantities by ocean tankers and pipeline. Natural gas is imported by pipeline from as far away as Canada. This demand stems from a combination of ever-rising population, lack of solid fuels, and the requirements of more than 10 million motor vehicles registered in the state.

Production of crude petroleum reached its peak in 1953 and began to decline the following year. It has recently averaged about 300 million barrels annually. Increasing emphasis on secondary recovery methods and federal oil and gas leasing on the ocean bottom miles seaward from older tidelands drilling are slowing the decline but have not fully compensated for the reduced output from older oilfields. More than a quarter of the crude oil being processed by California's two-score refineries now is obtained outside the state. Most of the in-state production is in the five adjoining counties of Los Angeles, Kern, Ventura, Orange, and Santa Barbara, although Fresno and Monterey counties to the north also report significant quantities.

California has begun exploring its offshore resources of oil and gas hidden in the submerged lands of the Outer Continental Shelf. Oil and gas reserves beneath the ocean's depths may open a promising source of fuel for California and the nation. With advanced technology, drilling for possible reserves in depths encountered outside the three-mile limit off the California coast has become practical.

1. Which of the following is one of California's chief mineral fuel resources?

   A. Coal   B. Lignite   C. Oil   D. Peat

2. Lignite's high content of montan wax is used

   A. in making shoe polish.
   B. in processing oil and gas.
   C. for fuel.
   D. for soil conditioning.

3. The rising demand for liquid fuels within California has been caused by all the following EXCEPT the

   A. increasing air pollution.
   B. increasing number of motor vehicles.
   C. increasing population.
   D. lack of solid fuels.

4. California's liquid fuels industry hopes to find new sources of liquid fuel by

   A. coal mining.
   B. offshore drilling.
   C. refining montan wax.
   D. tidelands drilling.

5. Which of the following statements about California's liquid fuel industry is TRUE?

   A. It is less important than California's solid fuel industry.
   B. It is increasingly capable of meeting the demands of California's consumers without relying on imports.
   C. It is increasingly involved in the processing of lignite.
   D. It is increasingly involved in exploring offshore resources of oil and gas.

Directions: Each of the following statements, questions, or problems is followed by four suggested answers or completions. Choose the *one* that best completes each of the statements or answers the question. Mark the oval on the answer sheet whose letter corresponds to the answer you have selected.

6. Pyramid Records is selling cassette tapes at $1 off its usual price of $8.35 per tape. What is the percentage reduction, to the nearest whole percent, on these tapes?

   A. 10%   B. 12%   C. 15%   D. 20%

Refer to the graph below to answer the next four questions.

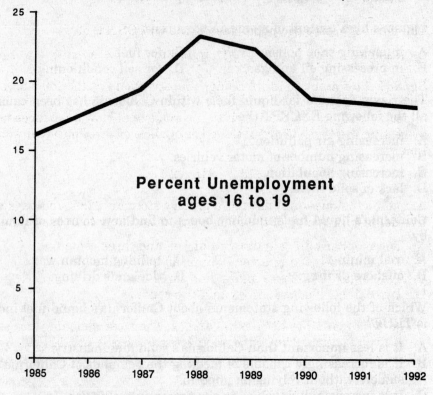

**Percent Unemployment
ages 16 to 19**

7. In which year on this graph was the unemployment rate for 16- to 19-year-olds the highest?

   A. 1987   B. 1988   C. 1989   D. 1990

8. Which year showed the greatest increase in teenage unemployment?

   A. 1986   B. 1987   C. 1988   D. 1989

9. Which statement below best describes the trends illustrated by this graph?

   A. Teenage unemployment first decreased and then increased.
   B. Teenage unemployment first increased and then decreased.
   C. Teenage unemployment increased and then leveled off.
   D. Teenage unemployment steadily decreased in these years.

10. Which of the following conclusions can be made from this graph?

   A. Throughout the first four years, at least a sixth of the teenage work-force was unable to find a job.
   B. At the height of the recession in 1988, nearly one out of every four workers was unemployed.
   C. It was harder for a teenager to get a job in 1985 than in 1989.
   D. More teenagers dropped out of school in 1988 than in 1991.

11. The word "rebuke" means the SAME as

A. answer   B. ignore   C. scold   D. tease

12. The phrase "beside the point" means the OPPOSITE of

A. feasible   B. logical   C. relevant   D. specific

13. *Sunday Magazine* offers its readers subscriptions at the following rates: one year for $15; two years for $27; and three years for $37. A man decides to get a three-year subscription to the magazine. How much does he save by getting the three-year subscription in place of three one-year subscriptions?

A. $3   B. $8   C. $15   D. $22

14. A man buys some vegetables at a grocery store for $2.67 and pays with a five-dollar bill. Which of the following is most likely to be his change?

A. Three dollar bills, a quarter, a nickel, and three cents.
B. Two dollar bills, a quarter, a dime, and two cents.
C. Two dollar bills, three dimes, and three cents.
D. Two dollar bills, two dimes, and two cents.

15. A family is planning a trip of 550 miles. Their car gets an average of 22 miles to the gallon. They expect to pay an average price of $1.40 for each gallon of gas they purchase. How much do they expect to spend on gas for the trip?

A. $30.80   B. $35.00   C. $66.95   D. $770.00

16. Which of the following conveys the most NEGATIVE or unfavorable meaning in describing a person's manners?

A. considerate   B. courteous   C. fawning   D. respectful

17. There may be an error in capitalization or punctuation in the following sentence.

Judy and <u>Aunt Mary</u> are going to the <u>Doctor's</u> office_later this afternoon.
         A   B   C

A. Underlined part A needs to be changed to make the sentence correct.
B. Underlined part B needs to be changed to make the sentence correct.
C. Underlined part C needs to be changed to make the sentence correct.
D. There is no change needed; the sentence is correct as written.

18. To find a map of a particular region, you would consult

    A. an almanac
    B. an atlas
    C. a bibliography
    D. a thesaurus

The following paragraph may not be in a logical sequence. Read the sentences and select the best order for them.

19. (1) Properly used for medically prescribed purposes, narcotic drugs are a great boon to mankind. (2) It is in misuse, and abuse, that narcotics are transformed from a boon to a bane. (3) A narcotic is a drug that, in proper doses, relieves pain and induces profound sleep. (4) In poisonous doses, however, such a drug induces stupor, coma, or convulsions.

    A. Correct as is
    B. 1, 4, 2, 3
    C. 3, 2, 4, 1
    D. 3, 4, 1, 2

20. Which of the following sentences is CORRECTLY punctuated?

    A. While Sarah enjoys most classical music she dislikes Bach.
    B. Doctor. Berman received her medical degree from Harvard University.
    C. The trouble with being an only child, is that you miss the chance to develop close ties with siblings.
    D. Few students study Latin; even fewer, French.

21. A woman is three times as old as her daughter and four times as old as her son. If the daughter is 12 years old, how old is the son?

    A. 8   B. 9   C. 10   D. 36

22. Martin Frobisher owns a house and land in Kern County. The full value of the land is $28,500; the full value of the improvements to the land (the house and any other structures put on the land) is $9,000. If locally assessed property in Kern County is assessed at 25% of full value, what is the *total* assessed value of Martin Frobisher's house and land there?

    A. $7,125   B. $9,375   C. $28,500   D. $37,500

23. The Wallaces have a circular pond in their backyard that is 20 feet across and has a depth of 2 feet. About how many cubic feet of water does it hold?

    A. 315   B. 525   C. 630   D. 2500

24. What is the next number in the sequence 7 10 14 19 25?

    A. 29   B. 31   C. 32   D. 36

25. A man travels from Kingston to Yorkville, a distance of 40 miles. For the first 30 miles he travels on the freeway, averaging a speed of 60 miles per hour. The last 10 miles he averages a speed of 30 miles per hour. How many minutes does it take him to travel from Kingston to Yorkville?

    A. 30 minutes
    B. 40 minutes
    C. 45 minutes
    D. 50 minutes

Directions: Refer to the following passage to answer the next five questions. You are to choose the *one* best answer, marked A, B, C, or D, to each question. Then, on your answer sheet, find the number of the problem and mark your answer clearly. Answer all the questions following a passage on the basis of what is *stated* or *implied* in the passage.

THE INDIANS OF CALIFORNIA

California's Indians have lived under the governments of three countries—Spain, Mexico, and the United States. Each of these governments recognized the rights of the Indians and attempted to deal fairly and justly with them, at least in theory, but their good intentions were never adequately administered.

Many Indians were held in peonage during the Spanish and Mexican regimes. The Spanish mission life into which the South California Indians were drawn cut their numbers by over 70 percent. For several decades after the United States acquired California, Indians were threatened with extinction by massacre and starvation. Nonetheless, Spain conceded the validity of the Indians' rights to use the land. Mexico recognized the Indians as Mexican citizens. When California became part of the United States, Indians were to become citizens and their liberty and property were to be accorded full protection under the laws of their new government.

Despite these good intentions, by 1860 the Indians of California were destitute, landless, and without any ratified treaties with the federal government. They remained in that unenviable position for the next 60 years until, in the early decades of the twentieth century, the insistence of a church group prompted the federal government to purchase homesites, or rancherias, for the "landless Indians of California."

The rancherias purchased were small, generally inadequate to support the residents, and scattered throughout the northern and central part of the state. Nevertheless, they were places to which the Indians could move, reasonably secure in the knowledge that no one could drive them away as they had so often been driven away from other homes.

26. The passage blames the injustices suffered by California's Indians on

A. Mexico's recognition of Indians as citizens.
B. the insistence of church groups.
C. the poor motivation of the Indians.
D. faulty administrative practices.

27. According to the above passage, Spanish mission life was so hard on Southern California Indians that

A. large numbers of them died.
B. their numbers increased by over 70 percent.
C. they chose to become ranchers.
D. they moved to the northern and central parts of the state.

28. In the 1860s, the Indians of California faced hardship because

A. they were held in peonage during the Spanish regime.
B. they were illegal aliens.
C. they had no ratified treaties with the federal government.
D. their homesites were scattered throughout the northern and central part of the state.

29.   Title to the Indians' rancherias was held by

A. a church group.
B. the federal government.
C. the three governments of Spain, Mexico, and the United States.
D. the residents of the homesites.

30.   One strong advantage of the rancherias was

A. their nearness to ancestral Indian hunting grounds in Southern California.
B. their stability as homesites from which the Indians could not be driven away.
C. the ability they had to support a large Indian population.
D. their ample size.

Refer to the following charts to answer the next two questions.

Consumer Installment Credit Outstanding and Mortgage Debt Outstanding: 1975 to 1985

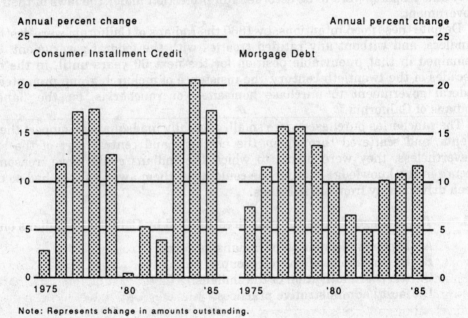

Note: Represents change in amounts outstanding.

31.   Which of the years below had the smallest change in consumer installment credit?

A. 1978   B. 1980   C. 1982   D. 1984

32.   Which of the following conclusions is supported by these graphs?

A. Mortgage debt and consumer credit follow the same pattern of increase and decrease.
B. More people owed money in 1985 than in 1975.
C. 1982 has one of the lowest increases in debt over the time shown on these graphs.
D. More Americans bought houses in 1977 than in 1982.

---

33. On his tenth birthday a boy stands 4 feet, 8 inches tall. On his twelfth birthday he stands 5 feet, 4 inches tall. What was his average growth per year in that period?

    A. 2 inches   B. 3 inches   C. 4 inches   D. 5 inches

34. A bank teller is asked to file 1,200 deposit slips. If he can file 180 deposit slips an hour, how long must he work before he finishes his assignment?

    A. $6\frac{1}{3}$ hours   B. $6\frac{1}{2}$ hours   C. $6\frac{2}{3}$ hours   D. 7 hours

---

Refer to the graph below for the next question.

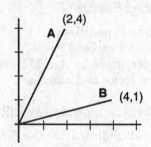

35. What is the ratio of the slope of line *A* to line *B*?

    A. 1:1   B. 2:1   C. 4:1   D. 8:1

Directions: Refer to the following passage to answer the next five questions. You are to choose the *one* best answer, marked A, B, C, or D, to each question. Then, on your answer sheet, find the number of the problem and mark your answer clearly. Answer all the questions following a passage on the basis of what is *stated* or *implied* in the passage.

SEATTLE

Nestled between the craggy Olympic Mountains to the west and the volcanic peaks of the Cascade Range to the east, the city of Seattle sits on a narrow strip of land between Puget Sound and 18-mile-long Lake Washington. Just north of downtown Seattle these bodies of water are linked by a system of locks and a ship canal leading into Lake Union, which bisects the city.

Although early maritime voyagers caught sight of the Washington coast before the close of the eighteenth century, Seattle itself was settled comparatively late. With an entire continent to cross, the first families did not reach what was to be Seattle until 1851, when they settled at Alki Point. The windswept town was soon moved around the point next to the protected waters of Elliott Bay.

The city prospered, but by 1865 it was noticeable something was missing: The busy lumberjacks, trappers, and traders had no brides. Asa Mercer, founder of the Territorial University, went east and recruited 11 brave and eligible young ladies to return with him; a second group of 57 women made their way to the growing city a year later.

Built almost entirely of wood, the young city was destroyed in 1889 when a painter's glue pot boiled over and started the Great Fire. Seattle was soon rebuilt, this time using more stone, iron, and concrete than wood. By 1893 the first transcontinental railroad had reached Seattle, and maritime trade had been established with the Orient.

Swift growth followed the 1897 Klondike gold rush, for which Seattle served as a jumping-off point. Seattle's population increased sixfold from 1890 to 1910; tide-flats were filled and steep slopes were leveled to create more livable areas. In 1909 the city was host to its first world's fair, the Alaska-Yukon-Pacific Exhibition; the University of Washington now occupies the site.

36. The main purpose of the opening paragraph is to

A. praise Seattle's scenic attractions.
B. portray Seattle as it was seen by the earliest explorers.
C. explain the basis of Seattle's economy.
D. introduce Seattle's geographic location.

37. The first families reached Seattle

A. as part of a maritime expedition.
B. after having taken an overland route.
C. after having been recruited by Asa Mercer.
D. through a system of locks and canals.

38. Why was the town of Seattle moved near Elliott Bay?

A. Because it needed rebuilding after the Great Fire of 1889.
B. Because the new site offered more shelter from wind.
C. Because Elliott Bay was closer to Alki Point.
D. Because women were expected to arrive shortly.

39. A "jumping-off point" (last paragraph) most likely is

A. a place from which one departs on a journey.
B. an introduction to a particular subject.
C. a steep slope that needs to be leveled.
D. a craggy mountain peak.

40. Population growth in the 1890s led to a need for

A. more industry.
B. trade with the Orient.
C. better housing sites.
D. stronger universities.

---

41. A right-angled triangle has two of its sides 2 inches long; which of the answers below is closest to the length of the other side?

A. 2 inches   B. 3 inches   C. 4 inches   D. 5 inches

42. Craig Leonard went with eight friends to Chang's Chinese Kitchen for lunch. All the others ordered the lunch special, but Craig had a dish (from the dinner menu) that cost $2 more than the others' lunches. If the bill came to $38.45, how much did Craig owe?

A. $3.80   B. $4.05   C. $6.05   D. $6.45

43. How many miles apart are the cities of Hilary and Powersville, shown on a map as $1\frac{3}{4}$ inches apart? The scale of miles on the map is 1 inch = 100 miles.

A. 125 miles   B. 134 miles   C. 175 miles   D. 1,340 miles

Refer to the table below to answer the next two questions.

1 gallon	4 quarts
1 gallon	3.785 liters
1 quart	2 pints
1 pint	4 cups
1 pint	16 ounces

44. A woman buys a half-gallon of milk. During the day, she drinks two 8-ounce glasses from the full container, and uses one cup of milk in cooking. How much milk does she have left in the container?

    A. 20 ounces   B. 28 ounces   C. 44 ounces   D. 108 ounces

45. Approximately how many ounces are there in a liter?

    A. 17 ounces   B. 34 ounces   C. 45 ounces   D. 64 ounces

---

Refer to the letter below in answering the three questions that follow.

> 5150 Fruitvale Boulevard
> Oakland, California 94602
> January 21, 1997

Mr. Mitchel Weiner
175 Ninth Avenue
New York, New York 10011

Dear Mr. Weiner,

    (1) I understand you own a house in Oakland on Montgomery Street near Pleasant Valley Road. (2) I am looking for new property to develop, and I would like to make an offer to buy this house. (3) I would be happy to purchase it in "as is" condition. (4) You would not even have to go to the trouble and expense of arranging for a termite inspection.

    (5) Let me assure you that I am not one of those fly by night operators who try to take advantage of property owners. (6) I am a licensed Realtor with long-term ties to the community. (7) Please consider my offer; and, even if you are not ready to sell right away, do not throw away this letter. (8) Save it in your rental property folder. (9) Then, when you are ready to sell, you can reach me at my office at Bob Willis Property Management.

    Sincerely,

    Bob Willis

46. Which of the following words or phrases contains an error in capitalization?

    A. "Valley" in sentence 1   C. "Realtor" in sentence 6
    B. "inspection" in sentence 4   D. "Management" in sentence 9

47. Which of the following terms contains an error in hyphenation?

    A. as is   B. fly by night   C. long-term   D. right away

48. Which of the following sentences contains an error in punctuation?

    A. Sentence 2   B. Sentence 4   C. Sentence 7   D. Sentence 9

---

49. A woman pays $396 a year for medical insurance. At the end of three years she is hospitalized briefly. The insurance company reimburses her for her hospital expenses, minus a deductible amount of $300. If the hospital bill was $2,278.60, how much money has she saved by carrying medical insurance?

    A. $396.00   B. $790.60   C. $800.00   D. $1090.60

50. Although I understand why airlines have to serve frozen foods to their passengers, I do not understand why I was served <u>a meal by a flight attendant that had been only partially defrosted.</u>

The sentence would be better if the underlined part were written as:

A. a meal by a flight attendant that had been only partially defrosted.
B. an only partially defrosted meal by a flight attendant.
C. a meal that only had been partially defrosted by a flight attendant.
D. by a flight attendant only a meal that had been partially defrosted.

Refer to the chart below to answer the next three questions.

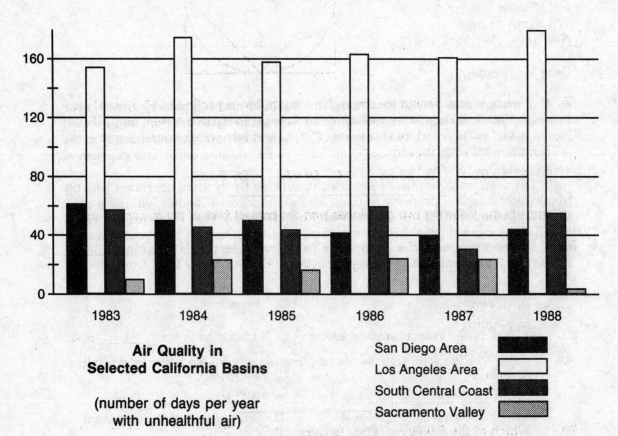

Air Quality in Selected California Basins

(number of days per year with unhealthful air)

San Diego Area
Los Angeles Area
South Central Coast
Sacramento Valley

51. About what fraction of the year does Los Angeles have unhealthful air quality?

    A. 1/4   B. 1/3   C. 1/2   D. 1/10

52. Which of the areas shown in this chart has had the fewest unhealthful days between 1983 and 1987?

    A. San Diego   C. South Central Coast
    B. Los Angeles   D. Sacramento Valley

53. Which of the areas shown reduced the number of unhealthful days every year from 1983 to 1987?

    A. San Diego   C. South Central Coast
    B. Los Angeles   D. Sacramento Valley

54. A circle has one square circumscribed around it and another one inscribed in it. What is the ratio of the area of the circumscribed square to that of the inscribed one?

    A. $\sqrt{2} : 1$
    B. $2 : 1$
    C. $3 : 1$
    D. $4 : 1$

55. Nancy is purchasing ice cream for a party, having collected $5 apiece from the six people who signed up to contribute to the ice cream fund. If the actual cost for the ice cream was $25, how much change does she owe each of the six contributors?

    A. $0.57   B. $0.83   C. $0.87   D. $0.89

Complete the following two sentences with the correct form of the missing word.

56. When we tore up the letter from Publishers' Clearing House, we _____ away our chance of winning the sweepstakes on Super Bowl Sunday.

    A. threw   C. throwed
    B. throw   D. thrown

57. I have never known anyone as nasty as Norbert; he is the _____ man in three counties.

    A. mean   C. meanest
    B. meaner   D. meanly

58. Which of the following terms is the most SPECIFIC?

    A. living creature   C. bird
    B. water fowl   D. seagull

59. Which of the following terms is the most GENERAL?

A. vehicle   C. automobile
B. motor vehicle   D. sedan

60. (1) Sir William Johnson was a British general during the mid-1700s. (2) Johnstown was founded by and named for him. (3) Johnstown has been a center of the glove-making industry since its earliest days.

Which answer below most effectively combines the above three sentences?

A. Sir William Johnson was a British general during the mid-1700s who founded Johnstown, which was named for him, and it has been a center of the glove-making industry since its earliest days.
B. A center of the glove-making industry since its earliest days, Johnstown was founded by and named for Sir William Johnson, a British general during the mid-1700s.
C. Johnstown was founded by and named for Sir William Johnson, a British general during the mid-1700s, which has been a center of the glove-making industry since its earliest days.
D. Sir William Johnson, a British general during the mid-1700s, founded and named after himself Johnstown, having been a center of the glove-making industry since its earliest days.

61. Raymond needs boards of $1\frac{3}{8}$ feet, $2\frac{3}{8}$ feet and $5\frac{1}{2}$ feet to complete a carpentry project. What is the total length of the boards he needs?

A. $8\frac{3}{8}$ feet   B. $9\frac{1}{4}$ feet   C. $9\frac{3}{8}$ feet   D. $9\frac{1}{2}$ feet

---

Refer to the following table to answer the next five questions.

	BUDGET AND EXPENSE RECORD							
	January		February		March		April	
ITEM	BUDGET	ACTUAL EXPENSE	BUDGET	ACTUAL EXPENSE	BUDGET	ACTUAL EXPENSE	BUDGET	ACTUAL EXPENSE
Rent	$125	$128.53	$125	$126.25	$125	$123.75	$125	$121.16
Food	$65	$62.48	$65	$64.18	$65	$60.43	$65	$62.35
Clothes	$20	$12.62	$20	$9.93	$20	$18.68	$50	$36.22
Phone	$5	$3.45	$5	$5.86	$5	$3.45	$5	$4.20

62. Martha Acton keeps a record of her monthly budget and expenses. The rent on her studio apartment varies from month to month, depending on how great her share of the utility bill is. In what month did the amount she paid in rent exceed the amount she had budgeted for rent?

A. February   C. April
B. March   D. None of the above

63. Martha needed to buy a new jacket and so she set aside extra money in her clothing budget one month. In what month did Martha purchase her jacket?

A. February   C. April
B. March   D. None of the above

64. How much more than the amount she budgeted did Martha pay for telephone service in February?

    A. $0.86   B. $1.55   C. $3.45   D. $5.00

65. What was Martha's total cost for telephone service during the 4-month period?

    A. $3.45   B. $5.86   C. $16.96   D. $17.06

66. What were Martha's total actual expenses in April?

    A. $215.00   B. $221.83   C. $223.93   D. $245.00

Directions: Refer to the following poem to answer the next four questions. You are to choose the *one* best answer, marked A, B, C, or D, to each question. Answer all questions on the basis of what is *stated* or *implied* in the poem.

A NARROW FELLOW IN THE GRASS

A narrow fellow in the grass
Occasionally rides;
You may have met him. Did you not,
His notice sudden is.

The grass divides as with a comb,
A spotted shaft is seen,
And then it closes at your feet
And opens further on.

He likes a boggy acre,
A floor too cool for corn,
Yet when a boy, and barefoot,
I more than once at noon

Have passed, I thought, a whip-lash
Unbraiding in the sun,
When, stooping to secure it,
It wrinkled, and was gone.

Several of nature's people
I know, and they know me;
I feel for them a transport
Of cordiality;

But never met this fellow,
Attended or alone,
Without a tighter breathing
And zero at the bone.

Emily Dickinson (1830–1886)

67. The "narrow fellow" of the title is most likely

A. a barefoot boy. C. a rider with a whip.
B. a blade of grass. D. a spotted snake.

68. In line 7, "it" most likely refers to

A. the comb. C. the shaft.
B. the grass. D. the narrow fellow.

69. Who is the speaker of this poem?

A. A young boy C. An adult male
B. An expert naturalist D. A woman who loves nature

70. What is the speaker's attitude toward the "narrow fellow" of the title?

A. Grudging respect C. Breathless wonder
B. Marked fear D. Cordial goodwill

Refer to the following graph to answer the next three questions.

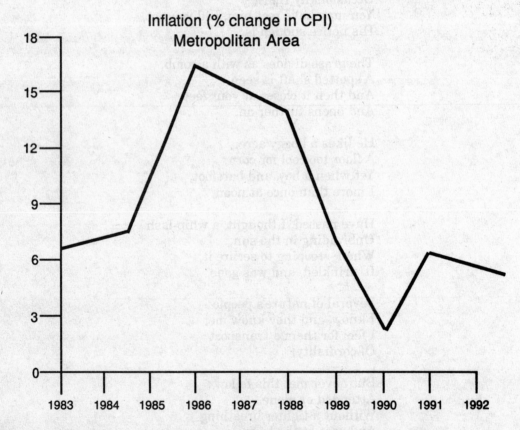

Inflation (% change in CPI)
Metropolitan Area

71. Which year saw the smallest change in the CPI in San Diego?

A. 1989   B. 1990   C. 1984   D. 1985

72. Which pattern best describes the trends shown by this graph?

    A. Increase, decrease, increase
    B. Decrease, increase, level off
    C. Level, decrease, increase
    D. Increase, decrease, level off

73. How much greater was the inflation rate at its highest than at its lowest point in the decade from 1983 to 1992?

    A. 3 times   B. 4 times   C. 5 times   D. 6 times

74. Kathy can wash a car in 15 minutes, and her friends Emily and Nancy can each wash a car in 20 minutes. If the girls work for three hours washing cars at a Student Council sponsored fund-raiser, what is the greatest number of cars they can wash during that time?

    A. 27   B. 30   C. 32   D. 36

75. A man bought a shirt priced at $45 and a pair of shorts priced at $15. If the store was giving a 10% discount on all items purchased that day, how much did he have to pay?

    A. $54   B. $57   C. $60   D. $66

76. There are 500 sheets of paper in a ream. A typist uses 3/4 of a ream of paper on a project. How many pieces of paper does she have left?

    A. 200   B. 133   C. 125   D. 100

77. Find the answer choice that matches the following definition.

Definition: obstacle or impediment; something that delays progress

    A. diversion   C. repression
    B. hindrance   D. conservation

78. Find the answer choice that matches the following definition.

Definition: not forced or planned; unrehearsed

    A. spontaneous   C. amateurish
    B. extravagant   D. momentary

79. Find the answer choice that matches the following definition.

Definition: use for one's own advantage

    A. undertake   C. disregard
    B. exploit   D. contribute

80. A woman bought a sedan for $16,700. In the first year she owned it, it depreciated 50% in value, and in the second year it depreciated an additional 20% of its original value. What was the car worth at the end of the second year?

    A. $3,340   B. $5,010   C. $8,350   D. $10,690

81. A box office cashier sells 528 theater tickets in six hours. What is his hourly average of theater tickets sold?

    A. 83   B. 87   C. 88   D. 93

82.   Examine the following arrangement of numbers:

> 1
> 1 2 1
> 1 3 3 1
> 1 4 6 4 1
> 1 5 10 ?

What number should appear next (at the question mark)?

A. 5   B. 10   C. 15   D. 20

83.   A woman is buying a house. The price of the house is $96,000. She makes a down payment of $17,500, and finances the rest by a loan. If she takes a home loan at an interest rate of 12% per year, what will the amount of interest be for the first year?

A. $942   B. $1,750   C. $9,420   D. $11,520

84.   In the triangle shown below, with two of the angles given in **degrees**, which is the longest side?

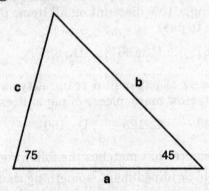

A. *a*   B. *b*   C. *c*
D. The longest side can't be determined from the data.

85.   A man knows he will have to pay $900 in property taxes on November 15. He decides to set aside $150 on the first of each month and save that money so that he can pay his taxes on November 15. On what date should he start saving if he is to follow his plan, skipping no month's deposit?

A. June 1   B. July 1   C. August 1   D. November 15

86.   A man has a choice of buying a digital watch for $31.95 in cash or of paying $15 down and three monthly payments of $7.95 each. How much will he save if he pays cash?

A. $6.90   B. $7.40   C. $7.80   D. $7.90

87.   LuckSafe Market makes a profit of 1.5% on all its sales. One week it sold $17,980 worth of merchandise. How much was its profit that week?

A. $268.60   B. $269.70   C. $2,696.00   D. $2,698.00

Directions: Refer to the following passage to answer the next four questions. You are to choose the *one* best answer, marked A, B, C, or D, to each question. Answer all questions on the basis of what is *stated* or *implied* in the passage.

ARMY RESERVE BENEFITS: MONEY FOR THE FUTURE

Maybe you're young and don't want to think about it now. Maybe you're not so young and are thinking about it. The "it" refers to life after service—your retirement and survivor benefits. Let's take a look at them.

Retirement Pay

As a Reservist attending regular monthly drills and two weeks of annual training, you are building up points toward retirement pay, pay that you are entitled to when you reach the age of 60 after 20 years of qualifying service. Retirement pay is something to think about, especially when it's tacked on to income from social security and a civilian or civil service pension.

Retirement Benefits

When you start drawing your retirement pay from the Reserve, the benefits don't stop there. In fact, some of them just begin or are an extension of those which you received prior to retirement. For example:

Medical Care. When you start receiving retirement pay, you and your legal dependents become eligible for medical care at a military medical facility. In some cases, medical care is authorized at a civilian hospital, for which the Army pays a major part of the cost.

Dental Care. Providing facilities are available, you can receive unlimited dental care. There are restrictions on the amount of care extended to dependents.

PX and Commissary Shopping Privileges. You and your spouse can make as many trips to these stores as you like, any time you like.

Travel. There may be other kinds of trips in store for you as well. One of the retirement benefits you and your dependents can enjoy is the chance to travel on military aircraft (space-available basis) anywhere in the world. When the cost of transportation can take a large chunk out of a vacation fund, this benefit can make the difference between going 50 miles or 5,000 miles from home.

There's More. There are other benefits, too, that you receive as a Reserve retiree drawing retirement pay. Some are limited but well worth exploring. These include legal assistance, veterinary aid, and use of recreation and other facilities (such as tennis courts and craft shops) on military posts. In addition, many military installations maintain recreation areas on lakes, by seashores, or in the mountains that are also available to retirees.

88. This article was probably taken from

    A. a congressional report on military spending.
    B. an Army Reserve combat training manual.
    C. an Army Reserve recruiting pamphlet.
    D. a civil service pension guide.

89. Which of the following statements are FALSE?

    I. A retired Reservist's wife may shop at the Commissary.
    II. Army Reserve retirees always are able to get on military flights.
    III. The Army pays only for medical treatments performed at military hospitals.

    A. Statements I and II only
    B. Statements I and III only
    C. Statements II and III only
    D. All of the statements

90. Which of the following is NOT a retirement benefit provided by the Reserve for its retirees?

    A. Care for sick pets
    B. Access to athletic facilities
    C. Help with legal difficulties
    D. Unlimited dental care for dependents

91. Which of the following statements is TRUE?

    A. The Reserve always provides dental treatment for retirees.
    B. The PX is a store used by both active and retired military personnel.
    C. You begin receiving your retirement pay 20 years after you reach the age of 60.
    D. Retirees are entitled to use only on-post military recreation facilities.

_____

92. A handyman has to cut a board one yard long into three unequal pieces. If the second piece he cuts is to be 1 inch longer than the first piece cut, and if the third piece is to be 1 inch longer than the second piece, how long should the first piece be?

    A. 11 inches   B. 12 inches   C. 13 inches   D. 14 inches

93. Six times as many boys as girls are enrolled in Court Hall Military Academy. The total enrollment of the military academy is 196. How many girls are enrolled?

    A. 26   B. 28   C. 44   D. 168

94. Myra could not decide <u>whether</u> she should wear her raincoat or her parka.

    A. The underlined word is spelled correctly.
    B. The underlined word is spelled incorrectly.

95. My aunt lived according to the strictest moral <u>principals</u>: she never did anything wrong.

    A. The underlined word is spelled correctly.
    B. The underlined word is spelled incorrectly.

_____

Refer to the following table to answer the next three questions.

MEDICAL INSURANCE PROGRAM
QUARTERLY RATES

MEMBER'S AGE ON PREMIUM DUE DATE	MEMBER ONLY	MEMBER & SPOUSE OR MEMBER & CHILDREN	MEMBER, SPOUSE, & CHILDREN
Less than 35	$43.86	$89.58	$128.08
35–39	$62.96	$128.72	$161.90
40–49	$68.48	$136.92	$175.44
50–59	$87.66	$175.34	$211.02
60–64	$112.88	$219.66	$252.40

Select the quarterly premium according to your current age. Include a check for that amount with your enrollment form. You will be billed thereafter for each quarterly premium, as it becomes due, at the rate appropriate to your age at that time.

96. A 58-year-old unmarried man enrolls in the Medical Insurance Program. What quarterly premium is he most likely to be paying?

    A. $68.48   B. $87.66   C. $112.88   D. $175.34

97. A 43-year-old man and his 28-year-old wife are both eligible to enroll in the Medical Insurance Program. They wish to pay the least expensive quarterly premium they can. What quarterly premium are they most likely to pay?

    A. $43.86   B. $68.48   C. $89.58   D. $136.92

98. By how much will their quarterly premium increase when the wife turns 35?

    A. $36.94   B. $39.12   C. $39.14   D. $62.96

---

99. A woman earns $21.60 an hour for a 30-hour work week. For any extra hours she works, she receives 60% of her regular hourly pay. If she works 33 hours one week and 35 hours the next, how much will she be paid for the two-week pay period?

    A. $699.84 B. $1,296.00 C. $1,399.68 D. $1,468.80

100. In the National League baseball standings, which of the following teams has a winning percentage of 45%?

    A. Los Angeles, Won 15, Lost 7   C. Houston, Won 10, Lost 12
    B. San Diego, Won 11, Lost 11   D. Atlanta, Won 5, Lost 17

ANSWER KEY   DIAGNOSTIC TEST

Part One: Essay

There are no "correct" answers to this part.

Part Two: Short-Answer Questions

1. C	21. B	41. B	61. B	81. C
2. A	22. B	42. C	62. A	82. B
3. A	23. C	43. C	63. C	83. C
4. B	24. C	44. C	64. A	84. B
5. D	25. D	45. B	65. C	85. A
6. B	26. D	46. C	66. C	86. A
7. B	27. A	47. B	67. D	87. B
8. C	28. C	48. C	68. B	88. C
9. B	29. B	49. B	69. C	89. C
10. A	30. B	50. B	70. B	90. D
11. C	31. B	51. C	71. B	91. B
12. C	32. C	52. D	72. A	92. A
13. B	33. C	53. A	73. D	93. B
14. C	34. C	54. B	74. B	94. A
15. B	35. D	55. B	75. A	95. B
16. C	36. D	56. A	76. C	96. B
17. B	37. B	57. C	77. B	97. C
18. B	38. B	58. D	78. A	98. C
19. D	39. A	59. D	79. B	99. C
20. D	40. C	60. B	80. B	100. C

ANSWER EXPLANATIONS   DIAGNOSTIC TEST

Part Two: Short-Answer Questions

1. Answer C. Oil

Question 1 asks whether coal, lignite, oil, or peat is one of California's chief mineral fuel resources; this is answered by the first sentence of the passage: "California's mineral fuel resources are primarily oil and gas." All the other resources mentioned are secondary. Gas is not one of the answers given, but oil is Choice C and is the correct answer.

2. Answer A. In making shoe polish

First, scan the passage for the key words "lignite" and "montan wax." "Lignite" occurs only in paragraph one, in a sentence discussing "the one remaining lignite mine" in the state. The last part of this sentence states that lignite is "now processed . . . for its high content of montan wax, used as an additive in making phonograph records, *shoe polish,* and rubber products. Montan wax serves as an ingredient in shoe polish; the correct answer is Choice A.

3. Answer A. Increasing air pollution

To answer this question, you must eliminate all those answer choices that do increase the demand for liquid fuels in California. You'll find the "rising demand for liquid fuels" discussed in paragraph 2. The last sentence of this paragraph gives the causes for the rising demand: "This demand stems from a combination of ever-rising population, lack of solid fuels, and the requirements of more than 10 million motor vehicles registered in the state." *Increasing population* creates a rising demand for liquid fuels; you can eliminate Choice C. *Lack of solid fuels* creates a rising demand for liquid ones; you can eliminate Choice D. With the increase in population you find a corresponding increase in the number of motor vehicles in the state, and, as the number of motor vehicles increases, that increases the demand for liquid fuel. Thus, you can eliminate Choice B. Only Choice A is left. *Increasing air pollution* is a *result* of increased fuel consumption, not a *cause* of an increased demand for fuel. The correct answer is Choice A.

4. Answer B. Offshore drilling

The final paragraph discusses California's offshore resources of oil and gas. Because California's liquid fuel industry cannot meet the state's rising demand for fuel, it "has begun exploring" these resources, hoping to find new fuel sources "hidden in the submerged lands of the Outer Continental Shelf." The off-shore oil and gas reserves "may open a promising source of fuel." The correct answer is clearly Choice B.

You can use the process of elimination to answer this question. Coal and montan wax are solid fuels, not liquid fuels; you can eliminate Choices A and C. While tidelands drilling is a source of liquid fuel, it is an old source, one declining in production. Thus, the tidelands are not a place where the industry could hope to find new sources of liquid fuel; you can eliminate Choice D. Only Choice B is left; it is the correct answer.

5. Answer D. It is increasingly involved in exploring offshore resources of oil and gas.

Once again, use the process of elimination to answer this question. Compare each of the answer choices with what the passage states or implies, and cross out the ones that seem false or unsupported by the passage.

A. The liquid fuel industry is less important than the solid fuel industry in California. FALSE. Paragraph 1 states that the chief mineral fuel resources in California are oil and gas, the liquid fuels. It also states there are only a few coal mines and no other solid fuel resources (since lignite and peal are not used as fuels). Paragraph 2 also mentions that lack of solid fuels. Everything in the passage indicates that California's liquid fuel industry is much more important than its solid fuel industry.

B. California's liquid fuel industry is increasingly capable of meeting the demands of California's consumers without relying on imports. FALSE. Paragraph 2 says "Crude petroleum and gasoline . . . must be imported each year in constantly increasing quantities."

C. California's liquid fuel industry is increasingly involved in the processing of lignite. FALSE. Lignite is not used as a fuel in California; therefore, the liquid fuel industry can hardly be increasingly involved in processing it.

D. California's liquid fuel industry is increasingly involved in exploring offshore resources of oil and gas. TRUE. The last paragraph explains that "with advanced technology, drilling for possible reserves in depths encountered outside the three-mile limit . . . has become practical."

6. Answer B. 12%

The percentage reduction is $100 \times$ amount off $\div$ original price. In this case, you need to find $100 \times 1 \div 8.35$ to the nearest whole percent. Anything between 11.5% and 12.4% rounds off to 12%.

$$
8.35 \overline{)100.00} \quad \rightarrow
$$

$$
\begin{array}{r}
11.9\ldots \\
835 \overline{)10000.0} \\
835 \\
\hline
1650 \\
835 \\
\hline
815\,0 \\
751\,5 \\
\end{array}
$$

7. Answer B. 1988

Look for the highest point on the graph; then look directly below that point to find the year labeled. It sometimes helps to use your pencil (or answer sheet) to help in this task. Lay it on the graph horizontally and move it up until all but one point of the graph is below it; then swing the pencil around parallel to the left edge of the graph and follow it down to the year label.

8. Answer C. 1988

The greatest increase in unemployment is shown on the graph by the steepest rise in the slope of the line, namely between 1987 and 1988. You can also estimate the values on the graph in order to see which year had the biggest increase:

1985 unemployment about 16%
1986 unemployment about 17%, increase from 1979 about 1%
1987 unemployment about 19%, increase from 1980 about 2%
1988 unemployment about 23%, increase from 1981 about 4%

Since unemployment went down in 1989, you can eliminate Choice D and see that Choice C must be correct.

9. **Answer B. Teenage unemployment first increased and then decreased.**

   As you look at the graph, you should notice that the points are higher each year until 1988 and then lower each year after that to 1992.

10. **Answer A.   Throughout the first four years, a sixth of the teenage workforce was unable to find a job.**

   From 1986 to 1991, the teenage unemployment shown on the graph was always 17% or more. One sixth $(\frac{1}{6})$ is equal to 0.1666 . . . or $16\frac{2}{3}$%.

11. **Answer C. Scold**

   To "rebuke" is to censure or chide. Its everyday synonym is to "scold."

12. **Answer C. Relevant**

   The phrase "beside the point" means unconnected or irrelevant. Its opposite therefore is "relevant" or to the point.

13. **Answer B. $8**

   The man gets a three-year subscription, which costs $37. The cost of three one-year subscriptions would be 3 × $15 = $45. The difference is how much he saves by getting the three-year subscription:

$$\begin{array}{r} \$\ 45 \\ -\ 37 \\ \hline \$\ \ 8 \end{array}$$

14. **Answer C.   Two dollar bills, three dimes, and three cents**

   The man needs $5 – $2.67 in change. That is $2.33. Look for the combination that adds up to this amount:

   A. 3 × $1 + $0.25 + $0.05 + 3 × $0.01 = $3.33 ($1 too much).
   B. 2 × $1 + $0.25 + $0.10 + 2 × $0.01 = $2.37 (4¢ too much).
   C. 2 × $1 + 3 × $0.10 + 3 × $0.01   = $2.33 (correct).
   D. 2 × $1 + 2 × $0.10 + 2 × $0.01   = $2.22 (11¢ too little).

15. **Answer B. $35.00**

   Calculate the number of gallons the family will need to complete the 550-mile trip and then multiply the number of gallons by the price ($1.40) they expect to pay per gallon. To find the number of gallons they will need, divide the length of the trip (550 miles) by the average mileage (22 miles per gallon) of their car:

$$\begin{array}{r} 25 \\ 22\overline{)550} \\ 44 \\ \hline 110 \\ 110 \\ \hline \end{array}$$
gallons; multiplying by $1.40 per gallon:

$$\begin{array}{r} \$\ \ 1.40 \\ \times\ \ \ \ 25 \\ \hline 7.00 \\ 28.00 \\ \hline \$35.00 \end{array}$$

16. **Answer C. Fawning**

   To be fawning is to act in an excessively, sickeningly respectful manner—to be a yes man (or woman), in short. Considerate or thoughtful behavior is good. Courteous or civil behavior is good. Respectful or polite behavior is good. But fawning or groveling behavior is too much. The word has strong negative connotations.

17. **Answer B.** **Underlined part "B" needs to be changed to make the sentence correct.**

   The use of the capital letter A in the name Aunt Mary is correct. There is no need for a comma or any other punctuation mark between the words "office" and "later." However, "Doctor" should not be capitalized. The rule is capitalize words that are part of proper names [as in "Doctor Brown's office"], but do not capitalize names of classes of persons ["the doctor's office"].

18. **Answer B.** **An atlas**

   An atlas is a book of maps.

19. **Answer D.** **3, 4, 1, 2**

   The paragraph makes the most sense read in the following order:
   (3) A narcotic is a drug that, in proper doses, relieves pain and induces profound sleep. (4) In poisonous doses, however, such a drug induces stupor, coma, or convulsions. (1) Properly used for medically prescribed purposes, narcotic drugs are a great boon to mankind. (2) It is in misuse, and abuse, that narcotics are transformed from a boon to a bane.

20. **Answer D.** **Sentence D is correctly punctuated.**

   Sentence A is incorrectly punctuated: there should be a comma between the words "music" and "she." Sentence B is incorrectly punctuated: the unabbreviated title "Doctor" does not end with a period. Sentence C is incorrectly punctuated: there should be no comma in the sentence.

21. **Answer B.** **9**

   The woman is three times as old as her daughter, and her daughter is 12 years old. Therefore we can figure out that the woman is $3 \times 12 = 36$ years old. The woman is four times as old as her son, and we are asked to find how old the son is. We can figure this out by an equation or by simply rephrasing the question until we see how to answer it.

   By equation: "The woman is four times as old as her son" becomes (woman's age) = $4 \times$ (son's age) or $36 = 4 \times s$. To find s (the son's age) divide both sides of the equation by 4:

   $$\frac{36}{4} = \frac{4 \times s}{4}$$

   $$\frac{36}{4} = 9$$

   By words: "The woman is four times as old as her son" means the same as "the son is $\frac{1}{4}$ as old as the woman," and (since we know she is 36) we can figure out $\frac{1}{4}$ of $36 = 36 \div 4 = 9$.

22. Answer B. $9,375

The total value of the house and land is $9,000 + $28,500 = $37,500. The assessed value is 25% of this, that is, one-quarter of $37,500.

```
      $ 9,375
  4)$37,500
      36
      ‾‾
      15
      12
      ‾‾
      30
      28
      ‾‾
      20
      20
      ‾‾
```

23. Answer C. 630

The pond is a cylinder, with a radius of 10 feet (20 feet across gives the diameter). The volume of a cylinder is $\pi r^2 h = \pi \times 10^2 \times 2 = 200 \times \pi \approx 200 \times 3.14 \ldots = 628$. You don't actually need to remember the formula for the volume of a cylinder if you know the general rule that the volume of a solid that has the same cross section at every height is the height times the area of the surface, in this case the area of the 20-foot diameter circle.

24. Answer C. 32

Find the change from each number to the next in the sequence (subtract each one from the following one).

$$10 - 7 = 3$$
$$14 - 10 = 4$$
$$19 - 14 = 5$$
$$25 - 19 = 6$$

At each step, the difference increases by 1; therefore the next number is 25 + 7 = 32.

25. Answer D. 50 minutes

The man traveled 30 miles at 60 miles per hour and the last 10 miles of his trip were at 30 miles per hour. To find how long the trip lasted, you need to calculate how much time each part of the trip took. The first part is easiest; if he was traveling at 60 miles per hour, he covered 30 miles (half of 60 miles) in half an hour—that is, the first part took 30 minutes. The second part is a bit harder to figure, but the same idea works; think of it as a proportion or fraction problem:

The man traveled 10 miles at 30 miles per hour, so in one hour he would have traveled 30 miles. He actually traveled only ⅓ of this distance (10 miles = ⅓ of 30 miles), so he must have taken ⅓ of an hour to go that far. ⅓ of 60 minutes = 20 minutes and adding this to the first part of the trip gives 30 minutes + 20 minutes for the total time in minutes for the man to travel from Kingston to Yorkville.

26. Answer D. Faulty administrative practices

The opening paragraph states that, although the various governments attempted to treat the Indians justly, the governments' "good intentions were never adequately administered." In other words, the injustices suffered by California's Indians were due to *faulty administrative practices*.

27. Answer A. Large numbers of them died.

The passage's second paragraph states that many Indians were held in peonage (this means that they were agricultural workers who were unable to leave the land they worked on) and that "mission life . . . cut their numbers by over 70 percent." This means that, for every hundred Indians who came under the control of the Spanish missionaries, at the end of the Spanish regime, fewer than thirty were left. Clearly, Spanish mission life was so hard on the Indians that "large numbers of them died."

28. Answer C.   They had no ratified treaties with the federal government.

Scan the passage for the key date "1860" or a phrase indicating the mid-nineteenth century. Does the opening sentence of the next-to-last paragraph jump out at you? Describing the situation of the Indians at that time, it states that "by 1860 the Indians of California were destitute, landless, and without any ratified treaties with the federal government." Checking the answers, you can immediately rule out Choice A: by 1860 the Spanish and Mexican regimes were past. You can also eliminate Choice B: once California became part of the United States its Indians were not foreign nationals or illegal aliens but natives who "were to become citizens." Similarly, you can cross out Choice D: by 1860, the Indians were landless; they had been driven away from their original territories. It was not until the early 1900s that the federal government purchased homesites for them in the northern and central parts of the state. Only Choice C is left. It is the correct answer. Lacking ratified treaties with the federal government, the Indians were at a major disadvantage.

29. Answer B.   The federal government

The homesites or rancherias were purchased in the early decades of the twentieth century at the insistence of a church group. The last paragraph describes the results of this program. The second sentence of that paragraph clearly states "Title to the lands was held by the federal government." The government owned the lands. Thus, Choice B is correct.

30. Answer B.   Their stability as homesites from which the Indians could not be driven away

Use the process of elimination to answer this question. Were the rancherias near ancestral Indian hunting grounds in Southern California? No. They were in the northern and central part of the state, not the south. Cross out Choice A. Were the rancherias capable of supporting a large Indian population? No. They were "generally inadequate to support the residents." Cross out Choice C. Were they ample or extensive in size? No. They were small. Cross out Choice D. Only Choice B is left. As the passage's last sentence states, "they were places to which the Indians could move, *reasonably secure* in the knowledge that no one could drive them away." Thus, they offered security or *stability as homesites*. The correct answer is Choice B.

31. Answer B.   1980

The bar chart on the left shows the change in consumer installment credit. The smallest bar (less than 1%) is directly over the year 1980.

32. Answer C.   1982 had one of the lowest increases in debt over the time shown on these graphs.

Check each answer for whether it is supported by the graphs:
A. Mortgage debt and consumer credit follow the same pattern.
   FALSE: There are years when one graph falls and the other graph rises (look at 1980 to 1981 and 1984 to 1985). It is true that the graphs are generally similar; you may want to keep this in mind until you see if there is a better choice.

B. More people owed money in 1985 than in 1975. FALSE. This statement may be true, but the graph shows nothing about the number of people with installment or mortgage debts.

C. 1982 had one of the lowest increases in debt.
TRUE. The sum of the increases in installment debt (about 4%) and mortgage debt (5%) is the lowest on the graph. You don't need to check all years to see this; the only other possibilities are 1975, 1980 and 1981, and all of these have larger increases.

D. More Americans bought houses in 1977 than 1982. FALSE. The graph says nothing about the number of homeowners.

33. Answer C.   4 inches

The boy's average growth rate for the two years (10th birthday to 12th birthday) is the total number of inches he grew divided by 2. Convert the heights to inches to make this easier:

at age 10 he was   4 feet 8 inches tall = $4 \times 12 + 8 = 48 + 8 = 56$ inches
at age 12 he was   5 feet 4 inches tall = $5 \times 12 + 4 = 60 + 4 = 64$ inches

The difference ($64 - 56 = 8$ inches) is the total growth; the average is $8 \div 2 = 4$ inches.

34. Answer C.   6⅔ hours

In one hour the teller can file a 180-slip part of the 1,200 deposit slip total; the number of hours it will take him to do the whole job is the number of times 180 goes into 1,200. That is, we want to find $1{,}200 \div 180$. It is a bit easier if we cancel 10 from both figures; this is all right because $\dfrac{1200}{180} = \dfrac{120}{18}$. We could continue cancelling to get the final answer, or just divide now:

$$
\begin{array}{r}
6\,\tfrac{12}{18} = 6\tfrac{2}{3} \\
18\overline{)120} \\
\underline{108} \\
12
\end{array}
$$

35. Answer D.   8 : 1

You need to find the slope of both lines to determine their ratio. Remember that the slope of a line is the "rise" divided by the "run"—that is, change in y over change in x. The slope of line A is 2, since it goes through the point (2,4) and the origin; that is a rise of 4 units divided by a run of 2 units. For line B, the rise is 1 over a run of 4, so the slope is 1/4. Therefore, the slope of A has the ratio of 2 : 1/4 to the slope of B. Reduce this to unit terms by multiplying both sides of the ratio by 4, and you get

slope (A) : slope $(B) = 4 \times (2 : 1/4) = 8 : 1$, which is Choice D.

36. Answer D.   Introduce Seattle's geographic location

Use the process of elimination to answer this question. Though the opening paragraph mentions several of Seattle's scenic attractions (Lake Washington, the Olympic Mountains, the Cascade Range), it merely names them; it does not praise them. You can cross off Choice A. Though the earliest explorers would have seen the mountains, they could not have seen the system of locks and canals built by later settlers. You can cross off Choice B. The opening paragraph explains nothing about Seattle's economy. You can cross off Choice C. With its emphasis on directions and physical dimensions ("to the west," "to the east," "18-mile-long"), the paragraph clearly tries to give the reader a sense of the city's physical setting and *introduce Seattle's geographic location*. The correct answer is Choice D.

37. Answer B. After having taken an overland route

Although the Washington coast was first glimpsed from the sea, Seattle's first settlers did not belong to a maritime expedition. Eliminate Choice A. Asa Mercer recruited brides for the unmarried lumbermen and traders 14 years after the first families settled at Alki Point. Eliminate Choice C. The system of locks and canals was built many years after Seattle's founding in 1851. Eliminate Choice D. Choice B is correct. The first families had "an entire continent to cross." They reached what was to be Seattle "after having taken an overland route."

38. Answer B. Because the new site offered more shelter from wind

The last sentence of paragraph 2 indicates why the first families moved their original settlement. The town's original location was "windswept." The settlers relocated the town "next to . . . protected waters." Clearly, they wanted *more shelter from the wind.*

39. Answer A. A place from which one departs on a journey

The news of the discovery of gold in the Klondike led thousands of people to head for Alaska to get rich quick. For these hopeful prospectors, Seattle was a jumping-off point, a place in which they could equip themselves for the goldfields and from which they could depart on their northern journey.

40. Answer C. Better housing sites

The "tideflats were filled and steep slopes . . . leveled to create more livable areas." Given the sudden growth in population, Seattle needed more dry, level places on which people could build homes. In other words, the city needed *better housing sites.*

41. Answer B. 3 inches

Try to eliminate the answers that do not work. If the other side is 2 inches, then all three sides are equal, and the triangle would be equilateral, with all angles 60°, not a right triangle. If the other side is 4 inches, then the 2-inch sides couldn't meet except by collapsing onto the 4-inch side, so that there is no triangle. A 5-inch side is even worse! The only good choice is B, 3 inches. You can also calculate the side by recognizing that it must be the diagonal of a square:

The side opposite the right angle has to be larger than the others (since the right angle is the largest angle). Now you can either use the Pythagorean formula, so that $x^2 = 2^2 + 2^2 = 8$; or remember that the diagonal of a square is $\sqrt{2}$ times the side, so that $x = 2\sqrt{2} = 2 \times 1.41 \ldots = 2.82$.

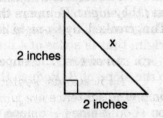

You don't need to be exact about the value of $\sqrt{2}$ or actually calculate the square root of 8 to see that 3 is closer to it than any of the other choices.

42. Answer C. $6.05

This question is a natural candidate for algebra, since the amount Craig and his friends paid for lunch is "unknown." Let x stand for the cost of the luncheon special, which Craig's eight friends had; then the cost of Craig's dish was $x + 2$ and the total cost has the equation:

$$8x + (x + 2) = 38.45$$
$$9x + 2 = 38.45$$
$$9x = 38.45 - 2 = 36.45$$

Therefore, $x = \$36.45/9 = \$4.05$, and Craig owed $x + 2 = \$6.05$.

43. Answer C.   175 miles

The cities are $1^3/4$ inches apart on the map, and 1 inch stands for 100 miles. Therefore, the cities are really $(1^3/4) \times 100$ miles apart = 100 miles + $(^3/4 \times 100)$ miles + 3×25 miles = 100 miles + 75 miles = 175 miles. (The 25 comes from cancelling, $\dfrac{3}{4} \times \overset{25}{\cancel{100}}$.)

44. Answer C.   44 ounces

Convert all the measures to the same unit, ounces in this case. A half-gallon = 2 quarts = 2×2 pints = 4×16 ounces, for a total of 64 ounces. The cup of milk used for cooking is 4 ounces (1 pint = 4 cups = 16 ounces; dividing by 4, $1/4$ pint = 1 cup = 4 ounces).

$$64 - 2 \times 8 - 4 = 64 - 16 - 4 = 44.$$

45. Answer B.   34 ounces

You have to find an equation relating ounces and liters. The table can be used as in the previous question to convert a larger unit (gallons in this case) into ounces, so that you can equate the number of liters and the number of ounces in a gallon.

1 gallon = 4 quarts = 4×2 pints = 8 pints = 8×16 ounces = 128 ounces.

Therefore, 128 ounces = 3.785 liters, and 1 liter is $128 \div 3.785$ liters. Instead of performing long division to work out the answer, notice that the result has to be between $128 \div 4$ and $128 \div 3$. Use these, which are easier to calculate, to make an inequality around the answer, x.

$128 \div 4 = 32 < x < 128 \div 3 = 42^2/3$, Only Choice B lies in this range.

46. Answer C.   "Realtor" in sentence 1

In sentence 1, the word "Realtor" should not be capitalized. When you are referring to the name of a class of persons, places, or things, you should not capitalize that word.

47. Answer B.   fly by night

Answer B contains an error in hyphenation: the word should be hyphenated. Here it is a compound adjective meaning unscrupulous in business dealings. It is written *fly-by-night*. Compare the following two sentences: "Military pilots fly by night." "That crooked, fly-by-night contractor took our money and never finished the job."

48. Answer C.   Sentence 7

As it stands, sentence 7 is incorrect. When two independent clauses in a compound sentence are joined by a coordinating conjunction (in this case, by *and*), you should place a comma between the clauses immediately before the conjunction. Rewrite sentence 7 as follows: Please consider my offer, and, even if you are not ready to sell right away, do not throw away this letter. (You can also rewrite sentence 7 as two separate sentences by eliminating the *and*: Please consider my offer. Even if you are not ready to sell right away, do not throw away this letter.)

49. Answer B. $790.60

The woman has paid $396 a year for three years, so she has spent $3 \times \$396$ = $1,188 for insurance. The insurance company paid her $2,278.60 – $300 = $1,978.60. The difference is

$$\begin{array}{r} 1,976.60 \\ -\ 1,188.00 \\ \hline 790.60 \end{array}$$

50. Answer B.   An only partially defrosted meal by a flight attendant

Choices A, C, and D either fail to correct the very common error of the misplaced modifier or introduce new errors. Ask yourself who or what has been partially defrosted. The answer is, of course, the meal, not the flight attendant.

51. Answer C.   ½

The white bars of the bar chart show the number of days of unhealthful air in Los Angeles. This bar is usually above 160; in 1988 it was about 180 (you can guess this by comparing the part of the bar above 160 with the scale on the left side). A year has 365 days, so that ¼ of a year is about 91 days, ⅓ is about 122 days, ½ is about 182 days, and ¹⁄₁₀ is about 36 days. The closest fraction for Los Angeles is Choice C, ½.

52. Answer D.   Sacramento Valley

Of the four regions in the chart, the one with the shortest bars, every year, is the one on the right. Comparing against the legend on the bottom right of the chart, we see that black represents San Diego, white is for Los Angeles, and medium gray is the South Central Coast, The rightmost bars stand for the Sacramento Valley, Choice D.

53. Answer A.   San Diego

To find which region was lower every year, you have to look at each color bar by itself without getting confused by the other colors. Notice that the question asks for reductions up to 1987, so a rise in 1988 won't affect the answer. San Diego (black bars) starts above 60 days per year in 1983 and is down to 40 in 1987. It is hard to tell if 1985 is lower than 1984, but it is no higher, so San Diego is a possible answer. A quick look at the other choices shows that each of them except San Diego went up in 1986; so the answer has to be Choice A, San Diego.

54. Answer B.   2 : 1

The inscribed square has its four corners on the circle, and the center of the square (where the diagonals cross) must be the center of the circle. The circumscribed square will have the centers of each side touching the circle, and again the square will be centered on the circle. Therefore, the diameter of the circle is a diagonal for the inside square and the same length as a side of the outside square. In other words the larger square has a side $\sqrt{2}$ times the side of the smaller square. The area of the larger square is then $\sqrt{2} \times \sqrt{2} = 2$ times the area of the smaller one.

55. Answer B. $0.83

Nancy collected $30 (6 × $5), so the amount to be divided among the contributors is that minus $25. $5 ÷ 6 can be done directly by long division, but it is simpler to multiply each answer in turn by 6 to check which one is best. Trying A gives 6 × $0.57 = $3.42; for B, 6 × $0.83 = 4.98; for C, 6 × $0.87 = $5.22; and for D the result will be even larger. Answer B is closest.

56. Answer A.   Threw

The missing word must be in the past tense. The simple past tense of the irregular verb *throw* is *threw*: I threw, you threw, he threw, she threw, we threw, they threw.

57. Answer C. Meanest

The missing word must be an adjective. Norbert is a mean man. However, he is not simply mean; he is extremely mean. In fact, he is the most mean or *meanest* man the writer knows. The adjective is in the superlative degree.

58. Answer D. Seagull

The correct order of the four terms, starting with the most SPECIFIC or particular and ending with the most GENERAL or encompassing is: seagull, water fowl, bird, living creature. A seagull is a specific kind of water fowl. A water fowl is a specific bird. A bird is a specific kind of living creature.

59. Answer D. Sedan

The correct order of the four terms, starting with the most GENERAL or encompassing and ending with the most SPECIFIC or particular is: vehicle, motor vehicle, automobile, sedan. A motor vehicle is one kind of vehicle. An automobile is a specific kind of motor vehicle. A sedan is a specific kind of automobile. (Other kinds of automobiles: convertibles, station wagons, coupes.)

60. Answer B. A center of the glove-making industry since its earliest days, Johnstown was founded by and named for Sir William Johnson, a British general during the mid-1700s.

Note the relative brevity of this answer choice. Five words shorter than the three original sentences, it retains all the ideas of the originals while combining them into a complex whole. Note also that Choice D, a very muddled sentence, introduces the new idea that it was Johnson who named the town after himself. The original sentence states that Johnstown was named for Johnson but gives no evidence about who actually did the naming. Eliminate answer choices that introduce information that is not provided in the original sentences.

61. Answer B. 9¼

Use the common denominator (8ths) to express all three lengths:

$$1\tfrac{3}{8} + 2\tfrac{3}{8} + 5\tfrac{1}{2} = (1 + 2 + 5) + (\tfrac{3}{8} + \tfrac{3}{8} + \tfrac{4}{8}) = 8 + \tfrac{10}{8} = 9\tfrac{2}{8}$$

Reduce the ²⁄₈ fraction to ¼; the sum is 9¼.

62. Answer A. February

You are looking for a month in which the actual expense is more than (exceeds) the budgeted amount of $125.

A. February. She paid $126.25, which is *more* than the budget.

This must be the answer to the question, and you don't need to go on to check the other choices.

63. Answer C. April

Look at her record to find what the clothes budget was in each of the four months: for January she budgeted $20, for February $20, for March $20, and for April $50. April is the month with a larger budget than usual.

64. Answer A. $0.86

The actual expense for phone service in February was $5.86. She had budgeted $5, and so the amount she paid was *more* than the budget by the difference:

$$\begin{array}{r} \$5.86 \\ -\ 5.00 \\ \hline \$0.86 \end{array}$$

This is Choice A.

65. Answer C. $16.96

To find the total cost for telephone service during the 4 months, we must add the 4 actual expense figures:

$ 3.45	for January
5.86	for February
3.45	for March
+ 4.20	for April
$16.96	total

66. Answer C. $223.93

Martha's total expenses for April were:

$121.16	for rent
62.35	for food
36.22	for clothes
+ 4.20	for phone
$223.93	total

67. Answer D. A spotted snake

Many clues in the poem lead you to this correct answer. The movement in the grass (think of the archetypal "snake in the grass"), the physical images (the spotted shaft, the supposed "whiplash" that wriggles off when the speaker tries to pick it up), the identification of the narrow fellow as one of "nature's people"—all these point to the narrow fellow's being *a spotted snake.*

68. Answer B. The grass

This question is tricky. You really need to know that the "spotted shaft" is the snake's body glimpsed through the grass and not a hole in the ground (like a mine shaft) that miraculously closes and then opens in a different place. What Dickinson is describing here is the snake's movement through the grass, which first parts or separates ("divides as with a comb") to let him through and then closes behind him once he's moved on.

69. Answer C. An adult male

In the third and fourth verses, the speaker refers to incidents in his youth, when he was "a boy, and barefoot." This suggests that he is now no longer a boy but *an adult male.* Despite his acquaintanceship with nature's people, however, there is no evidence that he is an expert naturalist.

70. Answer B. Marked fear

What causes the speaker's "tighter breathing" and his sense of being chilled to the core? His intense, *marked fear* of the snake. The correct answer is Choice B. Choice D is incorrect: though the speaker feels cordial goodwill toward other living creatures, he fears snakes.

71. Answer B. 1990

All other years except 1990 have a percent CPI change of 5% or more.

72. Answer A. Increase, decrease, increase

The inflation rate on this graph starts at about 6%, rises to 6.5%, and then to 10.5%, 15% and about 17% (in 1986). After that, it goes down to 13% in 1988, 6% in 1989, and 3% in 1990. Then it rises again to about 6% in 1991. There is a small decline in 1992, but the pattern described by A is closer to correct than any of the other choices. Choices B and C are clearly wrong. The graph doesn't begin with a decrease or with a level section and a decrease. Choice D is wrong because the inflation rate didn't level off at 1990, but instead rose again.

73. Answer D.   6 times

The low point for inflation was in 1990 at a value a little below 3%; the high point was in 1986 at about 17%. The fraction $\frac{17}{3} = 5\frac{2}{3}$ is closer to 6 than 5. (Since the 1990 rate is less than 3, the actual ratio is probably very close to 6; you don't need to figure it exactly.)

74. Answer B.   30

There are two different rates at which the girls wash the cars: Kathy washes four cars per hour (it takes her 15 minutes, ¼ hour, to wash a car) and the others each wash three cars per hour (20 minutes is $^{20}\!/_{60} = \frac{1}{3}$ hour.) At Kathy's rate, she can wash $4N$ cars in N hours. Emily and Nancy can each wash $3N$ cars in N hours. The total number of cars in three hours is $4 \times 3 + 3 \times 3 + 3 \times 3 = 12 + 9 + 9 = 12 + 18 = 30$. You could also solve this by simplifying the algebraic expression before multiplying by the three hours:

$$\text{Total cars} = 4N + 3N + 3N = (4 + 3 + 3)\,N = 10N.$$

For $N = 3$, this gives a total of 30.

75. Answer A. $54

His purchases were $45 + $15 = $60. A 10% discount means he got ¹⁄₁₀ taken off the listed price. ¹⁄₁₀ of $60 is $6, so he paid $60 − $6 = $54.

76. Answer C.   125

The typist used ¾ of the ream of 500 sheets. She is left with ¼ of that amount. $500 \div 4 = 125$.

77. Answer B.   Hindrance

A diversion is a distraction or an amusement, something that makes you turn away from your usual occupation: After sitting at the computer all day, Sharon found her phone call from Helen was a pleasant diversion. Therefore, Choice A is incorrect. Repression is the act of checking or keeping down feelings or actions or desires: Someone who tells you to keep a stiff upper lip advocates the repression of your natural emotions. It can also be the act of subduing or crushing disorder or treason: China's repression of student dissent shocked many Westerners. Choice C is also incorrect. Conservation is the act of preserving or saving something. During the drought, experts in water conservation told Californians to quit watering their lawns. Choice D is incorrect. A hindrance, however, is something that obstructs or prevents something, an obstacle or impediment. Marcel Marceau's lack of English was no hindrance to him onstage, for the language of pantomime is universal. Choice B is correct.

78. Answer A.   Spontaneous

Something extravagant is excessive or extreme; it may also be overpriced: Sally spent $100 on her extravagant Mohawk haircut. Wasn't that extravagant of Sally to spend so much? Choice B is incorrect. Amateurish is the opposite of professional: An amateurish production, however, isn't necessarily *unrehearsed*; it may simply be *badly* rehearsed. Choice C is incorrect. Something momentary lasts only for a moment; it may or may not be planned: Though Romeo caught only a momentary glimpse of Juliet, it was enough to make him fall in love with her.

Therefore, Choice D is incorrect. Something spontaneous, however, is unprepared; it's done without any premeditation. The correct answer is Choice A.

79. Answer B. Exploit

To undertake something is to tackle it, to take it on as a task or responsibility: Mother warned Billy not to undertake any job too big for him to handle. Choice A is incorrect. To disregard something is to pay no attention to it, to overlook or ignore it: Please disregard anything Tony says about his ex-wife; he's too upset about the divorce to speak rationally about her. Choice C is incorrect. To contribute something is to donate or furnish it: Marsha contributed a batch of brownies to the pot luck supper. Choice D is incorrect. To exploit something, however, is to take full advantage of it, possibly misusing it in the process: The movie star's son exploited his family connections to get a job in films. The Spanish conquerors exploited the natives, forcing them to work as peons. The correct answer is Choice B.

80. Answer B. $5,010

The car lost (50% + 20%) of its original value in the two years, or 70% altogether. Its value at the end of the two years is 100% − 70% = 30% of the original value, that is:

$$16,700 \times 0.3 = 1670 \times 3 = 5010.$$

81. Answer C. 88

The average number of tickets that he sells per hour is the total number of tickets sold divided by the total number of hours. That is 528 tickets ÷ 6 hours.

$$
\begin{array}{r}
88 \text{ tickets per hour} \\
6\overline{)528} \\
\underline{48} \\
48 \\
\underline{48} \\
\end{array}
$$

82. Answer B. 10

Look for the pattern in the number arrangement. Each row begins with 1, then goes on to the number of its line (3 is in the third line, *etc.*). In fact, each number is the sum of the numbers above it in the previous row. But you do not need to solve this puzzle completely to get the answer; the rows show a pattern of increase and decrease from left to center and from center to the right side. The second half of the row will be the same as the first half in reverse, that is 10, then 5, then 1. That is, the next number after 1, 5, and 10 will be Choice B, 10.

83. Answer C. $9,420

The woman takes out a loan for $96,000 minus the down payment of $17,500; that is, her loan is for $96,000 − $17,500 = $78,500. She must pay 12% of this amount in interest the first year. To find 12% of an amount, multiply the amount by 12%, which is the same as 0.12:

$$
\begin{array}{r}
\$\ 78,500 \\
\times\ .12 \\
\hline
157\ 000 \\
785\ 00 \\
\hline
\$9420.00 \\
\end{array}
$$

84. Answer B. _b_

In a triangle, the longest side is opposite the largest angle, and the smallest side is opposite the smallest angle. The sum of the angles is 180°, so the third angle is $180° - (75 + 45) = 180 - 120 = 60°$. The largest angle is the one marked 75, and the longest side is b, opposite this angle.

85. Answer A. June 1

The man wants to save $900 in installments of $150, making his last deposit on November 1 in order to have the whole $900 tax payment on November 15. He must make six deposits altogether because $150 goes into $900 exactly 6 times ($900 \div 150 = \frac{90}{15} = 6$). If he always makes the deposit on the first of the month and skips none of the deposits, he can figure out when to start by counting backwards from November 1 for six deposits:

(6)   November 1
(5)   October 1
(4)   September 1
(3)   August 1
(2)   July 1
(1)   June 1

The first deposit should be on June 1 (Choice A).

86. Answer A. $6.90

If the man pays $15 down and makes 3 monthly payments of $7.95 each, he will pay a total of $15 + (3 × $7.95) for the watch:

$ 7.95
× 3
$23.85 + $15 down = $ 38.85 total
− 31.95 (cash)
$ 6.90

If he pays cash ($31.95), he will save the difference.

87. Answer B. $269.70

To calculate the supermarket's profit of 1.5% on sales of $17,980, it is easiest to find 1% of the total sales and then find half of that 1% (½ of 1% = 0.5%) and add the two amounts together. It is also easy to find 1% of an amount—just shift the decimal point over two places to the left. 1% of $17,980 = $179.80. Half of this is:

$ 89.90
2)$179.80
16
19
18
18
18

Adding the two values together:

1.0% $179.80
+ 0.5%   + 89.90
1.5% $269.70

88. Answer C. An Army Reserve recruiting pamphlet

The passage discusses the pay and benefits to which a retired member of the Reserve is entitled. It talks about them in personal terms: they are *your* retirement and survivor benefits, good things that you can get if you serve in the Reserve for 20 years. Such a list showing the advantages of joining the service belongs most naturally in a Reserve recruiting pamphlet aimed at persuading potential reservists to enlist. The correct answer is Choice C. Though Choice D may appeal to you, it is incorrect—a civil service pension guide provides information about civilian administrative pensions, not military ones.

89. Answer C. Statements II and III only

Use the process of elimination to answer this question. Under the heading "PX and Commissary Shopping Privileges," the passage states that spouses (wives or husbands) may shop at these stores. Therefore Statement I is true. You can rule out Choices A, B, and D. Both Statements II and III are false. Under the heading "Travel," the passage states retirees may ride aircraft on a space-available basis. That means that, if a particular military flight were fully booked, the retiree would not be able to get on it. Similarly, under "Medical Care," the passage specifically states that medical treatments at civilian hospitals may sometimes be paid for by the Army.

90. Answer D. Unlimited dental care for dependents

Use the process of elimination to answer this question. The final paragraph lists veterinary aid as a benefit for retirees. Therefore, the Reserve does provide care for sick pets belonging to retirees. You can cross out Choice A. The paragraph also states retirees may use such on-post facilities as golf courses and tennis courts. Therefore, the Reserve does provide access to athletic facilities for its retirees. You can cross out Choice B. The paragraph also mentions legal assistance as a retirement benefit. You can cross out Choice C. Only Choice D is left. It is the correct answer. While the Reserve provides unlimited dental care for its retirees, it does not provide unlimited care for their dependents: "There are restrictions on the amount of care" dependents receive.

91. Answer B. The PX is a store used by both active and retired military personnel.

Again, use the process of elimination to reach the right answer. Note the phrase that begins the paragraph on dental care. *Providing facilities are available,* the Reserve offers dental treatment for retirees. If no facilities are available, the Reserve can't offer dental care. Therefore, it is false to claim that the "Reserve *always* provides dental treatment for retirees." Choice A is incorrect. The second paragraph states that you are entitled to retirement pay "when you reach the age of 60 after 20 years of qualifying service." If you've served for 20 years, you will begin receiving your retirement pay when you turn 60. It is false that you have to wait till you are 80 (20 years *after* you reach 60). Choice C is incorrect. According to the last paragraph, retirees can use military-maintained recreation areas "on lakes, by seashores, or in the mountains." Thus, they are entitled to use both off-post and on-post military recreation facilities, not just on-post ones. Choice D is incorrect. Only Choice B is left. It is true that both active and retired military personnel may shop at the PX. The correct answer is B.

92. Answer A. 11 inches

If the handyman cut the board into three *equal* pieces, each piece would be 12 inches long (since a yard is 36 inches and ⅓ of 36 inches = 12 inches). But one piece has to be an inch shorter and the third piece an inch longer than the second piece; if we "borrow" the extra inch for the third piece from the first piece, everything comes out right: the first piece is 1 inch shorter than the average, the second piece is just the average length, and the third piece is 1 inch longer than the average. 11 inches + 12 inches + 13 inches add up to 36 inches or 1 yard.

You can also do this as an equation, which you solve to find the length of the first piece; use the letter L to stand for the length of the first piece. The second piece is 1 inch longer than this, so its length is $L + 1$; and the third piece is 1 inch longer than the second, so its length is $L + 1 + 1 = L + 2$. We still don't know what L is, but we find out by adding all the lengths to make up 1 yard. $L + (L + 1) + (L + 2) = 36$. Adding the Ls together, we get $(3 \times L) + 1 + 2 = 36$ or $(3 \times L) + 3 = 36$. Subtract 3 from both sides: $3 \times L = 33$, and finally divide both sides by 3 to get

$$\frac{3 \times L}{3} = \frac{33}{3} = 11.$$

Therefore, the length of the first piece is 11 inches.

93. Answer B. 28

The number of boys is six times the number of girls, and the total enrollment is 196. Adding the boys and girls together we get # girls + # boys = 196. But # boys = 6 × # girls, so we have # girls + 6 × # girls = 196 or 7 × # girls = 196. Therefore the number of girls is 196 divided by 7:

$$7\overline{)196}^{28}$$

94. Answer A. The underlined word is spelled correctly.

"Whether" is a conjunction used to introduce the first of two (or more) alternatives. "Weather" refers to the state of the atmosphere. If the weather is bad enough (lots of snow, rain, etc.), it can cause stones to weather (crumble or disintegrate), unless the stones are solid enough to weather (survive or endure) such bad weather.

95. Answer B. The underlined word is spelled incorrectly.

Do you remember the old spelling formula: "The princi*pal* is your *pal* at school?" Similarly, a princi*ple* is a moral ru*le*. The sentence should read: "My aunt lived according to the strictest moral *principles*: she never did anything wrong.

96. Answer B. $87.66

The man is unmarried; so he is unlikely to make use of the plans for "Member & Spouse" or "Member & Children" or "Member, Spouse, & Children." The premium for the "Member Only" program for someone aged 58 is in the row marked 50–59; that is, $87.66, Choice B.

97. Answer C. $89.58

The insurance rate for a 28-year-old wife is less than that for a 43-year-old husband. Since both are eligible, by taking out the insurance in the wife's name, they are arranging that she is the member, and her husband then becomes insured as the member's spouse. Therefore, they will find the premium in the second column ("Member & Spouse") and in the first row because the wife is less than 35 years old. This place in the table shows that their premium will be $89.58.

98. Answer C. $39.14

When the wife turns 35, the premium goes up from $89.58 to $128.72. The increase is:

$128.72
$\underline{- 89.58}$
$ 39.14

99. Answer C. $1,399.68

In the two weeks, she works 2 × 30 = 60 regular hours, at the rate of $21.60 per hour, plus eight hours (three the first week, five the next) at the reduced rate. For the regular hours, she gets 60 × 21.60 = 6 × 216 = $1,296. Since she gets paid at the reduced rate for the extra eight hours, you can eliminate Choices A and B at this stage; only C or D could be correct. You could figure out exactly what she makes for the extra eight hours, but you can also estimate this as follows: 60% of $21.60 is somewhat more than half, say roughly $12 per hour. Then the eight hours are worth approximately 8 × $12 = $96. The correct answer, therefore, should be about $100 more than the $1296 for her regular 60 hours, giving Choice C.

For the exact calculation, find 60% of $21.60

21.6
$\underline{× 0.6}$
12.96

Then, her pay for the extra hours is

12.96
$\underline{×   8}$
103.68

and her total pay is $1,296.00 + $103.68 = $1,399.68.

100. Answer C.   Houston

A winning percentage of 45% means that less than half the games were won. From this, you can eliminate Choices A and B (Los Angeles won more than they lost; San Diego, the same number won and lost). 45% is not very much less than 50%, so Houston with ten wins should have a percentage not too far from San Diego's 50%. Check this by doing the division; if it isn't close to 45%, you can then try the remaining choice. It helps to reduce 10/22 to lowest terms, 5/11, to make the division easier:

$$\begin{array}{r} 0.45... \\ 11\overline{)5.00...} \\ \underline{4\,4} \\ 60 \\ \underline{55} \end{array}$$

CHAPTER 2
The Basics of Writing

You have 30 minutes in which to write a short essay. If you have not had to do much writing in high school or if you have received poor grades on the written work you have handed in, you may be worried about how well you will do on this part of the test. Relax. If you can talk coherently, you can write coherently. The trick is to involve yourself in what you write.

WHAT THE EXAMINERS LOOK FOR

The examiners at California Proficiency Testing are looking for someone who can communicate ideas. Basically, your essay tells the examiners whether you are able to put your thoughts on paper and get across a point to a friendly audience. The examiners don't expect perfection from you—they expect proficiency.

What is proficiency? Fundamentally, it is a combination of three elements:

1. **Fluency.** Fluency is smoothness and ease in communicating. In this case, it is your ability to set down a given number of words on paper within a limited period of time. If you freeze on essay examinations, writing only a sentence or two when whole paragraphs are called for, then you need to practice letting your words and ideas *flow*.

2. **Organization.** Organization is coherent arrangement. In this case, it is your ability to arrange your thoughts in order, following a clear game plan. If you jump from subject to subject within a single paragraph, if you leave out critical elements, or if you never manage to state exactly what you mean, then you need to practice outlining your position before you express it in paragraph form.

3. **Technical English.** Technical English is the part of English most students hate—grammar, spelling, punctuation, word usage. In this case, it is your ability to produce grammatically correct sentences in standard written English. If your English compositions come back to you with the abbreviations "frag" (fragment) or "agr" (agreement) or "sp" (spelling) scribbled in the margins, then you need to practice reading your papers to catch any technical mistakes.

4. **Completeness.** Completeness means just that. The essay topic often includes several questions. The examiners want you to answer every one of them. If you don't, you may lose up to half of the twelve points you could earn on the essay.

You will be asked to write one short essay in 30 minutes during your High School Proficiency Examination. Currently, the questions are in general expository rather than argumentative form. The questions require you to describe a person, thing, or event that has been important to you. It is possible, however, that you may be asked to take a position on an issue—older versions of the examination often required you to write an argumentative essay rather than an expository one. In order to be safe, you should be prepared to respond to either type of question.

HOW TO WRITE AN ESSAY IN 30 MINUTES

Minute One—Analyze

Look at the essay question. What is it asking you to do? Is it asking you to explain the reasons for an opinion of yours? Is it asking you to describe someone or something? Is it asking you to tell about a personal experience you have had? If you are being asked to argue for or against something, you may have an immediate gut reaction to what you're being asked. Pay attention to how you feel. If your immediate reaction is "Of course!" or "Never!" ask yourself why you feel that way.

See whether you can spot any key word or short phrase in the question that triggers your reaction. For example, consider the following essay question:

Write a brief essay explaining why you believe young persons should or should not be required to wear school uniforms.

What word or phrase triggers your reaction? "School uniforms."

Minutes Two to Three—Brainstorm

Write down the key word or phrase you spotted in the question. Circle it. Now write down other words and phrases that you associate with this key word or phrase. What words come to your mind, for example, when you think of school uniforms? Neutral words like <u>plaid</u>, <u>pleated skirts</u>, <u>blazers</u>? Negative words like <u>tacky</u>, <u>parochial</u>, <u>ugly</u>, <u>miserable</u>, <u>conformist</u>, <u>polyester</u>? Positive words like <u>noncompetitive</u>, <u>equal for everyone</u>, <u>no pressure</u>, <u>inexpensive</u>? Words like <u>soldiers</u>, <u>prisoners</u>, <u>police</u>, <u>guns</u>? Whether or not you ever had to wear a school uniform, you have some mental associations with the idea of uniforms and with wearing uniforms in school. By brainstorming, or clustering, as this process is sometimes called, you can tap these associations, call up the wealth of *ideas you already have,* and forget any worries you may have had about having nothing to say.

Note, by the way, in the illustration below, the many other words and phrases that branch off from the central phrase, "school uniforms." When you brainstorm, your mind leads you in innumerable directions, hinting at the whole range of what you already know about the subject at hand. If you feel like it, draw lines and arrows linking the various words and phrases to your key phrase. Don't worry about setting these words and phrases in any particular order. Just play with them, jotting them down and doodling around them—a sense of where you are going will emerge.

You have plenty to say. You have gut reactions to all sorts of questions. Let the brainstorming process tap the knowledge and feelings that lie within you.

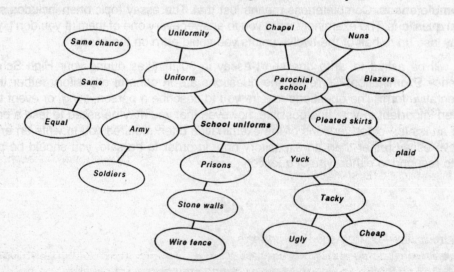

Minutes Four to Five—Define Your Position

After you have been brainstorming for a minute or so, something inside you is going to say "Now"—*now* I know what I'm going to write. Trust that inner sense. You know where you are going—now put it into words.

Look over your "map" or record of your mental associations and see what patterns have emerged. Just what is it that you have to say? Are you *for* school uniforms? Are you *against* them? Are your feelings *mixed?* What you are doing is coming up with a statement of your position—words to express your initial gut reaction—a *thesis sentence* for your essay.

<u>Thesis 1</u>: I believe students should be required to wear uniforms in school because wearing school uniforms lessens peer pressure and promotes social equality.

<u>Thesis 2</u>: I believe students should not be required to wear uniforms in school because school uniforms are unattractive outfits which no one likes.

<u>Thesis 3</u>: Although I was miserable wearing a uniform in elementary school, I still believe young people should be required to wear uniforms in school.

Here are three possible thesis sentences, one for, one against, one mixed. Note how their main clauses start: <u>I believe</u>, <u>I believe</u>, <u>I still believe</u>. In your opening sentence, *state your point*. Don't wait. The examiners want to see whether you can express your ideas clearly. Make your point clear to them from the start.

In a sense, the test-makers give you your opening sentence. All you have to do is take the question and rephrase it. This does not take much work. Remember, your job is to prove your writing competence, not demonstrate your literary style. You do not need to open your essay with a quotation ("Henry Thoreau warns us, 'Beware of all enterprises that require new clothes.'") or with a statement designed to startle your reader ("My school uniform hates me."). You simply need to state your thesis. In doing so, however, you must exercise some caution: you must limit your thesis to something you can handle in a couple of hundred words.

The one problem with brainstorming is that you may wind up feeling that you have too much to say. Your job is not to write *Everything You Ever Wanted to Know about School Uniforms (But Were Afraid to Ask)*. It is to write one or two pages and make a single clear point. Avoid starting with open-ended statements like "School uniforms are ugly" or "Everybody should wear uniforms." These are weak thesis statements—they are too broad to help you focus on the topic and too vague to show why you hold the opinion that you have.

In writing your thesis statement, limit yourself. State your point—and be ready to support it with reasons.

Minutes Six to Eight—Outline

Now take a minute to organize what you are going to say in outline form. In a sense, your thesis sentence sets up everything else you have to say. It you have a clear thesis, the essay almost writes itself.

See how each of the thesis sentences just discussed sets up the essay, in each case requiring a slightly different outline.

Outline 1

I.   Introduction—statement of your thesis
      I believe students should be required to wear uniforms in school because wearing school uniforms lessens peer pressure and promotes social equality.

II. Reasons
   A. Lessens Peer Pressure
      1. "Clothes wars"
      2. Pressure to keep up with Joneses
   B. Promotes Social Equality
      1. Rich and poor wear same clothes
      2. Clothes don't make the person

III. Conclusion—restatement of your thesis
To promote a spirit of equality among young people and to free them from pressures inspired by the fashion industry, students should be required to wear uniforms while they attend school.

Outline 2

I. Introduction—statement of your thesis
I believe students should not be required to wear uniforms in school because school uniforms are unattractive that outfits that no one likes.

II. Description of School Uniform
   A. Unbecoming Colors
   B. Unflattering Cut
   C. Mediocre Materials

III. Conclusion—restatement of your thesis
Young or old, nobody likes to wear unbecoming clothing. Young people should not be forced to wear unattractive uniforms that they heartily dislike.

Outline 3

I. Introduction—statement of your thesis
Although I was miserable wearing a uniform in elementary school, I still believe young people should be required to wear uniforms in school.
II. Elementary School Experience
III. Reasons for Change of Opinion
IV. Conclusion—restatement of your thesis
Being required to wear a school uniform distressed me in elementary school. Looking back, however, I can see it helped me as well. Thus, I believe that school uniforms are beneficial and that wearing them should be required.

Minutes Nine to Twenty-four—Write

You have 15 minutes to write your essay. You have your opening, your outline, and your conclusion all in mind. Devote this time to putting down your thoughts, writing approximately a page and a half. Try to write neatly, but don't worry so much about neatness that you wind up clenching your pencil for dear life. Just leave yourself room in the margins and know that there's no problem if you cross out or erase.

Minute Twenty-five—Read

Expert writers often test their work by reading it aloud. In the exam room, you cannot read out loud. However, when you read your essay silently, take your time and listen with your inner ear to how it sounds. Read to get a sense of your essay's logic and of its rhythm. Does one sentence flow smoothly into the next? Would they flow more smoothly if you were to add a transition word or phrase (therefore, however, nevertheless, in contrast, similarly)?

Do the sentences follow a logical order? Is any key idea or example missing? Does any sentence seem out of place? How would things sound if you cut out that awkward sentence or inserted that transition word?

Minute Twenty-six—React

Take this minute to act on your response to hearing your essay. If it sounded to you as if a transition word was needed, insert it. If it sounded to you as if a sentence should be cut, delete it. If it sounded to you as if a sentence was out of place, move it. Trust your inner ear, but do not attempt to do too much. You know your basic outline for the essay is good. You have neither the need nor the time to attempt a total revision.

Minute Twenty-seven—Reword

Look over your vocabulary in your essay. In your concern to get your thoughts on paper, have you limited yourself to an overly simple vocabulary? Have you used one word over and over again, never substituting a synonym? Try upgrading your vocabulary. Replace one word in the essay with a synonym—<u>detest</u> or <u>loathe</u> in place of <u>hate</u> in the sentence <u>Students hate school uniforms</u>, for example. Substitute a somewhat more specific adjective or adverb for a vague one—<u>gentle</u> or <u>considerate</u> in place of <u>nice</u>; <u>extremely</u> unflattering in place of <u>really</u> unflattering. Again, do not attempt to do too much. Change only one or two words. Replace them with stronger words *whose meanings you are sure you know.*

Minute Twenty-eight—Rescan

Think of yourself as an editor. You need to have an eye for errors that damage your text.

Take a minute to look over your essay for problems in spelling and grammar. From your English classes you should have an idea of particular words and grammatical constructions that have proved troublesome to you in the past. See whether you can spot any of these words or constructions in your essay. Correct those errors that you find.

Minute Twenty-nine—Reread

Now that you have looked over your essay like an editor, give yourself one final opportunity to hear your words again. Reread the composition to yourself, making sure that the changes you have made have not harmed the flow of your text.

Minute Thirty—Relax

You have just completed a basic essay. Now it is time to regroup your forces and relax before you go on to the next section of the test. Take a deep breath. Admire your essay. If you feel you have to do *something*, spend the time erasing stray marks on your paper or rewriting words that are hard to read. Do nothing major; at this point, you have earned a break.

DEVELOPING YOUR ESSAY WRITING SKILLS

You have just read about the process of writing a 30-minute essay. Now you should be ready to try writing a 30-minute essay of your own. Find a quiet corner where you will be undisturbed for the full 30 minutes—no phone calls, no MTV in the background, no soda breaks. You want to approximate exam conditions as closely as you can. In this practice session, however, you do get a choice of essay topics. Do not feel you have to write on all these topics. They are here to give you a wide choice and to make you aware of the range of topics on the CHSPE.

In the weeks to come, try writing on several of these topics. If you can, show your completed essays to a teacher or to a friend who does well in English. Get feedback on the organization of your essays, as well as on your technical mistakes. Make a check list of words you misspell. To write well is a valuable skill—the time you spend improving your ability as a writer will pay off, not only on the CHSPE, but throughout your adult life.

Argumentative Essay Topics

1. Many students today object to mandatory exercise and fitness classes. Write an essay explaining why you believe high school students should or should not be required to take physical education classes.

2. Write a short essay explaining why you believe young persons should or should not move away from home as soon as they are able to support themselves.

3. Write a short essay giving your opinion whether the speed limit should or should not be set at 55 miles per hour.

4. Write a short essay explaining why you believe young persons enrolled in school should or should not be limited to one hour of television viewing per day.

5. Write a short essay discussing why you did or did not enjoy a particular class you took in high school.

6. Many young people are involved in hobbies or pastimes, such as gardening or playing Dungeons and Dragons. Discuss a particular hobby or pastime with which you are acquainted, telling why you find it beneficial or harmful to participants.

7. Write a short essay explaining why you believe young people should or should not work part time while attending high school.

8. The automobile insurance industry considers teenage drivers risky clients and requires them to pay high rates. Write a short essay explaining why you believe teenage drivers are safer or less safe than elderly drivers are.

9. Write a short essay giving your opinion as to whether the drinking age should or should not be lowered in California.

10. Write a short essay explaining why you believe fraternities and sororities should or should not be permitted in high school.

Descriptive Essay Topics

1. Most young people in the course of their lives have been greatly influenced by a particular adult—a relative, a teacher, an employer, a coach. Choose a person who has been of great influence in your life, and write a short essay on him or her. Describe the person. Explain how he or she has influenced you. If you were to thank this person for his or her help, what would you say?

2. Write a short essay describing your ideal vacation. Where would you go? What would you do there? Explain why you would enjoy this trip.

3. People often have emotional reactions to the places where they live or work. Write a short essay about a place in your town that you particularly like. Describe the place. Explain what you like about it. Describe one of your experiences visiting this place.

4. Describe your dream job. What are the responsibilities of the position? Explain why you are well suited for the job. What training would you need to qualify for this job? Title your essay "Dream Job."

5. Every child has had a possession that he or she treasured in youth. Write a short essay describing a possession that you treasured as a child. What was it? How did you acquire it? Why was it special to you?

6. What is your favorite holiday? Explain what the holiday celebrates. Describe what you do to celebrate the holiday. Why is this holiday of special significance to you? Title your essay "Favorite Holiday."

7. Most of us have had a favorite teacher. Who is your favorite teacher? What class did he or she teach? What did you like most about this teacher? How has he or she influenced you? Title your essay "Favorite Teacher."

8. Imagine that you were to run for political office. For what position would you choose to run? What qualifications or skills would you bring to the job? What changes would you like to make once you were elected? Title your essay "My Life in Politics."

9. Most of us associate certain foods with special memories. Write a short essay about a food that brings back memories for you. Describe the food. When was it served to you? What memories does it trigger, and how does it make you feel?

10. Most of us have a special friend with whom we can share our frustrations and our triumphs. Who is your special friend? How did you meet him or her? What sets this friendship apart from others?

SAMPLE ESSAYS—ONE THAT SCORED HIGH AND ONE THAT SCORED LOW

ESSAY TOPIC 1   30 MINUTES

For many, reading is an exciting experience. For others, it is frustrating and even boring. Tell the story of your life as a reader. What were your earliest experiences with reading? What was your favorite book as a child? What role does reading play in your life today? Title your essay "Reading Autobiography."

READING AUTOBIOGRAPHY

Reading has always been a positive influence on my life. Originating in the early stages of my life, my interest in reading has grown as time has progressed. My experience as a reader has had both academic and entertaining effects on my life.

My first experiences in reading began while I was in preschool. Daily, my mother read stories to me. These stories captured my interest and motivated me to learn how to read on my own. Though I often got frustrated, I never gave up trying to read my first book, "The Cat in the Hat."

My ability to read advanced in stages, and along the way it has motivated my imagination. My favorite book as a child was "Grover Goes to the Museum," because the character Grover explored different areas of history and technology. I often pictured myself in Grover's place, and from this story and other stories I read, during my early years, I learned to allow my imagination to flow freely.

Reading has had many positive effects in my life, both past and present. Directly, it has been a form of enjoyment, but the indirect effects of my interest in reading have greater significance. Reading has boosted my vocabulary and taught me proper grammar. Without reading, there would be a void in my life that could never be filled.

Remarks: The first essay receives a relatively high score not because it is stylistically brilliant but because it is complete. It responds to all points of the topic. It is reasonably well organized. Each paragraph begins with a topic sentence that states what the paragraph will cover. There are no striking technical flaws: the essay contains few errors in spelling, punctuation, or grammar. The writer writes nothing that is particularly interesting, but he clearly makes his point.

ESSAY TOPIC 2   **30 MINUTES**

Most people have a favorite hobby or activity. Describe your favorite hobby or activity. Explain what you like best about it. How were you introduced to this hobby or activity? Title your essay "Favorite Hobby."

FAVORITE HOBBY

My favorite hobby is to play basketball. I like the exercise I get from it. I was introduced to the sport at elementary school.

Basketball is a sport where two opposing teams, five people per team, try to score points by shooting a ball into a basket. There is a set time limit for how long the game will be played. After time expires, the team with the greatest number of points win.

I like what this sport gives me. It gives me the physical and mental exercise I need in order to succeed in the future. I develop stronger muscles as I run up and down the court. I learn how to play as a team. I learned not to be selfish because being selfish will not help me win. I no longer get out of breath with running for a minute. These skills will help me later in my life, both in health and in my job.

I was first introduced to this hobby in elementary school. I saw all my friends playing and they ask me if I wanted to play. I nodded my head and stepped onto the court. I was pretty horrible at this game. But after a couple of months I was considered one of the best on my team.

All of the reasons above is why my favorite hobby is basketball. I play everyday in high school. The things I learned will always be apart of me.

Remarks: The second essay, though lively in tone, earns a significantly lower score than the first because it contains many technical flaws. Some problems are:

faulty idiom (The opening sentence should read: "My favorite hobby is playing basketball.")

flawed subject-verb agreement ("the team with the greatest number of points <u>win</u>," "All of the reasons above <u>is</u>");

incorrect sequence of tenses ("I <u>saw</u> all my friends playing and they <u>ask</u> me");

poor spelling ("apart" instead of "a part"; "everyday" instead of "every day").

ADVANCED OUTLINING

If you have been having trouble structuring your essays, you may find it helpful to consider the following typical ways in which essays are arranged. An essay may be arranged in one of several ways:

1.   It may be arranged in **chronological order**—an order following a time sequence.

2.   It may be arranged as a **comparison** or a **contrast**.

3.   It may be arranged according to an **ascending or descending order of importance**.

4.   It may be arranged to show a pattern of **cause and effect**.

Chronological order organizes details in the order in which they have happened, are happening, or should happen (will happen).

> On the first day God created light, and there was morning and evening on that day.
> On the second day God created the firmament.
> On the third day. . . .

This order is useful in telling a story or describing a process. Notice the sorts of words used to clarify transitions in a chronological paragraph: *first, second, third, fourth; in the beginning, next, then, after that; finally, last, in the end.* You want to use some of these transitional words to help your reader see the time sequence clearly..

When you **compare** two objects, you are trying to point out ways in which they resemble one another. When you **contrast** two objects, you are trying to point out ways in which they differ from one another. Transitional words useful in comparisons are *similarly, likewise, in like manner, in the same way, correspondingly.* Transitional words useful in contrasts are *however, but, in contrast, on the other hand, on the contrary, nevertheless.*

An **ascending order of importance** starts with the least important item in a series and works its way up to the most important. A **descending order of importance** starts with the most important item and works its way down to the least important. Both orders are useful in presenting an argument. In either case, you use transitional words like *first, second, third, fourth; most important, of the greatest importance, somewhat less important, significantly.*

Cause-and-effect order is particularly useful when you are trying to explain something. For example, if you were asked to write about the main reason for the decrease of interest in reading in America, you might write as follows:

> The invention of television has caused Americans to lose interest in reading. In the early days of television, few programs were available. People still had time to read. As television became more and more widespread, *however,* more hours of programming were available each day. *In consequence,* people who were attracted to the new medium found themselves with less time in which to read. They *therefore* read less and *as a result* spent less time developing their basic reading skills. *Consequently,* they never had enough practice to become truly skilled readers; reading, which had been a source of pleasure to previous generations, was just plain hard work to these television fans.

In addition to the italicized transitional words in the preceding paragraph, useful transitional words for cause-and-effect paragraphs are *because, thus, inasmuch as, hence, it follows that.*

Select an appropriate order for your composition.
Use transitional words to provide continuity.

ESSENTIAL GRAMMAR

If you have been having trouble spotting grammatical and other technical errors in your essays, you may find it helpful to work your way through some basic grammatical review. The remainder of this chapter presents the essentials of grammar and usage, describes common problems, and outlines the effects of punctuation marks on the meaning and structure of a sentence. Work through the sections in order. To understand how to avoid the common problems illustrated, you first must acquaint yourself with the technical grammatical terms used in the discussion.

1. **Nouns** are words that name or designate persons, places, things, states, or qualities. *John Jones, Africa, book,* and *justice* are examples of nouns.

2. **Pronouns** are words used in place of nouns. *He, we, them, who, which, this, what, each, everyone,* and *myself* are examples of pronouns.

3. **Verbs** are words or phrases that express action or state of being. *Eat, memorize, believe, feel,* and *seem* are examples of verbs.

4. **Adjectives** are words that serve as modifiers of nouns. *Famous, attractive, tall,* and *devoted* are examples of adjectives.

5. **Adverbs** are words that modify verbs, adjectives, or other adverbs. *Too, very, happily,* and *quietly* are examples of adverbs.

6. **Prepositions** are words used with nouns or pronouns to form phrases. *From, with, between, of,* and *to* are examples of prepositions.

7. **Conjunctions** are words that serve to connect words, phrases, and clauses. *And, but, when,* and *because* are examples of conjunctions.

8. **Articles** are the words *the, a,* and *an.* These words serve to identify as a noun the word that they modify.

9. **Interjections** are grammatically independent words or expressions. *Alas, wow,* and *oh my* are examples of interjections.

NOUNS

Nouns are inflected; that is, they change in form to indicate number and case. *Number* refers to the distinction between singular and plural; *case* refers to the way in which a noun is related to other elements in the sentence.

Number

Nouns are either singular or plural. To form the plural of a noun:

1. Add *s* to the singular.
   girl / girls   house / houses

2. Add *es* when the noun ends in *s, x, z, ch,* or *sh.*
   dish / dishes   church / churches

3. Add *s* when the noun ends in *o* preceded by a vowel.
   folio / folio<u>s</u>   trio / trio<u>s</u>

4. Add *es* when the noun ends in *o* preceded by a consonant.
   tomato / tomato<u>es</u>   potato / potato<u>es</u>
   (Exceptions to this rule: *contraltos, pianos, provisos, dynamos, Eskimos, sopranos.*)

5. Add *s* to nouns ending in *f* or *fe* after changing these letters to *ve*.
   knife / kni<u>ves</u>   shelf / shel<u>ves</u>
   (Exceptions to this rule: *chiefs, dwarfs, griefs, reefs, roofs, safes.*)

6. Add *s* to nouns ending in *y* preceded by a vowel.
   boy / boy<u>s</u>   valley / valley<u>s</u>

7. Add *es* to nouns ending in *y* preceded by a consonant and change the *y* to *i*.
   baby / bab<u>ies</u>   story / stor<u>ies</u>

8. Add *s* to the important part of a hyphenated word.
   brother-in-law / brother<u>s</u>-in-law   passer-by / passer<u>s</u>-by

9. Add *s* or *es* to proper nouns.
   Frank / Frank<u>s</u>   Smith / Smith<u>s</u>
   Jones / Jones<u>es</u>   Charles / Charles<u>es</u>
   (Note that the apostrophe (') is not used.)

10. Add *s* or *es* to either the title or the proper noun when both are mentioned.
    Doctor Brown / Doctor<u>s</u> Brown or Doctor Brown<u>s</u>
    Miss Smith / Miss<u>es</u> Smith or Miss Smith<u>s</u>

11. Add *'s* to form the plural of letters, numerals and symbols.
    e / e<u>'s</u>   9 / 9<u>'s</u>
    etc. / etc.<u>'s</u>   & / &<u>'s</u>

12. Change to a different form in the following cases:
    foot / feet   tooth / teeth
    goose / geese   woman / women
    louse / lice   child / children
    man / men   ox / oxen

13. Retain the foreign form with some words of foreign origin.
    alumna / alumnae   focus / foci
    alumnus / alumni   genus / genera
    analysis / analyses   hypothesis / hypotheses
    antithesis / antitheses   larva / larvae
    bacillus / bacilli   matrix / matrices
    bacterium / bacteria   monsieur / messieurs
    basis / bases   oasis / oases
    crisis / crises   parenthesis / parentheses
    criterion / criteria   thesis / theses
    erratum / errata   trousseau / trousseaux

Note: The correct formation or spelling of plurals is *not* directly tested on the CHSPE. However, you will need to be able to recognize singular and plural noun forms in order to detect certain grammatical errors.

Case

Nouns are also inflected to show possession. The possessive case of nouns is formed in the following manner:

1. If the noun ends in *s*, add an apostrophe (').

2. If the noun does not end in *s*, add an apostrophe (') and an *s*.
   The <u>doctor's</u> office (The office of the doctor)
   The <u>doctors'</u> office (The office of two or more doctors)
   The <u>girl's</u> books (The books of one girl)
   The <u>girls'</u> books (The books of two or more girls)

Note that in nouns of one syllable ending in *s*, either the apostrophe or the apostrophe and an *s* may be used.

<u>James'</u> hat and <u>James's</u> hat are both correct.

A noun preceding a gerund should be in the possessive case. (A gerund is a verb form—a verbal—that is used as a noun: <u>Slicing raw onions</u> made him cry.)

Incorrect: The teacher complained about <u>John</u> talking.
Correct: The teacher complained about <u>John's</u> talking.

PRONOUNS

Pronouns are classified as *personal, relative, interrogative, demonstrative, indefinite, intensive,* or *reflexive*.

Personal Pronouns

Personal pronouns indicate the person speaking, the person spoken to, or the person spoken about. They are inflected to indicate case and number. In the third person, they also indicate gender. *He* is the masculine pronoun, *she* is the feminine pronoun, and *it* is the neuter or common gender pronoun.

The *First Person*
(the person speaking or writing)

Case	Singular	Plural
Nominative	I	we
Possessive	my, mine	our, ours
Objective	me	us

The *Second Person*
(the person spoken or written to)

Case	Singular	Plural
Nominative	you	you
Possessive	your, yours	your, yours
Objective	you	you

The *Third Person*
(the person, place, or thing spoken or written about)
Third Person Masculine

Case	Singular	Plural
Nominative	he	they
Possessive	his	their, theirs
Objective	him	them

Third Person Feminine

Case	Singular	Plural
Nominative	she	they
Possessive	her, hers	their, theirs
Objective	her	them

Third Person Neuter

Case	Singular	Plural
Nominative	it	they
Possessive	its	their, theirs
Objective	it	them

Relative Pronouns

The relative pronouns are *who, which,* and *that.* They are used to relate a word in the independent clause (see the section on clauses later in this chapter) to a dependent clause. *Who* is used to refer to persons, *which* to things, and *that* to both persons and things. Like the personal pronouns, *who* has different forms according to case:

Case	Singular	Plural
Nominative	who	who
Possessive	whose	whose
Objective	whom	whom

Interrogative Pronouns

The interrogative pronouns are *who, which,* and *what.* They are used to ask questions. *Which* and *what* do not change according to case. *Who* follows the forms listed under "Relative Pronouns."

Demonstrative Pronouns

The demonstrative pronouns are *this, that, these,* and *those.* They serve to point out people, places, and things. The plural of *this* is *these;* the plural of *that* is *those.*

Indefinite Pronouns

The indefinite pronouns include *all, anyone, each, either, everyone, somebody, someone, whatever, whoever.* The objective case of *whoever* is *whomever;* all the other indefinite pronouns have the same form in the nominative and objective cases. The possessive case of any indefinite pronoun is formed by adding *'s: everyone's, somebody's.*

Intensive and Reflexive Pronouns

Intensive pronouns are used to intensify or emphasize a noun or pronoun.

I <u>myself</u> did it.

Reflexive pronouns refer back to the subject of the sentence.

> I taught <u>myself</u>.

The intensive and reflexive pronouns have the same singular and plural forms:

Person	Singular	Plural
First	myself	ourselves
Second	yourself	yourselves
Third	himself	themselves
	herself	themselves

Some Problems Involving Pronouns

The major grammatical problems concerning pronouns involve agreement and case. These are discussed in the following section.

An intensive pronoun should not be used without the noun or pronoun to which it refers.

> Incorrect: <u>Herself</u> baked the cake.
> Correct: <u>Mary herself</u> baked the cake.

Like nouns, a pronoun preceding a gerund should be in the possessive case.

> Incorrect: She objected to <u>me</u> going out too late.
> Correct: She objected to <u>my</u> going out too late.

VERBS

Conjugation of Verbs

Verbs change their forms to indicate person, number, tense, mood, and voice. The various changes involved are indicated when the verb is *conjugated*. In order to conjugate a verb, its *principal parts* must be known.

Principal Parts of *to talk*

Infinite: *to talk*
Present tense: *talk*
Present participle: *talking*
Past tense: *talked*
Past participle: *talked*

When the principal parts of a verb are listed, the infinitive and the present participle are often omitted.

CONJUGATION OF THE REGULAR VERB *TO CARRY*
(principal parts: *carry, carried, carried*)

Indicative Mood—Active Voice

Present Tense

Singular	Plural
I carry	We carry
You carry	You carry
He, she, it carries	They carry

Past Tense

Singular	Plural
I carried	We carried
You carried	You carried
He, she, it carried	They carried

Future Tense

Singular	Plural
I shall (will) carry*	We shall (will) carry*
You will carry	You will carry
He, she, it will carry	They will carry

Present Perfect Tense

Singular	Plural
I have carried	We have carried
You have carried	You have carried
He, she, it has carried	They have carried

Past Perfect Tense

Singular	Plural
I had carried	We had carried
You had carried	You had carried
He, she, it had carried	They had carried

Future Perfect Tense

Singular	Plural
I shall (will) have carried*	We shall (will) have carried*
You will have carried	You will have carried
He, she, it will have carried	They will have carried

* Some traditional grammarians assert that only the auxiliary verb *shall* is correct in the first person when simple future or future perfect meaning is intended. Most modern writers and grammarians do not accept this distinction, however, and *I will* may be regarded as equally correct.

Indicative Mood—Passive Voice

Present Tense

Singular	Plural
I am carried	We are carried
You are carried	You are carried
He, she, it is carried	They are carried

Past Tense

Singular	Plural
I was carried	We were carried
You were carried	You were carried
He, she, it was carried	They were carried

Future Tense

Singular	Plural
I shall (will) be carried*	We shall (will) be carried*
You will be carried	You will be carried
He, she, it will be carried	They will be carried

Present Perfect Tense

Singular	Plural
I have been carried	We have been carried
You have been carried	You have been carried
He, she, it has been carried	They have been carried

Past Perfect Tense

Singular	Plural
I had been carried	We had been carried
You had been carried	You had been carried
He, she, it had been carried	They had been carried

Future Perfect Tense

Singular	Plural
I shall (will) have been carried*	We shall (will) have been carried*
You will have been carried	You will have been carried
He, she, it will have been carried	They will have been carried

Subjunctive Mood—Active Voice

Present Tense

Singular	Plural
If I, you, he carry	If we, you, they carry

Past Tense

Singular	Plural
If I, you, he carried	If we, you, they carried

Subjunctive Mood—Passive Voice

Present Tense

Singular	Plural
If I, you, he be carried	If we, you, they be carried

Past Tense

Singular	Plural
If I, you, he were carried	If we, you, they were carried

Imperative Mood—Present Tense

Carry!

Note that most verbs form the past and past participle forms by adding *ed* to the present tense. Verbs ending in *y* preceded by a consonant (like *carry*) change the *y* to *i* before adding *ed*. Verbs ending in *e* (like *raise*) add *d* only.

Verbs that do not follow these rules are called *irregular*. The principal parts of the most common irregular verbs follow; when two or more forms are given, the first form is preferred.

PRINCIPAL PARTS OF IRREGULAR VERBS

Present Tense	Past Tense	Past Participle
arise	arose	arisen
awake	awoke, awaked	awaked, awoke, awoken
bear	bore	borne, born
beat	beat	beaten, beat
befall	befell	befallen
begin	began	begun
bend	bent	bent
bid (command)	bade	bidden
bid (make an offer)	bid	bid
bind	bound	bound
blow	blew	blown
break	broke	broken
bring	brought	brought
broadcast	broadcast, broadcasted	broadcast, broadcasted
build	built	built
burst	burst	burst
buy	bought	bought
cast	cast	cast
catch	caught	caught
choose	chose	chosen
cling	clung	clung
come	came	come
creep	crept	crept
deal	dealt	dealt
dive	dived, dove	dived
do	did	done
draw	drew	drawn
drink	drank	drunk
drive	drove	driven
eat	ate	eaten
fall	fell	fallen
feed	fed	fed
feel	felt	felt
fight	fought	fought
find	found	found
flee	fled	fled
fling	flung	flung
fly	flew	flown
forbear	forbore	forborne
forbid	forbade, forbad	forbidden
forget	forgot	forgotten, forgot
forgive	forgave	forgiven
forsake	forsook	forsaken
freeze	froze	frozen
get	got	got, gotten
give	gave	given

Present Tense	Past Tense	Past Participle
go	went	gone
grow	grew	grown
hang (an object)	hung	hung
hang (a person)	hanged	hanged
have	had	had
hit	hit	hit
hold	held	held
kneel	knelt, kneeled	knelt, kneeled
know	knew	known
lay	laid	laid
lead	led	led
leave	left	left
lend	lent	lent
lie	lay	lain
lose	lost	lost
make	made	made
meet	met	met
put	put	put
read	read	read
ring	rang	rung
rise	rose	risen
run	ran	run
see	saw	seen
seek	sought	sought
sell	sold	sold
send	sent	sent
set	set	set
shine	shone	shone
shrink	shrank, shrunk	shrunk, shrunken
sing	sang	sung
sink	sank	sunk
slay	slew	slain
sit	sat	sat
sleep	slept	slept
slide	slid	slid
sling	slung	slung
slink	slunk	slunk
speak	spoke	spoken
spring	sprang, sprung	sprung
steal	stole	stolen
stick	stuck	stuck
sting	stung	stung
stride	strode	stridden
strike	struck	struck
swear	swore	sworn
sweat	sweat, sweated	sweated, sweat
sweep	swept	swept
swim	swam	swum
swing	swung	swung
take	took	taken
teach	taught	taught
tear	tore	torn
telecast	telecast, telecasted	telecast, telecasted

Present Tense	Past Tense	Past Participle
tell	told	told
think	thought	thought
thrive	throve, thrived	thriven, thrived
throw	threw	thrown
wake	waked, woke	waked, woken, woke
wear	wore	worn
weep	wept	wept
win	won	won
wind	wound	wound
work	worked, wrought	worked, wrought
wring	wrung	wrung
write	wrote	written

How the Verb Tenses Are Used

In addition to the six tenses listed in the typical conjugation shown before (of the verb *to carry*), there are *progressive* and *intensive* forms for some of the tenses. These will be discussed as we consider the uses of each tense.

The present tense indicates that the action or state of being defined by the verb is occurring at the time of speaking or writing.

I plan to vote for the incumbent.

The present tense is used to state a general rule.

Honesty is the best policy.

The present tense is used to refer to artistic works of the past or to artists of the past whose work is still in existence.

Michelangelo is one of Italy's most famous artists.

The present tense is used to tell the story of a fictional work.

In *Gone with the Wind*, Rhett Butler finally realizes that Scarlett O'Hara is unworthy of his love.

The progressive form of the present tense (a combination of the present tense of the verb *to be* and the present participle) indicates prolonged action or state of being.

I am thinking about the future.
You are flirting with disaster.
He is courting my sister.
We are planning a trip to Yosemite National Park.
They are being stubborn.

The intensive form of the present tense (a combination of the verb *to do* and the infinitive) creates emphasis.

He does care.
We do intend to stay.

The past tense is used to indicate that an event occurred in a specific time in the past and that the event is completed.

I lived in New York in 1979.
I lived in that house for six years. (I no longer live there.)

The progressive form of the past tense combines the past tense of *to be* and the present participle. It indicates prolonged past action or state of being.

I, he, she, it was playing.
We, you, they were going.

The intensive form of the past tense combines the past tense of *to do* and the infinitive. It creates emphasis.

I <u>did know</u> the answer to the question.

The future tense makes a statement about a future event. As indicated in the conjugation of the verb *to carry*, traditional grammarians distinguish between the use of *shall* and *will* in the future tense. According to this rule, the simple future uses *shall* in the first person and *will* in the second and third persons.

I, <u>we shall go</u>.
You, he, <u>they will go</u>.

To show determination, promise, or command, *will* is used in the first person and *shall* in the second and third persons.

I <u>will pay</u> this bill on Friday.
You, he, <u>they shall comply</u> with this order.

However, most contemporary grammarians accept the use of *shall* and *will* interchangeably in the future tense.

The progressive form of the future tense combines the future tense of *to be* and the present participle.

I <u>shall be wearing</u> a white jacket.
He <u>will be going</u> with my brother.

The present perfect tense combines the present tense of *to have* and the past participle.

I <u>have gone</u>.
He <u>has eaten</u> his breakfast.

Whereas the past tense refers to a definite time in the past, the present perfect tense indicates that the event is perfected or completed at the present time.

The present perfect tense is also used to indicate that the event began in the past and is continuing into the present.

He <u>has attended</u> Yale University for three years. (He is still attending Yale.)

The progressive form of the present perfect tense combines the present perfect tense of *to be* and the present participle.

He <u>has been complaining</u> about a pain in his side for some time.

The past perfect tense is formed by combining the past participle of the verb and the past tense of the verb *to have*. It describes an event which was completely perfected at a definite time in the past. Its major use is to indicate that one event occurred before another in the past.

By the time the firemen arrived, the boys <u>had extinguished</u> the blaze. (The fire was put out before the firemen came.)

The progressive form of the past perfect tense is formed by combining the present participle of the verb and the past perfect tense of *to be*.

I <u>had been holding</u> this package for you for three weeks.

The future perfect tense is formed by combining the past participle of the verb and the future tense of the verb *to have*. It indicates that a future event will be completed before a definite time in the future.

By one in the afternoon, he <u>will have finished</u> his lunch and <u>will have returned</u> to the office.

The progressive form of the future perfect tense is formed by combining the present participle of the verb and the future perfect tense of *to be*.

They <u>will have been swimming</u> all afternoon.

Kinds of Verbs

Transitive verbs are verbs that require an object. The object is the receiver of the action.

He hit the boy. (The object <u>boy</u> has been hit.)
I received a letter. (The object <u>letter</u> has been received.)

Intransitive verbs do not require an object.

She is walking.

Copulative verbs are intransitive verbs with the special quality of connecting the subject to a noun, pronoun, or adjective. The most common copulative verb is *to be*.

Mr. Jones is the teacher.

It is I.

(In these two sentences, teacher and I are called predicate nominatives.)

The man is rich.

The actress is beautiful.

(Rich and beautiful are predicate adjectives.)

Predicate nominatives and predicate adjectives are normally called predicate complements because they complete the thought of the copulative verb. The predicate nominative represents the same person or thing as the subject of the verb *to be* and is in the nominative case.

He is the teacher.

The teacher is he.

The predicate adjective is connected to the subject by the copulative verb. The description, the *lame horse*, becomes a statement or sentence when the copulative verb is used as follows:

The horse is lame.

The other copulative verbs are *appear, become, feel, get, grow, look, seem, smell, sound,* and *taste*. These verbs should be followed by predicate adjectives.

This tastes good.

I feel sad.

This sounds too loud.

I became ill.

Be careful to distinguish between transitive and intransitive verbs. Words like *lie* and *lay, sit* and *set, rise* and *raise* often give students trouble.

1. *Lie* is an intransitive verb, meaning "to rest or recline." Its principal parts are *lie, lay, lain*.
   Lay is transitive and means "to place down." Its principal parts are *lay, laid, laid*.
   Incorrect: I lay the book on the table.
   Correct: I laid the book on the table.
   Incorrect: Because I am tired, I am going to lay down.
   Correct: Because I am tired, I am going to lie down.

2. *Sit* is intransitive. Its principal parts are *sit, sat, sat*.
   Set may be either transitive or intransitive. Its principal parts are *set, set, set*.
   Incorrect: I am going to sit this tripod on the floor.
   Correct: I am going to set this tripod on the floor (Transitive).
   Correct: The sun is going to set at 5:42 P.M. (Intransitive).

3. *Rise*, meaning "to come up," in intransitive. Its principal parts are *rise, rose, risen*.
   Raise, meaning "to lift up," is transitive. Its principal parts are *raise, raised, raised*.
   Incorrect: The delta lowlands were in danger of being flooded when the sea raised by three feet.
   Correct: The delta lowlands were in danger of being flooded when the sea rose by three feet.

Voice and Mood

Voice is a characteristic of transitive verbs. In the **active voice**, the subject is the doer of the action stated by the verb, and the object of the verb is the receiver of the action.

John caught the ball. (John is doing the catching and the ball is being caught.)

In the **passive voice**, the receiver of the action is the subject. The doer of the action may be identified by using a phrase beginning with *by*.

The ball was caught.

The ball was caught by John.

Some writers prefer the active voice and object to the use of the passive. However, both voices have their virtues and neither should be regarded as incorrect.

It is inadvisable to switch from one voice to the other in the same sentence.

Undesirable: The outfielder <u>raced</u> toward the wall and the ball <u>was caught</u>.

Preferable: The outfielder <u>raced</u> toward the wall and <u>caught</u> the ball.

Mood is used to indicate the intentions of the writer.

The **indicative mood** makes a statement or asks a question.

I <u>wrote</u> you a letter.

When <u>did</u> you <u>mail</u> it?

The **imperative mood** commands, directs, or requests.

<u>Go</u> home!

<u>Make</u> a left turn at the stop light.

Please <u>talk</u> more slowly.

The **subjunctive mood** is used when the writer desires to express a wish or a condition contrary to fact.

I wish I <u>were</u> able to go with you.

(I am not able to go.)

If he <u>were</u> less of a bore, people would invite him to their homes more frequently.

(He is a bore.)

It is also used after a verb which expresses a command or a request.

The governor has ordered that all pay increases <u>be</u> deferred.

She demanded that he <u>leave</u> immediately.

Verbals

The infinitive, present participle, and past participle are called non-finite verbs, or **verbals**. These forms of the verb cannot function as verbs without an auxiliary word or words.

Running is not a verb.

Am running, have been running, shall be running are verbs.

Broken is not a verb.

Is broken, had been broken, may be broken are verbs.

The **infinitive** (the verb preceded by *to*) is used chiefly as a noun. Occasionally, it may serve as an adjective or an adverb.

John wants <u>to go</u> to the movies. (<u>To go</u> to the movies is the object of <u>wants</u>. It serves as a noun.)

I have miles <u>to go</u> before I sleep. (<u>To go</u> modifies <u>miles</u>. It serves as an adjective.)

<u>To be honest</u>, we almost lost the battle. (<u>To be honest</u> modifies the rest of the sentence. It serves as an adverb.)

The **present participle** usually serves as an adjective.

<u>Flying</u> colors

<u>Singing</u> waiters

<u>Dancing</u> waters

(In each case, the participle modifies the noun it precedes.)

<u>Writing on the blackboard</u>, the scientist presented his arguments in favor of his thesis.

(<u>Writing on the blackboard</u> is a <u>participial phrase</u> modifying <u>scientist</u>.)

The present participle may also serve as a noun. When it does so, it is called a **gerund**.

<u>Jogging</u> is good exercise.

<u>Dieting</u> to lose weight requires discipline.

A noun or pronoun preceding a gerund should be in the possessive case.

<u>My</u> talking to Mary annoyed the teacher.

We were frightened by <u>Helen's</u> fainting.

The **past participle** serves as an adjective.

<u>Broken</u> homes
<u>Fallen</u> arches
<u>Pained</u> expressions

ADJECTIVES

Adjectives are words that limit or describe nouns and pronouns.

<u>Three</u> men
The <u>fourth</u> quarter
(<u>Three</u> and <u>fourth</u> limit the words they precede.)
A <u>pretty</u> girl (<u>Pretty</u> describes the word it precedes.)
A <u>daring young</u> man (<u>Daring</u> is a participle used as an adjective, and describes man; <u>young</u> describes <u>man</u>.)

Adjectives usually precede the word they limit or describe. However, for emphasis the adjective may follow the word it modifies.

One nation, <u>indivisible</u>

Adjectives are often formed from nouns by adding suffixes such as -al, -ish, -ly, and -ous.

Noun	Adjective
fiction	fictional
girl	girlish
friend	friendly
joy	joyous

Predicate adjectives are adjectives that follow the copulative verbs be, appear, become, feel, get, grow, look, seem, smell, sound, and taste. These adjectives follow the verb and refer to its subject.

The man is <u>tall</u>. (A tall man)
The lady looks <u>beautiful</u>. (A beautiful lady)

Adjectives are inflected; that is, they change form to indicate degree of comparison: *positive, comparative,* or *superlative.* The *positive degree* indicates the basic form without reference to any other object. The *comparative degree* is used to compare two objects. The *superlative degree* is used to compare three or more objects. Usually, *er* or *r* is added to the positive to form the comparative degree, *est* or *st* to form the superlative. Some adjectives of two syllables and all adjectives longer than two syllables use *more* (or *less*) to form the comparative degree and *most* (or *least*) to form the superlative.

Positive	Comparative	Superlative
tall	taller	tallest
pretty	prettier	prettiest
handsome	more handsome	most handsome
expensive	less expensive	least expensive

A few adjectives have irregular comparative and superlative forms. These include:

Positive	Comparative	Superlative
good	better	best
bad	worse	worst
ill	worse	worst

ADVERBS

Adverbs are words that modify verbs, adjectives, or other adverbs.

He spoke <u>sincerely</u>. (Sincerely modifies <u>spoke</u>.)

<u>Almost</u> any person can afford this kind of vacation. (<u>Almost</u> modifies the adjective <u>any</u>.)

He spoke <u>very</u> sincerely. (<u>Very</u> modifies the adverb <u>sincerely</u>.)

Most adverbs end in *ly* (*angrily, stupidly, honestly*). However, some adjectives also end in *ly* (*manly, womanly, holy, saintly*). Some commonly used words have the same form for the adjective and the adverb. These include *early, far, fast, hard, high, late, little, loud, quick, right, slow,* and *well*.

Adjective	Adverb
The *early* bird	He left *early*.
A *far* cry	You have gone too *far*.
He is a *fast* worker.	Don't go so *fast*.
This is *hard* to do.	He slapped him *hard*.
A *high* voice	Put it *high* on the agenda.
A *late* bloomer	He arrived *late*.
Men of *little* faith	He is a *little* late.
A *loud* explosion	He spoke *loud*.
A *quick* step	Think *quick*.
The *right* decision	Do it *right*.
A *slow* worker	Drive *slow*.
All is *well*.	He was *well* prepared.

Adverbs, like adjectives, change form to show comparison. The comparative degree uses the word *more* (or *less*); the superlative degree, the word *most* (or *least*). *Badly* and *well* have irregular comparative forms.

Positive	Comparative	Superlative
quickly	more quickly	most quickly
rapidly	less rapidly	least rapidly
badly	worse	worst
well	better	best

PREPOSITIONS

Prepositions are words that combine with nouns, pronouns, and noun substantives to form phrases that act as adverbs, adjectives, or nouns.

I arrived <u>at ten o'clock</u>. (Adverbial phrase)

The man <u>with the broken arm</u>. (Adjective phrase)

The shout came from <u>outside the house</u>. (Noun phrase acting as object of *from*)

The most common prepositions are:

about	behind	during	on	to
above	below	except	out	touching
after	beneath	excepting	over	toward
against	beside	for	past	under
along	besides	from	round	underneath
amid	between	in	save	up
among	beyond	into	since	with
around	but	notwithstanding	through	within
at	by	of	throughout	without
before	down	off	till	

Some verbs call for the use of specific prepositions. See the list of Idiomatic Expressions on page 125.

CONJUNCTIONS

Conjunctions are connecting words that join words, phrases, and clauses. There are two kinds of conjunctions:

Coordinating conjunctions connect words, phrases, and clauses of equal rank. They are *and, but, or, nor, for, whereas,* and *yet.* Pairs of words like *either . . . or, neither . . . nor, both . . . and, not only . . . but also* are a special kind of coordinating conjunction called *correlative conjunctions.*

Subordinating conjunctions connect dependent clauses to independent clauses. Some of the more common subordinating conjunctions are *although, as, because, if, since, so than, though, till, unless, until, whether,* and *while.* Also, when the relative pronouns *who, which, that* introduce a dependent clause, they act as subordinating conjunctions.

Independent and dependent clauses are discussed in the section on Sentence Sense later in this chapter.

ARTICLES

The three most frequently used adjectives—*a, an,* and *the*—are called **articles**. The *definite article* is *the.* The *indefinite articles* are *a* and *an. A* is used before a word beginning with a consonant sound. *An* is used before a word beginning with a vowel sound.

A bright light
An auspicious beginning
An RCA television set
A humble beginning (the h sound is pronounced)
An hour ago (the h sound is omitted)

INTERJECTIONS

Interjections are words that express emotion and have no grammatical relation to the other words in the sentence.

Alas, I am disconsolate.
Wow! This is exciting!
Eureka! I have found it.

Sentence Sense

The ability to write complete sentences without error is characteristic of a student who has mastered standard written English. Failure to write in complete sentences is a major weakness of students whose written compositions are considered unsatisfactory.

A sentence may be defined as a group of words that contains a subject and a predicate, expresses a complete thought, and ends with a period (.), a question mark (?), or an exclamation point (!).

The sentence must contain a finite verb that makes the statement or asks the question.

The soldiers fought a battle.
Halt!
Where are you going?
The students have gone home.
I have been thinking about your offer.
Why have you been making this accusation?
Who will take your place?

(The verbs in the preceding sentences are *fought, halt, are going, have gone, have been thinking, have been making,* and *will take.*)

The forms of the verb that are not finite are the *infinitive*, the *participle*, and the *gerund*. These three forms cannot act as finite verbs.

Clauses

A clause is a group of words containing a subject and a verb. There are two kinds of clauses:

Main clauses (also called **principal** or **independent clauses**): A main clause does not modify anything; it can stand alone as a sentence.

    I went to the theater.

    I failed my spelling test.

A sentence containing one main clause is called a *simple sentence*.

A sentence containing two or more main clauses is called a *compound sentence*. The clauses must be connected by a coordinating conjunction or by a semicolon (;).

    I went to the theater and I saw a good production of *Hamlet*.

    You must pass this test, or you will be suspended from the team.

    Four boys played tennis; the rest went swimming.

Subordinate clauses (also called **dependent clauses**): A subordinate clause cannot stand alone; to be a good sentence, it must always accompany a main clause. A sentence containing a main clause and one or more subordinate clauses is called a *complex sentence*. If the subordinate clause modifies a noun or pronoun, it is called an *adjective clause*. If it modifies a verb, it is an *adverb clause* or an *adverbial clause*. A clause that acts as the subject or the object of a verb or as the object of a preposition is called a *noun clause*.

    The book that is on the table belongs to my sister. (The clause that is on the table is an adjective clause because it modifies the noun book.)

    She quit school because she had to go to work. (The clause because she had to go to work is an adverbial clause because it modifies the verb quit.)

    I asked what the teacher did. (What the teacher did is a noun clause because it is the object of the verb asked.)

    Give this medal to whoever comes in first. (Whoever comes in first is a noun clause because it is the object of the preposition to.)

Phrases

A phrase is a group of words that lacks a subject and a predicate and acts as a unit. A phrase cannot serve as a complete sentence. These are the common types of phrases:

Prepositional phrases are introduced by a preposition and act as adjectives or adverbs.

    This is an overt act of war. (Of war is an adjective phrase modifying act.)

    Please come at 10:00 A.M. (At 10:00 A.M. is an adverbial phrase modifying come.)

Participial phrases are introduced by a participle and are used as adjectives to modify nouns and pronouns.

    Fighting his way through tacklers, he crossed the goal line. (Fighting his way through tacklers is a present participial phrase modifying the pronoun he.)

    Sung by this gifted artist, the words were especially stirring. (Sung by this gifted artist is a past participial phrase modifying the noun words.)

Gerund phrases are introduced by a gerund and are used as nouns.

    Smoking cigarettes is harmful to one's health. (Smoking cigarettes is a gerund phrase used as the subject of the verb is.)

Infinitive phrases are introduced by the infinitive form of the verb, usually preceded by *to*. They are used as nouns, adjectives, and adverbs.

To win a decisive victory is our goal. (To win a decisive victory is an infinitive phrase used as the subject of the verb is.)
I have a dress to alter. (To alter is an infinitive modifying the noun dress.)
The ice is too soft to skate on. (To skate on is an infinitive modifying the adjective soft.)

Grammarians disagree about the interpretation of sentences like *I want him to buy a suit.* Some regard *him to buy a suit* as an infinitive clause with *him* the subject of the infinitive *to buy.* Others regard *him* as the object of the verb *want* and *to buy a suit* as an infinitive phrase acting as an objective complement. No matter how the sentence is interpreted, *him* is correct.

COMMON PROBLEMS IN GRAMMAR AND USAGE

Common Problems in Grammar

SENTENCE FRAGMENTS

A sentence fragment occurs when a phrase or a dependent clause is incorrectly used as a sentence. Examples of sentence fragments and ways of correcting them follow:

1. When he walked into the room.

2. Apologizing for his behavior.

3. To discuss the problem amicably.

4. In our discussion of the problem.

5. Or yield to their demands.

In Example 1, we have a dependent clause used as a sentence. To correct, either remove the subordinating conjunction *when* or add an independent clause.
He walked into the room.
When he walked into the room, we yelled "Surprise."

In Example 2, we have a participial or gerund phrase used as a sentence. To correct, either change the phrase to a subject and a verb or add an independent clause.
He apologized for his behavior.
Apologizing for his behavior, he tried to atone for the embarrassment he had caused.

In Example 3, we have an infinitive phrase. To change this phrase to a complete sentence, either change the infinitive to a finite verb and add a subject, or add a subject and verb that will make a complete thought.
We discussed the problem amicably.
It is advisable to discuss the problem amicably.

In Example 4, we have a prepositional phrase. To correct this fragmentary sentence, add an independent clause to which it can relate.
We failed to consider the public's reaction in our discussion of the problem.

In Example 5, we have part of a compound predicate. To correct this, combine it with the other part of the compound predicate in a single complete sentence.
We must fight this aggressive act or yield to their demands.

PRACTICE

Correct the following sentence fragments, following the methods of correction shown for Example 1.
When she gave birth to her baby.

_____

_____

Although I like ice cream.

_____

_____

Correct the following sentence fragments, following the correction patterns shown for Example 2.

Substituting for the starting pitcher.

_____

_____

Expecting to go to the party.

_____

_____

_____

Correct the following sentence fragments, following the correction patterns shown for Example 3.

To remodel the kitchen completely.

_____

_____

To apologize to his father.

_____

_____

_____

Correct the following sentence fragments, following the correction pattern shown for Example 4.

In our enthusiasm for the team's victory.

_____

_____

At the conclusion of the history lesson.

_____

_____

_____

Correct the following sentence fragments, following the correction pattern shown for Example 5.

Or pay a cleaning deposit.

_____

_____

And save our money for a new car.

_____

_____

_____

RUN-ON SENTENCES

The run-on sentence has been given many different names by grammarians, including the *comma fault* sentence or *comma splice* sentence, and the *fused* sentence.

The jurors examined the evidence, they found the defendant guilty. (Comma fault sentence)
It is very cloudy I think it is going to rain. (Fused sentence)

The *comma fault* or *comma splice* sentence may be defined as a sentence in which two independent clauses are improperly connected by a comma. The first example given is an illustration of the comma fault sentence. The *fused* sentence consists of two sentences that run together without any distinguishing punctuation. The second example illustrates this kind of error.

Any of four methods may be used to correct run-on sentences:

1. Use a period at the end of the first independent clause instead of a comma. Begin the second independent clause with a capital letter.
   <u>The jurors examined the evidence</u>. They found the defendant guilty.
   <u>It is very cloudy</u>. I think it is going to rain.

2. Connect the two independent clauses by using a coordinating conjunction.
   The jurors examined the <u>evidence, and</u> they found the defendant guilty.
   It is very <u>cloudy, and</u> I think it is going to rain.

3. Use a semicolon between two main clauses not connected by a coordinating conjunction.
   The jurors examined the <u>evidence; they</u> found the defendant guilty.
   It is very <u>cloudy;</u> I think it is going to rain.

4. Use a subordinating conjunction to make one of the independent clauses dependent on the other.
   <u>When</u> the jurors examined the evidence, they found the defendant guilty.
   <u>Because</u> it is very cloudy, I think it is going to rain.

PRACTICE

Correct each of the following run-on sentences, using all four of the methods just shown.

The organist played the wedding march, the bride came down the aisle.

1. _____

2. _____

3. _____

4. _____

It is getting very late I had better go to bed.

1. _____

2. _____

3. _____

4. _____

(It is important to master method 4; if you are able to combine independent clauses in this way, you will be able to vary sentence structure and add interest to your paragraphs.)

PROBLEMS WITH AGREEMENT

Problems with agreement generally involve a violation of one of the two basic rules governing agreement.

Rule I: A verb and its subject must agree in person and number. A singular verb must have a singular subject; a plural verb must have a plural subject.

If you examine the conjugation of the verb *to carry* on pages 92—93, you will observe that this rule applies only to the present and present perfect tenses. The other tenses use the same form for each of the three persons and with both singular and plural subjects. Therefore, an error in agreement cannot occur in any tense other than the present or present perfect tense, with the exception of the verb *to be* The past tense of *to be* is:

Person	Singular	Plural
First	I was	We were
Second	You were	You were
Third	He, she, it was	They were

Rule I concerning agreement is simple and easy to remember. However, you should note the following:

1. The verb does *not* agree with the modifier of the subject or with a parenthetical expression introduced by *as well as, with, together with,* or a similar phrase.
   The father of the children is going to work. (The subject of the singular verb is going is the singular noun father. Children is part of the prepositional phrase of the children, which modifies father.)
   The pupils as well as the teacher are going to the zoo. (The subject of the plural verb are going is the plural noun pupils. Teacher is part of the parenthetical expression as well as the teacher. This parenthetical expression is not the subject.)

2. A plural verb is used with a compound subject (two or more nouns or pronouns connected by *and*).
   John and his friends are going camping.
   John and Mary are planning a party.
   However, when the compound subject can be considered as a single unit or entity, regard it as singular and follow it with a singular verb.
   "Jack and Jill" is a popular nursery rhyme.
   Bacon and eggs is one of the most popular breakfast dishes in America.

3. Collective nouns like *team, committee, jury, gang, class, army,* and so on are usually regarded as singular nouns.
   The team is practicing for the big game.
   The Revolutionary Army was at Valley Forge.
   When a collective noun is used to refer to the *individual members* of the group, it is considered a plural noun.
   The jury were unable to reach a verdict. (The individual jurors could not come to a decision.)

4. The words *billiards, economics, linguistics, mathematics, measles, mumps, news* and *physics* are considered singular nouns.
   Billiards is a game of skill.
   Mathematics is my most difficult subject.

5. The words *barracks, glasses, insignia, odds, pliers, scissors, tactics, tongs, trousers,* and *wages* are considered plural nouns.
   These barracks have been empty for some time.
   My glasses are fogged; I cannot see clearly.

6. The words *acoustics, ethics, gymnastics, politics,* and *statistics* are singular when they refer to specific fields of study or activity. They are plural at all other times.
   Ethics is part of our Humanities program.
   His ethics are questionable.

7. Names of organizations and titles of books and shows are singular.
   The Canterbury Tales was written by Chaucer.
   The United States now has a national debt that approaches a trillion dollars.

8. In a sentence beginning with *there* or *here,* the subject of the verb *follows* the verb in the sentence.
   There are many reasons for his failure. (Reasons is the subject of the plural verb are.)
   Here is my suggestion. (Suggestion is the subject of the singular verb is.)

9. The words *anybody, anyone, each, either, every, everyone, everybody, neither, nobody, no one,* and *someone* are regarded as singular and require a singular verb.
   Anyone of the students is welcome.
   Each of the songs he sang was memorable.
   Either of the two choices is satisfactory.
   Nobody in her classes likes her.

No one is going.
Someone in this group is a liar.

10. The words *few*, *many*, and *several* are regarded as plural and require a plural verb.
Many are called, but few are chosen.
Several have already been disqualified by the lawyers.

11. The expressions *the number* and *the variety* are regarded as singular and require a singular verb.
The number of people able to meet in this room is limited by the Fire Department.
The variety of food presented at this buffet is beyond imagination.

12. The expressions *a number* and *a variety* are regarded as plural and require a plural verb.
A number of new cases of malaria have been reported to the Health Department.
A variety of disturbances in the neighborhood have alarmed the homeowners.

13. *Either* and *neither* are regarded as singular (see item 9). However, when *either* or *neither* is coupled with *or* or *nor*, a different rule applies. In these sentences, the verb agrees with the noun or pronoun that follows the word *or* or *nor*.
Either Mary or John is eligible.
Either Mary or her sisters are mistaken.
Neither Harry nor you are eligible.
Neither you nor I was invited.

14. When using the copulative verb *to be*, be sure to make the verb agree with the subject and not with the predicate complement.
Our greatest problem is excessive taxes.
Excessive taxes are our greatest problem.

PRACTICE

Correct each of the following errors in agreement in accordance with the examples just shown.

1. The leader of the apes are swinging through the trees.

   _____

   The child as well as the parents are affected by a divorce.

   _____

2. Lassie and her pups is chasing rabbits.

   _____

   "Frankie and Johnny" are a love song.

   _____

3. The committee are meeting on Tuesday.

   _____

   The Latin class are studying Caesar.

   _____

4. Mumps are a dangerous disease.

   _____

   _____

Economics are a complete mystery to me.
_____
_____

5. My trousers is wrinkled; I need the iron.
_____

His tactics was too outmoded for modern warfare.
_____
_____

6. Statistics are a field worth studying.
_____

Their statistics is incorrect.
_____
_____

7. *Star Wars* were directed by George Lucas.
_____

Pacific Gas & Electricity have sent me a bill.
_____

8. Here is my answers to the question.
_____
_____

9. No one of the counselors are able to advise you.
_____

Neither of the clerks want to wait on him.
_____

Everybody from our office are going to the party.
_____

10. Several of the class has handed in the exercise.
_____

Many is unemployed, but few is getting unemployment insurance.
_____

11. The variety of grammatical errors possible are countless.
_____

The number of students taking the test are increasing.
_____

12. A number of bad. riots has troubled the city.
_____

A variety of attempts to remedy the situation was made.
_____
_____

13. Either the mayor or the city manager are in charge.

_____

_____

Either the teacher or his students is correct.

_____

Neither David nor you is welcome.

_____

Neither you nor I were elected.

_____

_____

14. A storekeeper's greatest worry are bad checks.

_____

Bad checks is a storekeeper's greatest worry.

_____

_____

Rule II: A pronoun must agree with its antecedent in person, number, and gender. (The antecedent is the noun or pronoun to which the pronoun refers.)

> The detectives arrested <u>Mrs. Brown</u> as <u>she</u> entered the building. (The antecedent <u>Mrs. Brown</u> is a third person singular feminine noun; <u>she</u> is the third person singular feminine pronoun.)

Rule II concerning agreement is also easy to remember. However, watch out for these potentially troublesome points:

1. When the antecedent is an indefinite singular pronoun (*any, anybody, anyone, each, either, every, everybody, everyone, nobody, no one, somebody,* or *someone*), the pronoun should be singular.
<u>Everybody</u> on the ship went to <u>his</u> cabin to get <u>his</u> life jacket.
<u>Neither</u> of the girls is writing <u>her</u> thesis.

2. When the antecedent is compound (two or more nouns or pronouns connected by *and*), the pronoun should be plural.
<u>Mary</u> and <u>Jane</u> like <u>their</u> new school.

3. When the antecedent is part of an *either . . . or* or *neither . . . nor* statement, the pronoun should agree with the nearer antecedent.
Either John or <u>Henry</u> will invite Mary to <u>his</u> home. (<u>Henry</u> is closer to <u>his</u>.)
Neither the seller nor the <u>buyers</u> have submitted <u>their</u> final offers. (<u>Buyers</u> is closer to <u>their</u>.)
Neither the buyers nor the <u>seller</u> has submitted <u>his</u> final offer. (<u>Seller</u> is closer to <u>his</u>.)

Note: in some sentences, Rules I and II are combined.
John is one of the boys who (is, are) trying out for the team. (In this sentence, the antecedent of <u>who</u> is <u>boys</u>, a third person plural noun. The verb should be <u>are</u> because <u>are</u> is the third person plural verb.)

PRACTICE

Correct each of the following errors in agreement in accordance with the examples just shown.

1. Everybody in the class went to their desk to get their essay.

_____

Neither of the teachers is correcting their tests.

_____

_____

2. Bob and Sue remodeled her new home.

_____

_____

3. Either John or Tom will donate their ball to the team.

_____

_____

Neither the students nor the teacher has picked up their tickets to the concert.

_____

_____

PROBLEMS WITH CASE

Nouns and pronouns have three cases:

The **nominative case** indicates that the noun or pronoun is being used as the subject of a verb, or as a word in apposition to the subject, or as a predicate nominative.

John is the batter. (John is in the nominative case, since it is the subject of the verb is.)
Jane, my younger sister, attends elementary school. (Sister is in the nominative case because it is in apposition with Jane, the subject of the verb attends.)
Mrs. Brown is the teacher. (Teacher is the predicate nominative of the verb is.)
The culprit is he. (He is the predicate nominative of the verb is.)

The **possessive case** indicates possession.

I broke Mary's doll.
John did not do his homework.

The **objective case** indicates that the noun or pronoun is the object (receives the action) of a transitive verb, a verbal, or a preposition.

John hit her. (Her is the object of the verb hit.)
Practicing the violin can be boring at times. (Violin is the object of the participle practicing.)
Please come with me. (Me is the object of the preposition with.)

Some special rules concerning case:

1. The subject of an infinitive is in the objective case.
I want him to go. (Him is the subject of the infinitive to go.)
I told her to stop talking. (Her is the subject of the infinitive to stop.)

2. The predicate nominative of the infinitive *to be* is in the objective case.
I want the leader to be him. (Him is the predicate complement of the infinitive to be.)

3. Nouns and pronouns used as parts of the compound subject of a verb are in the nominative case.
Mary and he are going to the party. (The two parts of the compound subject, Mary and he, are both in the nominative case.)
John and we are friends. (John and we, the two parts of the compound subject of the verb are, are both in the nominative case.)

4. Nouns and pronouns used as parts of the compound object of a verb, a verbal, or a preposition are in the objective case.
I met Mary and him at the party. (Mary and him are the objects of the verb met.)
Seeing Mary and him at the party was a treat. (Mary and him are the objects of the gerund seeing.)
Take the food to him and her. (Him and her are objects of the preposition to.)

5. A noun or pronoun immediately preceding a gerund is in the possessive case.
John's talking during the lesson was rude. (John's immediately precedes the gerund talking.)
John was afraid that his speaking in class would be reported to his father. (His immediately precedes the gerund speaking.)

6. In sentences using the conjunctions as or than to make comparisons, the clause following as or than is often truncated. Such clauses are called *elliptical clauses*. In these sentences, the case of the noun or pronouns following the conjunction is based on its use in the elliptical clause.
Mary is as tall as he. (The complete sentence is Mary is as tall as he is tall. The nominative case is used because he is the subject of the verb is.)
The twins are older than I. (The complete sentence is The twins are older than I am old. The nominative case is used because I is the subject of the verb am.)

7. The case of the relative pronouns who, whoever, and whosoever is determined by their use in the clause in which they belong.
Whom are you talking to? (The objective case is used because whom is the object of the preposition to.)
Whom did you take them to be? (The objective case is used because whom is the predicate complement of the infinitive to be.)
Give this book to whomever it belongs. (The objective case is used because whomever is the object of the preposition to.)
Give this award to whoever has earned it. (The nominative case is used because whoever is the subject of the verb has earned. In this sentence, the object of the preposition to is the noun clause whoever has earned it.)

PRACTICE

Correct each of the following errors in case in accordance with the examples just shown.

1. He asked she to go dancing.

_____

2. I want the leading lady to be she.

_____

3. Alice and him are going to get married.

Judy and me are roommates.

_____

4. I saw she and Stan at the restaurant.

Give the ice cream to Vicki and I.

_____

5. Toby leaving work early left us short-handed.

_____

6. John is as bright as me.

Susan is brighter than me.

_____

7. Who is he speaking to?

Who did you think them to be?

_____

Give this coat to whoever it fits.

_____

Give this kitten to whomever wants it.

_____

PROBLEMS WITH REFERENCE OF PRONOUNS

Since pronouns are words used in place of nouns, the words they refer to should be clear to the reader or speaker. Vagueness or ambiguity can be avoided by observing the following rules:

1. The pronoun should refer to only one antecedent.
   Vague: The captain asked him to polish his boots. (Whose boots are to be polished?)
   Clear: The captain said, "Polish your boots." The captain said, "Polish my boots."

2. The antecedent of the pronoun should be a single noun and not a general statement. The pronouns most often affected by this rule are *it, this, that,* and *which.*
   Vague: The ship was pitching and tossing in the heavy seas, and it made me seasick. (It refers to the entire clause that precedes the pronoun.)
   Clear: The pitching and tossing of the ship in the heavy seas made me seasick. (Combine the two clauses in order to eliminate the pronoun.)
   Clear: The ship was pitching and tossing in the heavy seas, and this motion made me seasick. (Replace the vague pronoun with a noun preceded by this, that, or which.)
   Vague: When the teacher walked into the room, the students were shouting, which made her very angry. (Which refers to the entire clause rather than to a single noun.)
   Clear: When the teacher walked into the room, the students' shouting angered her.
   Clear: When the teacher walked into the room, the students were shouting. This lack of control angered her. (A sentence has been substituted for the vague pronoun.)

3. The antecedent of the pronoun should be stated, not merely implied in the sentence.
   Vague: My accountant has been taking classes at law school, but he does not intend to become one. (One what?)
   Clear: My accountant has been taking classes at law school, but he does not intend to become a lawyer.

PRACTICE

Correct each of the following errors in pronoun reference in accordance with the examples just shown.

1. The hostess asked her to finish her dessert.

   _____

   _____

2. The cafeteria was filthy, and it made me lose my appetite.

   _____

   _____

3. My son has been studying the violin, but he doesn't want to be one.

   _____

   _____

PROBLEMS INVOLVING VERBS

Sequence of Tenses

In this section, we will discuss five errors in tense that can occur when two or more verbs are used in the same sentence. The following are examples of these errors:

1. When I called him, he doesn't answer the phone.

2. At the present time, I attended John Adams High School for two years.

3. Our attorney already presented our proposition to the Planning Commission by the time I arrived.

4. I hoped to have won first prize in the contest.

5. We had ought to pay our respects.

In Example 1, we have one verb in the past tense and another in the present tense. Since the actions described by both verbs have occurred or are occurring at the same time, the tenses of the two verbs should be the same:

When I called him, he didn't answer the phone. (Both verbs are in the past tense.)
When I call him, he doesn't answer the phone. (Both verbs are in the present tense.)

Example 2 confuses the use of the past and present perfect tenses. As stated in the section on Verbs in this chapter, the past tense should be used to indicate action completed in the past. The present perfect tense should be used to indicate action begun in the past and carried into the present. The phrase *At the present time* indicates that the speaker is still attending high school. Therefore, the present perfect tense is required:

At the present time, I have attended John Adams High School for two years.

Example 3 exemplifies the need for the past perfect tense. Two events are mentioned in this sentence. To differentiate between the time when the attorney spoke and the time when the speaker arrived, the past perfect tense should be used for the event that occurred first:

Our attorney had already presented our proposition to the Planning Commission by the time I arrived.

Example 4 is an example of the use of the present and the perfect infinitive. The tense of the infinitive is determined by its relation to the principal verb. At the time specified by the principal verb, *hoped*, the speaker was still expecting *to win*. Therefore, the correct form of the sentence is:

I hoped to win first prize in the contest.

Example 5 uses the expression *had ought*, which is never acceptable. *Ought* is a defective auxiliary verb. It has no other form. Thus the present and past tenses of *ought* are *ought*. The correct form of Example 5 is:

We ought to pay our respects.

PRACTICE

Correct each of the following errors in tense in accordance with the examples just shown.

1. When I asked her, she doesn't come to my party.

_____

_____

2. At the present time, I studied French for three years.

_____

_____

3. The life guard already performed artificial respiration by the time the ambulance got there.

_____

_____

4. I wanted to have found a new job.

_____

_____

5. We had ought to do our homework.

_____

_____

Mood

As noted earlier, verbs are conjugated in three moods: indicative, imperative, and subjunctive. Because the subjunctive mood is the least used, many students are not aware of the uses of the subjunctive:

1. The subjunctive mood is used to state a wish or a condition contrary to fact.
    I wish this party <u>were</u> over. (The party is <u>not</u> over.)
    If I <u>were</u> king, I would lower taxes. (I am <u>not</u> king.)
    If he <u>had been elected</u>, he would have served his full term. (He was <u>not</u> elected.)

2. The subjunctive mood is also used after a verb that expresses a command or a request.
    I insist that he <u>pay</u> me today. (<u>Pay</u> is in the subjunctive mood.)
    I ask that this discussion <u>be deferred</u>. (<u>Be deferred</u> is in the subjunctive mood.)

3. The most common error involving the subjunctive is the following:
    If he <u>would have known</u> about the side effects of this medicine, he would not have prescribed it for his patients.

    The expression *would have known* in the subordinate clause is incorrect. The subjunctive should be used:
    If he <u>had known</u> about the side effects of this medicine, he would not have prescribed it for his patients.

PRACTICE

Correct each of the following errors in mood in accordance with the illustrations just shown.

1. If I was President, I would end unemployment.

    _____
    _____

    I wish this Rolls Royce was inexpensive.

    _____
    _____

2. I insist that she gives up marijuana now.

    _____
    _____

3. If I would have heard about the radar trap, I would not have driven so fast on the highway.

    _____
    _____

Voice

In the active voice, the subject of the verb is the doer of the action. In the passive voice, the subject of the verb is the receiver of the action.
Active Voice: The linebacker <u>intercepted</u> the pass.
Passive Voice: The pass <u>was intercepted</u> by the linebacker.

Switching from one voice to the other within a sentence is regarded as an error in style and should be avoided.
Poor: He <u>likes</u> to play chess and playing bridge <u>is</u> also <u>enjoyed</u> by him.
Better: He <u>likes</u> to play chess and he also <u>enjoys</u> playing bridge.

> TIP: Avoid Errors in your Essay:
>
> 1. Stick to one tense.
>   (Give your opinion using the present tense.)
>   (Write a summary in the past tense.)
>
> 2. Use the active voice.

PROBLEMS INVOLVING MODIFIERS

Unclear Placement of Modifiers

In general, adjectives, adverbs, adjective phrases, adverbial phrases, adjective clauses, and adverbial clauses should be placed close to the word they modify. If these modifiers are separated from the word they modify, confusion may result. Here are some specific rules to apply:

1. The adverbs *only, almost, even, ever, just, merely,* and *scarcely* should be placed next to the word they modify.
   Ambiguous: I <u>almost</u> ate the whole cake. (Did the speaker eat any of the cake?)
   Clear: I ate <u>almost</u> the whole cake.
   Ambiguous: This house <u>only</u> cost $42,000.
   Clear: <u>Only</u> this house cost $42,000. (One house was sold at this price.)
   Clear: This house cost <u>only</u> $42,000. (The price mentioned is considered low.)

2. Phrases should be placed close to the word they modify.
   Unclear: The advertisement stated that a table was wanted by an elderly gentleman <u>with wooden legs</u>. (It is obvious that the advertisement was not written to disclose the gentleman's infirmity.)
   Clear: The advertisement stated that a table <u>with wooden legs</u> was wanted by an elderly gentleman.

3. Adjective clauses should be placed near the words they modify.
   Misplaced: I bought groceries at the Safeway store <u>that cost $29.47</u>.
   Clear: I bought groceries <u>that cost $29.47</u> at the Safeway store.

4. Words that may modify either a preceding or a following word are called *squinting modifiers*. In order to correct the ambiguity, move the modifier so that its relationship to only one word is clear.
   Squinting: He said that if we refused to leave <u>in two minutes</u> he would call the police.
   Clear: He said that he would call the police if we refused to leave in <u>two minutes</u>.
   Clear: He said that he would call the police <u>in two minutes</u> if we refused to leave.
   Squinting: We agreed <u>on Tuesday</u> to visit him.
   Clear: <u>On Tuesday</u>, we agreed to visit him.
   Clear: We agreed to visit him <u>on Tuesday</u>.

PRACTICE

Clear up the following ambiguous sentences, using the preceding examples as models.

1. I almost drank all the milk.

   _____

   This station wagon only seats five passengers.

   _____

2. The report mentioned that a man was wanted for murder with a wooden leg.

   _____

3. I found a roast at the supermarket that was big enough for eight.

   _____

4. We promised Mother on Sunday to go to church.

   _____

Dangling Modifiers

When modifying phrases or clauses precede the main clause of the sentence, good usage requires that they come directly before the subject of the main clause and clearly refer to the subject. Phrases and clauses that do not meet these requirements are called *dangling modifiers*. They seem to refer to a wrong word in the sentence, often with humorous or misleading results.

EXAMPLE 1:

Dangling participle: Walking through Central Park, the Metropolitan Museum of Art was seen. (Is the museum walking?)

Corrected: Walking through Central Park, the tourists saw the Metropolitan Museum of Art. (The participle <u>walking</u> immediately precedes the subject of the main clause <u>tourists</u>.)

EXAMPLE 2:

Dangling gerund phrase: Upon hearing the report that a bomb had been placed in the auditorium, the building was cleared. (Who heard the report?)

Corrected: Upon hearing the report that a bomb had been placed in the auditorium, the police cleared the building.

EXAMPLE 3:

Dangling infinitive phrase: To make a soufflé, eggs must be broken. (Do eggs make a soufflé?)

Corrected: To make a soufflé, you must break some eggs.

EXAMPLE 4:

Dangling elliptical construction: When about to graduate from elementary school, the teacher talked about the problems and joys of junior high school. (Is the teacher graduating?)

Corrected: When we were about to graduate from elementary school, the teacher talked about the problems and joys of junior high school.

PRACTICE

Correct the following dangling modifiers according to the corrections shown in the preceding examples.

1. Driving along the Monterey Peninsula, the cypress trees were beautiful.

   _____

   _____

2. On reading the report that cockroaches had been found in the school cafeteria, the kitchen was fumigated.

   _____

   _____

   _____

3. To repair a flat tire, the car must be jacked up.

   _____

   _____

4. When about to get married for the fourth time, the minister talked to the divorcee about the holiness of marriage.

   _____

   _____

   _____

PROBLEMS WITH PARALLEL STRUCTURE

Balance in a sentence is obtained when two or more similar ideas are presented in *parallel form*. A noun is matched with a noun, an active verb with an active verb, an adjective with an adjective, a phrase with a phrase. A lack of parallelism weakens the sentence.

EXAMPLE 1:

Not parallel: We are studying mathematics, French, and how to write creatively.
Parallel: We are studying mathematics, French, and creative writing. (All the objects of the verb <u>are studying</u> are nouns.)

EXAMPLE 2:

Not parallel: He told the students to register in his course, to study for the examination, and that they should take the test at the end of January.
Parallel: He told the students to register in his course, to study for the examination, and to take the test at the end of January. (The parallel elements are all infinitives.)

EXAMPLE 3:

Not parallel: The children ate all the candy and the birthday cake was devoured. (The use of the active voice in the first clause and the passive voice in the second clause creates a lack of parallelism.)
Parallel: The children ate all the candy and devoured the birthday cake. (The change in voice has been eliminated. The two verbs <u>ate</u> and <u>devoured</u> are both in the active voice.)

PRACTICE

Following the corrections shown in the preceding examples, correct the following unbalanced sentences to provide the parallel structure they lack.

1. The minister preached about sin, judgment, and how we needed to repent.

_____

_____

2. She told her husband to mow the lawn, to take out the trash, and that he should do the laundry.

_____

_____

3. The husband took out the trash, and the lawn was mowed.

_____

_____

Common Problems in Usage

WORDS OFTEN MISUSED OR CONFUSED

Errors in *diction*—that is, choice of words—often occur in student essays. Here are some of the most common diction errors to watch for.

accept/except. These two words are often confused. *Accept* means to receive; *except,* when used as a verb, means to preclude or exclude. *Except* may also be used as a preposition or a conjunction.

I will <u>accept</u> the award in his absence.
He <u>was excepted</u> from receiving the award because of his record of excessive lateness.
We all received awards <u>except</u> Tom.

affect/effect. *Affect* is a verb meaning (1) to act upon or influence, and (2) to feign or assume. *Effect,* as a verb, means to cause or bring about; as a noun, *effect* means result.

His poor attendance <u>affected</u> his grade.
To cover his embarrassment, he <u>affected</u> an air of nonchalance.
As he assumed office, the newly elected governor promised to <u>effect</u> many needed reforms in the tax structure.
What will be the <u>effect</u> of all this discussion?

aggravate. *Aggravate* means to worsen. It should not be used as a synonym for *annoy* or *irritate*. You will <u>aggravate</u> your condition if you try to lift heavy weights so soon after your operation. The teacher was <u>irritated</u> [not <u>aggravated</u>] by the whispering in the room.

ain't. *Ain't* is nonstandard English and should be avoided.

all the farther/all the faster. These are colloquial and regional expressions and so are considered inappropriate in standard English. Use *as far as* or *as fast as* instead.

already/all ready. These expressions are frequently confused. *Already* means previously; *all ready* means completely prepared.
I had <u>already</u> written to him.
The students felt that they were <u>all ready</u> for the examination.

alright. *All right* should be used instead of the misspelling *alright*.

altogether/all together. *All together* means as a group. *Altogether* means entirely, completely.
The teacher waited until the students were <u>all together</u> in the hall before she dismissed them.
There is <u>altogether</u> too much noise in the room.

among/between. *Among* is used when more than two persons or things are being discussed; *between*, when only two persons or things are involved.
The loot was divided <u>among</u> the three robbers.
This is <u>between</u> you and me.

amount/number. *Amount* should be used when referring to mass, bulk, or quantity. *Number* should be used when the quantity can be counted.
I have a large <u>amount</u> of work to do.
A large <u>number</u> of books were destroyed in the fire.

and etc. The *and* is unnecessary. Just write *etc.*

being as/being that. These phrases are nonstandard and should be avoided. Use *since* or *that*.

beside/besides. These words are often confused. *Beside* means alongside of; *besides* means in addition to.
Park your car <u>beside</u> mine.
Who will be at the party <u>besides</u> Mary and John?

between. See *among*.

but what. This phrase should be avoided. Use *that* instead.
Wrong: I cannot believe <u>but what</u> he will not come.
Better: I cannot believe <u>that</u> he will not come.

can't hardly. This phrase is a double negative that borders on the illiterate. Use *can hardly*.

complected. This word is nonstandard and should be avoided. Use *complexioned*.

continual/continuous. These words are used interchangeably by many writers; however, the careful stylist should make the distinction between the two words. *Continual* refers to a sequence that is steady but interrupted from time to time. A child's crying is *continual* because it does stop crying from time to time to catch its breath or to eat or sleep. *Continuous* refers to a passage of time or space that continues uninterruptedly. The roar of the surf at the beach is *continuous*.

could of. This phrase is nonstandard. Use *could have*.

different from/different than. Contemporary usage accepts both forms; however, *different from* remains the preferred choice.

effect. See *affect*.

except. See *accept*.

farther/further. *Farther* should be used when discussing physical or spatial distances; *further,* when discussing quantities.

We have six miles farther to go.
Further discussion will be futile.

fewer/less. *Fewer* should be used with things that can be counted; *less,* with things that are not counted but measured in other ways.

There are fewer pupils in this class than in the other group. (Note that you can count pupils— one pupil, two pupils, and so on.)
You should devote less attention to athletics and more to your studies.

former/latter. Use *former* and *latter* only when you are discussing a series of two. *Former* refers to the first item of the series and *latter* to the second. If you discuss a series of three or more, use *first* and *last.*

Both Judy and Charles are qualified for the position, but I will vote for the former.
Sam, Bob, and Harry invited Mary to the dance, but she decided to go with the first.

further. See *farther.*

had of. This phrase is nonstandard. Use *had.*

hanged/hung. Both words are the past participle of the verb *hang.* However, *hanged* should be used when the execution of a person is being discussed; *hung* when the suspension of an object is discussed.

The convicted murderer was scheduled to be hanged at noon.
When the abstract painting was first exhibited, very few noticed that it had been hung upside down.

healthful/healthy. These two words should not be confused. *Healthful* describes things or conditions that provide health. *Healthy* means in a state of health.

You should eat healthful foods like fresh vegetables, instead of the candy you have just bought.
To be healthy, you need good food, fresh air and sunshine, and plenty of sleep.

imply/infer. These are not synonyms. *Imply* means to suggest or indicate. *Infer* means to draw a conclusion.

Your statement implies that you are convinced of his guilt.
Do not infer from my action in this matter that I will always be this lenient.

in back of. Avoid this expression. Use *behind* in its place.

irregardless. This is nonstandard. Use *regardless* instead.

kind of/sort of. These phrases should not be used as adverbs. Use words like *quite, rather,* or *somewhat* instead.

Undesirable: I was kind of annoyed by her statement.
Preferable: I was quite annoyed by her statement.

last/latter. See *former.*

lay/lie. *Lay,* a transitive verb, means to place; *lie,* an intransitive verb, means to rest or recline. One way of determining whether to use *lay* or *lie* is to examine the sentence. If the verb has an object, use the correct form of *lay.* If the verb has no object, use *lie.*

He laid the book on the table. (Book is the object of the verb. The past tense of lay is correct.)
He has lain motionless for an hour. (The verb has no object. The present perfect tense of lie is correct.)

learn/teach. *Learn* means to get knowledge; *teach,* to impart information or knowledge.
I learned my lesson.
She taught me a valuable lesson.

leave/let. *Leave* means to depart; *let,* to permit.
Incorrect: Leave me go.
Correct: Let me go.

less. See *fewer*.

liable/likely. *Likely* is an expression of probability. *Liable* adds a sense of possible harm or misfortune.
    Incorrect: He is liable to hear you.
    Correct: He is likely to hear you.
    Incorrect: The boy is likely to fall and hurt himself.
    Correct: The boy is liable to fall and hurt himself.

lie. See *lay*.

mad/angry. These are not synonyms. Mad means *insane*.

number. See *amount*.

of. Don't substitute *of* for *have* in the expressions *could have, should have, must have*, and so on.

off of. The *of* is superfluous and should be deleted.
    Incorrect: I fell off of the ladder.
    Correct: I fell off the ladder.

prefer. This verb should not be followed by *than*. Use *to, before*, or *above* instead.
    Incorrect: I prefer chocolate than vanilla.
    Correct: I prefer chocolate to vanilla.

principal/principle. *Principal*, meaning chief, is mainly an adjective. *Principle*, meaning a rule or basic law, is a noun e.g., a Scientific Principle. In a few cases, *principal* is used as a noun because the noun it once modified has been dropped.
    principal of a school (Originally, the principal teacher.)
    principal in a bank (Originally, the principal sum.)
    a principal in a transaction (Originally, the principal person.)

raise/rise. *Raise* is a transitive verb (takes an object); *rise* is intransitive.
    Incorrect: They are rising the prices.
    Correct: They are raising the prices.
    Incorrect: The sun will raise at 6:22 A.M.
    Correct: The sun will rise at 6:22 A.M.

real. This word is an adjective and should not be used as an adverb.
    Incorrect: This is a real good story.
    Correct: This is a really [or very] good story.

the reason is because. This expression is ungrammatical. The copulative verb *is* should be followed by a noun clause; *because* introduces an adverbial clause.
    Incorrect: The reason I was late is because there was a traffic jam.
    Correct: The reason I was late is that there was a traffic jam.

same. Do not use *same* as a pronoun. Use *it, them, this, that* in its place.
    Incorrect: I have received your letter of inquiry; I will answer same as soon as possible.
    Correct: I have received your letter of inquiry; I will answer it as soon as possible.

sort of. See *kind of*.

teach. See *learn*.

try and. This phrase should be avoided. Use *try to* in its place.
    Incorrect: I will try and find your book.
    Correct: I will try to find your book.

unique. This adjective should not be qualified by *more, most, less*, or *least*.
    Incorrect: This was a most unique experience.
    Correct: This was a unique experience.

PRACTICE

Some, but not all, of the following sentences contain errors in diction. Underline the errors and correct the sentences, following the models in the previous section. (Corrections for the sentences containing errors follow the exercise.)

1. Stevie Wonder is the most unique singer I know.

2. He is a real exciting performer.

3. I cannot believe but what he will not have a new hit record every year.

4. He performs in clubs, concert halls, theaters, etc.

5. He is all together the finest singer I have ever seen.

6. I want to be in the audience when he excepts his award.

7. He already has won many awards for his music.

8. If he made less records, I would be unhappy.

9. I can't hardly wait until his next record comes out.

10. When a Stevie Wonder record comes out, I try and buy it right away.

11. People are liable to remember his music for a hundred years.

12. What singers do you admire besides Stevie Wonder and Elvis?

13. Stevie and Elvis are both great, but I prefer the former to the latter.

14. I would of gone to Stevie's last concert, but I didn't have the money.

15. Stevie Wonder's private life is kind of interesting.

_____

_____

16. He takes care of himself and only eats healthful foods.

_____

_____

17. He has strong moral principles.

_____

_____

18. He has not let his fame affect him badly.

_____

_____

19. The amount of fans he has is huge, but he nonetheless remains a simple, modest man.

_____

_____

20. In my book, he is alright.

_____

_____

21. Between you and me, I think he's wonderful.

_____

_____

22. I get really aggravated when someone criticizes him.

_____

_____

23. The reason I get angry is because his critics are wrong.

_____

_____

24. They will learn a great deal if they listen to him.

_____

_____

25. You can infer from everything I have said that I am a confirmed Stevie Wonder fan.

_____

_____

ANSWERS:

The following sentences contain errors in diction: 1, 2, 3, 5, 6, 8, 9, 10, 11, 14, 15, 19, 20, 22, 23.

Suggested corrections are:

1. . . . the most unusual singer I know (or . . . a unique singer).
2. . . . a highly exciting performer. (You may also omit the adverb *highly*.)
3. I cannot believe that he . . .
5. He is altogether the finest . . .
6. . . . when he accepts . . .
8. If he made fewer records, . . .
9. . . . I can hardly wait . . .

10. ... I try to buy it ...

11. People are likely to ...

14. I would have gone ...

15. ... life is somewhat interesting (or quite interesting, or rather interesting).

19. The number of fans he has ...

20. ... he is all right.

22. I get really angry ... (or I get really irritated ... Even better, drop the adverb really: I get angry ...)

23. The reason I get angry is that his critics ... (Better: I get angry because his critics ...)

IDIOMATIC EXPRESSIONS

An idiom is a form of expression peculiar to a particular language. Occasionally, idioms seem to violate grammatical rules; however, the common use of these expressions has made them acceptable. Some of the most common idioms in English involve prepositions. The following list indicates which preposition is idiomatically correct to use after each word:

accede to	desire for	observant of
accuse of	desirous of	partial to
addicted to	desist from	peculiar to
adhere to	different from	preview of
agreeable to	disagree with	prior to
amazement at	disdain for	prone to
appetite for	dissent from	revel in
appreciation of	distaste for	separate from
aside from	enveloped in	suspect of
associate with	expert in	tamper with
blame for	frugal of	try to
capable of	hint at	void of
characterized by	implicit in	weary of
compatible with	negligent of	willing to
conversant with	oblivious to	

PUNCTUATION FOR SENTENCE SENSE

Errors in punctuation are noticeable: they stand out. When you write, understanding the effects of various punctuation marks on the meaning and structure of a sentence is likely to be helpful. In this section, we will review the most commonly used punctuation marks and illustrate the ways they should be used.

End Punctuation

THE PERIOD (.)

1. The period is used to indicate the end of a declarative or imperative sentence.
   I am going home.
   Go home.

2. The period is used after initials and abbreviations.
   Mr. J. C. Smith
   John Rose, M.D.

3. The period is *not* used after contractions, initials of governmental agencies, chemical symbols, or radio and television call letters.

can't	HCl	didn't	Sn
IRS	WNBC	FBI	KPIX

4. A series of three periods is used to indicate the fact that material has been omitted from a quotation.
We, the People of the United States, In Order to form a more perfect union, . . . do ordain and establish this Constitution for the United States of America.

THE QUESTION MARK (?)

1. The question mark is used after a direct question.
Who is going with you?

2. The question mark should *not* be used when questions appear in indirect discourse.
He asked whether you would go with him.

3. The question mark should *not* be used when a polite or formal request is made.
Will you please come with me.

4. The question mark should *not* be used when the question is purely rhetorical (that is, asked only for effect, with no answer expected).
That's very good, don't you think.

Middle Punctuation

THE COMMA (,)

1. The comma is used to set off nouns in direct address.
Mr. Smith, please answer this question.
Tom, come here.

2. The comma is used to set off words or phrases in apposition.
Mr. Brown, our newly elected sheriff, has promised to enforce the law vigorously.
Dr. Alexander, my instructor, has written several authoritative books on this topic.

3. The comma is used to set off items in a series.
I bought milk, eggs, apples, and bread at the store.
Maine, Vermont, New Hampshire, Massachusetts, Rhode Island, and Connecticut are the states that make up New England.
The river tumbles down lofty mountains, cuts through miles of prairie land, and finally empties into the Atlantic Ocean.

4. The comma is used to separate the clauses of a compound sentence connected by a coordinating conjunction.
The bill to reduce taxes was introduced by Congressman Jones, and it was referred to the House Ways and Means Committee for consideration. (Note that the omission of the conjunction <u>and</u> would result in a run-on sentence.)

5. The comma is used to set off long introductory phrases and clauses that precede the main clause.
In a conciliatory speech to the striking employees, Mr. Brown agreed to meet with their leaders and to consider their complaints.
Because I was ignorant of the facts in this matter, I was unable to reach a decision.

6. The comma is used to set off unimportant (or *nonrestrictive*) phrases and clauses in a sentence.
My brother, who is a physician, has invited me to spend Christmas week with him.

7. The comma is used to set off parenthetical words like *first, therefore, however,* and *moreover,* from the rest of the sentence.
   I am, therefore, going to sue you in small claims court.
   More than two inches of rain fell last week; however, this was not enough to fill our reservoirs.

8. The comma is used to set off contrasting, interdependent expressions.
   The bigger they are, the harder they fall.

9. The comma is used to separate adjectives that could be connected by *and.*
   He spoke in a kind, soothing voice.

10. In sentences containing direct quotations, the comma is used to separate introductory words from quoted words.
    Mary said, "I hope you will understand my reasons for doing this to you."

11. The comma may be used to indicate omitted words whose repetition is understood.
    Tall and short are antonyms; rapid and swift, synonyms.

12. The comma is used to separate items in dates, addresses, and geographical names.
    January 5, 1981
    Detroit, Michigan
    My address is 5225 East 28 Street, Brooklyn, New York.

13. The comma is used to follow the salutation in a friendly letter.
    Dear Mary,

14. The comma follows the complimentary close in business and friendly letters.
    Your sincerely,
    Truly yours,

THE SEMICOLON (;)

1. The semicolon is used as a substitute for the comma followed by *and* that connects two independent clauses in a compound sentence.
   Mary won first prize in the contest, and John came in second.
   Mary won first prize in the contest; John came in second.

2. The semicolon is used before *namely, for instance,* and *for example* when they introduce a list.
   Four students were chosen to act as a committee; namely, John, Henry, Frank, and William.

3. When the words *however, nevertheless, furthermore, moreover,* and *therefore* are used to connect two independent clauses, they should be preceded by a semicolon.
   He worked diligently for the award; however, he did not receive it.

4. The semicolon is used to separate items in a list when the items themselves contain commas.
   Among the contributors to the book were Roy O. Billett, Boston University; Lawrence D. Brennan, New York University; Allan Danzig, Lafayette College; and Mario Pei, Columbia University.

THE COLON (:)

1. The colon is used to introduce a list, especially after the words *following* and *as follows.*
   On this tour, you will visit the following countries: England, France, Spain, Italy, Greece, and Israel.

2. The colon is used after the salutation in business letters.
   Dear Sir:
   Dear Dr. Brown:
   To Whom It May Concern:

3. The colon is used when time is indicated in figures.
   Please meet me at 3:30 P.M.

4. The colon is used to indicate ratios.
   2:5 :: 6:15

QUOTATION MARKS (" ")

1. Quotation marks are used to indicate the exact words of a speaker or writer. The introductory words are separated from the quotation by a comma or commas.
   Patrick Henry said, "Give me liberty or give me death."
   "Give me liberty," Patrick Henry said, "or give me death."
   "Give me liberty or give me death," Patrick Henry said.

2. When quotation marks are used, the capitalization of the original quotation should be retained.
   "I have always wanted," John said, "to ride a ten-speed bike." (And small t is used because to was not capitalized in the statement being quoted.)

3. If the quotation is a question, the question mark should appear inside the quotation marks.
   John asked, "When does the party start?"
   "When does the party start?" John asked.

CHAPTER 3
The Basics of Reading

HOW TO INTERPRET READING MATERIALS

Practical Reading

Practical reading, the reading you do in the course of your daily life, is primarily for purposes of information. *In the home,* you follow a recipe or read the label on a bottle of aspirin. You read a house plan or charts and tables dealing with storing food in a freezer. You read the warranty for an appliance you buy. You consult the newspaper when you look for a job. You read an advertisement from a bank offering different kinds of accounts. *On the road,* you read a train schedule or a road map.

We shall provide practice in all of these kinds of practical reading. *But what skills are required?* The skills are as varied as the different kinds of reading you are called upon to do. Here are some examples:

1. Recipe. You need to know how to follow instructions *in the order* in which they are given, using a basic cooking vocabulary.

2. Drug label. You must *locate essential details* as to dosage and dangers of misuse.

3. Charts and tables. You have to move up and down and back and forth to *locate* either *numbers* or numbers in their relationship to others.

4. Advertisements. You sometimes have to *know special abbreviations* when reading classified (or want) ads; you will have to *sort out* facts you need from all the *irrelevant material* presented.

5. Maps. In road maps, you have to *read symbols* indicating various locations and the distances between them.

6. Train and bus schedules. These are similar to charts and tables, but you must deal with time and a set of code letters or numbers that refer you to footnotes.

7. Warranties. You've heard of the expression "read the small print." Well, warranties are similar to contracts in that they constitute an agreement between the manufacturer and the user. You have to determine what you are offered by the manufacturer and under what conditions.

These are only some of the more common examples of practical reading, but they are similar to many others. Following directions in making bookends in a shop does not require different skills from those in following a recipe. Charts, tables, and maps are encountered in social studies.

Let us turn to three typical kinds of practical reading: reading a drug label, reading a recipe, and reading a bank newspaper advertisement.

ILLUSTRATION 1

ASPIRIN
TABLETS
(Analgesic)
5 grains each

For relief of minor headaches and neuralgia. Adults: 1 to 2 tablets with water every 3 or 4 hours, 5 to 6 times daily as required. Children 10–16 years: 1 tablet; 6–10 years: ½ tablet; 3–6 years: ¼ tablet. For children under 3 years of age, consult your physician. Indicated dosage for children may be repeated every 3 hours, but not more than 3 times in one day unless prescribed by the child's physician.

CAUTION: If pain persists or recurs, be sure to consult a physician.
WARNING: KEEP THIS AND ALL DRUGS OUT OF REACH OF CHILDREN.
IN CASE OF ACCIDENTAL OVERDOSE, SEEK PROFESSIONAL ASSISTANCE OR CONTACT A POISON CONTROL CENTER IMMEDIATELY.

1. The maximum dosage for adults in any 24-hour period is
   (1) 4 tablets
   (2) 6 tablets
   (3) 8 tablets
   (4) 10 tablets
   (5) 12 tablets

   1. 1 2 3 4 5
   ‖ ‖ ‖ ‖ ‖

2. According to the warning on the label, in case of an overdose, one should consider the symptoms to be the same as
   (1) the effects of a normal dosage of any other medicine
   (2) the effects of a normal dosage of àspirin
   (3) poisoning
   (4) a child's ailment
   (5) a minor headache or neuralgia

   2. 1 2 3 4 5
   ‖ ‖ ‖ ‖ ‖

3. From the words after CAUTION, it can be inferred that the meaning of *analgesic* is
   (1) painkiller
   (2) digestive
   (3) analytic
   (4) dangerous
   (5) headache

   3. 1 2 3 4 5
   ‖ ‖ ‖ ‖ ‖

Answers:

1. **5**   2. **3**   3. **1**

Answer Analysis:

1. **5** If, according to the instructions on the label, an adult takes the maximum dosage of 2 tablets every 3 or 4 hours for a maximum of 6 times daily, he or she will consume a total of 12 tablets.

2. **3** The instructions following the word WARNING suggest contacting a poison control center immediately or seeking professional assistance. This is the procedure followed in the event of poisoning.

3. **1** The words "CAUTION: If pain persists . . ." lead to the inference that aspirin is used to kill pain. *Analgesic,* therefore, means painkiller.

ILLUSTRATION 2

NUT BREAD

4 cups flour	2 cups milk
4 tsp. baking powder	3 eggs separated
1 tsp. salt	1 cup broken nuts
1½ cups sugar	

Mix flour, baking powder, salt and sugar; add milk, egg yolks and nuts; fold in stiffly beaten egg whites. Pour into bread pan and let rise 30 minutes. Bake about 45 minutes in slow oven.

1. Before beginning to bake the nut bread, one must do all of the following EXCEPT   **1.** 1 2 3 4 5
   (1) use a tablespoon
   (2) separate the egg white from the egg yolk
   (3) beat the egg white
   (4) break nuts
   (5) have a bread pan and a mixing bowl on hand

2. The correct order of actions required to make the nut bread is   **2.** 1 2 3 4 5
   (1) mix, add, pour, let rise, bake, fold
   (2) mix, add, let rise, bake, pour, fold
   (3) mix, add, fold, pour, let rise, bake
   (4) mix, add, bake, let rise, fold, pour
   (5) mix, add, pour, fold, let rise, bake

3. Preparing the nut bread requires approximately   **3.** 1 2 3 4 5
   (1) 30 minutes   (4) 1 hour and 15 minutes
   (2) 45 minutes   (5) 2 hours
   (3) 1 hour

Answers:

1. **1**   2. **3**   3. **4**

Answer Analysis:

1. **1** To arrive at this answer, one must make inferences from the steps indicated in the recipe and also apply a general knowledge of the abbreviations for teaspoon and tablespoon. If you must pour the mixture into a bread pan, the bread pan must be on hand, and if you have to mix the flour and baking powder, a mixing bowl is necessary. The only thing not needed from the choices given is a tablespoon.
2. **3** According to the recipe, the correct order for the six steps to make nut bread is: mix, add, fold, pour, let rise, and bake.
3. **4** According to the recipe, the rising time for the bread is 30 minutes and baking time is 45 minutes—a total of 1 hour and 15 minutes. Allowing time for mixing the ingredients, the approximate time might be 15 minutes more. Choices 1, 2, and 3 are all below the minimum 1 hour and 15 minute figure. Choice 5, 2 hours, is too long. The closest approximate time is 1 hour and 15 minutes, Choice 4.

ILLUSTRATION 3

8.17% effective annual yield on

7.75% a year — Time Deposit Savings Account 6 to 7 year term Minimum Deposit $1,000

7.90% effective annual yield on

7.50% a year — Time Deposit Savings Account 4 to 6 year terms Minimum Deposit $1,000

7.08% effective annual yield on

6.75% a year — Time Deposit Savings Account 2½ to 4 year terms Minimum Deposit $500

6.81% effective annual yield on

6.50% a year — Time Deposit Savings Account 1 to 2½ year terms Minimum Deposit $500

5.47% annual yield on

5.25% per year Daily Dividend—Grace Day dividend Savings Accounts

Put your money in our "Daily Dividend" account and take it out any time you like without losing a single day's earned dividends. We currently pay 5.25% from day of deposit to day of withdrawal compounded daily (as long as $5 remains to the end of the quarter).

OR

Deposit any amount before the 10th of any month in a Regular Grace Day Account and your dividends start from the 1st. Leave your money in, and daily compounding at the current 5.25% dividend rate adds up to an annual return of 5.47%.

On all accounts, interest/dividends are compounded daily and credited quarterly. To earn annual yields shown, interest/dividends must remain on deposit for a full year.

Withdrawals on time deposit accounts permitted before maturity, but Federal Deposit Insurance Corporation regulations require that a substantial penalty be imposed, i.e., that interest be reduced to regular savings account rate on amount withdrawn and three months' interest be forfeited.

1. To gain the maximum interest allowed, you must be prepared to deposit

    (1) $500 for 2½ years
    (2) $1,000 for 4 years
    (3) $1,000 for 6 years
    (4) $500 for 4 years
    (5) $1,000 for 1 year

1. 1 2 3 4 5
‖ ‖ ‖ ‖ ‖

2. If you deposit and withdraw money frequently, it is best for you to use a

2. 1 2 3 4 5
‖ ‖ ‖ ‖ ‖

(1) Daily Dividend Account
(2) Grace Day Account
(3) Time Deposit Savings Account
(4) Time Deposit Savings Account for 4 years
(5) Time Deposit Savings Account for 7 years

3. According to the chart in the advertisement, what is the maximum interest that can be earned if you have $100 to save and do not need the money for a year?

3. 1 2 3 4 5
‖ ‖ ‖ ‖ ‖

(1) 5.25%
(2) 5.47%
(3) 6.50%

(4) 6.81%
(5) 7.08%

Answers:

1. **3** 2. **1** 3. **2**

Answer Analysis:

1. **3** This question deals with the maximum interest for the smallest deposit allowable for that amount of interest. According to the ad, a minimum deposit of $1,000 for six years, Choice 3, will earn the highest possible yield, an effective annual yield of 8.17%.

2. **1** According to the ad, in a Daily Dividend Account, you may deposit or withdraw money any time you like without losing a single day's earned dividends.

3. **2** All annual yields higher than 5.47%, Choice 2, require $500 or $1,000 minimum deposits. Choice 1, 5.25%, is wrong because it doesn't represent the highest amount of interest that can be earned.

PRACTICE

Directions: **Each of the statements or questions based on the materials below is followed by five suggested answers or completions. In each instance, choose the one that best completes the statement or answers the question.   Mark the frame in the answer column whose number corresponds to the answer you have selected.**

Refer to the following directions on a can of liquid plastic clear gloss to answer the next four questions.

Keep contents away from heat and open flame.
Avoid prolonged contact with skin and breathing of vapors or
  spray mist.
Do not take internally.
Close container after each use.
Use only with adequate ventilation.

KEEP OUT OF REACH OF CHILDREN

Directions for Use

Be sure surface is absolutely dry, free from all wax, grease, and dirt. Sand with fine sandpaper and wipe off dust. Use LIQUIPLAST Liquid Plastic unthinned straight out of the can. If thinning is desired, use mineral spirits.

UNFINISHED WOOD SURFACES: Apply LIQUIPLAST directly to the unfinished wood. When using paste fillers, remove excess paste from the surface before finishing. When using LI-QUIPLAST Liquid Plastic as a sealer, sand before recoating to get the best finish.

LACQUERED, VARNISHED, OR STAINED SURFACES: Sand to remove surface imperfections and sheen from the previous coatings. Do not use LIQUIPLAST Liquid Plastic over shellac, lacquer sanding sealers, or fillers and stains containing stearates.

Under normal use, a three-coat application of LIQUIPLAST will wear well. Under conditions of severe wear, more coats may be necessary. Sand lightly between coats to eliminate sheen and allow fresh LIQUIPLAST to adhere.

Use paint thinner to clean brushes.

1. The minimum number of coats of LIQUIPLAST recommended for normal conditions of wear is
   (1) one coat
   (2) two coats
   (3) three coats
   (4) four coats
   (5) five coats

   1. 1 2 3 4 5

2. According to the warning on the label, you should NOT
   (1) close the container after each use.
   (2) apply LIQUIPLAST in a tightly sealed room
   (3) mix LIQUIPLAST with mineral spirits
   (4) use LIQUIPLAST out of the reach of children
   (5) sand LIQUIPLAST to remove sheen

   2. 1 2 3 4 5

3. From the directions about sanding between coats, it can be inferred that sheen
   (1) is a condition of severe wear
   (2) is a stain containing stearates
   (3) must be used unthinned from the can
   (4) may hinder the adhesion of LIQUIPLAST
   (5) may be increased by light sanding

   3. 1 2 3 4 5

4. LIQUIPLAST should NOT be
   (1) used unthinned straight out of the can
   (2) used to seal unfinished wood surfaces
   (3) used over lacquer sanding sealers
   (4) mixed with mineral spirits
   (5) used over paste fillers

   4. 1 2 3 4 5

Refer to the following recipe to answer the next four questions.

PEANUT BUTTER COOKIES

¼ c. butter	1½ c. all-purpose flour
⅞ c. peanut butter	½ tsp. baking soda
½ c. brown sugar	½ tsp. baking powder
½ c. white sugar	¼ tsp. salt
2 small eggs	

Blend the softened butter with the peanut butter. Cream the

sugars with the peanut butter mixture. Add the eggs and mix thoroughly. Sift the flour. Then resift it with the rest of the dry ingredients. Mix and knead the dry ingredients into the peanut butter mixture. Shape the dough with your fingers into small balls and place them (not too close together) on an ungreased baking sheet. Using a fork dipped into flour, press the balls flat in a crisscross pattern. Bake at 375°F. for 10–15 minutes. Watch the cookies carefully, as they brown quickly at the end of the baking period. Yield: 3–4 dozen cookies.

Note: For a cookie that tastes less "peanutty," reduce the amount of peanut butter and substitute an equal amount of butter.

5. The remaining dry ingredients to be sifted with the flour are
   (1) baking soda, baking powder, and salt
   (2) baking soda, baking powder, brown sugar, and salt
   (3) baking powder, brown sugar, white sugar, and salt
   (4) baking powder, baking soda, brown sugar, white sugar, and salt
   (5) baking soda, brown sugar, white sugar, and salt

5. 1 2 3 4 5
‖ ‖ ‖ ‖ ‖

6. The eggs are to be added to the peanut butter mixture
   (1) after the flour
   (2) before the sugars are creamed
   (3) after kneading is completed
   (4) after the sugars are combined with the butter and peanut butter
   (5) using a fork dipped in flour as a mixing tool

6. 1 2 3 4 5
‖ ‖ ‖ ‖ ‖

7. The greatest single ingredient in this recipe is
   (1) flour
   (2) sugars (both kinds)
   (3) butter
   (4) peanut butter
   (5) baking powder

7. 1 2 3 4 5
‖ ‖ ‖ ‖ ‖

8. To reduce the nutty taste of these cookies, the recipe advises you to
   (1) increase the amount of flour
   (2) bake the cookies for only ten minutes
   (3) substitute one egg for some of the peanut butter
   (4) replace some peanut butter with an equal quantity of butter
   (5) press the cookies flat in a crisscross pattern

8. 1 2 3 4 5
‖ ‖ ‖ ‖ ‖

Refer to the following chart to answer the next three questions.

SOURCES OF IRON	
Meat, Fish, & Poultry	**Milligrams**
Most poultry, lamb, fish (raw), 4 oz.	1.5
Sardine & shrimp (canned), 3 oz.	2.5
Beef & pork (raw), 4 oz.	2.8
Beef heart (raw), 4 oz.	4.5
Beans: red, white, or lima (canned), 1 cup	5.0
Beef liver (raw), 4 oz.	7.2
Pork liver (raw), 4 oz.	22.0

Breads & Cereals

Bread, 1 slice	0.5
Cereal (cooked), 1 cup	1.0

Fruit & Vegetables

Peas (cooked), ½ cup	1.5
Lima beans (cooked), ½ cup	2.0
Spinach (cooked), ½ cup	2.0
Prune juice, ½ cup	5.0

Other Foods

Brown sugar, 2 tablespoons	1.0
Molasses, 2 tablespoons	1.8
Chocolate (bitter), 1 oz.	1.9
Cocoa, 4 tablespoons	3.3

9. Which of the following contains the greatest amount of iron?
   (1) Three ounces of shrimp
   (2) Four ounces of spinach
   (3) Two ounces of bitter chocolate
   (4) Eight ounces of raw lamb
   (5) Four tablespoons of cocoa

9. 1 2 3 4 5
‖ ‖ ‖ ‖ ‖

10. Which of the following statements are true?
    I. An ounce of canned beans contains more iron than an ounce of bitter chocolate.
    II. Cooked spinach contains more iron than cooked lima beans do.
    III. Beef heart is a better source of iron than beef liver is.
    (1) Statements I and II only
    (2) Statements I and III only
    (3) Statements II and III only
    (4) All of the statements
    (5) None of the statements

10. 1 2 3 4 5
‖ ‖ ‖ ‖ ‖

11. Men between the ages of 18 and 75 years need 10 milligrams of iron per day. Which of the following food combinations would supply a twenty-year-old with his day's requirement of iron?
    (1) 2 slices of bread, 8 ounces of beef steak, and ½ cup of peas
    (2) 1 cup of cooked cereal, 2 tablespoons of brown sugar, 4 ounces of beef heart, and ½ cup of spinach
    (3) 2 slices of bread, ½ cup of peas, and 4 ounces of beef liver
    (4) 1 cup of cooked cereal, 4 tablespoons of cocoa, ½ cup of prune juice, and 3 ounces of shrimp
    (5) 2 ounces of bitter chocolate, ½ cup of cooked lima beans, 4 ounces of pork, and 1 slice of bread

11. 1 2 3 4 5
‖ ‖ ‖ ‖ ‖

Refer to the following chart to answer the next four questions.

Dishwasher
Capacity: Standard

ENERGYGUIDE

Estimates on the scale are based on
a national average electric rate of
4.97¢ per kilowatt hour and a
natural gas rate of 36.7¢ per therm

Only standard size
Dishwashers are used
in the scale.

Electric Water Heater

Model with lowest energy cost	$64	Model with highest energy cost
$41		$80
▼	THIS ▼ MODEL	▼

Estimated yearly energy cost

Gas Water Heater

Model with lowest energy cost	$30	Model with highest energy cost
$19		$39
▼	THIS ▼ MODEL	▼

Estimated yearly energy cost

Your cost will vary depending on your local energy rate and how you use the product. This energy cost is based on U.S. Government standard tests.

How much will this model cost you to run yearly?

with an electric water heater

Loads of dishes per week		2	4	6	8	12
Estimated yearly $ cost shown below						
Cost per kilowatt hour	2¢	$ 7	$13	$ 20	$ 26	$ 39
	4¢	$13	$26	$ 39	$ 52	$ 78
	6¢	$20	$39	$ 59	$ 78	$117
	8¢	$26	$52	$ 78	$104	$156
	10¢	$33	$65	$ 98	$130	$195
	12¢	$39	$78	$117	$156	$234

with a gas water heater

Loads of dishes per week		2	4	6	8	12
Estimated yearly $ cost shown below						
Cost per therm (100 cubic feet)	10¢	$ 5	$ 9	$14	$18	$27
	20¢	$ 6	$11	$17	$23	$34
	30¢	$ 7	$14	$21	$27	$41
	40¢	$ 8	$16	$24	$32	$48
	50¢	$ 9	$18	$28	$37	$55
	60¢	$10	$21	$31	$41	$82

Ask your salesperson or local utility for the energy rate (cost per kilowatt hour or therm) in your area, and for estimated costs if you have a propane or oil water heater.

2. The national average natural gas rate is
   (1) 3.67¢ per kilowatt hour
   (2) 4.97¢ per kilowatt hour
   (3) 36.7¢ per therm
   (4) 49.7¢ per therm
   (5) between $19 and $39

12. 1 2 3 4 5
    ‖ ‖ ‖ ‖ ‖

3. We may infer that the standard sources of energy for dishwashers are
   (1) oil and propane
   (2) electricity and oil
   (3) electricity and propane
   (4) propane and gas
   (5) gas and electricity

13. 1 2 3 4 5
    ‖ ‖ ‖ ‖ ‖

14. If you run eight loads in your dishwasher per week and the cost per therm is 30¢, your estimated annual cost of running your dishwasher is

(1) $23
(2) $27
(3) $32
(4) $52
(5) $78

15. Which of the following statements are true?
  I. Electric rates are measured in terms of kilowatt hours.
  II. Heating water with gas costs more than heating water with electricity.
  III. The U.S. government conducts standard tests of dishwasher models.

(1) Statements I and II only
(2) Statements I and III only
(3) Statements II and III only
(4) All of the statements
(5) None of the statements

Refer to the following recommendations to answer the next three questions.

HOW TO THAW A TURKEY

First, when do you want to cook your fresh frozen turkey?

Cook it immediately?
1. Remove wrap. Place frozen turkey on rack in shallow roasting pan.
2. Cook for 1 hour in preheated 325°F oven.
3. Take turkey from oven and remove neck and giblets from body cavity and wishbone area.
4. Immediately return turkey to oven and cook until done.

Later today?
1. Leave in original wrap.
2. Thaw in running water or water that is changed frequently.

Thawing Time

5–9 pounds	3–4 hours
Over 9 pounds	4–7 hours

3. Cook or refrigerate thawed turkey immediately.

Cook it tomorrow?
1. Leave in original wrap.
2. Place frozen turkey in brown paper bag or wrap in 2–3 layers of newspaper.

Thawing Time

Under 12 pounds	10–18 hours
Over 12 pounds	18–30 hours

3. Check turkey often during last hours of thawing and refrigerate immediately if completely thawed.

Cook it day after tomorrow?
1. Leave in original wrap and place on tray or drip pan.
2. Thaw in refrigerator. (Turkeys over 12 pounds may take up to 3 days.)

These suggestions were released by the Poultry and Egg National Board.

16. The fastest way to thaw a fresh frozen turkey is to
    (1) place it in a brown paper bag
    (2) refrigerate it on a drip pan
    (3) check it often during thawing
    (4) put it in running water
    (5) heat it in a 325° oven for one hour

16. 1 2 3 4 5

17. What is the longest a 20-pound turkey may take to thaw in the refrigerator?
    (1) 3–4 hours
    (2) 4–7 hours
    (3) 10–18 hours
    (4) 18–30 hours
    (5) Up to 3 days

17. 1 2 3 4 5

18. Before heating a fresh frozen turkey, you must be sure to
    (1) refrigerate it
    (2) thaw it
    (3) remove its original wrap
    (4) wrap it in 2–3 layers of newspaper
    (5) allow it to stand at room temperature

18. 1 2 3 4 5

Refer to the following provisions on a residential rental agreement to answer the following two questions.

RESIDENTIAL RENTAL AGREEMENT
(Month-to-Month Tenancy)

Upon not less than 24 hours' advance notice, Tenant shall make the demised premises available during normal business hours to Landlord or his authorized agent or representative, for the purpose of entering (a) to make necessary agreed repairs, decorations, alterations or improvements or to supply necessary or agreed services, and (b) to show the premises to prospective or actual purchasers, mortgagees, tenants, workmen or contractors. In an emergency, Landlord, his agent or authorized representative may enter the premises at any time without securing prior permission from Tenant for the purpose of making corrections or repairs to alleviate such emergency.

19. According to the residential agreement, the Landlord can enter the Tenant's apartment with less than 24 hours' notice
    (1) to show the unit to prospective buyers
    (2) to redecorate the premises
    (3) to deal with an emergency

19. 1 2 3 4 5

    (4) only after normal business hours
    (5) with an agent or authorized representative

20. Which of the following statements are false?

    I. Landlord has no right to show the premises to a future tenant while the current tenant resides there.

    II. The tenant normally must have more than 24 hours' notice before the Landlord enters the premises.

    III. Landlords must secure prior permission from the tenant to enter the premises in an emergency.

    (1) Statements I and II only
    (2) Statements I and III only
    (3) Statements II and III only
    (4) All of the statements
    (5) None of the statements

20. 1 2 3 4 5

Answer Key

1. 3	6. 4	11. 4	16. 5
2. 2	7. 1	12. 3	17. 5
3. 4	8. 4	13. 5	18. 3
4. 3	9. 3	14. 2	19. 3
5. 1	10. 5	15. 2	20. 2

General Reading

General reading is the reading you do in the course of your daily life. It may be the reading you do on the job or it may be the reading you do in the evening and on weekends to find out more about the things that interest you—cooking, woodworking, travel, etc. For this, you read magazines and the family living sections of newspapers. You also consult books which deal with subjects in which you are interested.

    This part of the examination tests your ability to read popular articles that deal with everyday topics. *What are the skills you will need to master?*

1.   ***You read to find the main idea of the selection.***   You find it in a variety of places. It may be stated directly in the first sentence (easy to find). It may be stated in the final sentence to which the others build up (a bit harder to find). It may have to be discovered within the passage (most difficult). An example of this (note the underscored words) may be found in the following paragraph:

> Several students were seriously injured in football games last Saturday. The week before, several more were hospitalized. <u>Football has become a dangerous sport</u>. The piling up of players in a scrimmage often leads to serious injury. Perhaps some rule changes would lessen the number who are hurt.

You may also find that the main idea is not expressed at all, but can only be inferred from the selection as a whole.

> The plane landed at 4 P.M. As the door opened, the crowd burst into a long, noisy demonstration. The waiting mob surged against the police guard lines. Women were screaming. Teenagers were yelling for autographs or souvenirs. The visitor smiled and waved at his fans.

The main idea of the paragraph is not expressed, but it is clear that some popular hero, movie or rock star is being welcomed enthusiastically at the airport.

To find the main idea of a passage, ask yourself any or all of these questions:
1. What is the *main idea* of the passage? (Why did the author write it?)
2. What is the *topic sentence* of the paragraph or paragraphs (the sentence that the other sentences build on or flow from)?
3. What *title* would I give this selection?

---

2. *You read to find the details that explain or develop the main idea.* How do you do this? You must determine how the writer develops the main idea. He may give examples to illustrate that idea, or he may give reasons why the statement which is the main idea is true. Or he may give arguments for or against a position stated as the main idea. The writer may define a complex term and give a number of qualities of a complicated belief (such as democracy). He may also classify a number of objects within a larger category. Finally, he may compare two ideas or objects (show how they are similar) or contrast them (show how they are different).

In the paragraph immediately above, you can see that the sentence "You must determine how the writer develops the main idea" *is* the main idea. Six ways in which the writer can develop the main idea follow. These are the details that actually develop the main idea of the paragraph.

To find the main details of a passage, the questions to ask yourself are these:
1. What examples illustrate the main point?
2. What reasons or proof support the main idea?
3. What arguments are presented for or against the main idea?
4. What specific qualities are offered about the idea or subject being defined?
5. What classifications is a larger group broken down into?
6. What are the similarities and differences between two ideas or subjects being compared or contrasted?

---

3. *You read to make inferences by putting together ideas which are expressed to arrive at other ideas which are not.* In other words, you draw conclusions from the information presented by the author. You do this by locating relevant details and determining their relationships (time sequence, place sequence, cause and effect).

How do you do this? You can put one fact together with a second to arrive at a third which is not stated. You can apply a given fact to a different situation. You can predict an outcome based on the facts given.

To make inferences from a passage, ask yourself the following questions:
1. From the facts presented, what conclusions can I draw?
2. What is being suggested, in addition to what is being stated?
3. What will be the effect of something which is described?
4. What will happen next (after what is being described)?
5. What applications does the principle or idea presented have?

Let's try to apply these skills to representative passages you will encounter in the general reading part of the test.

ILLUSTRATION

Camping

Family camping has been described as the "biggest single growth industry in the booming travel/leisure market." Camping ranges from backpacking to living in rolling homes with complete creature comforts. It is both an end in itself and a magic carpet to a wide variety of other forms of outdoor recreation.

Camping was once a June to September activity for the young and hardy. Today, it is a year-round fascination for big and small families, retired couples, the affluent, and the budget watchers, as nearly 800 manufacturers provide a camping rig to fit every pocketbook and camping need.

During the 1960's, the number of camping vehicles produced each year—travel trailers, camping trailers, truck campers, and motor homes—grew from less than 100,000 units to nearly half a million.

Until the 1960's, most campgrounds were owned and operated at public expense. For up to 10 months of each year the campground "ranger" may have been an area's only human resident. Today, nearly two-thirds of the nation's 15,000 campgrounds (800,000 campsites) are commercially operated and many include such conveniences as laundromats, supervised recreation programs, and babysitting services.

1. The article stresses the
   (1) role of the campground "ranger"
   (2) cost of camping
   (3) commercialization of camping
   (4) benefits of camping
   (5) growth of camping

1. 1 2 3 4 5
‖ ‖ ‖ ‖ ‖

2. A major change in camping, mentioned in the passage, has involved the
   (1) length of the camping season
   (2) kinds of vehicles produced
   (3) role of the campground "ranger"
   (4) increase of publicly operated campgrounds
   (5) wide variety in recreation provided

2. 1 2 3 4 5
‖ ‖ ‖ ‖ ‖

3. It can be inferred from the passage that the LEAST luxurious form of camping is

   (1) backpacking   (4) truck campers
   (2) travel trailers   (5) motor homes
   (3) camping trailers

3. 1 2 3 4 5
‖ ‖ ‖ ‖ ‖

Answers:

1. **5**   2. **1**   3. **1**

Answer Analysis:

1. **5** This question asks you to find the main idea of the passage. The first sentence of paragraph 1, the topic sentence, establishes the theme of growth—growth in appeal of camping to all kinds of people, growth in the number of camping vehicles, etc.

2. **1** Question 2 requires the location of an important detail. The key phrase is "mentioned in the passage." Since the second paragraph states that camping was once a June to September activity but is now a year-round event, Choice 1 is correct. There is no mention in the passage of a change in the kinds of vehicles produced, Choice 2. Nor is there a discussion of the role of the campground "ranger," Choice 3; the increase of publicly operated campgrounds, Choice 4; or a change in the variety of recreation available, Choice 5. Length of the camping season is the only change specifically mentioned.

3. **1** This question requires you to make an inference from the information in the passage. The second sentence in paragraph 1 refers to the range of camping—from backpacking to the "creature comforts" of rolling homes. From this, it can be inferred that backpacking is the least luxurious form of camping.

PRACTICE

Directions: **Read each of the following selections carefully. After each selection there are questions to be answered or statements to be completed. Select the best answer. Then blacken the appropriate space in the answer column to the right.**

Life insurance is a way to provide immediate financial protection for the loss of income through the death of the breadwinner. Once children are expected, the need arises for life insurance. Life insurance is usually purchased to cover the cost of the funeral and the expenses of the last illness, as well as to provide income for the survivors.

In planning for this type of financial protection be sure to consider all resources the survivors will have to use (earning ability as well as financial), the amount of income that will meet necessities, and finally the cost of such a program. Concentrate insurance dollars on the breadwinner and buy the type of insurance that will give the most protection for the cost.

A savings account is the second leg of the stool for a savings program. It is here where a family keeps the money that it may need immediately or plans to use within the near future.

Life insurance, savings accounts, and Government bonds have fixed value. They lose buying power during inflationary periods. However, they should form the basis of a family's savings program.

Some family finance professionals strongly suggest that a family should have 2 to 6 months' income reserved for emergencies.

After this is accomplished, a family is ready to consider other types of investments.

In times of inflation, your home may be one of the best protections against inflation. Of course, home ownership is not for everyone and all homes do not appreciate. Some lose value. In the sequence of selecting investments, a home is often chosen after life insurance and savings accounts.

Common stock, variable annuities, and real estate—either in a growth area or rental property—are the best investments for protection against inflation. These are the ones that can appreciate, but of course you must select them carefully.

1. The person most concerned about inflation should turn for protection to
   (1) life insurance
   (2) savings accounts
   (3) government bonds
   (4) corporate bonds
   (5) real estate

   1. 1 2 3 4 5
   ‖ ‖ ‖ ‖ ‖

2. The author gives first priority in planning family financial protection to
   (1) savings
   (2) life insurance
   (3) a home
   (4) common stock
   (5) variable annuities

   2. 1 2 3 4 5
   ‖ ‖ ‖ ‖ ‖

3. It can be inferred that the best financial protection for a family is
   (1) life insurance
   (2) fixed value investments
   (3) an emergency reserve
   (4) fixed and variable value investments
   (5) home ownership

   3. 1 2 3 4 5
   ‖ ‖ ‖ ‖ ‖

The new feminism will have two effects: an increased awareness of women's decision-making role within the family and society, and a drive on the part of women for more personal satisfaction through greater independence, self-expression, and personal achievement.

Many women will rediscover their personal autonomy and satisfaction in the wife-mother role in the family. This role will take on greater economic significance as society begins to place dollar value on family functions such as caring for children and providing services for family members.

The woman's contribution to the family will become increasingly important and complex because of the information she needs for decision making and the knowledge that the productivity and health of family members depends upon the quality of choices she makes.

The changing role of women assumes a corresponding change for men in attitudes and role identity. A more equal sharing of the decision making and more equal division of labor in the family are obvious changes. The male as authority figure and head of household may disappear. Children, as well as women, will become more directly involved in family decision making, will share the growing equality of the family, and will have a less dependent relationship with their parents.

4. The changing role in women will result in
   (1) abandonment of the wife-mother role
   (2) simpler contributions by the woman to the family
   (3) greater importance to the male
   (4) decreased monetary significance of the woman's contribution
   (5) increased equality of all family members

4. 1 2 3 4 5
‖ ‖ ‖ ‖ ‖

5. The changing role of the male will result in
   (1) greater independence
   (2) less labor in the family
   (3) stability in male role identity
   (4) increased economic importance to the family
   (5) greater self-expression

5. 1 2 3 4 5
‖ ‖ ‖ ‖ ‖

6. The new feminism will give many women all of the following EXCEPT
   (1) greater personal achievement
   (2) increased economic importance
   (3) greater decision-making power in the family
   (4) greater control over the children
   (5) greater self-expression

6. 1 2 3 4 5
‖ ‖ ‖ ‖ ‖

7. The women will assume all of the following roles, according to the passage, EXCEPT
   (1) decision-maker
   (2) wife-mother
   (3) services-provider
   (4) authority figure
   (5) raiser of children

7. 1 2 3 4 5
‖ ‖ ‖ ‖ ‖

You can become a more competent consumer when you consciously follow management and economic principles as you select, maintain, and use goods and services. These principles apply, regardless of what you purchase, but are especially important when the cost is large.

• *Plan what to buy.* Each decision to buy means that you do not have that money for something else. Fit purchases into the family's spending plan. Anticipate and set aside money for large future purchases.

• *Decide where and when to shop.* Buy from reputable dealers. Learn merchandising practices and use them to your advantage. Example: Dealers may give a greater discount on an automobile during the off-season.

• *Know how to buy.* Get information on cost, quality, grades, guarantees, annual percentage interest rate (if item is to be financed), and expected performance. Make price and feature comparison (especially on expensive items).

• *Be a responsible consumer.* Know about and use laws and regulations that protect consumers. Understand consumer rights and assume consumer responsibilities.

• *Develop family business skills.* Maintain a good credit record. Understand contracts and other legal business forms. Develop a workable system for family business papers, spending, income tax records, etc.

8. The best title for this selection is
   (1) "Do's for the Consumer"
   (2) "The Responsible Consumer"
   (3) "Principles for the Consumer"
   (4) "The Competent Consumer"
   (5) "The Knowledgeable Consumer"

   8. 1 2 3 4 5

9. Comparison shopping is most important, according to the passage, when you
   (1) have a family spending plan
   (2) shop in the off-season
   (3) buy on credit
   (4) learn merchandising practices
   (5) buy a costly item

   9. 1 2 3 4 5

10. An example of a family business skill, according to the passage, is a(an)
    (1) family spending plan
    (2) off-season purchase
    (3) feature comparison
    (4) consumer protection law
    (5) good credit record

    10. 1 2 3 4 5

11. All of the following kinds of information should be obtained according to the article EXCEPT
    (1) merchandising practices
    (2) consumer laws and regulations
    (3) consumer rights and responsibilities
    (4) income tax records
    (5) interest rates on financial items

    11. 1 2 3 4 5

The more sophisticated and advanced our culture becomes, the more we seem to need the relaxation of growing our own plants.

Gardening can be an easygoing hobby, a scientific pursuit, an opportunity for exercise and fresh air, a serious source of food to help balance the family budget, a means of expression in art and beauty, an applied experiment in green plant growth, or all of these things together.

You may be a city dweller whose yearning for green plants is satisfied by minigardens in the house or patio, a shut-in who can enjoy container grown plants, a homeowner in the suburbs whose garden is a basement, or someone in the wide open spaces who is letting loose his or her yearning for creativity.

Gardening has no bounds, no space limitations, no requirements that cannot be met readily in today's world. Not really needed are power tools, large areas of sunshine-bathed land, or even a strong back. A gardener is not restricted by any age limitations, training requirements, or any social background from doing "his thing." And many physically handicapped persons can garden.

12. The author's attitude toward gardening is
    (1) cautious   (4) irrational
    (2) pessimistic   (5) impractical
    (3) enthusiastic

12. 1 2 3 4 5 ‖ ‖ ‖ ‖ ‖

13. All of the following are made possible by gardening according to the passage EXCEPT
    (1) relaxation   (4) artistic expression
    (2) exercise   (5) hard work
    (3) experimentation

13. 1 2 3 4 5 ‖ ‖ ‖ ‖ ‖

14. Gardening is restricted by
    (1) age   (4) social class
    (2) availability of land   (5) no limitation at all
    (3) training

14. 1 2 3 4 5 ‖ ‖ ‖ ‖ ‖

15. All of the following are mentioned as possible places for a garden EXCEPT a
    (1) backyard   (4) wide open space
    (2) patio   (5) house
    (3) container

15. 1 2 3 4 5 ‖ ‖ ‖ ‖ ‖

Accidents are the major cause of death for all young people under 35 and the fourth most frequent cause of death for all age groups in this country—fourth only to heart disease, cancer, and stroke. Each year some 115,000 Americans are killed in accidents, over 400,000 are permanently crippled, and at least 11 million are disabled for a day or longer.

Each year about 55,000 of our fellow citizens lose their lives and 2 million suffer disabling injuries in traffic accidents. Over 14,000 die and 2.3 million are seriously maimed in accidents at work. And 28,000 deaths and over 4 million serious injuries result from accidents in the home.

Statistically, by far the most common types of home accidents are falls. Each year over 10,500 Americans meet death in this way, within the four walls of their home, or in yards around the house. Nine out of 10 of the victims are over 65, but people of all ages experience serious injuries as a result of home falls. It is impossible to estimate how many injuries result from falls, but they must run into the millions.

16. The most frequent cause of death for all age groups in this country is
    (1) accidents   (4) stroke
    (2) heart disease   (5) falls
    (3) cancer

16. 1 2 3 4 5 ‖ ‖ ‖ ‖ ‖

17. Falls most frequently result in death for
    (1) children   (4) adults over 65
    (2) adults under 35   (5) factory workers
    (3) all age groups

17. 1 2 3 4 5 ‖ ‖ ‖ ‖ ‖

18. The most frequent cause of death in accidents is

    (1) traffic accidents

    (2) accidents at work

    (3) accidents in the home

    (4) falls at home

    (5) falls in yards around the house

18. 1 2 3 4 5

19. Most serious injuries result from

    (1) traffic accidents

    (2) accidents at work

    (3) accidents in the home

    (4) falls in the home

    (5) falls in yards around the house

19. 1 2 3 4 5

20. People who are maimed are

    (1) under 35   (4) crippled

    (2) over 65   (5) killed

    (3) victims of falls

20. 1 2 3 4 5

Answer Key

1. 5	6. 4	11. 4	16. 2
2. 2	7. 4	12. 3	17. 4
3. 4	8. 3	13. 5	18. 1
4. 5	9. 5	14. 5	19. 3
5. 1	10. 5	15. 1	20. 4

CHAPTER 4
The Basics of Mathematics

INTERPRETING MATH PROBLEMS

It is helpful to use a systematic method of solving mathematics problems. You can use the following steps in almost all cases.

> **1.** Read the problem carefully.
> **2.** Collect the information that is given in the problem.
> **3.** Decide upon what must be found.
> **4.** Develop a plan to solve the problem.
> **5.** Use your plan as a guide to complete the solution of the problem.
> **6.** Check your answer.

The following examples will show you how to use this systematic method.

Arithmetic Problem Example

1. *Read the Problem carefully.* Mr. Bates bought a jacket and a shirt at a sale where all items were reduced 25% below the marked price. If the marked price of the jacket was $80 and the marked price of the shirt was $16, how much did Mr. Bates save by buying at the sale?

2. *Collect the information that is given in the problem.*

	Marked Price	Discount Percent
Jacket	$80	25%
Shirt	$16	25%

3. *Decide upon what must be found.* Find the amount of money saved.

4. *Develop a plan to solve the problem.* Find the amount of savings on the jacket. Then find the amount of savings on the shirt. Finally, add the two savings.

5. *Use your plan as a guide to complete the solution of the problem.*
   Savings on jacket = 25% of 80 = $1/_4$ of 80 = $20
   Savings on shirt = 25% of 16 = $1/_4$ of 16 = $4
   Total savings was 20 + 4 = $24.

6. *Check your answer.*
   Total of the two marked prices = 80 + 16 = $96
   Savings of 25% of marked prices = $1/_4$ of 96 = $24

Algebra Problem Example

1. *Read the problem carefully.* A father is 15 years more than twice the age of his daughter. If the sum of the ages of the father and daughter is 48 years, what is the age of the daughter?

2. *Collect the information that is given in the problem.*
   Age of father = twice age of daughter + 15
   Age of father + age of daughter = 48

3. *Decide upon what must be found.* We must find the age of the daughter.

4. *Develop a plan to solve the problem.* Set up an equation using the given facts. Then solve the equation.

5. *Use your plan as a guide to complete the solution of the problem.*
   Let n = age of daughter
   And $2n + 15$ = age of father.

   $$\text{age of daughter} + \text{age of father} = 48$$
   $$n + 2n + 15 = 48$$
   $$3n + 15 = 48$$
   $$3n + 15 - 15 = 48 - 15$$
   $$3n = 33$$
   $$n = 33/3$$
   $$n = 11$$

   The daughter's age is 11 years.

6. *Check your answer.*
   Age of daughter = 11
   Age of father = $2 \times 11 + 15 = 22 + 15 = 37$
   Age of father + age of daughter
   $$37 \quad + \quad 11 \quad = 48$$

Geometry Problem Example

1. *Read the problem carefully.* A room is 22 feet long, 14 feet wide, and 9 feet high. If the walls and ceiling of the room are to be painted, how many square feet must be covered by paint?

2. *Collect the information that is given in the problem.* Sometimes, it is helpful to draw a diagram to collect information. In this case, we have

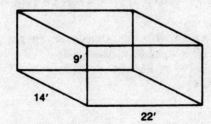

3. *Decide upon what must be found.* We must find the sum of the areas of the front and back, the two sides, and the ceiling of the room.

4. *Develop a plan to solve the problem.* Here again, diagrams are helpful. Front and back of room.

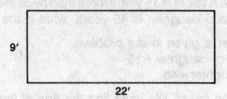

Sides of room

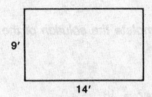

Ceiling of room.

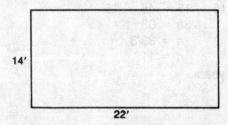

5. *Use your plan as a guide to complete the solution of the problem.*

Area of front = 9 × 22 = 198 square feet
Area of back = 9 × 22 = 198 square feet
Area of side = 9 × 14 = 126 square feet
Area of second side = 9 × 14 = 126 square feet
+ *Area of ceiling = 14 × 22 = 308 square feet*
Total Area = 956 square feet

6. *Check your answer.* In this case, the best method of checking is to go over your work carefully.

I. ARITHMETIC

I. A. The Number Line

A-1

It is often useful to pair numbers and collections (or sets) of numbers with points on a line, called the *number line*. Here is how this is done.

Draw a straight line and, on it, take a point and label it 0. This starting point is called the *origin*. Next, take a point to the right of the zero-point and label it 1, as follows. The arrows on the line indicate that the line extends infinitely in either direction.

Now, use the distance between 0 and 1 as a unit and mark off the next few counting numbers, as follows.

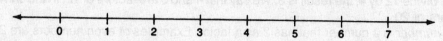

The number that is paired with a point is called the *coordinate* of that point. For example, the coordinate of point A on the number line below is 2.

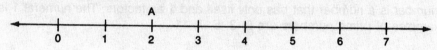

PRACTICE

Directions: Solve the following problems and blacken the space at the right under the number which corresponds to the one you have selected as the correct answer.

1. The number paired with the origin on the number line is
(1) 1
(2) 0
(3) 2
(4) 5
(5) 3

1. 1 2 3 4 5
‖ ‖ ‖ ‖ ‖

2. The coordinate of a point is a(n)
(1) number
(2) point
(3) letter
(4) line
(5) arrow

2. 1 2 3 4 5
‖ ‖ ‖ ‖ ‖

3. The collection (or set) of numbers whose graph is shown below is

3. 1 2 3 4 5
‖ ‖ ‖ ‖ ‖

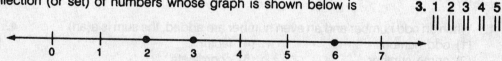

(Note: Collections [or sets] of numbers are often enclosed in braces, as shown below.)

(1) {0,2,3,6}
(2) {1,2,3,6}
(3) {2,3,4,5,6}
(4) {0,1,2,3,6}
(5) {2,3,6}

4. The set of numbers whose graph is shown below is

4. 1 2 3 4 5
‖ ‖ ‖ ‖ ‖

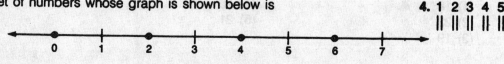

(1) {0,1,2,4}
(2) {0,2,4,6}
(3) {1,2,4,6}
(4) {0,1,2,4,6}
(5) {0,1,2,3,6}

Answers:

I. B.   Factors and Prime Numbers

B-1

When we divide 12 by 4, the result is 3. We say that 4 and 3 are *factors* of 12. In the same way, 5 and 4 are factors of 20.

An *even number* is a number that has 2 as a factor. Examples of even numbers are 2, 4, 6, 8, 10, 12 . . .

An *odd number* is a number that does not have 2 as a factor. Examples of odd numbers are 1, 3, 5, 7, 9, 11 . . .

A *prime number* is a number that has only itself and 1 as factors. The numeral 1 is not a prime number. Examples of prime numbers are 2, 3, 5, 7, 11 . . .

PRACTICE

Directions: Blacken the space at the right under the number which corresponds to the one you have selected as the correct answer.

1. A factor of 15 is
   (1) 4   (4) 10
   (2) 6   (5) 9
   (3) 5

1. 1 2 3 4 5
   ‖ ‖ ‖ ‖ ‖

2. The next greater even number than 20 is
   (1) 21   (4) 25
   (2) 24   (5) 22
   (3) 30

2. 1 2 3 4 5
   ‖ ‖ ‖ ‖ ‖

3. An example of a prime number is
   (1) 6   (4) 10
   (2) 1   (5) 39
   (3) 17

3. 1 2 3 4 5
   ‖ ‖ ‖ ‖ ‖

4. When an odd number and an even number are added, the sum is a(an)
   (1) odd number   (4) factor
   (2) prime number   (5) coordinate
   (3) even number

4. 1 2 3 4 5
   ‖ ‖ ‖ ‖ ‖

5. A factor of every even number is
   (1) 3   (4) 2
   (2) 4   (5) 7
   (3) 6

5. 1 2 3 4 5
   ‖ ‖ ‖ ‖ ‖

6. The next prime number in the series of prime numbers 7, 11, 13, 17 is
   (1) 18   (4) 20
   (2) 23   (5) 21
   (3) 19

6. 1 2 3 4 5
   ‖ ‖ ‖ ‖ ‖

Answers:

I. C. Whole Numbers

C-1

The process of division involves some ideas which should be recalled.

When we divide 18 by 3, we have $18 \div 3 = 6$. In this case, 18 is called the *dividend*, 3 is called the *divisor,* and 6 is called the *quotient.*

When we divide 27 by 4, we have $27 \div 4 = 6\frac{3}{4}$. In this case, 27 is the dividend, 4 is the divisor, 6 is the quotient, and 3 is called the *remainder.*

If you wish to check the answer to a division example, multiply the divisor by the quotient and add the remainder to obtain the dividend.

EXAMPLE: Divide 897 by 36, and check the result.

```
                    24 →quotient
divisor←36/ 897 →dividend
                    72
                   ───
                   177
                   144
                   ───
                    33 →remainder
```

CHECK: $36 \times 24 + 33$
$= 864 + 33$
$= 897$

PRACTICE

Addition:

1. 307	**2.** 49	**3.** 1769	**4.** $685.17
58	26	3205	48.09
129	7	467	103.15
984	38	5180	234.68
+236	+92	+2073	+580.80

Subtraction:

5. From 805, take 196 _____

6. Subtract 69 from 204 _____

7. Find the difference between 817 and 349 _____

8. Subtract 107 from 315 _____

Find The Products:

9. 4327	**10.** 3092	**11.** 283	**12.** 409
39	45	97	307

Divide and Check Your Results:

13. Divide 986 by 29 _____

14. Divide 29,040 by 48 _____

15. Divide 1,035 by 37 _____

16. Divide 47,039 by 126 _____

Answers:

1. 1,714	5. 609	9. 168,753	13. 34
2. 212	6. 135	10. 139,140	14. 605
3. 12,694	7. 468	11. 27,451	15. 27 36/37
4. $1,651.89	8. 208	12. 125,563	16. 373 41/126

I. D. Rational Numbers

D-1

A number obtained when a counting number or 0 is divided by a counting number is called a *rational number*. For example, ⅔, 9/7, and 5/1 (or 5), are rational numbers. Zero is also a rational number since 0 may be written as 0/6.

A *fraction* is a form in which a rational number may be written. That is, ⅔ is a rational number in fractional form. But 4 is a rational number which is not in fractional form. A fraction is a form which has a numerator and a denominator. For example, in the fraction ⅘, 4 is the numerator and 5 is the denominator. Every rational number has fractional forms. For example, the rational number 5 has the fractional forms 5/1, 10/2, etc.

All counting numbers and 0 are rational numbers. Rational numbers may be located on the number line, as shown below.

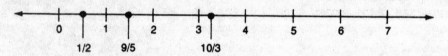

I. E. Fractions

E-1

In counting, we need only whole numbers. However, when we measure, we frequently have parts, and we need fractions. For example, consider the circle shown. The circle is divided into four equal parts, and each part is ¼ of the circle. Since the shaded portion contains three of these parts, we say that the shaded portion is ¾ of the circle. In this case, the denominator (4) tells us that the circle is divided into four equal parts. The numerator (3) tells us that we are considering 3 of these parts. In this section, you will obtain some practice in understanding the meaning of fraction.

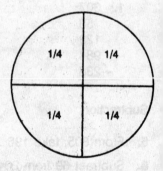

> **EXAMPLE:** A baseball team won 37 games and lost 15 games. What fractional part of the games played did the team win?
>
> The required fraction is
> $$\frac{\text{number of games won}}{\text{total number of games played}} = \frac{37}{37+15} = \frac{37}{52}$$

> **EXAMPLE:** A certain school has an enrollment of 500 students. Of these students, X are girls. What fractional part of the enrollment consists of boys?

Since the total enrollment is 500 and X students are girls, the number of boys is obtained by subtracting the number X from 500. Thus, the number of boys enrolled in the school is 500 − X.

The required fraction is
$$\frac{\text{number of boys}}{\text{total enrollment}} = \frac{500-X}{500}$$

PRACTICE

Directions: Solve the following problems and blacken the space at the right under the number which corresponds to the one you have selected as the right answer.

1. The Star Movie Theater has 650 seats. At one performance 67 seats were not occupied.. What fractional part of the theater seats were occupied?
   (1) 67/650
   (2) 583/650
   (3) 67/588
   (4) 67/717
   (5) 583/717

   1. 1 2 3 4 5
   ‖ ‖ ‖ ‖ ‖

2. Mr. Davis parked his car at 2:45 P.M. in a one-hour parking zone. If he drove away at 3:08 P.M., during what fractional part of an hour was his car parked?
   (1) 63/100
   (2) 53/60
   (3) 45/60
   (4) 8/60
   (5) 23/60

   3. 1 2 3 4 5
   ‖ ‖ ‖ ‖ ‖

3. Mr. Barnes spent *a* dollars for a jacket and $18 for a pair of slacks. What fractional part of the money spent was spent for the jacket?
   (1) $\frac{a}{18}$
   (2) $\frac{18}{a}$
   (3) $\frac{18}{a+18}$
   (4) $\frac{a}{a+18}$
   (5) $\frac{a+18}{a}$

   3. 1 2 3 4 5
   ‖ ‖ ‖ ‖ ‖

4. Mr. Stern planned to drive a distance of *x* miles. After driving 120 miles, Mr. Stern stopped for gas. What fractional part of the trip had Mr. Stern covered when he stopped?
   (1) $\frac{x}{120}$
   (2) $\frac{120}{x}$
   (3) $\frac{x}{x+120}$
   (4) $\frac{120}{x+120}$
   (5) $\frac{x+120}{x}$

   4. 1 2 3 4 5
   ‖ ‖ ‖ ‖ ‖

5. On a test taken by 80 students, *y* students failed. What fractional part of the students passed the test?
   (1) $\frac{80-y}{80}$
   (2) $\frac{y}{80}$
   (3) $\frac{80}{y}$
   (4) $\frac{y-80}{80}$
   (5) $\frac{80}{80-y}$

   5. 1 2 3 4 5
   ‖ ‖ ‖ ‖ ‖

6. A dealer bought a shipment of 150 suits. Of these, 67 were blue, 39 were brown, and the rest were gray. What fractional part of the shipment was made up of gray suits?
   (1) $\frac{67}{150}$
   (2) $\frac{106}{150}$
   (3) $\frac{39}{150}$
   (4) $\frac{44}{150}$
   (5) $\frac{83}{150}$

   6. 1 2 3 4 5
   ‖ ‖ ‖ ‖ ‖

7. A carpenter cut strips x inches wide from a board 16 inches wide. After he had cut 5 strips, what fractional part of the board was left? (Do not allow for waste.)

   (1) $\dfrac{5x}{16}$ (4) $\dfrac{5}{16x}$

   (2) $\dfrac{16-5x}{16}$ (5) $\dfrac{5}{16}$

   (3) $\dfrac{5}{16-x}$

8. A class has 35 students. If y pupils were absent, what fractional part of the class was present?

   (1) $\dfrac{y}{35}$ (4) $\dfrac{y-35}{35}$

   (2) $\dfrac{35}{y}$ (5) $\dfrac{y}{35+y}$

   (3) $\dfrac{35+y}{35}$

9. A family spent a dollars for food, b dollars for rent, and c dollars for all other expenses. What fractional part of the money spent was spent for food?

   (1) $\dfrac{a+b+c}{a}$ (4) $\dfrac{b}{a+c}$

   (2) $\dfrac{a}{a+b+c}$ (5) $\dfrac{a+c}{a+b+c}$

   (3) $\dfrac{a}{a+b}$

10. An electrical contractor used 6 men on a job. The men worked 5 days each at a salary of $45 per day. In addition, the contractor spent $687 for materials. What fractional part of the total cost of the job was spent for labor?

   (1) $\dfrac{270}{957}$ (4) $\dfrac{495}{2{,}037}$

   (2) $\dfrac{225}{912}$ (5) $\dfrac{1350}{2{,}037}$

   (3) $\dfrac{270}{2{,}037}$

11. A table and four chairs cost $735. If the cost of each chair was z dollars, what fractional part of the total cost was spent for chairs?

   (1) $\dfrac{z}{735}$ (4) $\dfrac{735}{4z}$

   (2) $\dfrac{735}{z}$ (5) $\dfrac{735-4z}{4z}$

   (3) $\dfrac{4z}{735}$

12. A hockey team won 8 games, lost 3 games, and tied x games. What fractional part of the games played were won?

   (1) $\dfrac{8}{11+x}$ (4) $\dfrac{8}{x+3}$

   (2) $\dfrac{8}{11}$ (5) $\dfrac{11}{11+x}$

   (3) $\dfrac{8+x}{11+x}$

Answers:

E-2

Operations With Fractions.   In order to be able to work with fractions, you must know how to perform operations with fractions. We will first explain the meanings of "improper fraction" and "mixed number," and then show how to reduce a fraction to lowest terms.

An *improper fraction* is a fraction in which the numerator is equal to, or greater than, the denominator. For example, $\frac{7}{3}$ and $\frac{8}{5}$ are improper fractions.

A *mixed number* consists of the sum of a whole number and a fraction. For example, $1\frac{1}{2}$ and $7\frac{3}{5}$ are mixed numbers.

In working with fractions, we will frequently use the multiplication property of 1. That is, when a number is multiplied by 1, the value of the number remains unchanged.

E-3

Changing an Improper Fraction to a Mixed Number.   It is sometimes necessary to change an improper fraction to a mixed number.

   EXAMPLE: Change $\frac{17}{5}$ to a mixed number.

$$\frac{17}{5} = \frac{2+15}{5} = \frac{2}{5} + \frac{15}{5} = 3\frac{2}{5}$$

You may obtain the same result by dividing the numerator 17 by the denominator 5.

$$5\,\overline{)17}\quad 3\tfrac{2}{5}$$

E-4

Changing a Mixed Number to an Improper Fraction.
   EXAMPLE: Change $2\frac{3}{7}$ to an improper fraction.

$$2\tfrac{3}{7} = 2 + \tfrac{3}{7}$$
$$2 = \tfrac{14}{7}$$
$$2\tfrac{3}{7} = \tfrac{14}{7} + \tfrac{3}{7} = \tfrac{17}{7}$$

The same result may be obtained by multiplying the whole number 2 by the denominator 7, and adding 3, to obtain the numerator. The denominator is unchanged.

$$2\tfrac{3}{7} = 2 \times 7 + 3 = 17 \rightarrow \text{numerator}$$
$$2\tfrac{3}{7} = \tfrac{17}{7}$$

E-5

Reducing a Fraction to Lowest Terms.   You may use the multiplication property of 1 to reduce a fraction to lowest terms.

   EXAMPLE: Reduce $\frac{21}{28}$ to lowest terms.

$$\frac{21}{28} = \frac{3 \times 7}{4 \times 7} = \frac{3}{4} \times \frac{7}{7} = \frac{3}{4} \times 1 = \frac{3}{4}$$

The same result may be obtained by dividing the numerator and the denominator of the fraction by the same number, 7.

$$\frac{21}{28} = \frac{21 \div 7}{28 \div 7} = \frac{3}{4}$$

PRACTICE

Change the following improper fractions to mixed numbers:

1. $\frac{8}{5}$ 2. $\frac{9}{8}$ 3. $\frac{22}{7}$ 4. $\frac{26}{9}$ 5. $\frac{17}{3}$ 6. $\frac{11}{10}$ 7. $\frac{29}{4}$ 8. $\frac{17}{8}$

Change the following mixed numbers to improper fractions:

9. $1\frac{2}{3}$ 10. $5\frac{3}{7}$ 11. $2\frac{7}{10}$ 12. $3\frac{5}{7}$ 13. $3\frac{1}{2}$ 14. $4\frac{5}{8}$ 15. $6\frac{1}{4}$ 16. $8\frac{3}{4}$

Reduce the following fractions to lowest terms:

17. $\frac{4}{6}$ 18. $\frac{16}{18}$ 19. $\frac{12}{32}$ 20. $\frac{36}{64}$ 21. $\frac{6}{12}$ 22. $\frac{15}{20}$ 23. $\frac{42}{63}$ 24. $\frac{76}{114}$

Answers:

1. $1\frac{1}{3}$ 2. $1\frac{1}{4}$ 3. $3\frac{3}{4}$ 4. $2\frac{5}{8}$ 5. $5\frac{4}{7}$ 6. $1\frac{1}{10}$ 7. $7\frac{1}{4}$ 8. $2\frac{5}{8}$

9. $\frac{5}{3}$ 10. $\frac{38}{7}$ 11. $\frac{27}{10}$ 12. $\frac{26}{7}$ 13. $\frac{7}{2}$ 14. $\frac{37}{8}$ 15. $\frac{25}{4}$ 16. $\frac{35}{4}$

17. $\frac{2}{3}$ 18. $\frac{8}{9}$ 19. $\frac{3}{8}$ 20. $\frac{9}{16}$ 21. $\frac{1}{2}$ 22. $\frac{3}{4}$ 23. $\frac{2}{3}$ 24. $\frac{2}{3}$

E-6

Multiplying Fractions. To multiply two or more fractions, multiply the numerators to obtain the numerator of the product. Then, multiply the denominators to obtain the denominator of the product.

EXAMPLE: Multiply $\frac{4}{7}$ by $\frac{3}{5}$.

$$\frac{4}{7} \times \frac{3}{5} = \frac{4 \times 3}{7 \times 5} = \frac{12}{35}$$

Sometimes, the process of multiplying fractions may be simplified by reducing to lowest terms before performing the multiplication.

EXAMPLE: Multiply $\frac{8}{15}$ by $\frac{5}{12}$.

$$\frac{8}{15} \times \frac{5}{12}$$

Since 8 and 12 can both be divided by 4, the result can be simplified by performing this division before multiplying. Similarly, 5 and 15 can both be divided by 5.

$$\frac{\cancel{8}^{2}}{\cancel{15}_{3}} \times \frac{\cancel{5}^{1}}{\cancel{12}_{3}} = \frac{2 \times 1}{3 \times 3} = \frac{2}{9}$$

If you are required to multiply a whole number by a fraction, you may write the whole number in fractional form with denominator 1 and proceed as before.

EXAMPLE: Multiply 12 by $\frac{5}{9}$.

$$12 \times \frac{5}{9} = \frac{12}{1} \times \frac{5}{9} = \frac{\cancel{12}^{4}}{1} \times \frac{5}{\cancel{9}_{3}} = \frac{4 \times 5}{1 \times 3} = \frac{20}{3}$$

If you are required to multiply two mixed numbers, you can convert the mixed numbers to improper fractions and proceed as before.

EXAMPLE: Multiply $3\frac{2}{3}$ by $1\frac{1}{5}$.

$$3\tfrac{2}{3} = \tfrac{11}{3} \text{ and } 1\tfrac{1}{5} = \tfrac{6}{5}$$

$$\frac{11}{3} \times \frac{6}{5} = \frac{11}{\cancel{3}} \times \frac{\cancel{6}^{2}}{5} = \frac{11 \times 2}{1 \times 5} = \frac{22}{5}$$

PRACTICE

Perform the following multiplications:

1. $\frac{2}{3} \times \frac{5}{7}$ 4. $\frac{3}{8} \times \frac{5}{12}$ 7. $12 \times \frac{5}{6}$ 10. $8 \times 1\frac{3}{4}$ 13. $1\frac{5}{8} \times 3\frac{1}{3}$

2. $\frac{1}{4} \times \frac{3}{10}$ 5. $15 \times \frac{2}{3}$ 8. $\frac{5}{8} \times 24$ 11. $2 \times 3\frac{5}{6}$ 14. $2\frac{3}{4} \times 3\frac{1}{5}$

3. $\frac{1}{6} \times \frac{4}{5}$ 6. $\frac{5}{6} \times \frac{9}{10}$ 9. $3 \times 2\frac{2}{5}$ 12. $1\frac{1}{3} \times 2\frac{1}{2}$ 15. $4\frac{1}{8} \times 3\frac{1}{3}$

Answers:

1. $\frac{10}{21}$ 2. $\frac{3}{40}$ 3. $\frac{2}{15}$ 4. $\frac{5}{32}$ 5. 10   6. $\frac{3}{4}$

7. 10   8. 15   9. $\frac{36}{5}$ 10. 14   11. $\frac{23}{6}$ 12. $\frac{10}{3}$

13. $\frac{65}{12}$ 14. $\frac{44}{5}$ 15. $\frac{55}{4}$

E-7

Dividing Fractions. Suppose we wish to divide $\frac{2}{5}$ by $\frac{3}{4}$. We may write this operation as $\frac{2/5}{3/4}$. Recall that you may multiply the numerator and denominator of a fraction by the same number. Notice what happens when you multiply the numerator and denominator of the above fraction by $\frac{4}{3}$:

$$\frac{\dfrac{2}{5}\times\dfrac{4}{3}}{\dfrac{3}{4}\times\dfrac{4}{3}}=\frac{\dfrac{2\times4}{5\times3}}{\dfrac{3\times4}{4\times3}}=\frac{\dfrac{8}{15}}{1}=\frac{8}{15}$$

Note that the final result was obtained by multiplying the dividend by the divisor inverted, $\frac{4}{3}$. This is a method for dividing one fraction by another fraction: **To divide one fraction by another fraction,** invert the divisor and multiply the resulting fractions.

EXAMPLE: Divide $\frac{2}{3}$ by $\frac{5}{6}$.

$$\frac{2}{3}\div\frac{5}{6}=\frac{2}{3}\times\frac{6}{5}=\frac{2}{\cancel{3}_1}\times\frac{\cancel{6}^2}{5}=\frac{4}{5}$$

EXAMPLE: Divide 8 by $\frac{6}{7}$. We write 8 in fractional form, as $\frac{8}{1}$, and proceed as before:

$$8\div\frac{6}{7}=\frac{8}{1}\times\frac{7}{6}=\frac{\cancel{8}^4}{1}\times\frac{7}{\cancel{6}_3}=\frac{28}{3}$$

EXAMPLE: Divide $3\frac{3}{5}$ by $2\frac{1}{10}$.

$$3\tfrac{3}{5}=\tfrac{18}{5},\text{ and }2\tfrac{1}{10}=\tfrac{21}{10}$$

$$\frac{18}{5}\div\frac{21}{10}=\frac{18}{5}\times\frac{10}{21}=\frac{\cancel{18}^6}{\cancel{5}_1}\times\frac{\cancel{10}^2}{\cancel{21}_7}=\frac{12}{7}$$

PRACTICE

Perform the following divisions:

1. $\frac{1}{3}\div\frac{1}{2}$
2. $\frac{2}{7}\div\frac{2}{3}$
3. $\frac{3}{4}\div\frac{5}{8}$

4. $\frac{7}{10}\div\frac{1}{5}$
5. $\frac{7}{8}\div\frac{9}{16}$
6. $5\div\frac{1}{2}$

7. $4\div\frac{2}{5}$
8. $1\frac{1}{8}\div\frac{9}{20}$
9. $\frac{5}{6}\div1\frac{1}{4}$

10. $\frac{7}{8}\div5\frac{1}{4}$
11. $2\frac{2}{5}\div3\frac{3}{10}$
12. $2\frac{3}{4}\div3\frac{1}{7}$

13. $3\frac{1}{3}\div4\frac{1}{6}$
14. $3\frac{3}{4}\div2\frac{2}{9}$
15. $5\frac{5}{6}\div2\frac{5}{8}$

Answers:

1. $\frac{2}{3}$
2. $\frac{3}{7}$
3. $\frac{6}{5}$

4. $\frac{7}{2}$
5. $\frac{14}{9}$
6. 10

7. 10
8. $\frac{5}{2}$
9. $\frac{2}{3}$

10. $\frac{1}{6}$
11. $\frac{8}{11}$
12. $\frac{7}{8}$

13. $\frac{4}{5}$
14. $\frac{27}{16}$
15. $\frac{20}{9}$

E-8

Adding Fractions. Two fractions may be added directly if they have the same denominator. For example,

$$\frac{1}{5}+\frac{2}{5}=\frac{1+2}{5}=\frac{3}{5}$$

The diagram below shows why this is true.

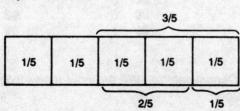

Next, consider the addition of two fractions with different denominators. Add $\frac{1}{2}$ and $\frac{1}{3}$, using the diagram below to help.

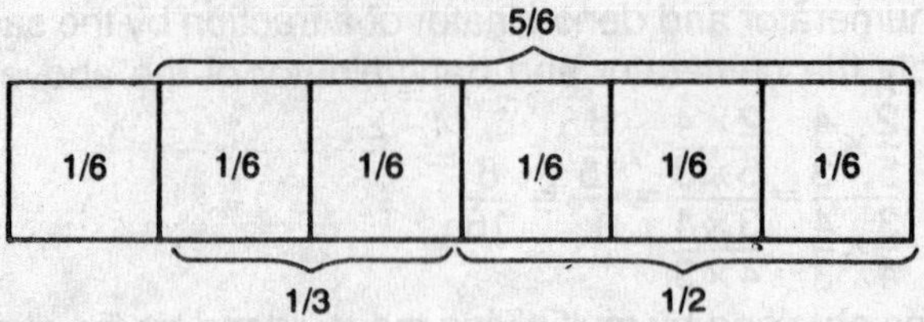

We see that $\frac{1}{2}+\frac{1}{3}=\frac{5}{6}$. Now, let us see how we may obtain the same result without the use of a diagram. Actually, we convert both $\frac{1}{2}$ and $\frac{1}{3}$ to equivalent fractions whose denominators are 6, by using the multiplication property of 1.

$$\frac{1}{2}=\frac{1}{2}\times\frac{3}{3}=\frac{3}{6}$$

$$\frac{1}{3}=\frac{1}{3}\times\frac{2}{2}=\frac{2}{6}$$

Therefore,

$$\frac{2}{6}+\frac{3}{6}=\frac{2+3}{6}=\frac{5}{6}$$

The denominator 6, which was used above, is called the *least common denominator*, or the *L.C.D.* for short. It is the smallest number into which each of the denominators of the fractions to be added can be divided evenly. For example, if we wish to add $\frac{3}{10}$ and $\frac{8}{15}$, the L.C.D. is 30 because 30 is the smallest number into which 10 and 15 may be divided evenly. Since finding the L.C.D. is most important, we will get some practice in this process.

We may use sets of multiples to find the L.C.D. Study the following examples:

EXAMPLE: Find the L.C.D. used in adding the fractions $\frac{2}{3}$ and $\frac{5}{7}$.

First, write the sets of multiples of the denominators of the two fractions:
The set of multiples of 3 is (3,6,9,12,15,18,21,24,27, . . .)
The set of multiples of 7 is (7,14,21, . . .)
The first number which is a multiple of both the denominators, 3 and 7, is the L.C.D. In this case, the L.C.D. is 21.

EXAMPLE: Find the L.C.D. used in adding the fractions $\frac{3}{8}$ and $\frac{7}{10}$.

The set of multiples of 8 is (8,16,24,32,40,48,56, . . .)
The set of multiples of 10 is (10,20,30,40, . . .)
The *L.C.D.* is 40.

PRACTICE

In each case, find the L.C.D.:

1. $\frac{2}{3}+\frac{1}{4}$	**4.** $\frac{1}{9}+\frac{1}{6}$	**7.** $\frac{1}{4}+\frac{5}{6}$	**10.** $\frac{2}{7}+\frac{1}{4}$	**13.** $\frac{3}{10}+\frac{7}{15}$
2. $\frac{1}{6}+\frac{1}{3}$	**5.** $\frac{3}{4}+\frac{7}{18}$	**8.** $\frac{5}{9}+\frac{1}{12}$	**11.** $\frac{1}{4}+\frac{5}{8}$	**14.** $\frac{5}{6}+\frac{1}{10}$
3. $\frac{5}{6}+\frac{3}{8}$	**6.** $\frac{1}{5}+\frac{7}{10}$	**9.** $\frac{1}{3}+\frac{2}{11}$	**12.** $\frac{3}{8}+\frac{1}{12}$	**15.** $\frac{7}{10}+\frac{1}{12}$

Answers:

1. **12**	4. **18**	7. **12**	10. **28**	13. **30**
2. **6**	5. **36**	8. **36**	11. **8**	14. **30**
3. **24**	6. **10**	9. **33**	12. **24**	15. **60**

E-9

Adding Fractions With Unlike Denominators. We are now ready to get some practice in adding fractions with unlike denominators.

EXAMPLE: Add $\frac{7}{8}$ and $\frac{5}{6}$.
The L.C.D. is 24.

$$\frac{7}{8}=\frac{7}{8}\times\frac{3}{3}=\frac{21}{24}$$

$$\frac{5}{6}=\frac{5}{6}\times\frac{4}{4}=\frac{20}{24}$$

$$\frac{21+20}{24}=\frac{41}{24} \text{ or } 1\frac{17}{24}$$

In adding mixed numbers, add the whole numbers and the fractions separately and then combine the results.

EXAMPLE: Add $3\frac{5}{6}$ and $2\frac{3}{4}$.
The L.C.D. is 12.

$$\frac{5}{6}=\frac{5}{6}\times\frac{2}{2}=\frac{10}{12}$$

$$\frac{3}{4}=\frac{3}{4}\times\frac{3}{3}=\frac{9}{12}$$

$$\frac{10+9}{12}=\frac{19}{12}$$

The result is $5\frac{19}{12}$, which can be written as $5+1+\frac{7}{12}$, or $6\frac{7}{12}$.

PRACTICE
Add the following:

1. $\frac{1}{12}+\frac{5}{12}$	**4.** $\frac{5}{6}+\frac{1}{3}$	**7.** $\frac{3}{10}+\frac{1}{5}$	**10.** $1\frac{1}{9}+\frac{5}{6}$	**13.** $4\frac{1}{3}+2\frac{2}{5}$	**16.** $\frac{1}{2}+\frac{1}{3}+\frac{1}{4}$
2. $\frac{3}{10}+\frac{1}{2}$	**5.** $\frac{3}{4}+\frac{1}{6}$	**8.** $\frac{5}{6}+\frac{3}{8}$	**11.** $2\frac{3}{8}+3\frac{1}{2}$	**14.** $1\frac{5}{6}+2\frac{1}{2}$	**17.** $\frac{2}{3}+\frac{1}{4}+\frac{5}{6}$
3. $\frac{7}{8}+\frac{2}{3}$	**6.** $\frac{2}{9}+\frac{2}{3}$	**9.** $\frac{3}{7}+\frac{1}{2}$	**12.** $2\frac{7}{10}+\frac{1}{6}$	**15.** $2\frac{5}{12}+3\frac{1}{9}$	**18.** $\frac{3}{5}+\frac{1}{6}+\frac{7}{10}$

Answers:

1. $\frac{6}{12}=\frac{1}{2}$ 2. $\frac{4}{5}=\frac{8}{10}$ 3. $\frac{37}{24}=1\frac{13}{24}$ 4. $\frac{7}{6}=1\frac{1}{6}$ 5. $\frac{11}{12}$ 6. $\frac{8}{9}$ 7. $\frac{5}{10}=\frac{1}{2}$ 8. $\frac{29}{24}=1\frac{5}{24}$ 9. $\frac{13}{14}$ 10. $2\frac{5}{6}$ 11. $5\frac{7}{8}$ 12. $2\frac{26}{30}=2\frac{13}{15}$ 13. $6\frac{11}{15}$ 14. $4\frac{1}{3}$ 15. $5\frac{19}{36}$ 16. $\frac{13}{12}=1\frac{1}{12}$ 17. $\frac{21}{12}=1\frac{3}{4}$ 18. $\frac{44}{30}=1\frac{7}{15}$

E-10
Subtracting Fractions. To subtract fractions which have the same denominator, subtract the numerators and retain the denominator.

EXAMPLE: From $\frac{6}{7}$, subtract $\frac{2}{7}$.

$$\frac{6}{7}-\frac{2}{7}=\frac{6-2}{7}=\frac{4}{7}$$

To subtract denominators which have unlike denominators, first find the L.C.D., next convert the fractions to equivalent fractions which have the same denominator, and then perform the subtraction (as in the last example).

EXAMPLE: From $\frac{8}{9}$, subtract $\frac{1}{6}$.
The L.C.D. is 18.

$$\frac{8}{9}=\frac{8}{9}\times\frac{2}{2}=\frac{16}{18}$$

$$\frac{1}{6}=\frac{1}{6}\times\frac{3}{3}=\frac{3}{18}$$

$$\text{Difference}=\frac{13}{18}$$

When mixed numbers are involved in subtraction it is sometimes necessary to borrow, as in this example:

EXAMPLE: From $4\frac{1}{8}$, subtract $1\frac{5}{12}$.
The L.C.D. is 24.

$$4\frac{1}{8} = 4\frac{3}{24}$$

$$1\frac{5}{12} = 1\frac{10}{24}$$

Since we cannot subtract $\frac{10}{24}$ from $\frac{3}{24}$, we write $4\frac{3}{24}$ as

$$3 + 1 + \frac{3}{24} = 3 + \frac{24}{24} + \frac{3}{24} = 3\frac{27}{24}$$

$$\begin{array}{r} 3\frac{27}{24} \\ -1\frac{10}{24} \\ \hline \text{Difference} = 2\frac{17}{24} \end{array}$$

PRACTICE

Perform the following subtractions:

1. $\frac{5}{9} - \frac{1}{9}$	4. $\frac{3}{4} - \frac{1}{3}$	7. $\frac{5}{8} - \frac{1}{6}$	10. $\frac{8}{9} - \frac{5}{6}$	13. $4\frac{5}{6} - 2\frac{3}{4}$
2. $\frac{11}{12} - \frac{7}{12}$	5. $\frac{5}{6} - \frac{1}{4}$	8. $\frac{2}{3} - \frac{1}{2}$	11. $\frac{9}{10} - \frac{5}{6}$	14. $3\frac{1}{8} - 1\frac{1}{4}$
3. $\frac{2}{3} - \frac{1}{6}$	6. $\frac{7}{10} - \frac{3}{5}$	9. $\frac{4}{5} - \frac{2}{3}$	12 $3\frac{1}{2} - 1\frac{1}{3}$	15. $5\frac{4}{9} - 2\frac{5}{6}$

Answers:

1. $\frac{4}{9}$	4. $\frac{5}{12}$	7. $\frac{11}{24}$	10. $\frac{1}{18}$	13. $2\frac{1}{12}$
2. $\frac{4}{12} = \frac{1}{3}$	5. $\frac{7}{12}$	8. $\frac{1}{6}$	11. $\frac{2}{30} = \frac{1}{15}$	14. $1\frac{7}{8}$
3. $\frac{3}{6} = \frac{1}{2}$	6. $\frac{1}{10}$	9. $\frac{2}{15}$	12. $2\frac{1}{6}$	15. $2\frac{11}{18}$

E-11

Problems Involving Fractions. In general, there are three types of problems involving fractions:
1. **To find a number that is a fractional part of a number.**

   EXAMPLE: A dealer sold 70 television sets one month. If $\frac{2}{5}$ of the sets were color sets, how many color sets were sold?

   The word *of* indicates that we are to multiply 70 by $\frac{2}{5}$.

   $$\frac{70}{1} \times \frac{2}{5} = \frac{\cancel{70}^{14}}{1} \times \frac{2}{\cancel{5}_1} = 28$$

   The dealer sold 28 color television sets.

2. To find what fractional part one number is of another.

   EXAMPLE: A hotel has 70 guest rooms. Of these, 15 are single rooms. What fractional part of the total number of rooms are the single rooms?

   We form a fraction as follows:

   $$\frac{\text{number of single rooms}}{\text{total number of rooms}} = \frac{15}{70}, \text{ or } \frac{3}{14}$$

3. To find a number when a fractional part of the number is known.

   EXAMPLE: In a town election, only $\frac{2}{3}$ of the registered voters cast ballots. If there were 1,620 cast, how many registered voters were there?

⅔ of the registered voters = 1,620.

⅓ of the registered voters = $\frac{1,620}{2}$ = 810.

Then, ³⁄₃ or the total number of registered voters = 810 × 3 = 2,430.
There were 2,430 registered voters.

PRACTICE

Directions: Solve the following problems and blacken the space at the right under the number which corresponds to the one you have selected as the correct answer.

1. The Globe Theater has 600 seats. At one showing, ⅘ of the seats were taken. How many seats were taken?
   (1) 400
   (2) 420
   (3) 450
   (4) 480
   (5) 750

   1. 1 2 3 4 5
   || || || || ||

2. At a sale, Mr. Morse bought a suit for $96. This was ¾ of the regular price of the suit. The regular price of the suit was
   (1) $72
   (2) $128
   (3) $120
   (4) $125
   (5) $80

   2. 1 2 3 4 5
   || || || || ||

3. An oil tank holds 640 gallons. When the tank is ⅝ full, the number of gallons of oil in the tank is
   (1) 240
   (2) 320
   (3) 350
   (4) 400
   (5) 450

   3. 1 2 3 4 5
   || || || || ||

4. A football team scored 35 points in a game. If the team scored 21 points in the first half, the fractional part of the total scored in the second half was
   (1) ⅗
   (2) ⁷⁄₁₂
   (3) ⅕
   (4) ⅖
   (5) ³⁄₇

   4. 1 2 3 4 5
   || || || || ||

5. The Star Company employs 17 engineers. If this is ⅓ of the total work force, the number of employees of the Star Company is
   (1) 20
   (2) 41
   (3) 47
   (4) 23
   (5) 51

   5. 1 2 3 4 5
   || || || || ||

6. The Mills family saves n dollars per year. The number of dollars saved in 5 months is
   (1) 5n
   (2) ⁵⁄₁₂n
   (3) 12n
   (4) n + 5
   (5) ⁵⁄₁₂

   6. 1 2 3 4 5
   || || || || ||

7. A plane contains 5 times as many second class seats as first class seats. The fractional part of second class seats on the plane is
   (1) ⅙
   (2) ⅕
   (3) ⅚
   (4) ⅗
   (5) ⅓

   7. 1 2 3 4 5
   || || || || ||

8. A baseball player hit 90 singles in one season. If this was ⅗ of his total number of hits, the number of hits the player made that season was

(1) 54   (4) 144
(2) 150   (5) 154
(3) 540

9. During a sale on radio sets, ¼ of the stock was sold the first day. The next day, ⅔ of the remaining sets were sold. The fractional part of the total stock sold during the second day was

(1) ⅔   (4) ½
(2) ¼   (5) ¹⁄₁₂
(3) ⅙

10. It takes a man n hours to complete a job. The fractional part of the job that he can complete in 3 hours is

(1) $3n$ (4) $3+n$
(2) $\dfrac{3}{n}$ (5) $\dfrac{1}{n+3}$
(3) $\dfrac{n}{3}$

11. The regular price for hats is x dollars each. If they are reduced by ⅕ of the regular price, the new price is

(1) ⅕ x (4) $x - $ ⅕
(2) $x + $ ⅕   (5) $5x$
(3) ⅘ x

12. On a motor trip Mr. Anderson covers ⅜ of the distance during the first day by driving 300 miles. The total distance to be covered by Mr. Anderson is

(1) 624 miles   (4) 750 miles
(2) 640 miles   (5) 800 miles
(3) 720 miles

13. The Palmer Shoe Company received a shipment of 288 pairs of shoes composed equally of black and brown shoes. If 36 pairs of the brown shoes are returned and replaced by pairs of black shoes, the fractional part of the shipment consisting of black shoes is

(1) ⅜   (4) ⅛
(2) ⅝   (5) ¾
(3) ⁷⁄₁₂

14. An auditorium contains 540 seats and is ⁴⁄₉ filled. The number of seats left unfilled is

(1) 240   (4) 200
(2) 60   (5) 300
(3) 120

15. At a dance, x boys and y girls attended. Of the total attendance, the fraction which represents the number of boys is

(1) $\dfrac{x}{y}$ (4) $\dfrac{x}{x+y}$
(2) $\dfrac{y}{x}$ (5) $\dfrac{x+y}{x}$
(3) $\dfrac{y}{x+y}$

16. Mr. Adams paid ¼ of his total monthly income for rent. If Mr. Adams earned y dollars per month, the number of dollars remaining after he paid his rent was

(1) ¼y

(2) y + 4

(3) ¾y

(4) 12y

(5) 3y

17. Mr. Benson is on a diet. For breakfast and lunch he consumed ⁴⁄₉ of his allowable number of calories. If he still had 1,000 calories left for the day, his daily allowance in calories was

(1) 1,500

(2) 1,800

(3) 1,200

(4) 2250

(5) 444 ⁴⁄₉

18. In his will, Mr. Mason left ½ of his estate to his wife, ⅓ to his daughter, and the balance, consisting of $12,000, to his son. The value of Mr. Mason's estate was

(1) $24,000

(2) $60,000

(3) $14,400

(4) $65,000

(5) $72,000

19. An oil tank is ³⁄₁₀ full. It takes 420 gallons more to fill the tank. The number of gallons the tank holds is

(1) 600

(2) 480

(3) 840

(4) 1,260

(5) 1,000

20. A family spends ¼ of its income for rent and ⅕ for food. The fractional part of its income left is

(1) ⁹⁄₂₀

(2) ¹⁹⁄₂₀

(3) ¹¹⁄₂₀

(4) ⁴⁄₅

(5) ⁸⁄₉

Answers:

20. 3	16. 3	12. 5	8. 2	4. 4
19. 1	15. 4	11. 3	7. 3	3. 1
18. 5	14. 5	10. 2	6. 2	2. 2
17. 2	13. 2	9. 4	5. 5	1. 4

E-12

Arranging Fractions in Order. We know that ½ and ³⁄₆ are equivalent fractions. This fact can be checked as follows:

$$\frac{1}{2} \diagdown \diagup \frac{3}{6}$$

$$1 \times 6 = 2 \times 3$$

We know that ¾ is greater than ⅖. This fact can be checked as follows:

$$\frac{3}{4} \diagup \diagdown \frac{2}{5}$$

3 × 5 is greater than 4 × 2.

The symbol > means is *greater than*.
Thus, we may write $\frac{3}{4} > \frac{2}{5}$ because $15 > 8$.
We know that $\frac{3}{7}$ is less than $\frac{5}{6}$. This fact can be checked as follows:

$$\frac{3}{7} \diagdown\diagup \frac{5}{6}$$

3×6 is less than 7×5.

The symbol < means *is less than*.
Thus, we may write $\frac{3}{7} < \frac{5}{6}$ because $18 < 35$.

PRACTICE

In each case, use the symbol $=$, $>$, or $<$ to show the relationship between the given fractions:

1. $\frac{3}{4}$	$\frac{7}{10}$	**4.** $\frac{5}{8}$	$\frac{4}{7}$	**7.** $\frac{7}{11}$	$\frac{13}{19}$	**10.** $\frac{8}{13}$	$\frac{5}{8}$	**13.** $\frac{15}{35}$	$\frac{12}{28}$
2. $\frac{6}{9}$	$\frac{40}{60}$	**5.** $\frac{4}{9}$	$\frac{7}{15}$	**8.** $\frac{7}{9}$	$\frac{15}{17}$	**11.** $\frac{5}{16}$	$\frac{10}{31}$	**14.** $\frac{6}{13}$	$\frac{11}{20}$
3. $\frac{2}{3}$	$\frac{11}{16}$	**6.** $\frac{12}{20}$	$\frac{3}{5}$	**9.** $\frac{21}{28}$	$\frac{24}{32}$	**12.** $\frac{4}{11}$	$\frac{8}{21}$	**15.** $\frac{9}{17}$	$\frac{5}{7}$

Answers:

1. $\frac{3}{4} > \frac{7}{10}$ 2. $\frac{6}{9} = \frac{40}{60}$ 3. $\frac{2}{3} > \frac{11}{16}$
4. $\frac{5}{8} > \frac{4}{7}$ 5. $\frac{4}{9} > \frac{7}{15}$ 6. $\frac{12}{20} = \frac{3}{5}$
7. $\frac{7}{11} > \frac{13}{19}$ 8. $\frac{7}{9} < \frac{15}{17}$ 9. $\frac{21}{28} = \frac{24}{32}$
10. $\frac{8}{13} > \frac{5}{8}$ 11. $\frac{5}{16} > \frac{10}{31}$ 12. $\frac{4}{11} < \frac{8}{21}$
13. $\frac{15}{35} = \frac{12}{28}$ 14. $\frac{6}{13} < \frac{11}{20}$ 15. $\frac{9}{17} < \frac{5}{7}$

I. F. DECIMALS

F-1

A *decimal fraction*, or *decimal*, is a fraction in which the denominator is not written. The denominator is a power of 10; the denominator may be 10, 100, 1,000, etc., and is shown by the way the decimal is written. For example,

Written as common fractions	Written as decimals
$\frac{3}{10}$	0.3
$\frac{19}{100}$	0.19
$\frac{7}{100}$	0.07
$\frac{163}{1,000}$	0.163

If a number consists of a whole number and a fraction, the whole number is written first and is then followed by the decimal. For example,

$$8\tfrac{3}{10} = 8.3$$
$$9\tfrac{7}{100} = 9.07$$

Note:

The value of a decimal is *not* changed by annexing zeros to the right of the decimal. For example,

$$\tfrac{1}{2} = 0.5 = 0.50 = 0.500 = 0.5000$$

One reason for the use of decimals is that they are convenient to write and to work with. For example, it is more convenient to add decimals than to add fractions: in adding decimals you don't need to find common denominators.

F-2

Addition of Decimals. Mrs. Gordon bought the following items at a supermarket: bread, $0.53; steak, $4.70; tomato juice, $0.60; fish, $2.20. When she checked the total cost she arranged her work as follows:

$0.53
4.70
0.60
+2.20
――――
$8.03

You can see that she followed this rule:

In adding decimals, always put the decimal points under each other.

F-3

Subtraction of Decimals. In subtracting decimals we follow the same rule.

EXAMPLE: Subtract 9.73 from 15.58.

15.58
−9.73
――――
5.85

F-4

Multiplication of Decimals. Mr. Burns figured that it cost him about 9.8 cents per mile for the expense of driving his car. He drives 286 miles to work and back each week. How much does it cost him to do this?

In order to obtain the result we must multiply 286 by 9.8 cents. Note that in this multiplication we write 9.8 cents as $0.098. Before we actually multiply we can see that the answer should be roughly in the neighborhood of $28: 9.8¢ is almost one-tenth of a dollar, and $\frac{1}{10}$ of 286 is slightly more than 28.

286
×$0.098
――――
2288
2574
――――
$28.028

Do you agree that the answer should be $28.028, or $28.03 to the nearest cent?

This example illustrates the following rule:

In multiplying decimals the number of decimal places in the product is the sum of the number of decimal places in the numbers being multiplied.

EXAMPLES:

0.02 (2 decimal places)
×0.3 (1 decimal place)
――――
0.006 (3 decimal places)

1.02 (2 decimal places)
×0.004 (3 decimal places)
――――
0.00408 (5 decimal places)

F-5

Division of Decimals. Consider the division $\frac{8.46}{0.2}$. Since we may multiply the numerator and denominator of a fraction by the same number without changing the value of the fraction, we may multiply the numerator and denominator of this fraction by 10 to obtain

$$\frac{8.46}{0.2} = \frac{84.6}{2}$$

This is often written as

$$0.2 \overline{)8.4.6} \quad \text{or} \quad 2 \overline{)84.6}^{\,42.3}$$

The result is 42.3.

In dividing decimals, multiply both the divisor and the dividend by whatever power of 10 (10, 100, 1,000, etc.) that is necessary to make the divisor a whole number, and then proceed with the division. The decimal point in the quotient is always in the same place as in the new dividend.

EXAMPLES:

$$6.93 \div .3 \qquad 35.75 \div 0.05 \qquad 0.08136 \div 0.006$$

$$\begin{array}{r} 23.1 \\ 0.3\overline{)\,6.9.3} \end{array} \qquad \begin{array}{r} 715. \\ 0.05\overline{)\,35.75.} \end{array} \qquad \begin{array}{r} 13.56 \\ 0.006\overline{)\,0.081.36} \end{array}$$

Sometimes, there is a remainder and you are told to find the answer to the nearest tenth, nearest hundredth, etc. In such cases, carry out the division to one more place than is called for. *Regarding remainders*— If the digit just to the right of the desired decimal place is 5 or greater, add 1 to the desired decimal place number. Otherwise, drop the digit to the right of the desired decimal place.

EXAMPLE: Divide 3.734 by 0.9, and express the answer to the nearest tenth.

$$\begin{array}{r} 4.14 \\ 0.9\overline{)\,3.7.34} \end{array} \quad \text{The answer is 4.1.}$$

EXAMPLE: Divide 2.4853 by 0.7 and express the answer to the nearest hundredth.

$$\begin{array}{r} 3.550 \\ 0.7\overline{)\,2.4.853} \end{array} \quad \text{The answer is 3.55.}$$

F-6

Conversion of Fractions to Decimals. It is sometimes necessary to change a fraction to a decimal. To do this, we divide the numerator by the denominator, placing zeros after the decimal point in the numerator when they are needed.

EXAMPLE: Change ⅜ to a decimal.

$$\begin{array}{r} 0.375 \\ 8\overline{)\,3.000} \end{array}$$

$$\text{⅜} = 0.375$$

EXAMPLE: Change ⁵⁄₁₂ to a decimal.

$$\begin{array}{r} 0.4166\ \text{⅔} \\ 12\overline{)\,5.0000} \end{array}$$

To the nearest tenth, ⁵⁄₁₂ = 0.4.
To the nearest hundredth, ⁵⁄₁₂ = 0.42.
To the nearest thousandth, ⁵⁄₁₂ = 0.417.

PRACTICE

1. Add 38.52 + 7.09 + 92.78 + 0.84. _____
2. Add 2.806 + 0.935 + 4.037 + 65 + 0.029. _____
3. From 1.907 subtract 0.023. _____
4. Take 3.79 from 12.82. _____
5. Multiply 5.68 by 2.9. _____
6. Multiply 3.14 by 0.015. _____
7. Divide 1.6357 by 0.37 and express the result to the nearest hundredth. _____
8. Divide 0.32277 by 5.3. _____
9. Convert ¹⁷⁄₂₀ to a decimal. _____
10. Convert ⁸⁄₁₅ to a decimal to the nearest hundredth. _____

Answers:

1. 139.23	3. 1.884	5. 16.472	7. 4.42	9. 0.85
2. 72.807	4. 9.03	6. 0.04710	8. 0.0609	10. 0.53

I. G. Percent

G-1

We have seen that rational numbers may be expressed as fractions or as decimals. A rational number may also be expressed as a percent. In this section, we will learn how to work with percents.

On a motor trip of 100 miles, 73 miles were on parkway. If we wish to indicate the part of the trip taken on a parkway, we may say that $^{73}/_{100}$ of the trip was on a parkway. Another way of stating the same fact is to say that 0.73 of the trip was taken on a parkway. A third way to express the same idea is to say that 73% of the trip was taken on a parkway. *Percent is just another way of writing a fraction in which the denominator is 100.* The % sign is used instead of writing the denominator 100. In short, 73% means $^{73}/_{100}$ or 0.73. It is a simple matter to change a percent to a fraction or to a decimal.

> EXAMPLE: Change 45% (a) to a decimal.
> $$45\% = 0.45$$
> (b) to a fraction.
> $$45\% = {}^{45}/_{100}, \text{ or } {}^{9}/_{20}$$

> EXAMPLES: Change 0.37 to a percent.
> $$0.37 = {}^{37}/_{100} = 37\%$$
>
> Change 0.025 to a percent.
> $$0.025 = {}^{2.5}/_{100} = 2.5\% \text{ or } 2\tfrac{1}{2}\%$$
>
> Change $^{3}/_{4}$ to a percent.
> We first change $^{3}/_{4}$ to a decimal and then to a percent.
> $$4\overline{)3.00}^{\;0.75}$$
>
> $$^{3}/_{4} = 0.75 = 75\%$$
>
> Change $^{5}/_{19}$ to a decimal and then to a percent.
> $$\begin{array}{r} 0.26 \\ 19\overline{)5.00} \\ \underline{3\ 8} \\ 1\ 20 \\ \underline{1\ 14} \\ 6 \end{array}$$
>
> $$^{5}/_{19} = 0.26^{6}/_{19} = 26^{6}/_{19}\%$$

PRACTICE

Fill in the following blanks.

	FRACTION	DECIMAL	PERCENT
1.	$\tfrac{1}{2}$	_____	_____
2.	_____	0.35	_____
3.	_____	_____	36%
4.	$^{3}/_{7}$	_____	_____
5.	_____	0.24	_____
6.	_____	_____	$4\tfrac{1}{2}\%$

7. $^5/_9$
8. _____   0.37 $^1/_2$
9. _____   _____   83$^1/_3$
10. 1$^1/_5$

Answers:

FRACTION	DECIMAL	PERCENT
1. $^1/_2$	0.50	50%
2. $\frac{35}{100} = ^7/_{20}$	0.35	35%
3. $\frac{36}{100} = ^9/_{25}$	0.36	36%
4. $^3/_7$	0.42$^1/_7$	42$^1/_7$%
5. $^6/_{25}$	0.24	24%
6. $\frac{4^1/_2}{100} = \frac{9}{200}$	0.04$^1/_2$ = .045	4$^1/_2$%
7. $^5/_9$	0.55%	55%
8. $\frac{37^1/_2}{100} = \frac{75}{200} = ^3/_8$	0.37$^1/_2$	37$^1/_2$%
9. $\frac{83^1/_3}{100} = \frac{250}{300} = ^5/_6$	0.83$^1/_3$	83$^1/_3$%
10. 1$^1/_5$	1.2	120%

Certain fractions and their equivalent percents are used frequently.

Helpful Equivalents to Memorize

$^1/_2 = 50\%$	$^3/_4 = 75\%$	$^4/_5 = 80\%$	$^3/_8 = 37^1/_2\%$
$^1/_3 = 33^1/_3\%$	$^1/_5 = 20\%$	$^1/_6 = 16^2/_3\%$	$^5/_8 = 62^1/_2\%$
$^2/_3 = 66^2/_3\%$	$^2/_5 = 40\%$	$^5/_6 = 83^1/_3\%$	$^7/_8 = 87^1/_2\%$
$^1/_4 = 25\%$	$^3/_5 = 60\%$	$^1/_8 = 12^1/_2\%$	

G-2

Problems on Percents. Since percents are fractions in another form, problems involving percents are similar to problems involving fractions.

1. To find a percent of a given number.

EXAMPLE: In a factory, 4,775 machine parts were manufactured. When these were tested, 4% of them were found to be defective. How many machine parts were defective?

In this case, the word *of* indicates that we are to multiply 4,775 by 4%. Since 4% = 0.04, we have

```
   4775  parts manufactured
  × .04  percent defective
 191.00  number of defective parts
```

191 machine parts were defective.

2. To find what percent one number is of another.

EXAMPLE: During the season, a professional basketball player tried 108 foul shots, and made 81 of them. What percent of the shots tried were made?

We form a fraction as follows:

$$\frac{\text{number of shots made}}{\text{total number of shots tried}} = \frac{81}{108}$$

This fraction may be expressed as a percent by changing $^{81}/_{108}$ to a decimal and then to a percent:

$$\begin{array}{r} 0.75 \\ 108\overline{\smash)81.00} \\ \underline{75\ 6} \\ 5\ 40 \\ \underline{5\ 40} \end{array}$$

$$^{81}/_{108} = 0.75 = 75\%$$

The player made 75% of his shots.

3. To find a number when a percent of it is given.

   EXAMPLE: A businessman decided to spend 16% of his expense budget for advertising. If he spent $2,400, what was his total expense?

We know that 16%, or $^{16}/_{100}$, of his expenses amounted to $2,400.

$$^{16}/_{100} \text{ of expense} = 2,400$$
$$^{1}/_{100} \text{ of expense} = {}^{2,400}/_{16} = 150$$
$$\text{then } ^{100}/_{100} \text{ or total expense} = 150 \times 100 = \$15,000.$$

PRACTICE

Directions: Solve the following problems and blacken the space at the right under the number which corresponds to the one you have selected as the right answer.

1. Of $500 spent by the Jones family one month, $150 was spent for clothing. The percent spent for clothing was
    (1) 33⅓%   (4) 12%
    (2) 40%   (5) 20%
    (3) 30%

1. 1 2 3 4 5
   || || || || ||

2. Mr. Frank bought a jacket for $48 and a pair of slacks for $12.50. If there was a sales tax of 3% added to his bill, the amount of the tax was
    (1) $18   (4) $0.18
    (2) $1.82   (5) $0.36
    (3) $0.63

2. 1 2 3 4 5
   || || || || ||

3. A TV dealer made 20% of his annual sales during the month before Christmas. If he sold 130 sets during this month, the number of sets he sold during the year was
    (1) 650   (4) 520
    (2) 260   (5) 390
    (3) 1,300

3. 1 2 3 4 5
   || || || || ||

4. Of 600 students in a high school graduating class, 85% plan to go on to college. The number of students planning to go on to college is
    (1) 5,100   (4) 500
    (2) 51   (5) 510
    (3) 540

4. 1 2 3 4 5
   || || || || ||

5. A motorist planned a trip covering 720 miles. After he had covered 600 miles, what percent of the trip was completed?
    (1) 80%   (4) 16⅔%
    (2) 83⅓%   (5) 85%
    (3) 60%

5. 1 2 3 4 5
   || || || || ||

6. A school library contained 3,200 books. Of these, 48% were books of fiction. The number of books of fiction that the library contained was
    (1) 1,200
    (2) 1,208
    (3) 1,536
    (4) 1,380
    (5) 1,300

    6. 1 2 3 4 5
    II II II II II

7. A homeowner figured that 60% of his expenses were taxes. If his tax bill was $900, the total expense of running his house was
    (1) $540
    (2) $5,400
    (3) $1,800
    (4) $1,500
    (5) $2,000

    7. 1 2 3 4 5
    II II II II II

8. The value of a new car decreases 35% during the first year. Mr. Ames paid $6,000 for a new car. The value of the car at the end of the first year was
    (1) $2,100
    (2) $3,100
    (3) $4,000
    (4) $4,200
    (5) $3,900

    8. 1 2 3 4 5
    II II II II II

9. In a large housing development there are 1,250 apartments. Of these, 250 were three-room apartments. The percent of three-room apartments in the development is
    (1) 16⅔%
    (2) 25%
    (3) 20%
    (4) 24%
    (5) 30%

    9. 1 2 3 4 5
    II II II II II

10. Mrs. Breen bought a dining room suite for $800. She agreed to pay 25% down and the rest in installments. Her down payment was
    (1) $400
    (2) $200
    (3) $150
    (4) $100
    (5) $250

    10. 1 2 3 4 5
    II II II II II

11. An oil tank contains 560 gallons. After 210 gallons of oil were used, the percent of oil left in the tank was
    (1) 37½%
    (2) 40%
    (3) 60%
    (4) 62½%
    (5) 58%

    11. 1 2 3 4 5
    II II II II II

12. When Mrs. Green had paid $600 for her fur coat, she had paid 40% of the total cost. The total cost of her fur coat was
    (1) $1,000
    (2) $1,200
    (3) $1,500
    (4) $2,400
    (5) $1,800

    12. 1 2 3 4 5
    II II II II II

13. Mrs. Miller received a bill for electricity for $24.50. She was allowed a discount of 2% for early payment. If Mrs. Miller paid promptly her payment was
    (1) $0.49
    (2) $19.60
    (3) $24.45
    (4) $24.01
    (5) $4.90

    13. 1 2 3 4 5
    II II II II II

14. A table usually sells for $72. Because it was slightly shopworn, it sold for $60. The percent of reduction was
    (1) 20%
    (2) 16⅔%
    (3) 80%
    (4) 30%
    (5) 12½%

    14. 1 2 3 4 5
    II II II II II

15. The sales tax on a lawn mower was $4.80. If the tax rate is 4%, the selling price of the mower was
(1) $19.20
(2) $192
(3) $124.80
(4) $120
(5) $115.20

15. 1 2 3 4 5
|| || || || ||

16. A bookstore sold 800 copies of a popular cookbook at $5 each. If the dealer made a profit of 40% on each sale, his total profit on the sale of the cookbooks was
(1) $160
(2) $960
(3) $240
(4) $1,200
(5) $1,600

16. 1 2 3 4 5
|| || || || ||

17. At an evening performance, 83⅓% of the seats in a movie house were occupied. If 500 people attended this performance, the seating capacity of the movie house was
(1) 600
(2) 500
(3) 583
(4) 650
(5) 750

17. 1 2 3 4 5
|| || || || ||

18. A food store made sales of $9,000 during one week. If 5% of the sales amount was profit, the profit for the week was
(1) $45
(2) $4,500
(3) $450
(4) $544.42
(5) $434.42

18. 1 2 3 4 5
|| || || || ||

19. The Blue Sox baseball team won 56 games and lost 28 games. The percent of the games won by the Blue Sox was
(1) 50%
(2) 66⅔%
(3) 33⅓%
(4) 40%
(5) 36%

19. 1 2 3 4 5
|| || || || ||

20. The Star Motel had 60 rooms occupied one night. This was 80% of the total number of rooms. The total number of rooms in the motel was
(1) 80
(2) 48
(3) 140
(4) 75
(5) 100

20. 1 2 3 4 5
|| || || || ||

Answers:

20. 4	**16.** 5	**12.** 3	**8.** 5	**4.** 5
19. 2	**15.** 4	**11.** 4	**7.** 4	**3.** 1
18. 3	**14.** 2	**10.** 2	**6.** 3	**2.** 2
17. 1	**13.** 4	**9.** 3	**5.** 2	**1.** 3

G-3

Business Applications of Percentage. Manufacturers will frequently suggest a price for which an article is to be sold. This is called the *list price.* Dealers will sometimes reduce the price in order to meet competition. The amount by which the price is reduced is called the *discount.* And the reduced price is called the *net price,* or *selling price.*

EXAMPLE: In a department store, a chair was marked as follows: "List Price $45. For sale at $31.50." What was the rate of discount?

The discount was $45.00 − $31.50 = $13.50.
To find the rate of discount, we use the fraction

$$\frac{\text{Discount}}{\text{List Price}} = \frac{13.50}{45.00}$$
$$= \frac{135}{450}$$
$$= \frac{3}{10}$$
$$= 30\%$$

The rate of discount was 30%.

PRACTICE

Directions: Solve the following problems and blacken the space at the right under the number which corresponds to the one you have selected as the right answer.

1. The list price of a coat was $120. Mr. Barr bought the coat at a discount of 10%. The net price of the coat was
(1) $132   (4) $118
(2) $12   (5) $100
(3) $108

1. 1 2 3 4 5
   || || || || ||

2. A men's store advertises a shirt that usually sells for $16.00 at a special price of $12.00. The rate of discount is
(1) 33⅓%   (4) 40%
(2) 25%   (5) 35%
(3) 20%

2. 1 2 3 4 5
   || || || || ||

3. A radio set is sold at a discount of 12½%. If the discount amounts to $6, the list price of the radio set is
(1) $42   (4) $50
(2) $45   (5) $48
(3) $54

3. 1 2 3 4 5
   || || || || ||

4. An electric toaster has a list price of $21. If it is sold at a discount of 33⅓% the net price is
(1) $7   (4) $25
(2) $28   (5) $16
(3) $14

4. 1 2 3 4 5
   || || || || ||

5. The net price of a watch was $40 after a discount of 20%. The list price of the watch was
(1) $50   (4) $35.20
(2) $30   (5) $45
(3) $48

5. 1 2 3 4 5
   || || || || ||

Answers:

1. 3   2. 2   3. 5   4. 3   5. 1

Sometimes a manufacturer will allow a *trade discount* and an additional discount on top of the trade discount. *Two or more discounts are called successive discounts.*

EXAMPLE: Mr. Boyd bought a table for a dealer. The list price was $180, and he was allowed a discount of 15%. In addition, he received a 2% discount for payment within 10 days. How much did Mr. Boyd pay for the table?

$180	list price
×0.15	rate of discount
900	
180	
$27.00	amount of discount

$180.00	list price
−27.00	amount of discount
$153.00	cost price

When we compute the second discount, we base it on the price after the first discount is taken off.

$153	cost price
×0.02	rate of discount
$ 3.06	discount for early payment

$153.00	cost price
−3.06	discount for early payment
$149.94	actual payment

PRACTICE

Directions: Solve the following problems and blacken the space at the right under the number which corresponds to the one you have selected as the right answer.

1. Mr. Mack bought a television set. The list price was $400. He was allowed successive discounts of 10% and 5%. How much did Mr. Mack actually pay for the television?
   (1) $340
   (2) $350
   (3) $352
   (4) $342
   (5) $324

1. 1 2 3 4 5
   || || || || ||

2. Mr. Drew bought a shipment of books. The list price of the books was $180. If Mr. Drew was allowed discounts of 15% and 5%, how much did he actually pay for the books?
   (1) $153
   (2) $171
   (3) $144
   (4) $150
   (5) $145.35

2. 1 2 3 4 5
   || || || || ||

3. On a purchase of $500, how much is saved by taking discounts of 20% and 10%, rather than discounts of 10% and 15%?
   (1) $40
   (2) $23.50
   (3) $22.50
   (4) $32.50
   (5) $35

3. 1 2 3 4 5
   || || || || ||

4. Mr. Benson bought a boat which had a list price of $120. He was allowed a 12½% discount and an additional 2% discount for cash. How much did Mr. Benson pay for the boat?
   (1) $102.90
   (2) $103.90
   (3) $112.90
   (4) $98.90
   (5) $105

4. 1 2 3 4 5
   || || || || ||

Answers:

1. 4   2. 5   3. 3   4. 1

When a businessman decides upon the price at which to sell an article, he must consider a number of items. First, the cost of the article is noted. Then the businessman must consider such items as rent, sales help salaries, and other expenses. This is called *overhead.* Any amount left over after taking account of cost and overhead is the *profit.* Thus, we have

$$\boxed{\text{Selling Price} = \text{Cost} + \text{Overhead} + \text{Profit}}$$

EXAMPLE: One week the Town Shoe Shop's sales amounted to $1,590. The merchandise sold cost $820, and the overhead was 20% of the sales. What was the profit?

$$20\% = 0.20$$
The overhead was $1,590 \times 0.20 = \$318.$

To obtain the profit, we must subtract the sum of the cost and the overhead from the selling price.

$820	cost of merchandise
+318	overhead
$1,138	cost + overhead

$1,590	selling price
−1,138	cost + overhead
$ 452	profit

The profit was $452.

PRACTICE

Directions: Solve the following problems and blacken the space at the right under the number which corresponds to the one you have selected as the right answer.

1. The cost of a chair is $68. The overhead is $10, and the profit is $18. The selling price is
   (1) $77.50 (4) $96
   (2) $86.50 (5) $92
   (3) $95

   1. 1 2 3 4 5
   ‖ ‖ ‖ ‖ ‖

2. A merchant buys lawn mowers at $43.50. He sells them at retail for $75. If his overhead is 12% of the selling price, his profit was
   (1) $9 (4) $61.50
   (2) $22.50 (5) $31.50
   (3) $23.50

   2. 1 2 3 4 5
   ‖ ‖ ‖ ‖ ‖

3. A merchant bought a shipment of cameras at a cost of $1,600 and sold the shipment for $2,500. If his profit was 25% of the cost of the shipment, his overhead expenses were
   (1) $900 (4) $500
   (2) $400 (5) $4,100
   (3) $650

   3. 1 2 3 4 5
   ‖ ‖ ‖ ‖ ‖

4. Raincoats cost a dealer $25 each. He plans to sell the raincoats at a profit of 30% on the cost. If his overhead on each sale is $2, the selling price of the raincoats is
   (1) $32.50 (4) $7.50
   (2) $30.50 (5) $35.10
   (3) $34.50

   4. 1 2 3 4 5
   ‖ ‖ ‖ ‖ ‖

5. The receipts of the Village Cafeteria for one week was $4,250. The cost of the merchandise sold was $1,560 and the overhead was 34% of the receipts. The profit was

(1) $3,005

(2) $1,245

(3) $1,445

(4) $1,545

(5) $1,255

Answers:

5. 2   4. 3   3. 4   2. 2   1. 4

We are often interested in finding the percent of increase or decrease.

EXAMPLE: The price of a bus ride was increased from $1.20 to $1.35. What was the percent of increase?

$$
\begin{array}{ll}
\$1.35 & \text{new fare} \\
-1.20 & \text{original fare} \\
\hline
\$0.15 & \text{increase in fare}
\end{array}
$$

To find the percent of increase we form the following fraction

$$\frac{0.15}{1.20} \quad \frac{\text{increase in fare}}{\text{original fare}}$$

We now change this fraction to a percent, as follows

$$\frac{0.15}{1.20} = \frac{15}{120} = \frac{3}{24} = \frac{1}{8}$$

$$\frac{0.125}{8\overline{)1.000}}$$

The percent of increase was 12½%.

EXAMPLE: During the past ten years the population of a small town decreased from 1,250 to 1,000. What was the percent of decrease?

$$
\begin{array}{ll}
1,250 & \text{original population} \\
-1,000 & \text{population after decrease} \\
\hline
250 & \text{actual decrease}
\end{array}
$$

To find the percent of decrease we form the following fraction

$$\frac{250}{1,250} \quad \frac{\text{actual decrease}}{\text{original population}}$$

We now change this fraction to a percent, as follows

$$
\begin{array}{r}
0.20 \\
1,250\overline{)250.00} \\
\underline{250\ 0} \\
0
\end{array}
$$

The percent of decrease was 20%.

Sometimes we have occasion to work with percents greater than 100%.

EXAMPLE: The profit of the X Corporation this year was 108% of its profit last year. If its profit last year was $250,000, what was its profit this year?

$250,000   profit last year
  1.08   percent this year
20000 00
250000 0
$270,000.00

Its profit this year was $270,000.

EXAMPLE: Mr. Fowler bought some stock at $40 per share. Three years later Mr. Fowler sold the stock at $90 per share. What percent of profit did Mr. Fowler make?

$90   selling price of stock per share
−40   cost of stock per share
$50   profit per share

$\frac{50}{40}$ profit per share
      original cost per share

          1.25
40$\overline{)50.00}$
      40
     100
      80
     200
     200

Mr. Fowler made a profit of 125%.

PRACTICE

Directions: Solve the following problems and blacken the space at the right under the number which corresponds to the one you have selected as the right answer.

1. A man bought a house for $40,000. Eight years later he sold the house for $64,000. What percent of profit did he make?
   (1) 40%   (4) 60%
   (2) 37½%   (5) 75%
   (3) 50%

   1. 1 2 3 4 5
   II II II II II

2. During a sale an overcoat was reduced from $120 to $102. What was the percent of reduction?
   (1) 18%   (4) 12%
   (2) 15%   (5) 16%
   (3) 50%

   2. 1 2 3 4 5
   II II II II II

3. A dealer sold a watch at 130% of his cost. If the sale price was $39, how much did the watch cost the dealer?
   (1) $5.70   (4) $30
   (2) $11.70   (5) $89.70
   (3) $16.50

   3. 1 2 3 4 5
   II II II II II

4. The price of a pound of coffee increased from $1.40 to $3.50. What was the percent of increase?
   (1) 250%   (4) 140%
   (2) 150%   (5) 200%
   (3) 125%

   4. 1 2 3 4 5
   II II II II II

5. Mr. Thorne's salary was $210 per week. He received a promotion and his salary rose to $375 per week. The percent of increase of his salary, to the nearest percent, is

(1) 79% (4) 179%
(2) 80% (5) 178%
(3) 78%

5. 1 2 3 4 5
|| || || || ||

6. 137½% of what number is 55?

(1) 50 (4) 45
(2) 39 (5) 42
(3) 40

6. 1 2 3 4 5
|| || || || ||

Answers:

3. 6.   1. 5.   2. 4.   4. 3.   2. 2.   4. 1.

I. H. Insurance

H-1

The amount of money paid for insurance is called the *premium.* It is usually paid annually. On many types of insurance the premium rate is stated as so many dollars per $100 or per $1,000 of insurance bought.

There are several types of life insurance sold. The ordinary life policy provides that the person buying the insurance continues to pay a premium for many years to come although dividends may reduce the premium as time goes on. The twenty-payment life policy provides that the person insured will pay the premium over a period of 20 years. The endowment policy provides that a person will pay premiums for a stated number of years. At the end of the period, he or she will receive a lump sum. During the period of the policy, he or she is protected by insurance. The rates are determined by the insurance company and given to the agent in tabular form. For example, the following figures are a portion of such a table.

Age in Years	Ordinary Life Premium per $1,000 of Insurance	Twenty-Payment Life Premium per $1,000 of Insurance	Endowment Premium per $1,000 of Insurance
20	$17.50	$23.40	$26.50
25	19.75	25.60	29.10
30	22.60	29.80	34.40
35	25.40	34.75	38.50
40	30.20	40.50	43.10

EXAMPLE: At the age of 30, a man buys a twenty-payment life policy for $7,500. What is his annual premium?

The table indicates that at age 30 the rate is $29.80 per $1,000. In 7,500 there are 7.5 thousands. His annual premium is 7.5 × $29.80 = $223.50.

PRACTICE

Directions: Solve the following problems and blacken the space at the right under the number which corresponds to the one you have selected as the right answer.

1. The annual premium rate on $6,500 worth of an ordinary life insurance policy is $28.24 per $1,000. The annual premium is
   - (1) $18.35
   - (2) $173.55
   - (3) $183.56
   - (4) $1,835.50
   - (5) $184.55

   1. 1 2 3 4 5
   || || || || ||

2. A house is insured against fire for 70% of its value. If the house has a value of $48,000 and the premium rate is $2.30 per $1,000, the annual premium is
   - (1) $772.80
   - (2) $77.28
   - (3) $75.28
   - (4) $77.08
   - (5) $75.08

   2. 1 2 3 4 5
   || || || || ||

3. A car is insured for fire and theft for $5,700. If the annual premium rate is $1.04 per $100, the annual premium is
   - (1) $59.28
   - (2) $79.80
   - (3) $58.24
   - (4) $60.32
   - (5) $79.28

   3. 1 2 3 4 5
   || || || || ||

4. The annual premium rate for a twenty-payment life policy is $36.40 per $1,000. The total amount paid in premiums over a twenty-year period for a $6,500 policy is
   - (1) $236.60
   - (2) $573.20
   - (3) $4,532
   - (4) $6,532
   - (5) $4,732

   4. 1 2 3 4 5
   || || || || ||

5. The annual premium on a fire insurance policy for $12,000 is $22.80. The premium rate per $100 is
   - (1) $1.90
   - (2) $3.74
   - (3) $0.19
   - (4) $37.46
   - (5) $0.29

   5. 1 2 3 4 5
   || || || || ||

Answers:

1. 3   2. 2   3. 1   4. 5   5. 3

I. I. Investments

I-1

The most common form of investment is the placement of money in a savings bank where it draws interest. In order to compute interest, we use the following formula.

$$Interest = Principal \times Rate \times Time$$

which is often written

$$I = P \times R \times T, \text{ or } I = PRT$$

The principal is the amount invested, the annual rate is the percent of the principal given to the investor each year, and the time is stated in years.

EXAMPLE: What is the interest on $1,200 at $4\frac{1}{2}$% for 9 months?

$$I = PRT$$

In this case, $\begin{cases} P = 1{,}200 \\ R = \dfrac{4\frac{1}{2}}{100} \\ T = \dfrac{9}{12} \text{ or } \dfrac{3}{4} \end{cases}$

Therefore, $I = 1{,}200 \times \dfrac{4\frac{1}{2}}{100} \times \dfrac{3}{4}$

Then, if you multiply the numerator and the denominator of $\dfrac{4\frac{1}{2}}{100}$ by 2, you have $\dfrac{9}{200}$.

$$I = 1{,}200 \times \dfrac{9}{200} \times \dfrac{3}{4}$$

$$I = {}^{3}\!\!\!\!/1{,}200 \times \dfrac{9}{200_1} \times \dfrac{3}{4_2} = \dfrac{81}{2} \text{ or } 40\frac{1}{2}$$

The interest is $40.50.

If the interest is added to the principal we have the *amount*.

In this case, the amount is $1,200 + $40.50, or $1,240.50.

Many banks *compound interest* every three months. That is, they add the interest to the principal at the end of three months. Then they compute interest for the next three months on an increased principal. This computation is made from tables. Interest that is not compounded is called *simple interest*.

A corporation is owned by stockholders who own *shares of stock*. Many such shares are traded on a stock exchange and are listed in the newspapers with current prices. For example,

American Telephone—63
United States Steel—48½

Stocks such as these pay dividends based upon the earnings of the company.

A corporation may borrow money by selling *bonds* to the public. Bonds carry a fixed rate of interest and are issued for a certain number of years. At the *maturity date* of the bond the corporation pays back the borrowed amount to the bondholder. Thus, a shareholder is a part owner of a company but a bondholder is a creditor.

EXAMPLE: Mr. Black owns 45 shares of stock in Company A. The stock pays an annual dividend of $1.60 per share. How much does Mr. Black receive in dividends per year?

To obtain the amount of dividends we multiply 45 by $1.60.

$$45 \times 1.60 = \$72.00$$

Mr. Black received $72 in dividends.

EXAMPLE: Mr. Glenn owns six $1,000 bonds that pay 8½% interest each year. How much does Mr. Glenn receive in interest each year?

This is a problem in computing simple interest. The principal is 6 × $1,000 or $6,000, the rate is 8½% and the period is 1 year.

$$\text{Interest} = 6{,}000 \times \dfrac{8\frac{1}{2}}{100} \times 1$$

$$= 6{,}000 \times \dfrac{17}{200} \times 1$$

$$= {}^{30}\!\!\!\!6{,}000 \times \dfrac{17}{200_1} \times 1 = 510$$

Mr. Glenn receives $510 in interest.

PRACTICE

Directions: Solve the following problems and blacken the space at the right under the number which corresponds to the one you have selected as the right answer.

1. Simple interest on $2,400 at 4½% for 3 years is
   (1) $288
   (2) $32.40
   (3) $3,240
   (4) $324
   (5) $314

   1. 1 2 3 4 5
   ‖ ‖ ‖ ‖ ‖

2. Mr. Payne borrowed $5,200 from a friend for 1 year and 3 months. He agreed to pay 5½% simple interest on the loan. The amount of money that he paid back at the end of the loan period was
   (1) $5,553.50
   (2) $357.50
   (3) $5,557.50
   (4) $4,842.50
   (5) $5,000

   2. 1 2 3 4 5
   ‖ ‖ ‖ ‖ ‖

3. Mrs. Holden kept $3,800 in a savings bank for 9 months at 5% simple interest. The interest on her money was
   (1) $142.50
   (2) $285
   (3) $3,942.50
   (4) $1.43
   (5) $1,425

   3. 1 2 3 4 5
   ‖ ‖ ‖ ‖ ‖

4. Mrs. Moss bought 80 shares of X Corporation at 28¾ and sold the shares a year later at 31½. Her profit, before paying commission, was
   (1) $22
   (2) $220
   (3) $140
   (4) $180
   (5) $242

   4. 1 2 3 4 5
   ‖ ‖ ‖ ‖ ‖

5. Mr. Kern owns 120 shares of Y Corporation. The corporation declared a dividend of $1.35 per share. The amount Mr. Kern received in dividends was
   (1) $16.20
   (2) $121.35
   (3) $135
   (4) $162
   (5) $1,620

   5. 1 2 3 4 5
   ‖ ‖ ‖ ‖ ‖

6. Mr. Cooper owns 280 shares of Z Corporation. The corporation pays a quarterly dividend of $0.35 per share. The amount Mr. Cooper receives in dividends for the year is
   (1) $98
   (2) $9.80
   (3) $392
   (4) $196
   (5) $280

   6. 1 2 3 4 5
   ‖ ‖ ‖ ‖ ‖

7. Mrs. Ross owns eight $1,000 bonds that pay 8½% interest each year. The amount of interest Mrs. Ross receives each year is
   (1) $645
   (2) $680
   (3) $68
   (4) $640
   (5) $85

   7. 1 2 3 4 5
   ‖ ‖ ‖ ‖ ‖

8. Mr. Dolan borrows $960 at 7½% for 3 months. The total amount that he will have to repay is
   (1) $1,032
   (2) $942
   (3) $1,140
   (4) $978
   (5) $967.50

   8. 1 2 3 4 5
   ‖ ‖ ‖ ‖ ‖

Answers:

1. 4   2. 3   3. 1   4. 2   5. 4   6. 3   7. 2   8. 4

I. J. Taxation

J-1

We ordinarily pay many kinds of taxes. In this section we will consider the more common types of taxes.

Many states in the United States have a *sales tax* on articles bought at retail. This may be 3%, 4%, 5% or a higher percent of the retail price of an article.

> **EXAMPLE:** Mrs. Horn buys a small rug for $39.95. If she has to pay a sales tax of 3%, what is the total cost of the rug?

$$3\% \text{ of } \$39.95 = 0.03 \times \$39.95 = \$1.1985$$

In a case such as this the amount of tax is rounded off to the nearest penny. In this case, the tax is $1.20. Mrs. Horn must pay $39.95 + $1.20, or $41.15.

A homeowner must pay a *real estate tax*. This tax is based upon the assessed valuation of the home. The assessed valuation of a home is determined by town or city authorities. The tax rate may be expressed as a percent or in the form "$4.70 per $100." In many localities, there is a separate school tax which is also based on the assessed valuation of the home.

> **EXAMPLE:** Mr. Martin's home is assessed at $43,500. His realty tax is $3.89 per $100, and his school tax is $1.09 per $100. What is Mr. Martin's total tax on his home?

We note that there are 435 hundreds in $43,500 since $43,500 = 435 \times 100$.

$$\text{The realty tax is } 435 \times 3.89 = \$1,692.15$$
$$\text{The school tax is } 435 \times 1.09 = \underline{+474.15}$$
$$\textit{Total tax} \quad \$2,166.30$$

The federal government and most state governments levy an *income tax*. Every person or business with an income above a certain minimum amount must file a tax return. The tax is based upon taxable income which is obtained after certain allowable deductions are taken off the gross income. For federal income taxes and some state income taxes, employers are required to withhold part of a worker's wages. Employers are also required to deduct a certain amount for social security taxes. After all deductions are made, the amount the employee gets is called "take–home pay."

> **EXAMPLE:** Mr. Dean's weekly salary is $285. Each week his employer deducts 5.9% of his salary for social security. He also deducts $15.70 for his federal withholding tax. What is Mr. Dean's weekly take–home pay?

$$5.9\% \text{ of } \$285 = \$16.82$$
$$\text{Total deductions} = \$16.82 + \$15.70 = \$32.52$$
$$\text{Mr. Dean's take–home pay is } \$285 - \$32.52 = \$252.48.$$

> **EXAMPLE:** Mr. Stark earns $16,400 per year. In paying his tax, he has allowable deductions of $3,750. On his state tax he pays 2% on the first $3,000 of taxable income, 3% on the next $3,000 of taxable income and 4% on the balance of his income. What is his state tax?

Mr. Stark's taxable income: $16,400 (Gross income)
  $\underline{-3,750}$ (Allowable deductions)
  $12,650 (Taxable income)

Tax on first $3,000:	$3,000
	×0.02
	$ 60

Tax on next $3,000:	$3,000
	×0.03
	$ 90

Balance:	$12,650
	−6,000 (Taxed income)
	$ 6,650

Tax on $6,650:	$6,650
	×0.04
	$ 266

Total Tax =	$60
	90
	+266
	$416

PRACTICE

Directions: Solve the following problems and blacken the space at the right under the number which corresponds to the one you have selected as the right answer.

1. Mr. Minor buys an overcoat for $137.50. If he must pay a sales tax of 3%, the total cost of the coat is
   (1) $178.80   (4) $133.37
   (2) $141.63   (5) $141.03
   (3) $137.92

   1. 1 2 3 4 5

2. On a purchase of a table for $64, Mrs. Morton paid a sales tax of $2.56. The rate of sales tax was
   (1) 3%   (4) 2½%
   (2) 3½%   (5) 4%
   (3) 2%

   2. 1 2 3 4 5

3. Mr. Powell's home is assessed at $36,500. The realty tax rate is $3.97 per $100. Mr. Powell's realty tax is
   (1) $144.91   (4) $14,490.50
   (2) $1,439.05   (5) $145
   (3) $1,449.05

   3. 1 2 3 4 5

4. Mrs. Olson bought a house for $32,000. It was assessed at 80% of her purchase price. If the school tax is $1.93 per $100, Mrs. Olson's school tax was
   (1) $494.08   (4) $49.41
   (2) $617.60   (5) $515.28
   (3) $61.76

   4. 1 2 3 4 5

5. Mr. Emerson sets aside $80 per month to cover his realty and school taxes. His home is assessed at $29,400. His realty tax is $3.14 per $100, and his school tax is $1.19 per $100. The amount he must add at the end of the year to cover both taxes is

(1) $303.02   (4) $313.02
(2) $213.02   (5) $473.02
(3) $31.32

6. Mrs. Howe has a gross income of $9,800 per year. Her deductions amount to $3,650. She pays state income taxes at the rate of 2% on the first $1,000 of taxable income, 3% on the next $2,000 of taxable income and 4% on the balance. Her total tax is

(1) $146   (4) $140
(2) $126   (5) $137.50
(3) $206

7. Mr. Robinson earns $235 per week. Each week his employer deducts 5.9% of his salary for social security. He also deducts $14.85 for his federal withholding tax. Mr. Robinson's weekly take-home pay is

(1) $221.13   (4) $249.85
(2) $206.28   (5) $205.28
(3) $210.15

8. Mrs. Tobin's taxable income is $8,900. On this, she must pay 2% on the first $3,000, 3% on the next $3,000 and 4% on the balance for state income tax. During the year her employer had withheld $4.50 per week. To settle her tax bill at the end of the year, Mrs. Tobin had to pay an additional

(1) $32   (4) $226
(2) $31   (5) $225
(3) $59

Answers:

1. 2   2. 5   3. 3   4. 1   5. 4   6. 3   7. 2   8. 1

II. ALGEBRA

II. A. Fundamentals

A-1

As we have seen earlier, we frequently use letters to represent numbers in algebra. For example, in the formula

$$I = P \times R \times T$$

I represents interest, P represents principal, R represents rate, and T represents time.

This is done because it enables us to solve many kinds of problems. That is, P may be $5,000 in one problem and $786 in another problem. In indicating multiplication in arithmetic we also use the $\times$ sign. For example, 5×6. In indicating multiplication in algebra, three methods are used:

1. Use the multiplication symbol. For example, $P \times R$.
2. Use a raised dot. For example, $P \cdot R$.
3. Place the numbers and letters next to each other. For example, $7a$ means $7 \times a$ or $7 \cdot a$; bc means $b \times c$ or $b \cdot c$

For other operations we use the same symbols as are used in arithmetic. In order to use algebra effectively, you must learn how to translate from ordinary language into symbols and letters.

EXAMPLE: John is x years old. How old will he be 7 years from now?
ANSWER: $x + 7$

EXAMPLE: An apple costs a cents. What is the cost of 6 apples?
ANSWER: $6 \times a$, or $6 \cdot a$, or $6a$ ($6a$ is preferred)

EXAMPLE: Alice weighed y pounds a year ago. Since then she has lost 9 pounds. What is her present weight?
ANSWER: $y - 9$

EXAMPLE: Take a number z. Increase it by 2. Multiply the result by 6.
ANSWER: $6(z + 2)$. Notice that the number represented by $(z + 2)$ is to be multiplied by 6. The answer might also be written $(z + 2)6$.

PRACTICE

Directions: Solve the following problems and blacken the space at the right under the number which corresponds to the one you have selected as the right answer.

1. A sweater costs $18. The cost of c sweaters is
   (1) $18 + c$ (4) $18c$
   (2) $18 \div c$ (5) $c - 18$
   (3) $c \div 18$

   1. 1 2 3 4 5
   || || || || ||

2. Fred is x years old. Bill is 4 years younger. Bill's age is
   (1) $x + 4$ (4) $4x$
   (2) $x - 4$ (5) $4x - 4$
   (3) $4 - x$

   2. 1 2 3 4 5
   || || || || ||

3. A car travels y miles per hour. The distance covered by the car in z hours is
   (1) $y + z$ (4) $y \div z$
   (2) $y - z$ (5) $z \div y$
   (3) yz

   3. 1 2 3 4 5
   || || || || ||

4. Bob had $15 and spent x dollars. The amount he had left was
   (1) $x - 15$ (4) $x \div 15$
   (2) $15x$ (5) $15 - x$
   (3) $15 \div x$

   4. 1 2 3 4 5
   || || || || ||

5. If 12 eggs cost a cents, the cost of one egg is
   (1) $12a$ (4) $12 + a$
   (2) $12/a$ (5) $a - 12$
   (3) $a/12$

   5. 1 2 3 4 5
   || || || || ||

6. Paul bought 3 ties at x dollars each. The change that he received in dollars from a $20 bill was
   (1) $3x$ (4) $20 - 3x$
   (2) $20 + 3x$ (5) $3x \div 20$
   (3) $3x - 20$

   6. 1 2 3 4 5
   || || || || ||

7. Mr. Barry bought a suit for y dollars. The sales tax rate on the purchase was 3%. The sales tax was

    (1) 0.03y   (4) $y \div 3$

    (2) 3y   (5) $y + 0.03y$

    (3) $0.03 + y$

7. 1 2 3 4 5

    || || || || ||

8. Bill had y dollars. He bought a articles at b dollars each. The number of dollars Bill had left was

    (1) $ab - y$ (4) y/ab

    (2) $ab + y$ (5) aby

    (3) $y - ab$

8. 1 2 3 4 5

    || || || || ||

Answers:

1. 4   2. 2   3. 3   4. 5   5. 3   6. 4   7. 1   8. 3

II. B. Exponents and Evaluations

B-1

There are times when we wish to multiply a number by itself. Of course, if we wish to multiply 7 by itself, we can write 7×7. However, in modern science where we may have occasion to multiply a number by itself many times, it becomes awkward to write such numbers as $7 \times 7 \times 7 \times 7 \times 7 \times 7 \times 7 \times 7 \times 7$. Instead, we use a shortcut and write the product of nine sevens as 7^9. In this case, 9 is known as an *exponent* and 7 is called the *base*.

> EXAMPLES: 6^3 means $6 \times 6 \times 6$.
>
> a^5 means $a \times a \times a \times a \times a$.
>
> $3b^4$ means $3 \times b \times b \times b \times b$.

We often wish to find the numerical value of an algebraic expression when we know the numerical value assigned to each letter of the expression. The following examples show how this is done.

> EXAMPLE: Find the numerical value of $5x + 3y - 7z$ when $x = 6$, $y = 4$, and $z = 1$.
>
> $$5x + 3y - 7z = (5 \cdot 6) + (3 \cdot 4) - (7 \cdot 1)$$
> $$= 30 + 12 - 7$$
> $$= 35$$

> EXAMPLE: Find the value of $4a^3 - 2b + 9c^2$ when $a = 5$, $b = 3$, and $c = 2$.
>
> $$4a^3 - 2b + 9c^2 = (4 \cdot 5^3) - (2 \cdot 3) + (9 \cdot 2^2)$$
> $$= (4 \cdot 125) - (6) + (9 \cdot 4)$$
> $$= (500) - (6) + (36)$$
> $$= 530$$

> EXAMPLE: Find the value of $5(x^3 - 2y^2)$ when $x = 4$ and $y = 3$.
>
> $$5(x^3 - 2y^2) = 5(4^3 - 2 \cdot 3^2) = 5(64 - 18)$$
> $$= 5 \cdot 46$$
> $$= 230$$

PRACTICE

Directions: Solve the following problems and blacken the space at the right under the number which corresponds to the one you have selected as the right answer.

In the following examples, $x = 5$, $y = 4$, $z = 3$, $a = 2$, and $b = 1$.

1. The value of $2x^3 + 3y$ is
   - (1) 112
   - (2) 32
   - (3) 47
   - (4) 262
   - (5) 98

   1. 1 2 3 4 5
   || || || || ||

2. The value of $3x + 5a - 7b$ is
   - (1) 18
   - (2) 17
   - (3) 15
   - (4) 20
   - (5) 37

   2. 1 2 3 4 5
   || || || || ||

3. The value of $3ab + x^2y$ is
   - (1) 9
   - (2) 32
   - (3) 11
   - (4) 15
   - (5) 106

   3. 1 2 3 4 5
   || || || || ||

4. The value of $2x^2 - y^2 + 5ab$ is
   - (1) 54
   - (2) 94
   - (3) 44
   - (4) 92
   - (5) 78

   4. 1 2 3 4 5
   || || || || ||

5. The value of $3x^2y^3z$ is
   - (1) 8,100
   - (2) 14,400
   - (3) 96
   - (4) 900
   - (5) 1,800

   5. 1 2 3 4 5
   || || || || ||

6. The value of $\dfrac{y^2}{a^2}$ is
   - (1) 8
   - (2) 2
   - (3) 16
   - (4) 4
   - (5) 36

   6. 1 2 3 4 5
   || || || || ||

7. The value of $\dfrac{a^3}{y} + 2xz$ is
   - (1) 23
   - (2) 31
   - (3) 9
   - (4) 32
   - (5) 54

   7. 1 2 3 4 5
   || || || || ||

8. The value of $\dfrac{4x^2}{5a} + 3y^2 - z^3$ is
   - (1) 21
   - (2) 29
   - (3) 32
   - (4) 46
   - (5) 31

   8. 1 2 3 4 5
   || || || || ||

Answers:

5 **8.** 4 **7.** 2 **6.** 1 **5.** 3 **4.** 5 **3.** 2 **2.** 4 **1.**

II. C. Formulas

C-1

Mr. Wells had a garden 60 feet long and 40 feet wide. He wished to fence in the garden. How many feet of fencing did he need?

We can see that Mr. Wells needed two lengths of 60 feet each and two widths of 40 feet each.

Thus, he needed $(2 \times 60) + (2 \times 40)$, or $120 + 80 = 200$ feet.

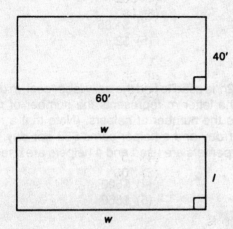

Now, suppose that we wish to find a formula to find the distance around the *rectangle* (called "the *perimeter*"). A rectangle is a figure having four sides and four right angles. If we represent the perimeter by P, the length by l, and the width by w,

> **Perimeter of a Rectangle**
> $P = l + w + l + w$
> or $P = 2l + 2w$

We can write this as $P = 2(l + w)$.
$P = 2l + 2w$, or $P = 2(l + w)$, is an example of a *formula* in mathematics.

EXAMPLE: The formula $C = 40 + 8(n - 3)$ gives the cost of borrowing a book from a circulating library. The minimum number of days is 3 and the minimum cost is 40 cents. In this formula, $C = $ cost, in cents, and $n = $ the number of days for which the book is borrowed. What is the cost of borrowing a book for 7 days?

$$C = 40 + 8(n - 3)$$
$$C = 40 + 8(7 - 3)$$
$$C = 40 + 8(4)$$
$$C = 40 + 32 = 72 \text{ cents}$$

PRACTICE

Directions: Solve the following problems and blacken the space at the right under the number which corresponds to the one you have selected as the right answer.

1. Mr. Dale wishes to fence in a rectangular lawn which is 60 feet long and 30 feet wide. He uses the formula $P = 2(l + w)$ to obtain the result. The perimeter, in feet, is

   (1) 90   (4) 180
   (2) 120   (5) 200
   (3) 150

1. 1 2 3 4 5
‖ ‖ ‖ ‖ ‖

2. The formula $A = \dfrac{a+b+c}{3}$ is used to find the average (A) of three numbers a, b, and c. The average of 95, 119, and 104 is

   (1) 108   (4) 104⅔
   (2) 106   (5) 110
   (3) 160

2. 1 2 3 4 5
‖ ‖ ‖ ‖ ‖

3. The formula $C = 80 + 15(n-4)$ is used to find the cost, C, of a taxi ride where n represents the number of $\frac{1}{4}$ miles of the ride. The cost of a taxi ride of $2\frac{3}{4}$ miles is
(1) $0.95
(2) $3
(3) $1.65
(4) $1.85
(5) $2

3. 1 2 3 4 5 || || || || ||

4. The formula $C = 72m + 32h$ is used to find the daily labor cost, in dollars, of a job in carpentry. The letter m represents the number of master carpenters; h represents the number of helpers. (Note that a master carpenter earns $72 per day and a helper earns $32 per day.) On a certain job, 6 master carpenters are used and 4 helpers are used. The daily labor cost is
(1) $480
(2) $550
(3) $650
(4) $600
(5) $560

4. 1 2 3 4 5 || || || || ||

5. The formula for the relationship between the length (L) and width (W) of a certain flag is $L = 1.8W$. A flag has a width of 5 feet. Its length is
(1) 2.3 feet
(2) 9 feet
(3) 90 feet
(4) 1.3 feet
(5) 8 feet

5. 1 2 3 4 5 || || || || ||

6. The weight of an adult is given by the formula $W = 1\frac{1}{2}(h-60) + 110$ where W = weight in pounds and h = height in inches. If Mr. Conrad is 68 inches tall, he should weigh, in pounds,
(1) 144
(2) 164
(3) 154
(4) 174
(5) 184

6. 1 2 3 4 5 || || || || ||

Answers:

3. 6   2. 5   5. 4   4. 3   2. 2   4. 1

II. D. Solving Equations

D-1

The ability to solve equations is important because it enables us to solve many different types of problems. In this section, you will learn how to solve some of the simpler kinds of equations. In a later section you will apply these skills in problem solving.

| An equation states that two quantities are equal |

Consider the equation

$$3x + 2 = 20$$

This tells us that $3x + 2$ and 20 name the same number. If this is so, then x must represent the number 6 since

$$3 \times 6 + 2 = 20$$

And 6 is the only number which will replace x and make $3x + 2$ equal 20. The number 6, which makes the statement $3x + 2 = 20$ true, is called the *root of the equation* and is said to satisfy the equation, or to *balance* the equation.

PRACTICE

Directions: Solve the following problems and blacken the space at the right under the number which corresponds to the one you have selected as the right answer.

In each case, select the root of the equation.

1. $x + 2 = 9$
   (1) 5
   (2) 9
   (3) 7
   (4) 3
   (5) 10

2. $x - 3 = 5$
   (1) 5
   (2) 3
   (3) 2
   (4) 10
   (5) 8

3. $2x = 10$
   (1) 8
   (2) 5
   (3) 20
   (4) ⅕
   (5) 9

4. $\dfrac{x}{3} = 4$
   (1) 12
   (2) ⁴⁄₃
   (3) ¾
   (4) 1
   (5) 6

5. $2x + 1 = 7$
   (1) 4
   (2) 3½
   (3) 5
   (4) 3
   (5) 6

6. $2x - 1 = 9$
   (1) 10
   (2) 8
   (3) 5
   (4) 4
   (5) 3

7. $\dfrac{x}{2} + 3 = 7$
   (1) 4
   (2) 8
   (3) 1½
   (4) 2½
   (5) 20

8. $\dfrac{x}{3} - 1 = 5$
   (1) 18
   (2) 12
   (3) 2
   (4) 6
   (5) 15

9. $\dfrac{2x}{5} + 1 = 9$
   (1) 8
   (2) 50
   (3) 20
   (4) 6
   (5) 4

10. $\dfrac{3x}{4} - 2 = 1$
    (1) 5
    (2) 6
    (3) 12
    (4) 4
    (5) 9

11. $2x + 3 = 10$
   (1) 4
   (2) $6\frac{1}{2}$
   (3) $3\frac{1}{2}$
   (4) $7\frac{1}{2}$
   (5) 5

11. 1 2 3 4 5
   || || || || ||

12. $3x - 4 = 6$
   (1) $3\frac{1}{3}$
   (2) $\frac{2}{3}$
   (3) 2
   (4) $3\frac{1}{2}$
   (5) 7

12. 1 2 3 4 5
   || || || || ||

Answers:

1. 3	3. 2	5. 4	7. 2	9. 3	11. 3
2. 5	4. 1	6. 3	8. 1	10. 4	12. 1

We will now study **systematic methods of finding the root of an equation.**

Consider the equation $x + 2 = 5$. This tells us that a certain number added to 2 will give us the result of 5. We can see that $x = 3$. Now, how can we get from
$$x + 2 = 5$$
to $x = 3$?
To get from $x + 2$ to x, we need only to subtract 2 from $x + 2$. Thus, $x + 2 - 2 = x$. Since $x + 2$ and 5 name the same number, we may subtract the same number from $x + 2$ and from 5 to obtain equal results.
$$x + 2 - 2 = 5 - 2$$
$$\text{or } x = 3$$
Consider the equation $x - 1 = 5$. In order to obtain x on the left side of the equation, we add 1 to $x - 1$. Since $x - 1$ and 5 name the same number, we may add 1 to both $x - 1$ and 5 to obtain equal results.
$$x - 1 + 1 = 5 + 1$$
$$\text{or } x = 6$$
Consider the equation $2x = 12$. In order to obtain x on the left side of the equation we must divide $2x$ (twice x) by 2. Since $2x$ and 12 name the same number, we divide both $2x$ and 12 by 2 to obtain equal results.
$$2x = 12$$
$$\frac{2x}{2} = \frac{12}{2}$$
$$1x, \text{ or } x = 6$$

Consider the equation $\frac{y}{3} = 4$. In order to obtain y on the left side of the equation, we must multiply $\frac{y}{3}$, or $\frac{1}{3}$ of y, by 3. Since $\frac{y}{3}$ and 4 name the same number, we multiply both $\frac{y}{3}$ and 4 to obtain equal results.
$$\frac{y}{3} = 4$$
$$3 \times \frac{y}{3} = 3 \times 4$$
$$y = 12$$

To remember these procedures, note the following:

> *Methods of Finding the Root of an Equation*
>
> **1.** Subtract when there is a sum. For example, $x + 2 - 2 = 5 - 2$.
>
> **2.** Add when there is a difference. For example, $x - 1 + 1 = 5 + 1$.
>
> **3.** Divide when there is a product. For example, $\frac{2x}{2} = \frac{12}{2}$.
>
> **4.** Multiply when there is a quotient. For example, $3 \times \frac{y}{3} = 3 \times 4$.

PRACTICE

Solve the following equations:

1. $x+1=3$, $x=$___	**6.** $x-3=4$, $x=$___	**11.** $x-2=9$, $x=$___	**16.** $x-1=5$, $x=$___
2. $x-2=4$, $x=$___	**7.** $5x=10$, $x=$___	**12.** $x+4=7$, $x=$___	**17.** $3x=21$, $x=$___
3. $3x=12$, $x=$___	**8.** $x/4=2$, $x=$___	**13.** $x/5=2$, $x=$___	**18.** $x+4=7$, $x=$___
4. $x/2=5$, $x=$___	**9.** $x+2=9$, $x=$___	**14.** $3x=18$, $x=$___	**19.** $x/4=3$, $x=$___
5. $x+5=7$, $x=$___	**10.** $5x=15$, $x=$___	**15.** $x+9=11$, $x=$___	**20.** $x-5=11$, $x=$___

Answers:

1. 2	**5.** 2	**9.** 7	**13.** 10	**17.** 7
2. 6	**6.** 7	**10.** 3	**14.** 6	**18.** 3
3. 4	**7.** 2	**11.** 11	**15.** 2	**19.** 12
4. 10	**8.** 8	**12.** 3	**16.** 9	**20.** 16

D-2

Solving More Difficult Equations. In order to solve interesting problems, it is necessary to be able to solve more difficult equations.

EXAMPLE: Solve the equation $5x+2x=28$.

Since $5x+2x=7x$, we have

$$7x=28$$
$$x={}^{28}/_7$$
$$x=4$$

EXAMPLE: Solve the equation $\frac{2}{3}x=16$.

In order to obtain x on the left side, we must multiply $\frac{2}{3}x$ by $\frac{3}{2}$. Since $\frac{2}{3}x$ and 16 name the same number, we multiply both $\frac{2}{3}x$ and 16 to obtain equal results.

$$\frac{\cancel{3}}{\cancel{2}} \cdot \frac{\cancel{2}}{\cancel{3}}x = \frac{3}{2} \cdot 16$$
$$x = 24$$

EXAMPLE: Solve the equation $2x+3=15$.

$$2x+3=15$$
$$2x+3-3=15-3$$
$$2x=12$$
$$\frac{2x}{2}=\frac{12}{2}$$
$$x=6$$

EXAMPLE: Solve the equation $\frac{3}{5}x-1=8$.

$$\frac{3}{5}x-1=8$$

$$\frac{3}{5}x-1+1=8+1$$

$$\frac{3}{5}x=9$$

$$\frac{\cancel{5}}{\cancel{3}} \cdot \frac{\cancel{3}}{\cancel{5}}x=\frac{5}{3} \cdot 9$$

$$x=15$$

PRACTICE

Solve the following equations:

1. $2x + 3x = 40$, $x =$ _____
2. $\frac{2}{3}x = 12$, $x =$ _____
3. $4x - 1 = 27$, $x =$ _____
4. $x/5 + 4 = 6$, $x =$ _____
5. $3x - 5 = 16$, $x =$ _____
6. $3x + 7 = 37$, $x =$ _____
7. $4x - 2 = 22$, $x =$ _____
8. $x/2 - 3 = 5$, $x =$ _____

9. $2x + x + 5 = 17$, $x =$ _____
10. $\frac{4}{5}x + 2 = 30$, $x =$ _____
11. $\frac{2}{3}x + 5 = 7$, $x =$ _____
12. $5x - 2x + 4 = 31$, $x =$ _____
13. $x/7 + 5 = 6$, $x =$ _____
14. $3x + 2x + 1 = 21$, $x =$ _____
15. $2x + x - 3 = 12$, $x =$ _____
16. $\frac{3}{4}x - 7 = 8$, $x =$ _____

Answers:

1. 8   3. 7   5. 7   7. 6   9. 4   11. 3   13. 7   15. 5
2. 18   4. 10   6. 10   8. 16   10. 35 12. 9   14. 4   16. 20

II. E. Solving Word Problems

We may use equations to solve problems stated in words, such as the following.

EXAMPLE: A plumber must cut a pipe 50 inches long into two pieces so that one piece will be 12 inches longer than the other piece. Find the length of each piece.

Let x = the length of one piece
And $x + 12$ = the length of the other piece.
Since the sum of the two pieces is 50 inches, we have

$$x + x + 12 = 50$$
$$2x + 12 = 50$$
$$2x + 12 - 12 = 50 - 12$$
$$2x = 38$$
$$\frac{2x}{2} = \frac{38}{2}$$
$$x = 19$$

One piece is 19 inches long and the other piece is 31 inches long.

EXAMPLE: Divide an estate of $46,000 among three sons so that the second son gets $6,000 more than the youngest, and the eldest son gets three times as much as the youngest.

Let x = amount the youngest son gets
And $x + 6,000$ = amount the second son gets
And $3x$ = amount the eldest son gets.

$$x + x + 6,000 + 3x = 46,000$$
$$5x + 6,000 = 46,000$$
$$5x + 6,000 - 6,000 = 46,000 - 6,000$$
$$5x = 40,000$$
$$\frac{5x}{5} = \frac{40,000}{5}$$
$$x = 8,000$$

The youngest son gets $8,000.
The second son gets $8,000 + $6,000 = $14,000.
The eldest son gets $3 \times $8,000 = $24,000.

EXAMPLE: Eighteen coins, consisting of nickels and dimes, have a total value of $1.25. How many dimes are there?

Let x = the number of dimes
And $18 - x$ = the number of nickels.
$10x$ = the value of the dimes
$5(18-x)$ = the value of the nickels

$$10x + 5(18-x) = 125$$
$$10x + 90 - 5x = 125$$
$$5x + 90 = 125$$
$$5x + 90 - 90 = 125 - 90$$
$$5x = 35$$
$$\frac{5x}{5} = \frac{35}{5}$$
$$x = 7$$

There are 7 dimes.

EXAMPLE: A dealer has some candy worth 75 cents per pound, and some candy worth 55 cents per pound. He wishes to make a mixture of 80 pounds that will sell for 60 cents per pound. How many pounds of each type of candy should he use?

Let x = the number of pounds of 75-cent candy
And $80-x$ = the number of pounds of 55-cent candy.
$75x$ = the value of the 75-cent candy
$55(80-x)$ = the value of the 55-cent candy
80×60, or 4,800 cents = the value of the mixture

$$75x + 55(80-x) = 4800$$
$$75x + 4400 - 55x = 4800$$
$$20x + 4400 = 4800$$
$$20x + 4400 - 4400 = 4800 - 4400$$
$$20x = 400$$
$$\frac{20x}{20} = \frac{400}{20}$$
$$x = 20$$

The dealer uses 20 pounds of the 75-cent candy.
The dealer uses $80-20$, or 60 pounds, of the 55-cent candy.

EXAMPLE: An investment of $12,500, part at 8% and part at 7%, earns a yearly income of $955. Find the amount invested at each rate.

Let x = the amount invested at 8%
And $12,500 - x$ = the amount invested at 7%.
$0.08x$ = the income on the 8% investment
$0.07(12,500 - x)$ = the income on the 7% investment

$$0.08x + 0.07(12,500 - x) = 955$$
$$0.08x + 875 - 0.07x = 955$$
$$0.01x + 875 = 955$$
$$0.01x + 875 - 875 = 955 - 875$$
$$0.01x = 80$$
$$\frac{1}{100}x = 80$$
$$100(\frac{1}{100}x) = 100 \times 80$$
$$x = 8,000$$

$8,000 was invested at 8%.
$12,500 - $8,000 = $4,500 was invested at 7%.

EXAMPLE: Two cars start at the same time from two cities 480 miles apart and travel toward each other. One car averages 35 miles per hour, and the other car averages 45 miles per hour. In how many hours will the two cars meet?

Let x = the number of hours it takes the two cars to meet.

In problems involving motion, it is convenient to collect our information in a box as shown below, with the formula Rate × Time = Distance.

	RATE	×	TIME	=	DISTANCE
FIRST CAR	35		x		$35x$
SECOND CAR	45		x		$45x$

Since the sum of the two distances covered is 480 miles, we have

$$35x + 45x = 480$$
$$80x = 480$$
$$\frac{80x}{80} = \frac{480}{80}$$
$$x = 6$$

The cars will meet in 6 hours.

PRACTICE

Solve the following problems:

1. Two partners in a business earn $60,000 one year. If the senior partner's share is 3 times that of the junior partner, what is the junior partner's share? _____

2. A wooden beam is 58 inches long. A carpenter must cut the beam so that the longer part is 8 inches longer than the shorter part. How long is the shorter part? _____

3. A certain kind of concrete contains five times as much gravel as cement. How many cubic feet of each of these materials will there be in 426 cubic feet of the concrete? _____

4. The length of a field is 3 times its width. If the perimeter (distance around the field) of the field is 312 feet, what is the width of the field? _____

5. A master carpenter earns $5 more per hour than his helper. Together they earn $119 for a 7-hour job. How much does the helper earn per hour? _____

6. A boy has $3.75 in nickels and dimes. If he has 6 more dimes than nickels, how many dimes does he have? _____

7. Mr. Dale asked his son to deposit $495 in the bank. There were exactly 70 bills, consisting of 10-dollar bills and 5-dollar bills. Find the number of 10-dollar bills he had to deposit. _____

8. The perimeter of a triangle is 27 inches. One side is 3 inches longer than the shortest side, and the longest side is twice the length of the shortest side. What is the length of the shorter side? _____

9. The sum of two numbers is 50. If the larger one is 5 more than twice the smaller number, what is the smaller number? _____

10. A dealer wishes to mix candy worth 90 cents per pound with candy worth 65 cents per pound in order to obtain 40 pounds of candy to be sold at 75 cents per pound. How many pounds of the 90-cent candy should he use? _____

11. Mr. Charles invests $20,000, part at 5% and the rest at 4%. If he obtains an annual income of $920, how much does he invest at each rate? _____

12. Tickets at a movie house cost $2 for adults and $1 for children. For a matinee performance, 800 tickets were sold, and the receipts were $1,150. How many adult tickets were sold? _____

13. At a sale, some radio sets were sold for $50 each and the rest for $35 each. If 175 sets were sold and the receipts were $7,250, how many $50 sets were sold? _____

14. Mr. Carter invested a sum of money at 4%. He invested a second sum, $400 more than the first sum, at 6%. If the total annual income was $184, how much did he invest at each rate? _____

15. In basketball, a foul basket counts 1 point and a field basket counts 2 points. A team scored 73 points, making 8 more field baskets than foul baskets. How many foul baskets did the team make? _____

16. A sofa was marked for sale at $270. This was a discount of 25% on the original sale price. What was the original sale price? _____

17. The sum of the ages of a father and son is 62. If the father is 11 years more than twice the age of the son, how old is the son? _____

18. A boy has $4.35 in nickels and dimes. If he has 12 more dimes than nickels, how many nickels does he have? _____

19. The perimeter of a rectangular field is 204 feet. If the length is 3 feet less than 4 times the width, what is the width of the field? _____

20. A dealer wishes to mix candy selling for $1.32 per pound with candy selling for $1.20 per pound to produce a mixture of 20 pounds that will sell for $1.29 per pound. How many pounds of $1.32 candy should he use? _____

21. Two cars start at the same time to travel toward each other from points 440 miles apart. If the first car averages 42 miles per hour and the second car averages 46 miles per hour, in how many hours will they meet? _____

22. Two trains start at the same time and travel in opposite directions. The first train averages 39 miles per hour and the second train averages 43 miles per hour. In how many hours are the trains 574 miles apart? _____

23. Two trains are 800 miles apart. They start at 9:00 A.M. traveling toward each other. One train travels at an average rate of 45 miles per hour and the other train travels at an average rate of 55 miles per hour. At what time do the trains meet? _____

24. Two motorboats start at the same time from the same place and travel in opposite directions. If their rates are 12 miles per hour and 16 miles per hour respectively, in how many hours will they be 140 miles apart? _____

Answers:

1. $15,000	9. 15	16. $360
2. 25 inches	10. 16	17. 17
3. 71 cubic feet of cement	11. $12,000 at 5%	18. 21
355 cubic feet of gravel	$8,000 at 4%	19. 21 feet
4. 39 feet	12. 350	20. 15
5. $6	13. 75	21. 5 hours
6. 27	14. $1,600 at 4%	22. 7 hours
7. 29	$2,000 at 5%	23. 5:00 P.M.
8. 6 inches	15. 19	24. 5 hours

II. F. Solving Inequalities

F-1

Recall that the symbol > means *is greater than* and that the symbol < means *is less than*. For example, 9>5 and 3<8.

An inequality is a statement in which two quantities are unequal. Consider the inequality
$$3x + 1 > 7$$
This tells us that $3x + 1$ names a number that is greater than 7. If this is so, then x must represent a number that is greater than 2. If $x = 2$, we have $3 \cdot 2 + 1 = 7$. When $x > 2$, $3x + 1 > 7$. For example, when $x = 5$, $3x + 1 = 16$. Thus, the solution of the inequality $3x + 1 > 7$ is $x > 2$. Note that the inequality $3x + 1 > 7$ has an infinite number of solutions. For example, some solutions are 2.1, 4, 5½, 7, and 8.67 since the replacement of x by any of these numbers will make the inequality true.

PRACTICE

Directions: In each case, select the number which is a solution of the given inequality.

1. $2x + 3 > 11$
   - (1) 4
   - (2) 1
   - (3) 2½
   - (4) 5
   - (5) 3

   1. 1 2 3 4 5
   ‖ ‖ ‖ ‖ ‖

2. $3x - 1 > 5$
   - (1) 1
   - (2) 2
   - (3) 6
   - (4) 1½
   - (5) 0

   2. 1 2 3 4 5
   ‖ ‖ ‖ ‖ ‖

3. $x + 2 < 7$
   - (1) 6
   - (2) 8
   - (3) 5
   - (4) 3
   - (5) 10

   3. 1 2 3 4 5
   ‖ ‖ ‖ ‖ ‖

4. $2x - 3 < 5$
   - (1) 2
   - (2) 5
   - (3) 7
   - (4) 6
   - (5) 4

   4. 1 2 3 4 5
   ‖ ‖ ‖ ‖ ‖

5. $5x + 2 > 17$
   - (1) 1
   - (2) 3
   - (3) 4
   - (4) 2
   - (5) 0

   5. 1 2 3 4 5
   ‖ ‖ ‖ ‖ ‖

6. $4x - 3 < 9$
   - (1) 5
   - (2) 2
   - (3) 4
   - (4) 7
   - (5) 9

   6. 1 2 3 4 5
   ‖ ‖ ‖ ‖ ‖

Answers:

1. 4 2. 3 3. 4 4. 1 5. 3 6. 2

We will now study systematic methods of solving inequalities.

Consider the inequality $x + 3 > 7$. This tells us that when certain numbers are added to 3, the result is greater than 7. We can see that x must be greater than 4, or $x > 4$. Now, how can we get from
$$x + 3 > 7$$
to $x > 4$?

To get from $x + 3$ to x we need only to subtract 3 from $x + 3$. Since subtracting the same quantity from both members of an inequality does not change the sense of the inequality, we may subtract 3 from 7 to get the result:
$$x + 3 - 3 > 7 - 3$$
$$x > 4$$

Consider the inequality $x-2<4$. In order to obtain x on the left side, we add 2 to $x-2$. Since adding the same quantity to both members of an inequality does not change the sense of the inequality, we may add 2 to 4 to obtain the result:

$$x-2+2<4+2$$
$$x<6$$

Consider the inequality $2x<10$. In order to obtain x on the left side of the inequality, we must divide $2x$ by 2. Since dividing both members of an inequality by a positive number does not change the sense of the inequality, we may divide 10 by 2 to obtain the result:

$$\frac{2x}{2}<\frac{10}{2}$$
$$x<5$$

Consider the inequality $\frac{y}{3}>2$. In order to obtain y on the left side of the inequality, we must multiply $\frac{y}{3}$ by 3. Since multiplying both members of an inequality by a positive number does not change the sense of the inequality, we may multiply 2 by 3 to obtain the result:

$$3\times\frac{y}{3}>3\times2$$
$$y>6$$

EXAMPLE: Solve the inequality $x+5>7$.
$$x+5>7$$
$$x+5-5>7-5$$
$$x>2$$

EXAMPLE: Solve the inequality $y-1<4$.
$$y-1<4$$
$$y-1+1<4+1$$
$$y<5$$

EXAMPLE: Solve the inequality $3x<18$.
$$3x<18$$
$$\frac{3x}{3}<\frac{18}{3}$$
$$x<6$$

EXAMPLE: Solve the inequality $\frac{y}{4}>2$.

$$\frac{y}{4}>2$$

$$4\times\frac{y}{4}>4\times2$$

$$y>8$$

PRACTICE

Solve the following inequalities:

1. $x+2>5$, $x>$_____
2. $x-3>1$, $x>$_____
3. $2y<8$, $y<$_____
4. $y/2>6$, $y>$_____
5. $y-3<2$, $y<$_____
6. $y/4>3$, $y>$_____
7. $x-5>2$, $x>$_____
8. $2y<12$, $y<$_____
9. $y+1<10$, $y<$_____
10. $x-3<4$, $x<$_____

Answers:

1. $x>3$	3. $y>4$	5. $y>5$	7. $x>7$	9. $y>6$
2. $x<4$	4. $y>12$	6. $y>12$	8. $y>6$	10. $x>7$

F-2
Solving more difficult inequalities.

EXAMPLE: Solve the inequality $2y+3>11$.

$$2y+3-3>11-3$$
$$2y>8$$
$$\frac{2y}{2}>\frac{8}{2}$$
$$y>4$$

EXAMPLE: Solve the inequality $\frac{y}{4}-1<5$.

$$\frac{y}{4}-1<5$$
$$\frac{y}{4}-1+1<5+1$$
$$\frac{y}{4}<6$$
$$4\times\frac{y}{4}<4\times6$$
$$y<24$$

PRACTICE

Solve the following inequalities:

1. $2x+1>7$, $x>$_____
2. $3y-2<4$, $y<$_____
3. $4x-7>5$, $x>$_____
4. $y/2+1<5$, $y<$_____
5. $y/3-4>1$, $y>$_____
6. $5y+1<6$, $y<$_____
7. $7y-2>19$, $y>$_____
8. $y/4+3>5$, $y>$_____

Answers:

1. $x>3$	2. $y<2$	3. $x>3$	4. $y<8$	5. $y>15$	6. $y<1$	7. $y>3$	8. $y>8$

II. G. RATIO AND PROPORTION

G-1

We may compare two numbers by subtraction or by division. For example, Mr. Carson earns $48 per day and Mr. Burns earns $36 per day. We may say that Mr. Carson earns $12 per day more than Mr. Burns. Or, we may say that the ratio of Mr. Carson's earnings per day to Mr. Burns' earnings per day is $^{48}/_{36}$. We may reduce $^{48}/_{36}$ to $^4/_3$, which indicates that Mr. Carson earns $1\frac{1}{3}$ times as much per day as Mr. Burns.

The comparison of the two pay rates may be written as $^{48}/_{36}$ or as $48:36$. In general, the ratio of a number a to a number b (b cannot be 0) is a/b, or $a:b$.

EXAMPLE: At a party there are 12 men and 8 women. What is the ratio of men to women? The ratio is $^{12}/_8$ or $12:8$. In simplest form, this is $^3/_2$, or $3:2$.

The Basics of Mathematics • **165**

EXAMPLE: At the same party, what is the ratio of women to men?
The ratio is $^8/_{12}$ or $8:12$. In simplest form, this is $^2/_3$, or $2:3$.

EXAMPLE: At the same party, what is the ratio of men to the number of people at the party?
The ratio is $^{12}/_{20}$ or $12:20$. In simplest form, this is $^3/_5$, or $3:5$.

EXAMPLE:

If $AB:BC=2:3$ and if $BC = 24$ inches, what is the length of AB?

Let $AB = 2x$
And $BC = 3x$.

We know that $3x = 24$
$$\tfrac{1}{3}(3x) = \tfrac{1}{3}(24)$$
$$x = 8$$
Since $x = 8$, $2x\ (AB) = 2 \cdot 8 = 16$
Therefore, $AB = 16$ inches.

Consider the following problem:
A baseball team wins 15 games out of 30 games played. If the team continues to win at the same rate, how many games will it win out of 40 games played?
Let n = number of games team will win in 40 games played.
The ratio of games won to games already played is $^{15}/_{30}$. Since the ratio of games won to games played is to remain the same, we may write this ratio as $n/40$. These ratios may also be written as $15:30$ and $n:40$.
We may now write the equation $^{15}/_{30} = n/40$. Such an equation, which tells us that one ratio is equal to another ratio, is called a *proportion*. Of course, in this case we know that $n = 20$, since the team wins $\tfrac{1}{2}$ of the games it plays.
Proportions have a very useful property which we will investigate. Consider the proportion
$$\tfrac{1}{3} = \tfrac{2}{6} \text{ or } 1:3 = 2:6$$
The two inside terms (3 and 2) are called the *means* of the proportion, and the two outside terms (1 and 6) are called the *extremes* of the proportion. Notice that if we multiply the two means, we obtain $3 \times 2 = 6$. Also, if we multiply the two extremes, we obtain $1 \times 6 = 6$. This illustrates the following property of proportions:

In a proportion, the product of the means is equal to the product of the extremes.

This property is very useful in solving problems.

EXAMPLE: The ratio of alcohol to water in a certain type of antifreeze is $3:4$. If a tank contains 24 quarts of alcohol, how many quarts of water must be added to make the antifreeze mixture?
Let x = the number of quarts needed.
$$\frac{\text{alcohol}}{\text{water}}\quad \frac{3}{4} = \frac{24}{x}$$
Now, we may use the property of proportions to find x.
$$3:4 = 24:x$$
$$3x = 4 \times 24$$
$$3x = 96$$
$$\tfrac{1}{3}(3x) = \tfrac{1}{3}(96)$$
$$x = 32 \text{ quarts of water}$$

Note: We may use the same property in the form

$$\frac{3}{4}\underset{x}{\overset{24}{\cancel{\times}}}$$

$$3x = 4 \times 24$$
$$3x = 96$$
$$x = 32$$

The following examples will indicate how we may use ratio and proportion to solve problems.

EXAMPLE: If 3 ties cost $12.57, what is the cost of 5 ties at the same rate?

Let $y =$ the cost of 5 ties.
We form the proportion

$$3 : 12.57 = 5 : x$$
$$\frac{3}{12.57} = \frac{5}{x}$$
$$3x = 5 \times 12.57 = 62.85$$
$$\frac{1}{3}(3x) = \frac{1}{3}(62.85)$$
$$x = \$20.95$$

5 ties cost $20.95 at the same rate.

EXAMPLE: The scale on a map is 1 inch to 60 miles. If the distance between two cities is $2\frac{3}{4}$ inches on the map, what is the actual distance between the two cities?

Let $d =$ the actual distance between the cities.

$$1 : 60 = 2\frac{3}{4} : d$$
$$1 \times d = 60 \times 2\frac{3}{4}$$
$$d = 60 \times \frac{11}{4} = 165$$

The actual distance is 165 miles.

EXAMPLE: Two numbers are in the ratio $9 : 5$. Their difference is 28. Find the numbers.

Let $9x =$ the larger number
And $5x =$ the smaller number.

Then $9x - 5x = 28$
$$4x = 28$$
$$\frac{1}{4}(4x) = \frac{1}{4}(28)$$
$$x = 7$$

The larger number is $9x$, or $9 \cdot 7 = 63$.
The smaller number is $5x$, or $5 \cdot 7 = 35$.

EXAMPLE: The numerator and denominator of a fraction are in the ratio $3 : 7$. If 2 is added to both the numerator and the denominator, the ratio becomes $1 : 2$. Find the original fraction.

Let $3n =$ the numerator of the fraction
And $7n =$ the denominator of the fraction.

If we add 2 to both the numerator and the denominator, the numerator becomes $3n + 2$ and the denominator becomes $7n + 2$. Thus, we have

$$\frac{3n+2}{7n+2} = \frac{1}{2}$$
$$1(7n + 2) = 2(3n + 2)$$
$$7n + 2 = 6n + 4$$
$$7n + 2 - 2 = 6n + 2$$
$$7n - 6n = 6n - 6n + 2$$
$$n = 2$$

The original denominator was 3n, or 3×2=6.
The original numerator was 7n, or 7×2=14.
The original fraction was ⁶/₁₄.

PRACTICE

Directions: Solve the following problems and blacken the space at the right under the number which corresponds to the one you have selected as the right answer.

1. At a dance, the ratio of the number of boys to the number of girls is 4:3. If there are 32 boys present, the number of girls present is
   (1) 36
   (2) 40
   (3) 20
   (4) 24
   (5) 28

   1. 1 2 3 4 5
   || || || || ||

2. John earned $150 one week and spent $120. The ratio of the amount John saved to the amount John spent is
   (1) 1:5
   (2) 1:4
   (3) 4:1
   (4) 4:5
   (5) 5:4

   2. 1 2 3 4 5
   || || || || ||

3. On a trip, a motorist drove x miles on a local road and y miles on a parkway. The ratio of the number of miles driven on the parkway to the total number of miles driven was
   (1) $\dfrac{y}{x}$
   (2) $\dfrac{x}{y}$
   (3) $\dfrac{y}{x+y}$
   (4) $\dfrac{x}{x+y}$
   (5) $\dfrac{x+y}{y}$

   3. 1 2 3 4 5
   || || || || ||

4. The ratio of a father's age to his son's age is 9:2. If the son's age is 12 years, the age of the father, in years, is
   (1) 45
   (2) 36
   (3) 63
   (4) 50
   (5) 54

   4. 1 2 3 4 5
   || || || || ||

5. On the line RS, RT=4 and RT:TS = 2:5. The length of RS is
   (1) 10
   (2) 12
   (3) 7
   (4) 9
   (5) 14

   5. 1 2 3 4 5
   || || || || ||

   R————————T——————————————————S

6. A picture measures 2 inches by 1½ inches. If the picture is enlarged so that the 2-inch dimension becomes 3 inches, the other dimension becomes
   (1) 2¼ inches
   (2) 2½ inches
   (3) 2 inches
   (4) 1¾ inches
   (5) 3¼ inches

   6. 1 2 3 4 5
   || || || || ||

7. If 3 shirts cost $23, the cost of a dozen shirts at the same rate is
   (1) $95
   (2) $84
   (3) $276
   (4) $92
   (5) $98.50

   7. 1 2 3 4 5
   || || || || ||

8. On a map, the scale is 1 inch to 80 miles. The actual distance between two cities is 200 miles. The distance between the cities, on the map, is

(1) 2 inches
(2) 3 inches
(3) 2½ inches
(4) 3½ inches
(5) 4 inches

8. 1 2 3 4 5

9. A certain recipe that will yield 4 portions calls for 1½ ounces of sugar. If the recipe is used to yield 6 portions, then the amount of sugar needed is

(1) 2½ ounces
(2) 2¼ ounces
(3) 2¾ ounces
(4) 2 ounces
(5) 3 ounces

9. 1 2 3 4 5

10. A gallon of paint covers 240 square feet of surface. If a living room contains 906 square feet of paintable surface and a kitchen contains 334 square feet of surface, the number of gallons of paint needed for the living room and kitchen is

(1) 6
(2) 4½
(3) 5⅙
(4) 5½
(5) 6½

10. 1 2 3 4 5

11. A recipe for hot chocolate calls for 2 ounces of chocolate, 4 cups of milk, and 4 tablespoons of sugar. If only 3 cups of milk are available, the number of ounces of chocolate to be used is

(1) 3
(2) ⅔
(3) 1½
(4) 6
(5) ¾

11. 1 2 3 4 5

12. Mr. Ash finds that he spends $47.50 for gas for each 1,000 miles that he drives his car. One month he drives his car 1,800 miles. The amount he spends for gas during that month is

(1) $855
(2) $95
(3) $82.50
(4) $85.50
(5) $8.55

12. 1 2 3 4 5

13. An artist finds that he obtains the most pleasing result when the ratio of the length of a painting to its width is 8 : 5. If the length of a painting is 2 feet 8 inches, then its width should be

(1) 2 feet
(2) 1 foot 8 inches
(3) 2 feet 8 inches
(4) 3 feet
(5) 2 feet 5 inches

13. 1 2 3 4 5

14. A recipe for chocolate fudge calls for ¾ cup of corn syrup and ½ teaspoon of salt. If 1 cup of corn syrup is used, the number of teaspoons of salt to be used is

(1) ⅔
(2) 1⅓
(3) ⅜
(4) 2⅔
(5) ¾

14. 1 2 3 4 5

15. It takes a train c hours to cover d miles. If the train travels k miles at the same rate, the number of hours it takes is

(1) cdk
(2) $\dfrac{d}{ck}$
(3) $\dfrac{dk}{c}$
(4) $\dfrac{ck}{d}$
(5) $\dfrac{cd}{k}$

15. 1 2 3 4 5

16. A man finds that he spends a total of y dollars per month for heating oil during 7 months of cold weather. If he wishes to prorate his cost over a 12-month period, the cost per month is

(1) $\dfrac{12}{7y}$

(2) $\dfrac{y}{12}$

(3) $\dfrac{12y}{7}$

(4) $\dfrac{7y}{12}$

(5) $84y$

17. A 25-acre field yields 375 bushels of wheat. How many acres should be planted to yield 525 bushels of wheat?

(1) 33

(2) 32

(3) 45

(4) 35

(5) 75

18. A house which is assessed at $30,000 is taxed $1,170. At the same rate, the tax on a house which is assessed for $40,000 is

(1) $992.50

(2) $156

(3) $1,560

(4) $2,340

(5) $1,360

19. A family consumes q quarts of milk each week. The number of quarts this family consumes in 10 days is

(1) $\dfrac{7q}{10}$

(2) $\dfrac{10g}{7}$

(3) $\dfrac{70}{q}$

(4) $\dfrac{10}{7q}$

(5) $\dfrac{q}{70}$

20. In making a certain type of concrete, the ratio of cement to sand used is $1:4$. In making x barrels of this concrete, the number of barrels of cement used is

(1) $\dfrac{x}{5}$

(2) $\dfrac{x}{4}$

(3) x

(4) $4x$

(5) $\dfrac{1}{5x}$

Answers:

20. 1	16. 4	12. 4	8. 3	4. 5
19. 2	15. 4	11. 3	7. 4	3. 3
18. 3	14. 1	10. 3	6. 1	2. 2
17. 4	13. 2	9. 2	5. 5	1. 4

III. GRAPHS

Pictures or graphs are often used in reports, magazines, and newspapers to present a set of numerical facts. This enables the viewer to make comparisons and to draw quick conclusions. In this section, we will learn how to interpret *pictographs, bar graphs, line graphs, circle graphs,* and *formula graphs.*

III. A. Pictographs

A-1

A *pictograph* is a graph in which objects are used to represent numbers.

EXAMPLE:

Population of Various Cities in a Certain State

City A

City B

City C

City D

City E

Each House Symbol Represents 10,000 People

1. Which city has the largest population?

ANSWER: City E

2. By how many people does the population of the largest city exceed the population of the next largest city?

ANSWER: City E has 80,000 people.
City C has 60,000 people.
City E has 20,000 people more than City C.

3. What is the ratio of the population of City B to City C?

ANSWER: City B has a population of 45,000.
City C has a population of 60,000.
Ratio is 45,000:60,000.
This ratio can be simplified to 3:4.

4. If City D's population is increased by 40%, what will its population be?

ANSWER: City D has a population of 25,000. If the population is increased by 40%, we have 25,000 × 0.4 = 10,000 more people.
City D's population will become 35,000.

III. B. Bar Graphs

B-1

Bar graphs are used to show relationships in a set of quantities. Here, bars are used very much like pictures in a pictograph.

EXAMPLE: In a recent year, a large industrial concern used each dollar of its sales income as shown in the graph below.

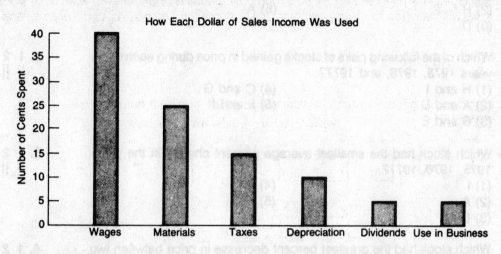

How Each Dollar of Sales Income Was Used

1. How many cents of each dollar of sales income did the company use to pay wages?
   ANSWER: $0.40

2. How many more cents of each sales dollar were spent on wages than on materials?
   ANSWER: $0.15

3. What percent of the sales dollar was spent for depreciation and dividends?
   ANSWER: 15%

4. The amount of money the company paid in taxes was how many times the amount of money it paid in dividends?
   ANSWER: 3 times

5. What percent of the sales dollar was spent on wages, materials, and taxes?
   ANSWER: Wages, 40%
   Materials, 25%
   Taxes, 15%
   Total, 80%

EXAMPLE:

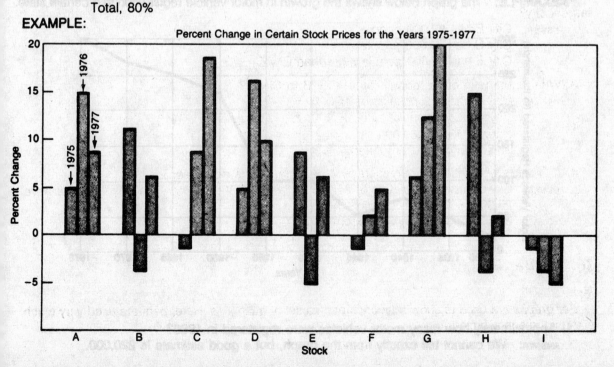

Percent Change in Certain Stock Prices for the Years 1975-1977

1. Which stock had the greatest percent increase in price during any year?

(1) B   (4) G
(2) H   (5) A
(3) D

1. 1 2 3 4 5
‖ ‖ ‖ ‖ ‖

2. Which of the following pairs of stocks gained in price during each of the years 1975, 1976, and 1977?

(1) H and I   (4) C and G
(2) A and D   (5) F and I
(3) B and E

2. 1 2 3 4 5
‖ ‖ ‖ ‖ ‖

3. Which stock had the smallest average percent change in the years 1975, 1976, 1977?

(1) I   (4) G
(2) A   (5) H
(3) C

3. 1 2 3 4 5
‖ ‖ ‖ ‖ ‖

4. Which stock had the greatest percent decrease in price between two consecutive years?

(1) B   (4) E
(2) D   (5) A
(3) F

4. 1 2 3 4 5
‖ ‖ ‖ ‖ ‖

Answers:

1. 4   2. 2   3. 1   4. 4

III. C. Line Graphs

C-1

A *line graph* is especially helpful in showing changes over a period of time.

EXAMPLE: The graph below shows the growth in motor vehicle registration in a certain state.

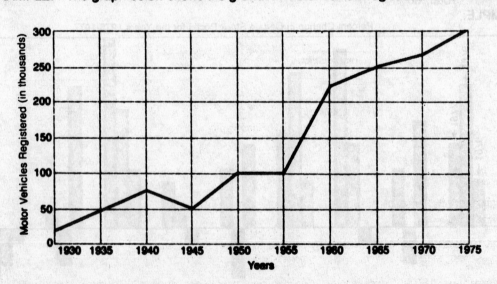

1. Approximately how many motor vehicles were registered in 1960?

ANSWER: We cannot tell exactly from the graph, but a good estimate is 220,000.

2. Approximately how many times as many motor vehicles were registered in 1965 as in 1935?

ANSWER: Registered in 1965—250,000
Registered in 1935—50,000

There were 5 times as many motor vehicles registered in 1965 as in 1935.

3. What percent of increase in registration took place between 1945 and 1975?

ANSWER: Registered in 1945—50,000
Registered in 1975—300,000
Increase in registration—250,000

$$\text{Percent of increase} = \frac{\text{Increase}}{\text{Original}} = \frac{250,000}{50,000} = \frac{5}{1}, \text{ or } 500\%.$$

4. Between what two periods shown was the increase the greatest?

ANSWER: Between 1955 and 1960. This is shown on the graph by the sharpest rise in the line.

5. Between what two periods shown was there no increase?

ANSWER: Between 1950 and 1955. This is shown by the horizontal (or flat) line between 1950 and 1955.

III. D. Circle Graphs

D-1

A *circle graph* is used when a quantity is divided into parts, and we wish to make a comparison of the parts. Recall that a complete revolution is divided into 360°. Thus, if we wish to mark off one-quarter of the circle, the angle at the center must be $\frac{1}{4} \times 360°$, or 90°. For the same reason, a part of the circle with an angle at the center of 60° will be $^{60}/_{360}$, or $\frac{1}{6}$ of the circle.

EXAMPLE: The circle graph below shows how the wage earners in a certain city earned their living in a certain year.

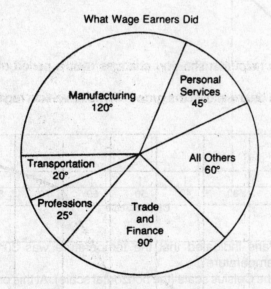

What Wage Earners Did

Manufacturing 120°
Personal Services 45°
Transportation 20°
All Others 60°
Professions 25°
Trade and Finance 90°

1. What fractional part of the labor force works in professions?

ANSWER: $^{25}/_{360} = \frac{5}{72}$

2. What fractional part of the labor force works in personal services?

ANSWER: $^{45}/_{360} = \frac{1}{8}$

3. If there were 180,000 workers in the city, how many are engaged in manufacturing?

ANSWER: The fractional part of the workers engaged in manufacturing was $^{120}/_{360} = \frac{1}{3}$.
$\frac{1}{3}$ of 180,000 = 60,000 workers engaged in manufacturing.

4. What is the ratio of the number of workers in transportation to the number of workers in personal services?

ANSWER: The ratio is 20:45, or more simply, 4:9.

5. What percent of the workers are in trade and finance?

ANSWER: The fractional part of the total number of workers in trade and finance is $^{90}/_{360} = ^{1}/_{4}$. The fraction $^{1}/_{4}$, written as a percent, is 25%.

III. E.   Formula Graphs

E-1

In working with a formula we may have occasion to obtain a number of bits of information. Instead of using the formula each time it may be easier to work from a graph of the formula *(formula graph)*.

In most parts of Europe and in all scientific work, the scale used to measure temperature is the Celsius scale. In the United States, the Fahrenheit scale is still used but mention is frequently made of the Celsius scale. We sometimes find it necessary to convert from one scale to the other. The graph below shows how the scales are related.

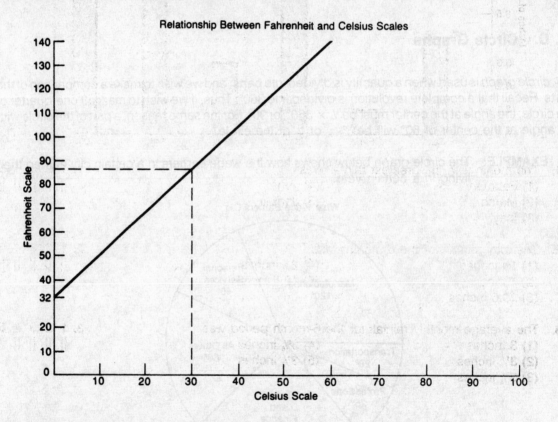

Relationship Between Fahrenheit and Celsius Scales

1. A weather report in Paris indicated that the temperature was 30° Celsius. What was the corresponding Fahrenheit temperature?

ANSWER: Locate 30° on the Celsius scale (the horizontal scale). At this point draw a line so that it is perpendicular to the Celsius scale line (as shown in the diagram).

You can read the corresponding Fahrenheit temperature by drawing a line perpendicular to the Fahrenheit scale line from the point where the first line cuts the graph. The answer is 86°.

2. What Celsius reading corresponds to a Fahrenheit reading of 77?

ANSWER: 25°

3. During one day the temperature rose from 41° to 68° Fahrenheit. What was the corresponding rise in the temperature on the Celsius scale?

ANSWER: The Celsius temperature rose from 5° to 20°.

PRACTICE

Directions: Blacken the space at the right under the number which corresponds to the one you have selected as the correct answer.

For questions 1-3:

The bar graph below shows the average monthly rainfall, in inches, for the first 6 months of a year in a certain city.

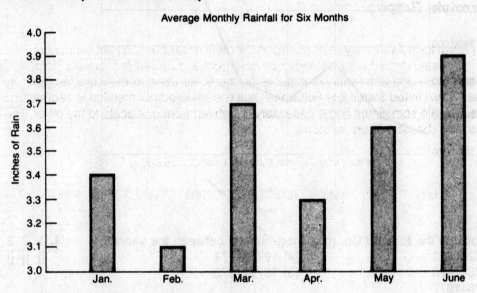

Average Monthly Rainfall for Six Months

1. The month with the greatest rainfall was
   (1) February
   (2) March
   (3) May
   (4) June
   (5) January

   1. 1 2 3 4 5
   ‖ ‖ ‖ ‖ ‖

2. The total rainfall for the 6 months was
   (1) 10 inches
   (2) 19 inches
   (3) 19.6 inches
   (4) 21 inches
   (5) 18.5 inches

   2. 1 2 3 4 5
   ‖ ‖ ‖ ‖ ‖

3. The average monthly rainfall for the 6-month period was
   (1) 3 inches
   (2) 3½ inches
   (3) 3⅙ inches
   (4) 3⅚ inches
   (5) 3⅓ inches

   3. 1 2 3 4 5
   ‖ ‖ ‖ ‖ ‖

For questions 4-6:
The graph below shows the record of profits of the Beacon Co. for a period of 8 years.

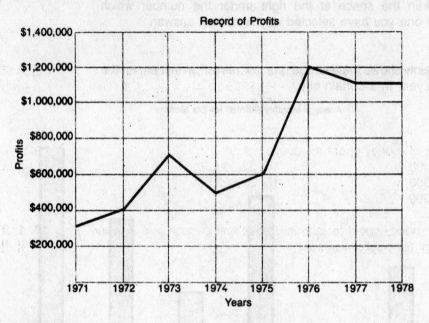

Record of Profits

4. The profits of the Beacon Co. rose most sharply between the years
   (1) 1972–1973
   (2) 1975–1976
   (3) 1976–1977
   (4) 1973–1974
   (5) 1971–1972

   4. 1 2 3 4 5
   || || || || ||

5. The year when the profits of the Beacon Co. were about $700,000 was
   (1) 1975
   (2) 1978
   (3) 1974
   (4) 1973
   (5) 1976

   5. 1 2 3 4 5
   || || || || ||

6. The profits of the Beacon Co. dropped most sharply between the years
   (1) 1977–1978
   (2) 1974–1975
   (3) 1973–1974
   (4) 1971–1972
   (5) 1976–1977

   6. 1 2 3 4 5
   || || || || ||

For questions 7-10:
7. In a large city, the breakdown of the $30,000,000 raised by means of real estate taxes for all purposes, except schools, is shown in the graph. To raise this sum, the tax rate was set at $21.95 per $1,000 of assessed valuation.

   7. 1 2 3 4 5
   || || || || ||

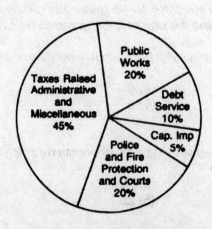

The angle at the center for the public works sector measures
(1) 90°   (4) 80°
(2) 72°   (5) 75°
(3) 100°

8. Mr. Mitchell's home is assessed at $18,000. His real estate tax bill is   **8.** 1 2 3 4 5
   (1) $385.10   (4) $395.10 || || || || ||
   (2) $394.10   (5) $375
   (3) $3,951

9. The amount of money spent for public works is   **9.** 1 2 3 4 5
   (1) $5,000,000   (4) $3,000,000 || || || || ||
   (2) $1,500,000   (5) $2,500,000
   (3) $6,000,000

10. The ratio of money spent for administrative and miscellaneous to the   **10.** 1 2 3 4 5
    money spent for public works is || || || || ||
    (1) 9:4   (4) 5:9
    (2) 4:9   (5) 2:1
    (3) 9:5

For questions 11-13:

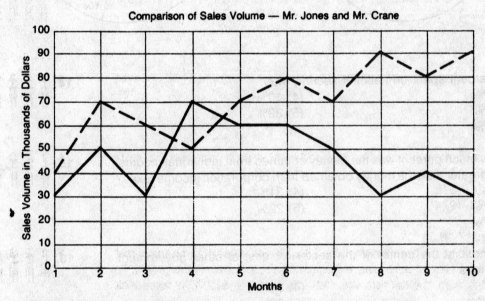

Comparison of Sales Volume — Mr. Jones and Mr. Crane

11. Mr. Jones and Mr. Crane are salesmen. They kept a record of their sales   **11.** 1 2 3 4 5
    over a 10-month period. The solid line on the graph above represents || || || || ||
    Mr. Jones' volume of sales, and the broken line represents Mr. Crane's
    volume of sales.
        Mr. Jones' greatest sales volume for the 10-month period occurred in
    the month numbered
    (1) 3   (4) 6
    (2) 4   (5) 9
    (3) 7

12. How much greater volume was Mr. Crane's best month over Mr. Jones'   **12.** 1 2 3 4 5
    best month? (in thousands) || || || || ||
    (1) 10   (4) 90
    (2) 30   (5) 20
    (3) 50

13. How much greater was Mr. Crane's average for the 10 months than Mr. Jones' average for this period? (in thousands)

(1) 44
(2) 70
(3) 25

(4) 36
(5) 16

13. 1 2 3 4 5

For questions 14-17:

The graphs below were published by the federal government to show where the tax dollar comes from and where it goes.

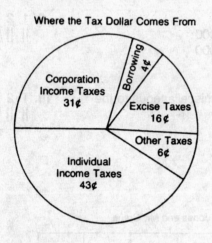

Where the Tax Dollar Comes From

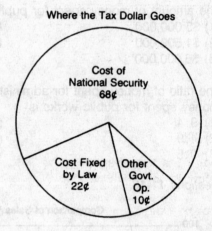

Where the Tax Dollar Goes

14. The percent spent on national security was

(1) 78%
(2) 90%
(3) 68%

(4) 10%
(5) 32%

14. 1 2 3 4 5

15. By how much percent was the money obtained from individual income taxes greater than the money obtained from corporation income taxes?

(1) 6%
(2) 12%
(3) 43%

(4) 31%
(5) 22%

15. 1 2 3 4 5

16. The angle at the center of the sector for cost of other government operations is

(1) 10°
(2) 20°
(3) 40°

(4) 36°
(5) 80°

16. 1 2 3 4 5

17. The percent of income derived from both corporation income taxes and individual income taxes is

(1) 84%
(2) 12%
(3) 75%

(4) 82%
(5) 74%

17. 1 2 3 4 5

Answers:

1. 4		2. 4		4. 2		7. 2		10. 1		11. 2		13. 3		14. 3		16. 4
3. 2		5. 4		6. 3		8. 4		9. 3		12. 5		15. 2		17. 5

IV. MEASURES

IV. A. Length
A-1

> The most *common measures of length* are
>
> 12 inches = 1 foot   5,280 feet = 1 mile
> 3 feet = 1 yard   1,760 yards = 1 mile

EXAMPLE: A plumber has a pipe $\frac{3}{4}$ yard in length. If he cuts off a piece 23 inches long, how much pipe does he have left?

$$\frac{3}{4} \text{ yard} = \frac{3}{4} \times 36 = 27 \text{ inches}$$

The plumber has 4 inches of pipe left.

PRACTICE

Directions: Blacken the space at the right under the number which corresponds to the one you have selected as the correct answer.

1. A plane flies at a height of 23,760 feet. In miles, this is
   (1) 4
   (2) $4\frac{2}{3}$
   (3) $4\frac{1}{4}$
   (4) $4\frac{1}{2}$
   (5) $4\frac{3}{4}$

   1. 1 2 3 4 5
   ‖ ‖ ‖ ‖ ‖

2. Mrs. Bryant buys 6 yards of linen. The number of towels 27 inches in length that she can cut is
   (1) 8
   (2) 6
   (3) 12
   (4) 9
   (5) 15

   2. 1 2 3 4 5
   ‖ ‖ ‖ ‖ ‖

3. A room is 18 feet long and 12 feet wide. The number of rubber tiles measuring 8 inches by 8 inches needed to cover the floor is
   (1) 45
   (2) 27
   (3) 486
   (4) 286
   (5) 304

   3. 1 2 3 4 5
   ‖ ‖ ‖ ‖ ‖

4. A lecture room is 50 feet wide. On each side of the room, there is an aisle 40 inches wide. The number of seats, 20 inches wide, that can be fitted across the room is
   (1) 20
   (2) 26
   (3) 40
   (4) 30
   (5) 35

   4. 1 2 3 4 5
   ‖ ‖ ‖ ‖ ‖

5. A long-distance race covers $6\frac{3}{4}$ miles. The number of yards covered is
   (1) 10,560
   (2) 12,000
   (3) 11,000
   (4) 11,880
   (5) 14,350

   5. 1 2 3 4 5
   ‖ ‖ ‖ ‖ ‖

Answers:

1. 4   2. 1   3. 3   4. 2   5. 4

IV. B. Time

B-1

The most *common measures of time* are

60 seconds = 1 minute	12 months = 1 year
60 minutes = 1 hour	365 days = 1 year

EXAMPLE: A man works from 9:45 A.M. until 1:30 P.M. How many hours does he work?

From 9:45 A.M. to 10:00 A.M. is 15 minutes, or ¼ hour.
From 10:00 A.M. to 1:00 P.M. is 3 hours.
From 1:00 P.M. to 1:30 P.M. is 30 minutes, or ½ hour.
The time the man worked is ¼ + 3 + ½ = 3¾ hours.

PRACTICE

Directions: Blacken the space at the right under the number which corresponds to the one you have selected as the correct answer.

1. A man is paid $6.50 per hour. He works from 10:45 A.M. until 3:15 P.M. He earns
   (1) $30.50   (4) $27.75
   (2) $16.25   (5) $22.75
   (3) $29.25

   1. 1 2 3 4 5
   ‖ ‖ ‖ ‖ ‖

2. A bell rings every 45 minutes. The number of times the bell rings in 15 hours is
   (1) 18   (4) 12
   (2) 20   (5) 25
   (3) 11

   2. 1 2 3 4 5
   ‖ ‖ ‖ ‖ ‖

3. A man leaves New York on a plane at 10:40 A.M. bound for Los Angeles. If he gains 3 hours in time and the trip takes 5 hours and 50 minutes, he arrives in Los Angeles at
   (1) 1:30 P.M.   (4) 3:10 P.M.
   (2) 2:30 P.M.   (5) 2:50 P.M.
   (3) 3:30 P.M.

   3. 1 2 3 4 5
   ‖ ‖ ‖ ‖ ‖

4. In flight, a plane covers 1 mile in 10 seconds. At the same rate of speed, the number of miles the plane covers in 1 hour is
   (1) 100   (4) 300
   (2) 200   (5) 360
   (3) 720

   4. 1 2 3 4 5
   ‖ ‖ ‖ ‖ ‖

5. On March 5, a man borrows $900 from a bank for 90 days. He must repay the loan on
   (1) June 1   (4) June 8
   (2) June 5   (5) June 9
   (3) June 3

   5. 1 2 3 4 5
   ‖ ‖ ‖ ‖ ‖

Answers:

5. 3   4. 5   3. 1   2. 2   1. 3

IV. C. Weight

C-1

The most commonly used measures of weight are

16 ounces = 1 pound   2,000 pounds = 1 ton

EXAMPLE: How many 2-ounce portions of candy can be obtained from a 10-pound box?

Since there are 16 ounces in 1 pound, each pound of candy will yield $^{16}/_2$, or 8 portions. Therefore, 10 pounds of candy will yield 8×10, or 80 portions.

PRACTICE

Directions: Blacken the space at the right under the number which corresponds to the one you have selected as the correct answer.

1. Bread sells for $0.32 per pound. The cost of a bread weighing 3 pounds 6 ounces is
   (1) $0.98   (4) $0.78
   (2) $1.08   (5) $1.15
   (3) $1.12

   1. 1 2 3 4 5
   ‖ ‖ ‖ ‖ ‖

2. A 12-ounce package of cheese costs $0.69. What is the cost of one pound of the same cheese?
   (1) $0.78   (4) $0.92
   (2) $0.95   (5) $1.04
   (3) $0.96

   2. 1 2 3 4 5
   ‖ ‖ ‖ ‖ ‖

3. A shipment of coal weighs 9,500 pounds. What is the cost of the shipment if 1 ton of coal costs $26.40?
   (1) $125.40   (4) $104.55
   (2) $106.85   (5) $112.60
   (3) $110.70

   3. 1 2 3 4 5
   ‖ ‖ ‖ ‖ ‖

4. A certain cut of meat costs $1.18 per pound. What is the cost of this cut of meat weighing 1 pound 13 ounces?
   (1) $2.05   (4) $1.92
   (2) $1.98   (5) $2.14
   (3) $2.20

   4. 1 2 3 4 5
   ‖ ‖ ‖ ‖ ‖

5. A truckload of steel bars weighs $3\frac{1}{4}$ tons. If each bar weighs 26 pounds, the number of bars on the truck is
   (1) 25   (4) 250
   (2) 2,500   (5) 270
   (3) 240

   5. 1 2 3 4 5
   ‖ ‖ ‖ ‖ ‖

Answers:

1. 2   2. 4   3. 1   4. 5   5. 4

IV. D. Liquid Measure

D-1

The most commonly used liquid measures are

16 fluid ounces = 1 pint   2 measuring cups = 1 pint
2 pints = 1 quart   4 quarts = 1 gallon

EXAMPLE: A snack bar sells half-pint bottles of milk at 15 cents a bottle. If 3 gallons of milk are sold one morning, how much money is taken in?

Since half-pint bottles sell for 15 cents, a full pint sells for 30 cents. Thus, one quart sells for 60 cents, and 1 gallon sells for $2.40. And, 3 gallons sell for 3 × $2.40 = $7.20.

PRACTICE

Directions: Blacken the space at the right under the number which corresponds to the one you have selected as the correct answer.

1. The number of measuring cups of milk in a 5-gallon can is
   (1) 40   (4) 100
   (2) 60   (5) 160
   (3) 80

   1. 1 2 3 4 5
   || || || || ||

2. A can of orange juice contains 36 ounces. The number of pints of orange juice is
   (1) 2   (4) 2¼
   (2) 2½   (5) 3
   (3) 1¼

   2. 1 2 3 4 5
   || || || || ||

3. A punch bowl contains 3½ gallons of punch. The number of 4-ounce portions that can be obtained from the punch bowl is
   (1) 102   (4) 115
   (2) 112   (5) 156
   (3) 204

   3. 1 2 3 4 5
   || || || || ||

4. A restaurant cook uses 150 measuring cups of milk in one day. The cost of the milk at $0.40 per quart is
   (1) $15   (4) $150
   (2) $30   (5) $15.20
   (3) $14.80

   4. 1 2 3 4 5
   || || || || ||

5. The number of fluid ounces in 1 gallon is
   (1) 64   (4) 96
   (2) 48   (5) 128
   (3) 100

   5. 1 2 3 4 5
   || || || || ||

Answers:

5. 5   4. 1   3. 2   2. 4   1. 3

IV. E.   Dry Measure

E-1

Such commodities as berries, apples, and potatoes are often sold by the quart or bushel.

The most commonly used dry measures are

2 pints = 1 quart   8 quarts = 1 peck   4 pecks = 1 bushel

EXAMPLE: A dealer received a shipment of 60 bags of apples, each bag containing 1 peck. If 1 bushel of the apples weighed 48 pounds and the dealer sold them at a price of 3 pounds for 85 cents, how much did he receive?

The dealer received 60 pecks of apples. This is $^{60}/_4$, or 15 bushels. Since each bushel weighed 48 pounds, the total weight of the shipment was 15×48, or 720 pounds.

At 3 pounds for 85 cents, the dealer received

$$^{720}/_3 \times 0.85, \text{ or } 240 \times 0.85 = \$204.00$$

PRACTICE

Directions: Blacken the space at the right under the number which corresponds to the one you have selected as the correct answer.

1. A storekeeper paid $5.60 for a bushel of potatoes. If 1 peck of potatoes weighs 15 pounds and the storekeeper sold the potatoes in 5-pound bags at $0.86 per bag, his profit on the deal was
    (1) $6.72   (4) $4.32
    (2) $4.52   (5) $10.02
    (3) $4.72

    1. 1 2 3 4 5
    || || || || ||

2. If a bushel of coal weighs 80 pounds and coal sells for $24 per ton, the cost of a bushel of coal is
    (1) $1   (4) $0.96
    (2) $0.98   (5) $1.02
    (3) $2

    2. 1 2 3 4 5
    || || || || ||

3. A fruiterer received a truckload of berries containing 15 bushels. If he sold the berries at $0.42 per pint, the amount he received for the berries was
    (1) $403.20   (4) $253.20
    (2) $201.60   (5) $25.32
    (3) $40.32

    3. 1 2 3 4 5
    || || || || ||

4. A fruiterer paid $19.20 for 2 bushels of apples. If he sold the apples for $3.60 per peck, his profit was
    (1) $7.60   (4) $9.60
    (2) $8.90   (5) $11.60
    (3) $9

    4. 1 2 3 4 5
    || || || || ||

Answers:

4. 4   3. 1   2. 4   1. 3

IV. F. The Metric System

F-1

The metric system of measures is used in most scientific work and in all European countries. It is especially useful because its units are related by multiples of 10. In this section, we will consider the most frequently used metric measures. However, please be aware that memorization of the metric system is *not* necessary for the California High School Proficiency Examination. We are introducing this section so that you will not be surprised by metric references in various problems. *You need not know any metric equivalences for this examination.*

The important unit of length in the metric system is the *meter.* The meter is a little bigger than 1 yard. In fact,

1 meter = approximately 39.37 inches

The *kilometer,* or 1,000 meters, is used for measuring large distances, like the distance between two cities.

1 kilometer = approximately ⅝ mile

The important unit of liquid measure in the metric system is the *liter*.

1 liter = approximately 1.1 liquid quarts

The basic unit of weight in the metric system is the *gram*. The gram is used extensively in the science laboratory. In practice, the *kilogram,* or 1,000 grams, is used extensively in weighing foods and other merchandise.

1 kilogram = approximately 2.2 pounds

To sum up, *the following metric equivalencies are important:*

1 meter = approximately 39.37 inches
1 kilometer = approximately ⅝ mile
1 liter = approximately 1.1 liquid quarts
1 kilogram = approximately 2.2 pounds

EXAMPLE: In traveling on a European road, an American motorist notes that the speed limit is 70 kilometers per hour. Approximately how fast is this, in miles per hour?

Since 1 kilometer = approximately ⅝ mile

$$⅝ × 70 = {}^{350}⁄_8 = 43¾$$

This is approximately 43¾ miles per hour.

PRACTICE

Directions: Blacken the space at the right under the number which corresponds to the one you have selected as the correct answer.

1. A package from Europe is marked to contain 3½ kilograms. In pounds, this is
   (1) 77
   (2) 770
   (3) 7.7
   (4) 6.6
   (5) 14

   1. 1 2 3 4 5
   ‖ ‖ ‖ ‖ ‖

2. If you weigh 160 pounds, your weight in kilograms, to the nearest kilogram, is
   (1) 72
   (2) 73
   (3) 352
   (4) 35
   (5) 70

   2. 1 2 3 4 5
   ‖ ‖ ‖ ‖ ‖

3. A motorist bought 50 liters of gasoline. The number of gallons bought, to the nearest gallon, is
   (1) 14
   (2) 13
   (3) 11
   (4) 12
   (5) 15

   3. 1 2 3 4 5
   ‖ ‖ ‖ ‖ ‖

4. If a plane is flying at the rate of 760 kilometers per hour, its rate of speed in miles per hour is
   (1) 1,216
   (2) 1,200
   (3) 675
   (4) 455
   (5) 475

   4. 1 2 3 4 5
   ‖ ‖ ‖ ‖ ‖

5. A building lot, rectangular in shape, is 35 meters in length and 15 meters in width. Its perimeter, in feet, to the nearest foot, is
   (1) 3,937
   (2) 328
   (3) 109
   (4) 984
   (5) 394

   5. 1 2 3 4 5
   ‖ ‖ ‖ ‖ ‖

6. The distance between two European cities is 440 kilometers. At an average speed of 50 miles per hour, the number of hours it would take a motorist to cover this distance is

(1) 5

(2) 8⅘

(3) 10

(4) 5½

(5) 6

Answers:

6. 4   **5.** 2   **4.** 5   **3.** 1   **2.** 2   **1.** 3

IV. G. Operations with Measures

G-1

It is often necessary to add, subtract, multiply, and divide with measures. The following examples indicate how this is done.

EXAMPLE: A woman bought a steak weighing 2 lb. 14 oz. and another steak weighing 3 lb. 6 oz. How many pounds of steak did she buy?

$$\begin{array}{r} 2 \text{ lb. } 14 \text{ oz.} \\ +3 \text{ lb. } 6 \text{ oz.} \\ \hline 5 \text{ lb. } 20 \text{ oz.} \end{array}$$

Since there are 16 ounces in 1 pound, we have

5 lb. 20 oz. = 5 lb. + 1 lb. + 4 oz. = 6 lb. 4 oz.

EXAMPLE: A plumber had a piece of pipe 6 ft. 3 in. long. If he cut off a piece 2 ft. 7 in. in length, what was the length of the pipe that was left?

6 ft. 3 in. = 5 ft. + 1 ft. + 3 in. = 5 ft. 15 in.

$$\begin{array}{r} 5 \text{ ft. } 15 \text{ in.} \\ -2 \text{ ft. } 7 \text{ in.} \\ \hline 3 \text{ ft. } 8 \text{ in.} \end{array}$$

The piece of pipe that was left was 3 ft. 8 in.

EXAMPLE: A butcher cuts steaks each of which weighs 1 lb. 9 oz. What is the weight of 5 such steaks?

$$\begin{array}{r} 1 \text{ lb. } 9 \text{ oz.} \\ \times 5 \\ \hline 5 \text{ lb. } 45 \text{ oz.} \end{array}$$

5 lb. 45 oz. = 5 lb. + 32 oz. + 13 oz. = 7 lb. 13 oz.

EXAMPLE: Mrs. Gordon buys a bolt of cloth 21 ft. 8 in. in length. She cuts the bolt into four equal pieces to make drapes. What is the length of each drape?

$$4\overline{)21 \text{ ft. } 8 \text{ in.}} = 4\overline{)20 \text{ ft.} + 1 \text{ ft.} + 8 \text{ in.}}$$
$$= 4\overline{)20 \text{ ft. } 20 \text{ in.}}$$
$$= 5 \text{ ft. } 5 \text{ in.}$$

Each drape is 5 ft. 5 in.

PRACTICE

Directions: **Blacken the space at the right under the number which corresponds to the one you have selected as the correct answer.**

1. A picture frame is 2 ft. 6 in. long and 1 ft. 8 in. wide. The perimeter of the frame is

(1) 4 ft. 2 in.

(2) 8 ft. 8 in.

(3) 8 ft. 6 in.

(4) 8 ft.

(5) 8 ft. 4 in.

2. A movie show lasts 2 hr. 15 min. A movie house has 5 such shows daily. The time consumed by the 5 shows is
   (1) 11 hrs.
   (2) 11 hrs. 15 min.
   (3) 10 hrs. 15 min.
   (4) 12 hrs. 30 min.
   (5) 12 hrs.

   2. 1 2 3 4 5
   || || || || ||

3. On a certain day the sun rises at 6:48 A.M. and sets at 7:03 P.M. The time from sunrise to sunset is
   (1) 12 hrs. 15 min.
   (2) 12 hrs. 5 min.
   (3) 11 hrs. 45 min.
   (4) 12 hrs. 25 min.
   (5) 10 hrs. 15 min.

   3. 1 2 3 4 5
   || || || || ||

4. If 6 cans of orange juice weigh 15 lb. 6 oz., the weight of 1 can of orange juice is
   (1) 2 lb. 6 oz.
   (2) 2 lb. 7 oz.
   (3) 2 lb. 1 oz.
   (4) 2 lb. 9 oz.
   (5) 2 lb. 3 oz.

   4. 1 2 3 4 5
   || || || || ||

5. A jug contains 2 gallons, 3 quarts of milk. The number of 8 oz. glasses that can be filled from this jug is
   (1) 24
   (2) 32
   (3) 44
   (4) 36
   (5) 40

   5. 1 2 3 4 5
   || || || || ||

6. A carpenter has a board 5 ft. 3 in. in length. He cuts off a piece 2 ft. 7 in. in length. The length of the piece that is left is
   (1) 3 ft. 6 in.
   (2) 2 ft. 6 in.
   (3) 2 ft. 3 in.
   (4) 2 ft. 8 in.
   (5) 2 ft. 5 in.

   6. 1 2 3 4 5
   || || || || ||

7. A set of books weighs 7 lb. 10 oz. The weight of 4 such sets is
   (1) 28 lb. 4 oz.
   (2) 30 lb. 8 oz.
   (3) 29 lb. 8 oz.
   (4) 29 lb. 10 oz.
   (5) 29 lb. 11 oz.

   7. 1 2 3 4 5
   || || || || ||

8. A store sold 6 gal. 2 qt. of ice cream on one day and 7 gal. 3 qt. the next day. The amount of ice cream sold on both days was
   (1) 15 gal. 2 qt.
   (2) 14 gal. 3 qt.
   (3) 14 gal. 1 qt.
   (4) 15 gal. 1 qt.
   (5) 13 gal. 2 qt.

   8. 1 2 3 4 5
   || || || || ||

Answers:

1. 5   2. 2   3. 1   4. 4   5. 3   6. 4   7. 2   8. 3

V. GEOMETRY

V. A. Lines and Angles

A-1

Geometry studies simple shapes that are often used as component parts of more complicated figures and structures. We have seen isolated examples earlier in this chapter, in formulas for the perimeter of a rectangle and questions about ratio and proportion. The number line is an example of geometrical reasoning about numbers.

Lines are imagined as infinitely long and composed of a continuous set of points. In diagrams, only segments of a line are shown, sometimes with a few points distinguished by a dot to mark their position:

Dots or other markers for points are not meant to suggest that these points are bigger than any of the others; all points are *dimensionless*, with no height or width or depth. The line above is a straight line, meaning that if you imagined picking up a copy of it and moving that along the original, they would keep on matching no matter how far you moved the copy.

Two straight lines in the same plane (such as the surface of a piece of paper) are called *parallel* if they never intersect, however far they are imagined as extending in both directions. If they do intersect, they form *angles*:

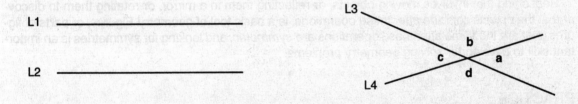

In the diagram above, L1 and L2 are parallel; L3 and L4 intersect forming four angles (*a*, *b*, *c*, and *d*). Angles are measured by rotation; if you imagine keeping L4 fixed but rotating L3 counterclockwise around the point of intersection, L3 would coincide with L4 after rotating by *c* degrees. Angles *a* and *b* fit together along one side of straight line L3; their combined angle makes a rotation of 180 degrees, also called a *straight angle*. That is, $a + b = 180°$. The sum of all four angles is one complete circle, $360°$.

Notice that *b* and *c* also form a straight angle, as do *c* and *d*, and *d* and *a*. As a good first example of geometrical reasoning, we see

$a + b = 180 = b + c$; therefore (cancelling *b*) $a = c$. Similarly, $b = d$.

NOTE: The *opposite* angles of intersecting lines are equal.

Pairs of angles that add up to 180° are known as *supplementary* angles; they needn't be adjacent angles lying along a line for this relationship to hold. The angles to the right are supplementary.

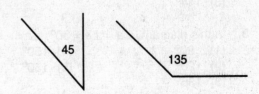

There is a special case of intersecting lines, where all four angles are equal; each angle must be 90° (each pair adds up to 180°, but since the two are equal, $r = 180/2°$). Angles of 90° are called *right angles*, and lines intersecting at right angles are described as *perpendicular*.

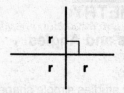

If a line intersects two parallel lines, there are several important relations among the angles that are formed:

The opposite angles at the intersections are equal, as above. But if you could take the intersection of L1 and L3 and move it down and to the right, always keeping L1 parallel to L2, and moving L3 along its own length, you would get L1 eventually lying exactly on L2, and the two intersections will exactly coincide. That is, angle a = angle m. Similarly, the unmarked angles are also equal. The angles a and m are called *alternate interior* angles.

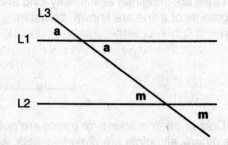

NOTE: Alternate interior angles formed when a line intersects two parallel lines are equal in measure.

You don't need to know the terminology to answer any questions on the test, but this is one of the facts that will help you find correct answers when a geometry problem has parallel lines.

Reasoning that involves moving objects, or reflecting them in a mirror, or rotating them to discover that the objects coincide after these operations, is a basic tool of geometry. Figures, or parts of figures, that are the same after these operations are *symmetric*, and looking for symmetries is an important skill to develop for solving geometry problems.

PRACTICE

Directions: Solve the following problems and blacken the space at the right under the number that corresponds to the one you have selected as the right answer.

1. In this diagram, angle s equals
   (1) p
   (2) q
   (3) r
   (4) $90° - p$
   (5) $180° - q$

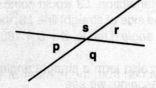

1. 1 2 3 4 5
|| || || || ||

2. Which angle is supplementary to an angle of 36°?
   (1) 54°
   (2) 90°
   (3) 144°
   (4) 180°
   (5) 360°

2. 1 2 3 4 5
|| || || || ||

3. In this diagram, $\angle a = \angle e = 30°$; $\angle c =$
   (1) 90°
   (2) 120°
   (3) 135°
   (4) 150°
   (5) 160°

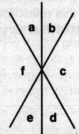

3. 1 2 3 4 5
|| || || || ||

4. If line *L* is parallel to line *M* and ∠1 = 50°, ∠2 =

(1) 50°   (4) 110°
(2) 70°   (5) 130°
(3) 90°

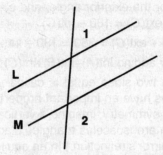

4. 1 2 3 4 5
‖ ‖ ‖ ‖ ‖

5. If line *V* is perpendicular to line *W*, how big is the angle *a* around their outside?

(1) 90°   (4) 270°
(2) 135°   (5) 360°
(3) 180°

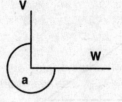

5. 1 2 3 4 5
‖ ‖ ‖ ‖ ‖

Answers:

1. 2   2. 3   3. 4   4. 5   5. 4

V. B. Figures Made of Straight Lines

B-1

When three or more lines in the same plane intersect each other, there is a central region with the lines as a boundary. The points of intersection are called *vertexes* (or *vertices*), and the line segments between vertexes are called *edges*. These points and line segments are emphasized in the diagram below:

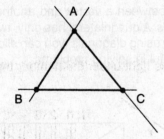
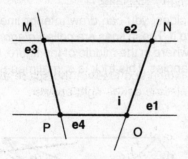
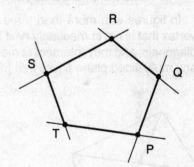

The figures are named from the number of edges (or angles; there is one angle for every edge): *triangles* have three edges and three angles, *quadrilaterals* have four, *pentagons* have five, etc. These names are derived from Latin or Greek words meaning three angles, four edges, and five angles, respectively.

There is an angle less than 180° on the inside of a plane figure like these, between any two successive edges. This is called an *interior* angle; the angle *i* between the edges *PO* and *ON* in the quadrilateral is an example of an interior angle. If you look at the extension of edge *PO* past the boundary of the quadrilateral, you see that the angle *e1* is supplementary to *i*; It is called an *exterior* angle of the figure. The exterior angle is the amount you would have to turn (rotate) if you walked along edge *PO* and then along *ON*. If you make a complete circuit of the figure, you will have made four turns, totaling 360°. On a circuit of the pentagon, you'd make five turns, but again the total will be 360°. The sum of the exterior angles in a plane figure (like these, with all the interior angles less than 180°) is 360°. As a result of this, we get one of the most basic facts from plane geometry:

NOTE: The sum of the interior angles in a triangle is 180°.

This follows because each interior angle and its exterior angle are supplementary. Each exterior angle is 180° minus the interior angle. In the triangle shown, use int(*A*) to stand for the interior angle at A and ext(A) for the exterior angle, and so on around the triangle. ext(A) = 180 – int(A), ext(B) = 180 – int(B), and ext(C) = 180 – int(C).

ext(A) + ext(B) + ext(C) = 360 = 180 – int(A) + 180 – int(B) + 180 – int(C).

Simplify this by adding int(A)+int(B)+int(C) to both sides, and subtracting 360.

A triangle with two sides equal is called *isosceles*; if all three sides are equal, it is *equilateral*. Isosceles triangles have an important property: the angles opposite the equal sides are equal. (You can see this from symmetry; imagine a vertical mirror going through the top vertex in the three triangles below, which are isosceles triangles placed with the third side horizontal. Each side will match the other in the mirror's reflection.) In an equilateral triangle, all the sides are equal; so all the angles are, too.

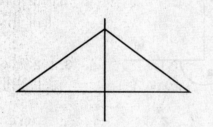 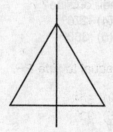 

NOTE: The angles opposite the equal sides of an isosceles triangle are equal.
NOTE: An equilateral triangle has each of its angles equal to 60º.

These facts reflect a more general rule:

NOTE: In any triangle, the largest side is opposite the largest angle and the smallest side is opposite the smallest angle.

In figures with more than three sides, you can draw interior lines between a vertex and another vertex that is not immediately next to it. These lines are called *diagonals*. A quadrilateral has only two diagonals, and they intersect somewhere in the middle of the figure. By using diagonals, you can slice any multi-sided plane figure into triangles. This trick is sometimes useful in solving problems.

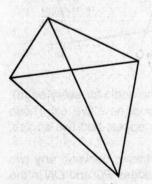 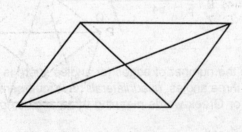 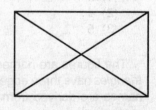

Some kinds of quadrilaterals are given special names from their distinctive properties. The most important of these are parallelograms, which have two sets of parallel lines as their opposite edges, and rectangles, in which all four angles are right angles. In the diagram above, the middle figure is a parallelogram and the one on the right is a rectangle. Rectangles are also parallelograms. In a rectangle, the diagonals are equal.

PRACTICE

Directions: Solve the following problems and blacken the space at the right under the number that corresponds to the one you have selected as the right answer.

1. What is the average size of an angle in any triangle?
   (1) 30º
   (2) 60º
   (3) 90º
   (4) 180º
   (5) Cannot be determined

   1. 1 2 3 4 5
   ‖ ‖ ‖ ‖ ‖

2. Triangle *ABC* has ∠*A* = 65º, and ∠*B* = 35º; ∠*C* is
   (1) 60º
   (2) 70º
   (3) 80º
   (4) 90º
   (5) 100º

   2. 1 2 3 4 5
   ‖ ‖ ‖ ‖ ‖

3. In triangle *PQR*, side *PQ* is equal to side *PR*.
   If ∠*P* = 48º, ∠*Q* =
   (1) 48º
   (2) 52º
   (3) 60º
   (4) 66º
   (5) 90º

   3. 1 2 3 4 5
   ‖ ‖ ‖ ‖ ‖

   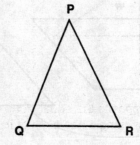

4. In rectangle *EFGH*, diagonal *EG* = 5 feet.
   Diagonal *FH* is
   (1) 5 feet
   (2) 6 feet
   (3) 7 feet
   (4) 8 feet
   (5) Cannot be determined

   4. 1 2 3 4 5
   ‖ ‖ ‖ ‖ ‖

5. How many distinct diagonals can be drawn
   in pentagon *NOPQR*?
   (1) 3
   (2) 4
   (3) 5
   (4) 6
   (5) 7

   5. 1 2 3 4 5
   ‖ ‖ ‖ ‖ ‖

   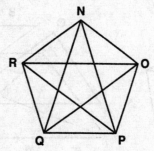

Answers:

1. 2   2. 3   3. 4   4. 1   5. 3

B-2

Perimeter and Area

The *perimeter* of a plane figure is the total length of its sides. Parallelograms (and rectangles, which are a special case of parallelograms) have two pairs of equal sides, so their perimeter is $2(a+b)$ if one of the sides has length a and the adjacent side has length b. A *regular* figure is one that has all its sides equal. Equilateral triangles are regular figures, as are squares, regular pentagons, regular hexagons, etc. The perimeter of a regular n-sided polygon is n times the length of each side.

The *area* of a figure is a measure of its two-dimensional content. If you divide a rectangle 3 inches by 4 inches into squares 1-inch on a side, you can fit $3 \times 4 = 12$ such unit-squares into its interior. Its area is 12 square inches.

NOTE: The area of a rectangle is its width times its height ($A = w \times h$).

If you take a parallelogram and slice off the part that doesn't fit in a rectangle of the same height, and move that to the other side of the parallelogram, you get a rectangle.

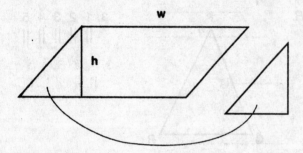

The measure of area remains unchanged by this, so the fact above generalizes to:

NOTE: The area of a parallelogram is its width times its height. All parallelograms with the same width and height have the same area. $A = w \times h$

Any triangle can be put inside a parallelogram by reflecting it around one side as a diagonal for the parallelogram. The triangle is obviously one-half of the resulting parallelogram.

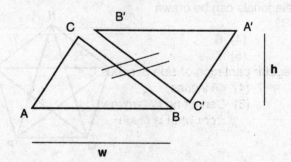

NOTE: The area of a triangle is 1/2 its width times its height. $A = (w \times h)/2$.

PRACTICE

Directions: Solve the following problems and blacken the space at the right under the number that corresponds to the one you have selected as the right answer.

1. What is the perimeter of a parallelogram with one side 15 inches and one side 5 inches?
   (1) 10 inches   (4) 40 inches
   (2) 20 inches   (5) 50 inches
   (3) 30 inches

   1. 1 2 3 4 5
   ‖ ‖ ‖ ‖ ‖

2. The area of the figure in this diagram is
   (1) 18   (4) 54
   (2) 36   (5) 70
   (3) 42

   2. 1 2 3 4 5
   ‖ ‖ ‖ ‖ ‖

   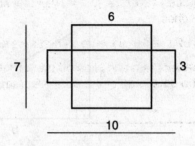

3. Rectangle *PQRS* shares a side with triangle *QST.* The area of △*QST* is
   (1) 10   (4) 30
   (2) 15   (5) 45
   (3) 20

   3. 1 2 3 4 5
   ‖ ‖ ‖ ‖ ‖

   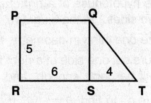

4. Which triangle in the rectangle *ABCD* has the smallest area?
   (1) △*ABC*   (4) △*ABD*
   (2) △*ADC*   (5) △*ABE*
   (3) △*AEC*

   4. 1 2 3 4 5
   ‖ ‖ ‖ ‖ ‖

   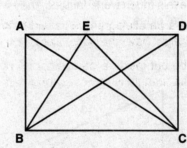

5. The perimeter of a regular pentagon of side 8 inches is
   (1) 24 inches   (4) 48 inches
   (2) 32 inches   (5) Cannot be determined
   (3) 40 inches   from what is given

   5. 1 2 3 4 5
   ‖ ‖ ‖ ‖ ‖

Answers:

5. 3   4. 5   3. 1   2. 4   1. 4

B-3

Right Triangles

An important special case of triangles occurs when one of the angles is a right angle; since the sum of all three angles is 180°, when one of the angles is 90°, the others add up to 90°, so each of them must be less than 90°. (Angles whose sum is 90° are called *complementary* angles.) A right-angled triangle, or *right triangle*, is half of a rectangle. The longest side of the triangle, opposite the right angle, is called the *hypotenuse*; and the sides that form the right angle are called the *legs* of the right triangle. There is an extremely important relationship that holds for the sides of a right triangle; it is known as the Pythagorean Theorem:

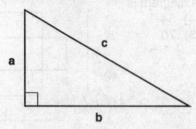

NOTE: The square of the hypotenuse of a right triangle is equal to the sum of the squares of the legs (the other two sides.) In the diagram, $c^2 = a^2 + b^2$.

If you can only memorize *one* thing in geometry, *this* is the one to memorize!

You may be asked to figure out one side of a right triangle given two of the other sides. Sometimes, an approximate answer will be good enough, and you won't have to do complex calculations of squares and square roots (e.g., to find $a = \sqrt{(c^2 - b^2)}$. The most likely cases of right triangles you will see will not require this much work. Instead, they will use a few special cases. There are some right triangles that have "nice" sides:

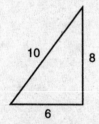 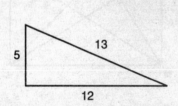 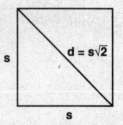 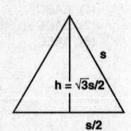

3-4-5 triangle. $3^2 + 4^2 = 9 + 16 = 25 = 5^2$. Any triangle with sides of length 3, 4 and 5 (in any units) satisfies the Pythagorean Theorem, and the sides of length 3 and 4 are the legs, with the side of length 5 as the hypotenuse. You are very likely to see triangles that have sides of length 3, 4 and 5, or some small multiples of these values. Be on the lookout for 6-8-10 and 9-12-15 triangles as well as 3-4-5 triangles!

5-12-13 triangle. $5^2 + 12^2 = 25 + 144 = 169 = 13^2$. This is another special case with simple whole number sides in a right triangle. Triangles with this ratio of the sides are less common on tests than 3-4-5 triangles, but be alert for them; here also you may see small multiples (10-24-26, for example). Reduce to lowest terms to see what you are dealing with.

half-square (or **isosceles right triangle**). In a square of side *s*, the diagonal *d* is found from the Pythagorean rule to be: $d^2 = s^2 + s^2 = 2s^2$; $d = s\sqrt{2}$. Since the other angles of this triangle are equal, they must be 45°; and this triangle is also known as a 45 degree right triangle. It comes up often enough that you should memorize the relation of the hypotenuse to the sides (the relation of the diagonal of a square to its sides), namely $\sqrt{2} = 1.414\ldots$ For most problems, it is good enough to know that $\sqrt{2}$ is about 1.4.

half-equilateral (30-60-90) triangle. Any isosceles triangle is made up of two right triangles, by drawing a line from the vertex between the equal side to its base (the third side.) The most likely case of this to show up on tests uses the equilateral triangle. Splitting this in half gives a right triangle with angles of 30° and 60°. If the side of the equilateral triangle is s, the base is $s/2$, and the other leg of the triangle is given by:

$$s^2 = (s/2)^2 + h^2$$

From this, $h^2 = s^2 - s^2/4 = 3s^2/4$, so $h = s\sqrt{3}/2$. Or, in other words, the height is $\sqrt{3}$ times the base (which is 1/2 the side of the equilateral triangle.) $\sqrt{3} = 1.732\ldots$; again you can usually get by remembering that $\sqrt{3}$ is about 1.7.

PRACTICE

Directions: Solve the following problems and blacken the space at the right under the number that corresponds to the one you have selected as the right answer.

1. A right triangle has each of its short legs 6 inches long; its hypotenuse is about
   - (1) 6.5 inches
   - (2) 7.5 inches
   - (3) 8.5 inches
   - (4) 9.5 inches
   - (5) 10.5 inches

   1. 1 2 3 4 5
   ‖ ‖ ‖ ‖ ‖

2. In △LMN, side MN is approximately
   - (1) 5
   - (2) 7
   - (3) 9
   - (4) 11
   - (5) 13

   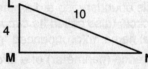

   2. 1 2 3 4 5
   ‖ ‖ ‖ ‖ ‖

3. In △PQR, RS is perpendicular to PQ. Side SQ has length
   - (1) 16
   - (2) 17
   - (3) 18
   - (4) 19
   - (5) 20

   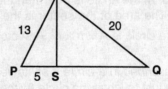

   3. 1 2 3 4 5
   ‖ ‖ ‖ ‖ ‖

4. The area of an equilateral triangle with side 20 feet is about
   - (1) 10 square feet
   - (2) 14 square feet
   - (3) 15 square feet
   - (4) 17 square feet
   - (5) 20 square feet

   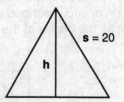

   4. 1 2 3 4 5
   ‖ ‖ ‖ ‖ ‖

5. An isosceles triangle has a base of 8 inches, and the equal sides are each 10 inches. The area of the triangle is
   - (1) 6 square inches
   - (2) 12 square inches
   - (3) 18 square inches
   - (4) 24 square inches
   - (5) 40 square inches

   5. 1 2 3 4 5
   ‖ ‖ ‖ ‖ ‖

Answers:

1. 3   2. 3   3. 1   4. 4   5. 2

V. C. Circles

C-1

In addition to plane figures made up of straight lines, geometry also studies figures with curved boundaries. The most important of these is a *circle*, a continuous set of points all at the same distance (the *radius*) from a *center* point.

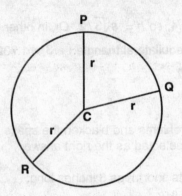

In this diagram, *C* is the center, and points *P, Q* and *R* are on the circle at radius *r* from the center at *C*. A line through the center from one side of a circle to the other is called a *diameter* of the circle; it is the largest line that can be drawn inside a circle. A diameter extends in both directions from the center of the circle to its boundary; so a diameter is exactly twice the length of a radius.

The perimeter of a circle (also called its *circumference*) always has the same ratio to its diameter. That ratio has a special name, π (pronounced "pie").

NOTE: The circumference (perimeter) of a circle is $C = \pi \times D = 2\pi \times r$.

A slice of the circle, like the figure *QCP* with the curved arc from *P* to *Q* and the radial lines *PC* and *QC*, is called a *sector* of the circle. The arc *PQ* has the same ratio to the circumference that the angle *PQC* has to 360°. If the angle is 80°, then the length of *PQ* is 80/360 = 8/36 = 2/9 (about 22%) of the circumference. The area of the sector is the same fraction of the area of the whole circle.

NOTE: The area of a circle is $A = \pi \times r^2$. A sector of a circle with angle *n* degrees at its center has area $(n/360) \times \pi \times r^2$.

A plane figure is *inscribed* in a circle if all its vertexes lie on the circle; it is *circumscribed* around the circle if each edge just touches the circle (without cutting across the curve.) In the diagram below, the figure on the left is inscribed and the figure on the right is circumscribed. If a square or other regular figure is inscribed in or circumscribed around a circle, its center (the intersection of its diagonals) will be the same point as the center of the circle.

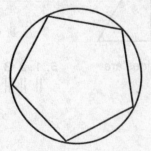 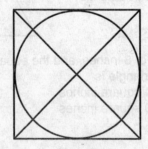 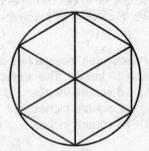

For inscribed and circumscribed squares, you should be able to figure out the relation between the radius or diameter of the circle and a side or a diagonal of the square. In the diagram above, for example, the side of the square is equal to the diameter (and, therefore, to twice the radius) of the circle.

The regular hexagon case is also worth remembering; here, the hexagon divides into 6 equilateral triangles with all the sides equal to the radius of the circle.

If you are asked to compare the areas of some figure with a circle, use a sketch or your imagination to see if the circle can fit around or inside the figure. In the diagram above, the circle obviously has less area than the square and more area than the pentagon or hexagon, and you can conclude that without knowing any formulas for the areas.

PRACTICE

Directions: Solve the following problems and blacken the space at the right under the number that corresponds to the one you have selected as the right answer.

1. A circle has area 4π; its circumference is
    (1) π   (4) 4
    (2) 2   (5) 4π
    (3) 2π

    1. 1 2 3 4 5
    ‖ ‖ ‖ ‖ ‖

2. In this diagram, the rectangle is formed by joining the centers of the circles. The circles each have area π; the perimeter of the rectangle is
    (1) 2   (4) 4π
    (2) 2π   (5) 6
    (3) 4

    2. 1 2 3 4 5
    ‖ ‖ ‖ ‖ ‖

3. Triangle *ABC* has a diameter of the circle as its base, and *AC* = *BC*. The area of *ABC* is
    (1) 5   (4) 25
    (2) 2√5   (5) 50
    (3) 5√2

    3. 1 2 3 4 5
    ‖ ‖ ‖ ‖ ‖

4. A circle is inscribed in a square of side 10; what is the area inside the square but outside the circle?
    (1) 100 − 25π   (4) π
    (2) 25π − 100   (5) 100 − 10π
    (3) 100 − 100π

    4. 1 2 3 4 5
    ‖ ‖ ‖ ‖ ‖

5. A wheel is 4 feet in diameter; about how far does it travel in 12 revolutions?
    (1) 100 feet   (4) 175 feet
    (2) 125 feet   (5) 200 feet
    (3) 150 feet

    5. 1 2 3 4 5
    ‖ ‖ ‖ ‖ ‖

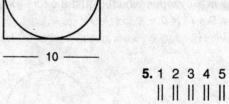

Answers:

3. 5   1. 4   4. 3   5. 2   5. 1

V. D. Solid Figures and Volume

D-1

Geometry also studies figures that are not totally in one plane, but have depth as well as height and width. These figures are harder to deal with, but are more like the ordinary objects around us in our three-dimensional world. You do not have to expect many questions about solid figures on the test, but you should know some basic facts about rectangular solids and about cylinders and spheres.

The simplest solid figures are rectangular solids; these are rectangles extruded (extended) from one plane into a perpendicular direction behind the surface of the original rectangle. Solid figures are usually sketched with their depth dimension hinted at by angling away from the straight up-and-down of a plane figure.

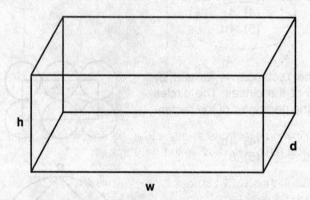

Just as we measure the area of a plane figure by filling it with unit squares (or fractions of unit squares), we measure the solid content (the *volume*) of a three-dimensional figure by filling it with unit cubes. If the rectangular solid above is 6 inches long, 4 inches high, and 3 inches deep, there will be $6 \times 4 \times 3 = 72$ cubes, each one 1 inch on a side, filling it. Its volume is 72 cubic inches.

NOTE: The volume of a rectangular solid is width $\times$ height $\times$ depth, $V = w \times h \times d$.

Just as in the case of a parallelogram, a solid can be made up of parallel planes that are not at right angles to each other; however, the volume will still be $w \times h \times d$ if you measure each dimension along perpendicular axes rather than along the edges of the solid.

In general, if you know the area of a plane figure, and you extend it perpendicularly into the depth dimension, the volume will be the area of the figure times its depth. The most common example of this is a *cylinder*, which is just a circle extended into the third dimension. The volume of a cylinder is $V = \pi \times r^2 \times d$.

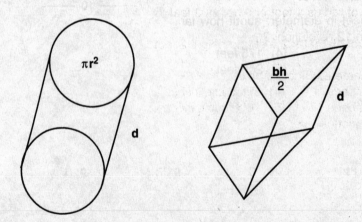

The solid on the right is a *triangular prism* (a triangle extended in depth). This figure has volume

$V = b \times h \times d/2$, where b is the base of the triangle, h is its height, and d is the depth in the third dimension. This is just the area of the triangle ($1/2\ b \times h$) times the depth.

A *sphere* is a solid figure formed by rotating a circle around a diameter as an axis. It is just barely possible that you may need to know the volume of a sphere, which is $V = 4/3\ \pi \times r^3$. It is more likely that you will be asked to compare spheres with other solids such as cylinders and cubes. Like area problems involving circumscribed and inscribed figures, the key here is to see which figures fit inside the others. For example, a sphere of diameter 10 fits inside a cylinder with radius 5 and height 10.

PRACTICE

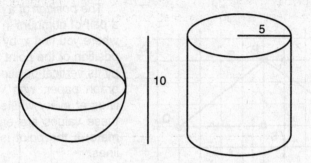

Directions: Solve the following problems and blacken the space at the right under the number that corresponds to the one you have selected as the right answer.

1. A shipping box is 36 inches by 24 inches by 18 inches; how many cubic feet can it hold?
    (1) 8
    (2) 9
    (3) 10
    (4) 12
    (5) 15

    1. 1 2 3 4 5
    ‖ ‖ ‖ ‖ ‖

2. A cylinder has a diameter of 2 feet and a height of 10 feet. Its volume is approximately
    (1) 31.5 ft^3
    (2) 40 ft^3
    (3) 63 ft^3
    (4) 94 ft^3
    (5) 126 ft^3

    2. 1 2 3 4 5
    ‖ ‖ ‖ ‖ ‖

3. Which of the following is too big to fit in a box 2 feet by 2 feet by 3 feet?
    (1) a sphere of radius 1 foot
    (2) a cube of side 2 feet
    (3) a cylinder of radius 1 foot and height 3 feet
    (4) a sphere of radius 2 feet
    (5) a cylinder of diameter 2 feet and height 2 feet

    3. 1 2 3 4 5
    ‖ ‖ ‖ ‖ ‖

4. A sphere of diameter 6 inches holds
    (1) 25 cubic inches
    (2) 36 cubic inches
    (3) 25π cubic inches
    (4) 36π cubic inches
    (5) 1000 cubic inches

    4. 1 2 3 4 5
    ‖ ‖ ‖ ‖ ‖

Answers:

4. 4   3. 4   2. 1   1. 2

V. E. Coordinate Geometry

E-1

The number line is a one-dimensional graph, with an imagined grid marking whole number positions. We can extend the graph into two dimensions by taking a horizontal number line and a vertical number line that intersects it at right angles, with the zero-point of both lines as the intersection. This point is called the *origin*, and the number lines are the *axes*. The horizontal *axis* is usually labeled *x*, and the vertical axis is labeled *y*.

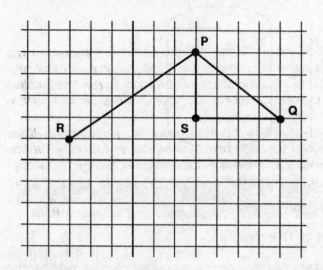

The *position* of a point is given by writing a pair of numbers in parentheses, as (*x,y*), where you find *x* by locating the horizontal position of the point along the *x*-axis and *y* by its vertical position along the *y*-axis. On graph paper, with vertical and horizontal lines at every whole number on the axes, these values are easy to find (or to estimate) if the point is not exactly on these lines.

In this diagram, *P* is (3,5), *Q* is (7,2) and *R* is (−3,1).

Coordinate graphs like this are set up to allow right triangle calculations using the Pythagorean Theorem. For example, a line from *P* to *Q* is the hypotenuse of a right triangle where the legs are segments of coordinate grid lines, drawn a bit thicker in the diagram to emphasize them. The third vertex of this right triangle is at *S,* which has the coordinates (3,2). Similarly, *P* and *R* form a right triangle with a point one unit below *S* at coordinates (3,1). To find the distance from *P* to *Q*, notice that the leg *PS* has length 3 and the leg *SQ* has length 4. So you should recognize that *PQS* is a 3-4-5 right triangle, and so *PQ* has length 5. In general, use the Pythagorean Theorem:

$$RP^2 = 6^2 + 4^2 = 36 + 16 = 52; \text{ therefore } RP = \sqrt{52} = 2\sqrt{13}.$$

NOTE: The distance between points $(x1, y1)$ and $(x2, y2) = \sqrt{(x1 - x2)^2 + (y1 - y2)^2}$.

$(x1 - x2)$ is the horizontal part of the distance; $(y2 - y1)$ is the vertical part. These are the legs of the right triangle, and the distance is the hypotenuse of that triangle.

You can find the midpoint of the line between *P* and *Q* by going halfway in the *x*-direction (2 units) and halfway in the *y*-direction (1½ units). The coordinates can be found by averaging the original (*x,y*) coordinates:

NOTE: The midpoint of the line from $(x1, y1)$ to $(x2, y2) = [\frac{1}{2}(x1 + x2), \frac{1}{2}(y1 + y2)]$.

E-2

Slope

The *slope* of a line is a measure of how steep it is. A horizontal line has slope 0, and a line that starts at the origin and goes through (1,1), (2,2), (3,3), etc., is going up in the *y*-direction exactly as rapidly as it covers horizontal distance in the *x*-direction. The definition is:

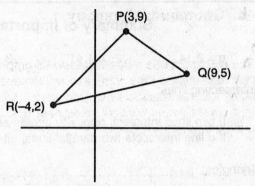

NOTE: The slope of the line from $(x1, y1)$ to
$(x2, y2) = (y2 - y1) / (x2 - x1)$.

Less formally, the slope is "rise" over "run," where "rise" means the change in vertical position and "run" means the change in horizontal position. Either the numerator or the denominator can be negative in this formula, and you must be careful to use the coordinates in the correct order (subtract the first point from the second; put another way, the change is what you have to add to the first point to get to the second one).

The line from *R* to *Q* has slope $(5 - 2) / [9 - (-4)] = 3/13$. It is rising gently, at a small fraction (slope = 1 means rising at a 45° angle from the horizontal; the angle here must be smaller than 45°). The line from *P* to *Q* has slope $(5 - 9) / (9 - 3) = -4/6 = -2/3$. The negative slope indicates that the line is dropping (negative rise) as it goes to the right. In a horizontal line, $(y2 - y1) = 0$, so the slope is 0; in a vertical line $(x2 - x1) = 0$, and division by it is undefined. You may think of it as "infinite"—as the angle of the line with the horizontal increases toward 90°, the slope gets larger and larger, without limit.

PRACTICE

Directions: Solve the following problems and blacken the space at the right under the number that corresponds to the one you have selected as the right answer.

1. The distance between the points (2,1) and (5,7) is
   (1) 9
   (2) $\sqrt{5}$
   (3) $\sqrt{9}$
   (4) $\sqrt{54}$
   (5) $\sqrt{74}$

   1. 1 2 3 4 5
   ‖ ‖ ‖ ‖ ‖

2. A circle of radius 4 with its center at the origin passes through all of the following points *except*
   (1) (−4,0)
   (2) (4,4)
   (3) (0,4)
   (4) (4,0)
   (5) (0,−4)

   2. 1 2 3 4 5
   ‖ ‖ ‖ ‖ ‖

3. The midpoint of the line from (−2,3) to (6,5) is
   (1) (4,8)
   (2) (8,2)
   (3) (2,4)
   (4) (3,3)
   (5) (0,0)

   3. 1 2 3 4 5
   ‖ ‖ ‖ ‖ ‖

4. The slope of the line from (2,7) to (9,1) is
   (1) −6/7
   (2) 7/6
   (3) 9/7
   (4) 1
   (5) 0

   4. 1 2 3 4 5
   ‖ ‖ ‖ ‖ ‖

5. The slope of the line through the points (2,−3) and (2,7) is
   (1) 2
   (2) −3/5
   (3) 5/3
   (4) 1
   (5) undefined

   5. 1 2 3 4 5
   ‖ ‖ ‖ ‖ ‖

Answers:

5. 5   4. 1   3. 3   2. 2   1. 4

Summary of Important Facts from Geometry

$\pi = 3.14\ldots$ $\sqrt{2} = 1.41\ldots$ $\sqrt{3} = 1.73\ldots$

Intersecting lines:

If two lines intersect, opposite angles are equal.
If a line intersects two parallel lines, alternate interior angles are equal.

Triangles:

The sum of the interior angles in a triangle is 180°.
An equilateral triangle has each of its angles equal to 60°.
The angles opposite the equal sides of an isosceles triangle are equal.
In any triangle, the largest side is opposite the largest angle and the smallest side is opposite the smallest angle.

Right Triangles:

In a right triangle, $c^2 = a^2 + b^2$ (Pythagorean Theorem).
Triangles with sides in the ratio 3:4:5 are right triangles.
Triangles with sides in the ratio 5:12:13 are right triangles.
A 45° right triangle (half-square) of side s has hypotenuse $s\sqrt{2}$.
A 30°-60°-90° triangle with short side s has height $s\sqrt{3}$.

Area and Volume:

Area of a rectangle or parallelogram with base b and height h, $A = b \times h$.
Area of a square of side s, $A = s^2$.
Area of a triangle with base b and height h, $A = (b \times h)/2$.
Area of a circle of radius r, $A = \pi r^2$ (circumference $C = 2\pi r$).

Volume of a rectangular solid or parallelepiped with base b, height h and depth d, $V = b \times h \times d$.
Volume of a cube of side s, $V = s^3$.
Volume of a cylinder of radius r and height h, $V = \pi r^2 h$.
Volume of a sphere of radius r, $V = \pi r^3$.

Coordinate Geometry:

The distance between points $(x1, y1)$ and $(x2, y2) = \sqrt{(x1 - x2)^2 + (y1 - y2)^2}$.
The midpoint of the line from $(x1, y1)$ to $(x2, y2) = [^{1}/_{2}(x1 + x2), ^{1}/_{2}(y1 + y2)]$.
The slope of the line from $(x1, y1)$ to $(x2, y2) = (y2 - y1) / (x2 - x1)$.

CHAPTER 5
Model Test A

ANSWER SHEET

Part One: Essay

Use the space allowed following the test question to write your answers to each of the essay questions.

Part Two: Short-Answer Questions

1. Ⓐ Ⓑ Ⓒ Ⓓ	26. Ⓐ Ⓑ Ⓒ Ⓓ	51. Ⓐ Ⓑ Ⓒ Ⓓ	76. Ⓐ Ⓑ Ⓒ Ⓓ
2. Ⓐ Ⓑ Ⓒ Ⓓ	27. Ⓐ Ⓑ Ⓒ Ⓓ	52. Ⓐ Ⓑ Ⓒ Ⓓ	77. Ⓐ Ⓑ Ⓒ Ⓓ
3. Ⓐ Ⓑ Ⓒ Ⓓ	28. Ⓐ Ⓑ Ⓒ Ⓓ	53. Ⓐ Ⓑ Ⓒ Ⓓ	78. Ⓐ Ⓑ Ⓒ Ⓓ
4. Ⓐ Ⓑ Ⓒ Ⓓ	29. Ⓐ Ⓑ Ⓒ Ⓓ	54. Ⓐ Ⓑ Ⓒ Ⓓ	79. Ⓐ Ⓑ Ⓒ Ⓓ
5. Ⓐ Ⓑ Ⓒ Ⓓ	30. Ⓐ Ⓑ Ⓒ Ⓓ	55. Ⓐ Ⓑ Ⓒ Ⓓ	80. Ⓐ Ⓑ Ⓒ Ⓓ
6. Ⓐ Ⓑ Ⓒ Ⓓ	31. Ⓐ Ⓑ Ⓒ Ⓓ	56. Ⓐ Ⓑ Ⓒ Ⓓ	81. Ⓐ Ⓑ Ⓒ Ⓓ
7. Ⓐ Ⓑ Ⓒ Ⓓ	32. Ⓐ Ⓑ Ⓒ Ⓓ	57. Ⓐ Ⓑ Ⓒ Ⓓ	82. Ⓐ Ⓑ Ⓒ Ⓓ
8. Ⓐ Ⓑ Ⓒ Ⓓ	33. Ⓐ Ⓑ Ⓒ Ⓓ	58. Ⓐ Ⓑ Ⓒ Ⓓ	83. Ⓐ Ⓑ Ⓒ Ⓓ
9. Ⓐ Ⓑ Ⓒ Ⓓ	34. Ⓐ Ⓑ Ⓒ Ⓓ	59. Ⓐ Ⓑ Ⓒ Ⓓ	84. Ⓐ Ⓑ Ⓒ Ⓓ
10. Ⓐ Ⓑ Ⓒ Ⓓ	35. Ⓐ Ⓑ Ⓒ Ⓓ	60. Ⓐ Ⓑ Ⓒ Ⓓ	85. Ⓐ Ⓑ Ⓒ Ⓓ
11. Ⓐ Ⓑ Ⓒ Ⓓ	36. Ⓐ Ⓑ Ⓒ Ⓓ	61. Ⓐ Ⓑ Ⓒ Ⓓ	86. Ⓐ Ⓑ Ⓒ Ⓓ
12. Ⓐ Ⓑ Ⓒ Ⓓ	37. Ⓐ Ⓑ Ⓒ Ⓓ	62. Ⓐ Ⓑ Ⓒ Ⓓ	87. Ⓐ Ⓑ Ⓒ Ⓓ
13. Ⓐ Ⓑ Ⓒ Ⓓ	38. Ⓐ Ⓑ Ⓒ Ⓓ	63. Ⓐ Ⓑ Ⓒ Ⓓ	88. Ⓐ Ⓑ Ⓒ Ⓓ
14. Ⓐ Ⓑ Ⓒ Ⓓ	39. Ⓐ Ⓑ Ⓒ Ⓓ	64. Ⓐ Ⓑ Ⓒ Ⓓ	89. Ⓐ Ⓑ Ⓒ Ⓓ
15. Ⓐ Ⓑ Ⓒ Ⓓ	40. Ⓐ Ⓑ Ⓒ Ⓓ	65. Ⓐ Ⓑ Ⓒ Ⓓ	90. Ⓐ Ⓑ Ⓒ Ⓓ
16. Ⓐ Ⓑ Ⓒ Ⓓ	41. Ⓐ Ⓑ Ⓒ Ⓓ	66. Ⓐ Ⓑ Ⓒ Ⓓ	91. Ⓐ Ⓑ Ⓒ Ⓓ
17. Ⓐ Ⓑ Ⓒ Ⓓ	42. Ⓐ Ⓑ Ⓒ Ⓓ	67. Ⓐ Ⓑ Ⓒ Ⓓ	92. Ⓐ Ⓑ Ⓒ Ⓓ
18. Ⓐ Ⓑ Ⓒ Ⓓ	43. Ⓐ Ⓑ Ⓒ Ⓓ	68. Ⓐ Ⓑ Ⓒ Ⓓ	93. Ⓐ Ⓑ Ⓒ Ⓓ
19. Ⓐ Ⓑ Ⓒ Ⓓ	44. Ⓐ Ⓑ Ⓒ Ⓓ	69. Ⓐ Ⓑ Ⓒ Ⓓ	94. Ⓐ Ⓑ Ⓒ Ⓓ
20. Ⓐ Ⓑ Ⓒ Ⓓ	45. Ⓐ Ⓑ Ⓒ Ⓓ	70. Ⓐ Ⓑ Ⓒ Ⓓ	95. Ⓐ Ⓑ Ⓒ Ⓓ
21. Ⓐ Ⓑ Ⓒ Ⓓ	46. Ⓐ Ⓑ Ⓒ Ⓓ	71. Ⓐ Ⓑ Ⓒ Ⓓ	96. Ⓐ Ⓑ Ⓒ Ⓓ
22. Ⓐ Ⓑ Ⓒ Ⓓ	47. Ⓐ Ⓑ Ⓒ Ⓓ	72. Ⓐ Ⓑ Ⓒ Ⓓ	97. Ⓐ Ⓑ Ⓒ Ⓓ
23. Ⓐ Ⓑ Ⓒ Ⓓ	48. Ⓐ Ⓑ Ⓒ Ⓓ	73. Ⓐ Ⓑ Ⓒ Ⓓ	98. Ⓐ Ⓑ Ⓒ Ⓓ
24. Ⓐ Ⓑ Ⓒ Ⓓ	49. Ⓐ Ⓑ Ⓒ Ⓓ	74. Ⓐ Ⓑ Ⓒ Ⓓ	99. Ⓐ Ⓑ Ⓒ Ⓓ
25. Ⓐ Ⓑ Ⓒ Ⓓ	50. Ⓐ Ⓑ Ⓒ Ⓓ	75. Ⓐ Ⓑ Ⓒ Ⓓ	100. Ⓐ Ⓑ Ⓒ Ⓓ

MODEL TEST A

Part One: Essay

30 MINUTES

Directions: The following two essay questions are designed to test your knowledge of written English. Read each question carefully, and then select one as your essay topic. You have 30 minutes to write a short essay on the topic you choose.

ESSAY TOPICS

Topic A

What is your favorite television program? Describe the show. Explain what you like most about this program. If you could talk to one of its creators, what would you ask him or her? Title your essay "Favorite Television Program."

Topic B

Imagine that you are stranded on a desert island. If you could have only one person with you, whom would you choose? Explain your reasons for your choice of companion. How would you and your companion pass the time? Title your essay "Desert Island Companion."

_____

_____

_____

_____

_____

_____

_____

_____

_____

_____

_____

_____

_____

_____

_____

Part Two: Short-Answer Questions 2 HOURS, 30 MINUTES

The kinds of questions used on this part of the test are varied. Be sure you read the directions carefully before beginning to answer the questions that follow.

Directions: Refer to the following passage to answer the next five questions. You are to choose the *one* best answer, marked A, B, C, or D, to each question. Then, on your answer sheet, find the number of the problem and mark your answer clearly. Answer all questions following a passage on the basis of what is *stated* or *implied* in that passage.

OFF-HIGHWAY VEHICLES: THE NEW RECREATION CHALLENGE

Over the last decade, Californians have witnessed the explosive growth of a new form of outdoor recreation—the use of off-highway recreational vehicles. The most common types of off-highway recreational vehicles are motorcycles, dune buggies, and four-wheel-drive vehicles. These key types of recreational vehicles, along with their derivatives (minibikes, go-karts) and a few exotics (gyrocopters, hovercraft) are now estimated to number more than a million and a half in California.

Field surveys have shown that the popularity of this recreational activity is tremendous. While some participants are interested only in competition and in the machines themselves, the majority of users prefer more casual touring and sight-seeing or using their vehicles as an aid in such other activities as hunting, fishing, and camping. For such people, off-highway vehicles are popular because they allow them great mobility in the out-of-doors, as well as a variety of satisfactions ranging from socialization with fellow vehicle users to the development of personal skills in mechanical repair work.

Despite its popularity, however, off-highway vehicle recreation is not without its problems. There has been a good deal of public protest and opposition to uncontrolled use of these vehicles. Property owners are sensitive to trespass, especially when off-highway vehicle use results in property destruction. Many observers are offended by the noise created by these vehicles, noise that is especially intrusive in the natural outdoor setting. Conservationists and land management officials are most concerned with the harm that unrestricted off-highway vehicle use may cause through soil erosion, vegetative damage, and disruption of wildlife patterns. All of these interests call for some limitation of the use of off-highway vehicles.

1. Which of the following off-highway recreational vehicles is LEAST commonly in use?

   A. Dune buggy   C. Gyrocopter
   B. Four-wheel-drive vehicle   D. Motorcycle

2. Most off-highway-vehicle users enjoy the vehicles because they allow them

   A. a chance to compete.
   B. great mobility in the out-of-doors.
   C. inexpensive urban transportation.
   D. opportunities for property destruction.

3. Conservationists fear unrestricted off-highway vehicle use may damage the land through

   A. mechanical problems.   C. socialization.
   B. public protest.   D. soil erosion.

4.   Property owners are concerned about off-highway vehicle use because vehicle users

A. develop skills in mechanical repair work.
B. disrupt wildlife patterns in wilderness areas.
C. prevent vegetative damage.
D. trespass on private property.

5.   If current problems caused by off-highway vehicle recreation continue, we may see

A. an expansion of off-highway vehicle use.
B. a lessening of public protest.
C. the proportion of gyrocopters to dune buggies increase.
D. restrictions placed on off-highway vehicle use.

Directions: Each of the following statements, questions, or problems is followed by four suggested answers or completions. Choose the *one* that best completes each of the statements or answers the question. Mark the oval on the answer sheet whose letter corresponds to the answer you have selected.

6.   The Carpenters bought an air conditioner on sale for $390, receiving a discount of 25% on the list price. What is the ratio of the sale price to the list price?

A. 2:3   B. 3:5   C. 3:4   D. 1:3

7.   If it takes 3.3 quarts to water 1 square foot of a vegetable garden, how many gallons does it take to water a garden 10 feet by 12 feet?

A. 96   B. 99   C. 39.6   D. 396

Refer to the graph below to answer the next three questions.

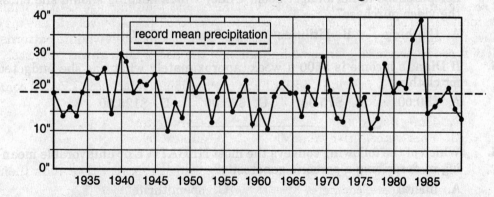

Annual Precipitation, San Joaquin Drainage, 1931-1989

8.   The lowest recorded precipitation (rainfall) in the San Joaquin Valley during this period was about

A. 10 inches   B. 15 inches   C. 20 inches   D. 25 inches

9.   The average annual precipitation in the San Joaquin Valley during this period was about

A. 15 inches   B. 20 inches   C. 25 inches   D. 30 inches

10. Roughly how many years shown in this graph had precipitation less than 15 inches?

    A. 10   B. 15   C. 20   D. 25

11. The word "refined" means the OPPOSITE of

    A. expensive   C. definite
    B. coarse   D. postponed

12. The phrase "under the weather" means the SAME as

    A. aboveboard   C. unwell
    B. turbulent   D. obscure

Refer to the following diagram to answer the next three questions.

DIAGRAM OF DIANA'S BUDGET

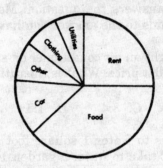

13. Approximately what portion of her monthly budget does Diana spend on rent?

    A. 1/10   B. 1/4   C. 1/3   D. 1/2

14. Diana buys her mother a video for her birthday and enters the amount of her purchase in her budget book. Under which heading should she enter the video purchase?

    A. Clothing   B. Utilities   C. Rent   D. Other

15. If Diana's income is $500 a week, approximately what has she budgeted for clothes?

    A. $50.00   B. $75.00   C. $85.00   D. $125.00

16. Which of the following conveys the most NEGATIVE or unfavorable meaning in describing a person's generosity?

    A. liberal   C. spendthrift
    B. unselfish   D. bountiful

17. There may be an error in capitalization or punctuation in the following sentence.

The United States Military <u>A</u>cademy at West Point is one of
                             A

the schools_that have been established to train the men and
            B

women who will become the officer<u>s</u> in our armed forces.
                           C

  A. Underlined part A needs to be changed to make the sentence correct.
  B. Underlined part B needs to be changed to make the sentence correct.
  C. Underlined part C needs to be changed to make the sentence correct.
  D. There is no change needed; the sentence is correct as written.

18. To find a synonym for a particular noun, you would consult
  A. an almanac.
  B. an atlas.
  C. an encyclopedia.
  D. a thesaurus.

The following paragraph may not be in a logical sequence. Read the sentences and select the best order for them.

19. (1) In the early days of television, few programs were available and people still had time to read. (2) The invention of television has caused Americans to lose interest in reading. (3) In consequence, people who were attracted to the new medium found themselves with less time in which to read. (4) As television became more and more widespread, however, more hours of programming were available each day.
  A. Correct as is
  B. 3, 1, 2, 4
  C. 4, 2, 1, 3
  D. 2, 1, 4, 3

20. Which of the following sentences is CORRECTLY punctuated?
  A. Mrs Williams baked a cake for the pot luck supper.
  B. Kim Phan, who was born in South Vietnam, moved to the United States as a child.
  C. Although Kareem enjoyed playing basketball he did not want to play professionally.
  D. The idea of running for Congress, has decidedly captured my imagination.

21. What part of a quarter is two nickels?
  A. 2/25
  B. 5/25
  C. 2/5
  D. 25/10

22. If 24 neighbors joined the neighborhood association and the remaining six did not, what percent of the neighbors did NOT join?
  A. 6%   B. 20%   C. 25%   D. 30%

23. If a man who is x years old now is three times the age of his son, how old will his son be five years from now?
  A. $(x + 15)$ years
  B. $(3x + 5)$ years
  C. $(x + 5/3)$ years
  D. $(x/3 + 5)$ years

24. Which of the following solid figures has the greatest volume?
    A. A rectangular solid 11 inches by 13 inches by 1 foot
    B. A sphere 1 foot in diameter
    C. A cone 1 foot in diameter and 1 foot high
    D. A cube 1 foot on a side

Refer to the following table for the next question.

BLEACH-O PRODUCTS		
Product	Amount	Price
Regular Size	1 Quart	$0.75
Family Size	1/2 Gallon	$1.14
Giant Economy Size	1 Gallon	$1.80

25. Which size bottle of Bleach-O should one buy to get the greatest quantity for the least amount of money?
    A. Regular Size
    B. Family Size
    C. Giant Economy Size
    D. All cost the same per quart

Directions: Refer to the following passage to answer the next five questions. You are to choose the *one* best answer, marked A, B, C, or D, to each question. Answer all questions on the basis of what is *stated* or *implied* in the passage.

GRAY WATER: USE EVERY DROP

"Gray water" is slightly used water—the water you have collected at the bottom of the tub after you have showered or the rinse water from the washing machine. It is still useful, and we cannot afford to let it go down the drain.

The best use for soapy water is in stretching your irrigation water allotment. The University of California Agricultural Cooperative Extension advises that gray water, regardless of whether it has detergent or soap in it, can be used on your plants without too much worry. There are some things to remember, however:

1) Don't put the soapy rinse water directly on the plant. Pour it on the earth at the base of the plant, but not on the leaves. You should not pour it on the lawn or on leafy ground covers.
2) If the rinse water contains borax soap, do not use it for irrigation.
3) If chlorine bleach is in the rinse water, you can use it for irrigation, but you should be sure to pour it on different spots each day. Too much chlorine is not good; letting the rinse water stand for a day will help.

Plumbing and health codes also have a few requirements:

1) Don't rearrange your plumbing to lead the gray water outside. Use buckets or trash pails to carry it outdoors. A garden hose siphon will work handily to get the used water outside where you need it.
2) There must not be any way for gray water to contaminate the water system. To avoid this, don't pump used water into the sprinkler system, and don't hook up a pump to any part of the household plumbing.
3) You may not allow the gray water to flow onto your neighbor's property. Keep it on your own plants and there is no problem.

26. Which of the following is an example of gray water?
    A. Carbonated water
    B. Rain water
    C. Soapy water
    D. Tap water

27. What is NOT a good use for gray water?
   A. Drinking
   B. Irrigating fields
   C. Rinsing sidewalks
   D. Watering house plants

28. Rinse water should not be used for irrigation if it
   A. contains borax soap.
   B. contains chlorine bleach.
   C. does not contain borax soap.
   D. does not contain chlorine bleach.

29. The health department does not wish gray water to
   A. be used for irrigation.
   B. be carried outdoors in buckets.
   C. contain detergent or soap.
   D. pollute the water system.

30. To get used water outside your home, you should
   A. let it flow onto your neighbor's property.
   B. pump it into your sprinkler system.
   C. rearrange your plumbing to lead the gray water outdoors.
   D. use a garden hose siphon or buckets.

---

31. A man drove 50 miles in two hours and then 150 miles in three hours. What was his average speed?
   A. 25 mph   B. 37.5 mph   C. 40 mph   D. 50 mph

32. What is the eighth number in the sequence below?

   2 5 8 11 14 . . .

   A. 17   B. 20   C. 23   D. 29

33. In the diagram to the right, Rosebud Avenue meets San Simeon at an angle of 30°, and 23rd Street crosses San Simeon at right angles. Rosebud runs for 60 yards between 23rd and San Simeon. Approximately how long is the stretch on San Simeon between the intersections?

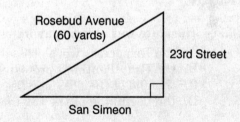

   A. 30 yards   B. 50 yards   C. 52 yards   D. 60 yards

34. If the price of grapes drops 30¢ per pound, you will be able to buy six more pounds for $8 than you were able to when you paid the higher price. What was the original, higher price per pound?
   A. 50¢   B. 60¢   C. 80¢   D. $1

35. A man who owns one-third of a business receives $20,000 as his share of the profits one year. He has five partners, each of whom owns an equal part of the remaining two-thirds of the business. How much should each of his partners receive in profits that year?
   A. $5,000   B. $8,000   C. $10,000   D. $20,000

Directions: Refer to the article below to answer the next five questions. You are to choose the *one* best answer, marked A, B, C, or D, to each question. Answer all questions on the basis of what is *stated* or *implied* in the article.

BUDGET BATTLE: NO ONE BUDGES

California legislators remained deadlocked for the second week in a row as disabled and unemployed people protested the budget battle that has delayed over 300,000 disability and unemployment checks.

Members of the American Federation of Teachers and the Gray Panther Party joined hundreds of protesters in wheelchairs who have been picketing the capitol building since the fiscal year began on July 1.

The teachers and Gray Panthers are protesting the delays in payments to retired teachers and in the issuance of Medi-Cal service checks to hospitals and nursing homes throughout the state.

Meanwhile, in the capital, Republicans and Democrats held separate press conferences to reiterate that the budget crisis was the fault of the other side.

Democratic Assembly Speaker Bustamente put the blame squarely on Republican shoulders, saying the lack of a speedy resolution of the budget impasse was due to a refusal by Republican Assembly members to compromise.

Republican Assembly leader Curt Pringle contradicted Bustamente, maintaining that the majority (Democratic) party never had intended to resolve the problem.

The state has been unable to pay any of its bills since Friday, June 30, because the Democratic legislators and the Republican governor have been unable to agree on a budget.

Republican legislators oppose any Democratic-backed legislation that would increase taxes; Democratic legislators oppose voting for even a Democrat-fashioned budget because they fear Governor Wilson will veto more than $1 billion from it to eliminate the necessity of a tax increase.

Sources claimed yesterday that Governor Wilson and top Democratic leaders were discussing the possibility of compromise.

"We must have a budget," said a source, "but first everyone must find a way to save face."

36. The state was able to pay its bills until

    A. the Democrats were elected.
    B. the Gray Panthers protested.
    C. the end of the previous fiscal year.
    D. the beginning of the tax increase.

37. All of the following groups have been adversely affected by the budget deadlock *except*

    A. handicapped persons.   C. retired teachers.
    B. nursery schools.   D. people out of work.

38. Which of the following statements are true?

    I. California has been without a budget since July 1.
    II. Curt Pringle leads the Republicans in the State Senate.
    III. Medi-Cal payments to hospitals have been delayed.

    A. Statements I and II only
    B. Statements I and III only
    C. Statements II and III only
    D. All of the statements

39. Which of the following statements are false?

    I. 300,000 unemployed and disabled persons picketed the capitol build-ing.

    II. Democratic Assembly leader Bustamente supports Republican Governor Wilson on the tax issue.

    III. Democratic legislators are ready to vote for a budget fashioned by Democrats.

    A. Statements I and II only
    B. Statements I and III only
    C. Statements II and III only
    D. All of the statements

40. A synonym for the word "impasse" is

    A. passage   C. compromise
    B. resolution   D. deadlock

41. Which answer below is closest to the area of this figure?

    A. 600 square feet
    B. 757 square feet
    C. 914 square feet
    D. 1256 square feet

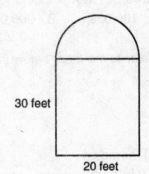

30 feet

20 feet

42. If you multiply the numbers A and B on the number line below, approximately where would you find the point representing $A \times B$?

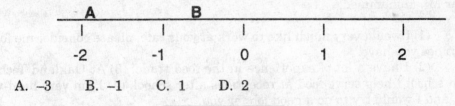

    A. –3   B. –1   C. 1   D. 2

Refer to the graph below to answer the next three questions.

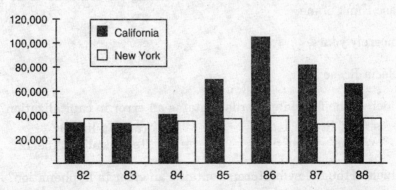

Persons Naturalized as U.S. Citizens in New York and California, 1982–88

43. In which year did New York naturalize more U.S. citizens than California did?

A. 1982   B. 1984   C. 1986   D. 1988

44. Which statement below best describes the number of citizens naturalized in California during this period?

A. The number of citizens naturalized each year increased throughout the period.

B. The number of citizens naturalized each year decreased steadily after 1982.

C. The number of citizens naturalized increased and then decreased during the period.

D. The number of citizens naturalized decreased and then increased during the period.

45. About how many citizens were naturalized in California from 1982 through 1988?

A. 100,000   B. 200,000   C. 300,000   D. 400,000

Refer to the letter below in answering the three questions that follow.

1542 Webster street
Oakland CA 94607
January 14, 1997

Marcus Mohammed
College Avenue Cafe
6220 College
Oakland CA 94618

Dear Mr. Mohammed,

(1) I would very much like to work at your cafe, please consider me for any openings you have.

(2) I have a lot of experience in the food trade. (3) At Oakland Technical high school I help serve food at receptions after school. (4) I am very hard-working, and I would try to do a good job for you.

(5) My English teacher, Mrs. Cooper, says she will be happy to give me a letter of reference. (6) I work for her as a classroom aide.

(7) If you are shorthanded and are looking for someone to do part-time work, please think of me.

Sincerely yours,

Felecia Reese

46. Which of the following words contains an error in capitalization?

A. "street" in line 1   C. "cafe" in line 9
B. "Avenue" in line 5   D. "Technical" in line 12

47. Which of the following terms contains an error in hyphenation?

A. hard-working   C. shorthanded
B. classroom aide   D. part-time

48. Which of the following sentences contains an error in punctuation?

A. Sentence 1   C. Sentence 5

B. Sentence 4   D. Sentence 7

---

49. Every three minutes on the average someone sets off a false alarm. Approximately how many false alarms are set off during an eight-hour shift?

A. 160   B. 120   C. 24   D. 16

50. Before starting an exercise program, <u>a consultation with your physician is advisable.</u>

The sentence would be better if the underlined part were written as:

A. a consultation with your physician is advisable.

B. it is advisable to get a consultation with your physician.

C. a physician's consultation is advisable.

D. you should consult your physician.

51. Phil buys some items at the local ReadyMart for a total purchase of $9.53. If he pays with a $10 bill, what is the *smallest* number of coins he could get as correct change?

A. 5   B. 6   C. 7   D. 8

52. What is the slope of line L in the graph below?

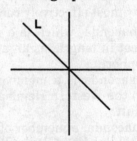

A. –2   B. –1   C. 1   D. 2

53. A man bought a suit priced at $200 and a pair of slacks priced at $30. If the store was giving a 10% discount on all items purchased that day, how much did he have to pay?

A. $23   B. $207   C. $210   D. $227

54. In the National League baseball standings, one of the following teams has a percentage of .333. Which team is it?

A. San Diego: Won 11, Lost 7

B. Houston: Won 10, Lost 8

C. Atlanta: Won 6, Lost 12

D. Los Angeles: Won 5, Lost 13

55. A man buys a condo for $63,000. He pays $2,500 for plumbing and $4,000 for rewiring. If he wants to make a profit of 20%, at what price must he sell the condo?

A. $70,000   B. $75,600   C. $83,400   D. $83,600

Complete the following two sentences with the correct form of the missing word.

56. Although Sally had told Bill she would supply all the refreshments for the party, he _____ some additional cheese and crackers for her to serve.
   A. bringed   C. brought
   B. brings   D. brung

57. Helen's good score on the proficiency test made her parents very _____.
   A. happily   C. happiness
   B. happy   D. happier

---

58. Which of the following terms is the most GENERAL?
   A. food   C. melon
   B. cantaloupe   D. fruit

59. Which of the following terms is the most SPECIFIC?
   A. dwelling place   C. ranch house
   B. building   D. house

60. (1) The common anaconda is the largest snake in the Western Hemisphere. (2) It is a member of the boa family. (3) It may reach 20 feet in length as an adult.

   Which answer below most effectively combines the above three sentences?
   A. The common anaconda, which is a member of the boa family which may reach 20 feet in length, as an adult it is the largest snake in the Western Hemisphere.
   B. The common anaconda is a member of the boa family, which is the largest snake in the Western Hemisphere, possibly reaching 20 feet in length as an adult.
   C. The common anaconda, a member of the boa family, which may reach 20 feet in length as an adult, is the largest snake in the Western Hemisphere.
   D. The largest snake in the Western Hemisphere, a member of the boa family which may reach 20 feet in length as an adult, is the common anaconda.

61. Al has $5 more cash with him than Jay has. After each of them has spent $4 on lunch, Al winds up with twice as much cash as Jay. How much cash did Al have to start with?
   A. $5   B. $10   C. $12   D. $14

62. A car is to make a 240-mile trip. The driver estimates he will be traveling at an average rate of 25 miles per hour in the city, but at an average of 50 miles per hour on the freeway. If only 15 miles will be driven in city traffic, how long will it take this driver to make the 240-mile trip if everything goes according to his estimate?
   A. 5 hours and 6 minutes   C. 4 hours and 30 minutes
   B. 4 hours and 48 minutes   D. 4 hours and 21 minutes

63. Mrs. Brown is 20 years older than her daughter. Five years ago, she was three times as old. How old is the daughter now?
   A. 15   B. 16   C. 18   D. 20

64. Amy's living room is 25 feet by 30 feet, with the ceiling 10 feet high. If she is painting the walls and ceiling the same color, what is the area she must buy paint to cover?

    A. 750 square feet   C. 1750 square feet

    B. 1500 square feet   D. 1850 square feet

65. A triangle has one angle of 55° and one of 40° What is the third angle?

    A. 75°   B. 85°   C. 90°   D. 95°

66. A man wishes to purchase some fabric to make a robe. The clerk tells him that if he washes the fabric it will shrink 25%. The man knows he will need 3 yards of the fabric for his robe. How many yards of fabric must he buy if he is to have 3 yards left after shrinkage?

    A. 3   B. 3¼   C. 4   D. 4½

Directions: Refer to the poem below to answer the next four questions. You are to choose the *one* best answer, marked A, B, C, or D, to each question. Answer all questions on the basis of what is *stated* or *implied* in the poem.

        EIGHT O'CLOCK*

        He stood, and heard the steeple
         Sprinkle the quarters on the morning town.
        One, two, three, four, to market place and people
         It tossed them down.

        Strapped, noosed, nighing his hour,
         He stood and counted them and cursed his luck;
        And then the clock collected in the tower
         Its strength, and struck.

                      A. E. Housman (1859-1936)

*Eight A.M. was the customary time in England for executions.

67. In line 1, "He" most likely refers to

    A. an observer.   C. the executioner.

    B. the condemned man.   D. a guard.

68. The "quarters" referred to in line 2 are

    A. coins.   C. divisions of an hour.

    B. housing accommodations.   D. districts of a city.

69. The poem's central character curses his luck because he

    A. dislikes having to wait.   C. has just lost a bet.

    B. is late for an appointment.   D. cannot escape his fate.

70. The poem provides information about all of the following EXCEPT

    A. the emotions of the condemned man.

    B. the manner of his execution.

    C. the nature of his crime.

    D. the physical setting.

Refer to the following graph to answer the next six questions.

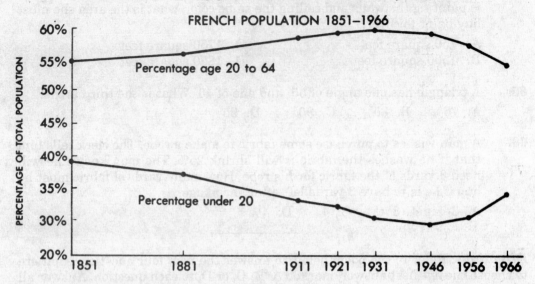

71. Which of the following statements about the makeup of the French population in the period from 1851 to 1966 is true?

    A. The percentage of the French population under 20 decreased, while the percentage between the ages of 20 and 64 increased.

    B. The percentage of the French population between the ages of 20 and 64 remained the same, while the percentage under 20 changed.

    C. The percentage of the French population under 20 decreased and then increased, while the percentage of the population between the ages of 20 and 64 first increased and then decreased.

    D. The percentage of the French population under 20 increased and then decreased; the percentage of the population between the ages of 20 and 64 did the same.

72. In what year was the percentage of the French population under 20 years of age at its *highest* point?

    A. 1966   B. 1946   C. 1881   D. 1851

73. In 1851, approximately what percentage of the total population was made up of persons between the ages of 20 and 64?

    A. 38%   B. 40%   C. 55%   D. 60%

74. In 1851, approximately what percentage of the total population was made up of persons aged 65 and over?

    A. 7%   B. 12%   C. 38%   D. 55%

75. Which of the following statements about the percentage of the French population aged 65 and over is true for the period from 1851 to 1966?

    A. The percentage of the French population aged 65 and over decreased.

    B. The percentage of the French population aged 65 and over remained the same.

    C. The percentage of the French population aged 65 and over increased steadily from about 7% to about 12% of the total population.

    D. It is impossible to determine any information about the percentage of the French population aged 65 and over from the graph given.

76. Which of the following statements about the percentage of the French population under the age of 20 is obviously *false*?

A. In the year 1851, persons under 20 made up approximately 38% of the total French population.

B. In the year 1931, the percentage of the French population under 20 was lower than it was in 1946.

C. In the year 1931, the percentage of the French population under 20 was higher than it was in 1966.

D. In the years after 1946, the portion of the French population under 20 grew as a result of the post-World War II baby boom.

---

77. Find the answer choice that matches the following definition:

Definition: recognize as different; set apart clearly

A. alienate   C. realize
B. distinguish   D. shun

78. Find the answer choice that matches the following definition:

Definition: a person with no prior training or experience in an activity

A. performer   C. novice
B. visionary   D. referee

79. Find the answer choice that matches the following definition:

Definition: strongly determined; set in one's purpose

A. enthusiastic   C. poised
B. evenhanded   D. resolute

80. A woman works a 40-hour week, with a pay rate of $8.90 an hour. What are her gross wages if she is paid every two weeks?

A. $89   B. $178   C. $356   D. $712

81. Three women eat lunch together, each ordering a salad plate and cup of coffee. Their total bill comes to $10.20, not counting the tip. If they leave a 15% tip, how much should each of the women pay?

A. $3.40   B. $3.74   C. $3.91   D. $11.73

Refer to the following table to answer the next three questions.

QUARTERLY EARNINGS	
QUARTER	AMOUNT EARNED
First quarter (October–December 1995)	$2,500
Second quarter (January–March 1996)	$4,750
Third quarter (April–June 1996)	$3,600
Fourth quarter (July–September 1996)	$4,360

82. Weekly unemployment benefits range from $25 to $90 a week, depending on how much the unemployed person has earned during a 12-month "base period." There are four quarters in each base period. The quarter in which the person had been paid the highest wages is used to set his weekly unemployment benefit amount. During his base period, a man earned the above amounts. Which quarter was used to set his weekly unemployment benefit amount?

A. First quarter   C. Third quarter
B. Second quarter   D. Fourth quarter

83. How many months make up an unemployed person's base period?

    A. 3   B. 4   C. 12   D. 25

84. How much did the man earn during the third quarter of his base period?

    A. $2,500   B. $3,600   C. $4,360   D. $4,750

85. A woman has made 12 gallons of strawberry preserves. How many quart jars does she need in order to store the preserves?

    A. 36   B. 40   C. 44   D. 48

86. A meter is approximately 39.36 inches. About how many meters are there in 100 yards?

    A. 50   B. 91   C. 110   D. 300

Refer to the diagram below for the next question.

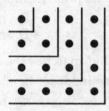

87. Johnny is arranging coins in the pattern shown and has done four repetitions of the pattern. How many additional coins are needed to complete the fifth repetition?

    A. 5   B. 9   C. 12   D. 25

Directions: Refer to the passage below to answer the next four questions. You are to choose the *one* best answer, marked A, B, C, or D, to each question. Answer all questions on the basis of what is *stated* or *implied* in the passage.

SYSTEMS OF BREEDING

In planning a breeding program for rabbits, you first need to understand the concept of the *gene pool*. Any breed or other foundation stock selected for breeding constitutes a pool or group of many, perhaps thousands, of hereditary units, commonly referred to as genes. The genes are specifically located in the chromosomes, very small threadlike bodies found in every cell of the body. In the rabbit there are 22 pairs, and their segregation (one member of each pair going to each egg or sperm) in the production of eggs or sperm, plus the ultimate union of egg and sperm at mating and conception, provides the mechanism for transmission of hereditary characteristics from one generation to the next. It also provides the mechanism that in nature insures sufficient variability for adaptation of the species to minor changes in the environment and for its perpetuation.

The gene pool of the rabbit has been modified in many ways by domestication and by selection to establish the different breeds. This pool, in the rabbits at hand, is the breeder's capital stock, and intelligent breeding depends on knowing as much as possible about the pool. How well does it perpetuate itself? How much variation does it transmit that is either good, bad, or indifferent, particularly with respect to reproductive capacity? How much of it is immediately apparent to the breeder, and how much can become apparent only after long breeding experience? In spite of all that humans know about genetics and reproduction, nature is still the most successful breeder. If this were not so, we would not have the infinite number and variety of species that exist in the world, many of which are known to have existed for many, many centuries. But even nature slips. Species have been lost as a result of circumstances with which they were unable to cope; malformed offspring occur sometimes in the wild. Nature's success is essentially due to the size of the gene pools of each species, plus the ruthless elimination of the unfit as they appear. These combine to insure a high proportion of successful individuals, including some individuals adaptable to any ordinary change that may occur in the environment in which they live. The ability to adapt to differing environments is the feature that helps promote survival and is the mechanism by which species have evolved.

88. This article is probably addressed to
    A. professional geneticists.
    B. commercial rabbit raisers.
    C. successful individuals.
    D. hereditary units.

89. What are chromosomes?
    A. Genes
    B. Species
    C. Types of rabbits
    D. Parts of cells

90. Which of the following statements are TRUE?
    I. Breeders need genetic information to plan breeding programs intelligently.
    II. The gene pool consists of 22 chromosome pairs.
    III. Successful species survive by adapting to their environment.

    A. Statements I and II only
    B. Statements I and III only
    C. Statements II and III only
    D. All of the statements

91. What does the phrase "even nature slips" most nearly mean?
    A. It is natural to slide.
    B. Nature is uniformly successful.
    C. Even nature moves gradually.
    D. Even nature makes mistakes.

92. What is the slope of the line in the diagram below?

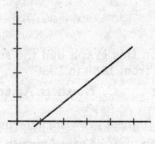

    A. 3/5   B. 3/4   C. 4/5   D. 3

93. A Marin County resident goes shopping and purchases $56 worth of goods, only $8 of which is taxable. How much will his total bill be, including the 6% sales tax?

    A. $48.00   B. $56.48   C. $60.48   D. $64.00

94. I was deeply <u>effected</u> by the news of his death.

    A. The underlined word is spelled correctly.

    B. The underlined word is spelled incorrectly.

95. Please save all your <u>reciepts</u> so that we can reimburse you.

    A. The underlined word is spelled correctly.

    B. The underlined word is spelled incorrectly.

Refer to the graph below to answer the next five questions.

World Population – Annual Growth Rate, by
Continent: 1960 to 1986

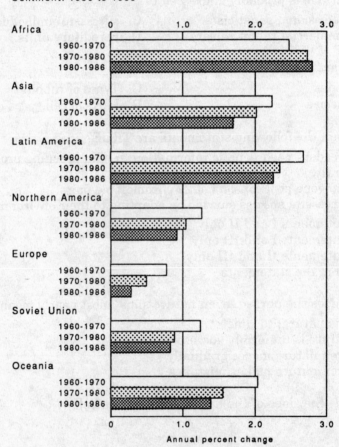

96. Which region shown on this graph had the smallest annual growth rate throughout the period from 1960 to 1986?

    A. Africa   B. Asia   C. Northern America   D. Europe

97. Which region had the highest growth rate from 1970 to 1980?

    A. Africa   B. Asia   C. Latin America   D. Oceania

98. Which region showed the smallest change in growth between the seventies and the eighties?

    A. Soviet Union   C. Northern America

    B. Latin America   D. Europe

99. Which of the conclusions below is NOT supported by this graph?

    A. Population is increasing in all major regions of the world.

    B. Growth rates have decreased everywhere since the sixties.

    C. No region's population is growing more than 3% per year.

    D. Europe's growth rate is less than half that of other regions.

100. Approximately how many times greater was the population growth rate in Africa than in Europe during the seventies?

    A. 2   B. 3   C. 4   D. 5

ANSWER KEY

TEST A

Part One: Essay

There are no "correct" answers to this part.

Part Two: Short-Answer Questions

1. C	21. C	41. B	61. D	81. C
2. B	22. B	42. C	62. A	82. B
3. D	23. D	43. A	63. A	83. C
4. D	24. D	44. C	64. D	84. B
5. D	25. C	45. D	65. B	85. D
6. C	26. C	46. A	66. C	86. B
7. B	27. A	47. A	67. B	87. B
8. A	28. A	48. A	68. C	88. B
9. B	29. D	49. A	69. D	89. D
10. B	30. D	50. D	70. C	90. B
11. B	31. C	51. A	71. C	91. D
12. C	32. C	52. B	72. D	92. B
13. B	33. C	53. B	73. C	93. B
14. D	34. C	54. C	74. A	94. B
15. A	35. B	55. C	75. C	95. B
16. C	36. C	56. C	76. B	96. D
17. D	37. B	57. B	77. B	97. A
18. D	38. B	58. A	78. C	98. A
19. D	39. D	59. C	79. D	99. B
20. B	40. D	60. C	80. D	100. D

ANSWER EXPLANATIONS   TEST A

Part Two: Short-Answer Questions

1. Answer C.   Gyrocopter

When you are answering questions about a reading passage, it is a good plan to read the passage quickly, or to skim over it paying special attention to the first and last paragraphs and to the opening and closing sentences of each paragraph. In this passage, the first paragraph introduces the topic (the growth in the number of off-highway recreational vehicles) and then goes on to give the main types of these vehicles and to estimate their numbers. The second paragraph says that these vehicles are tremendously popular and then goes on to give some of the reasons for their popularity. The last paragraph says that these vehicles cause problems and goes on to list some of the problems. The very last sentence says that various interests "call for the limitation of the use of off-highway vehicles." If you have a good overview of what the passage says and where it says it, you will be able to find the answers to detailed questions more easily.

Question 1 asks which of four possible choices is the least commonly used recreational vehicle. Turn back to the first paragraph, which introduces the different types of vehicles. Its second sentence says "The most common off-highway recreational vehicles are motorcycles, dune buggies, and four-wheel-drive vehicles." You are looking for the *least* commonly used recreational vehicle. Therefore, you should be able to rule out the most commonly used vehicles, Choices A, B, and D. The gyrocopter, Choice C, was not listed as one of the most commonly used vehicles. This suggests that, of the four vehicles given, it may be the one least commonly in use. In fact, later in the paragraph, gyrocopters are listed with hovercraft among the "few exotics." They are unusual recreational vehicles, far less common than dune buggies, four-wheel-drive vehicles, and motorcycles.

2. Answer B.   Great mobility in the out-of-doors

The second paragraph of the reading passage gives people's reasons for liking off-highway vehicles. Read through these reasons and compare them with the possible answers to determine the reason most users enjoy their vehicles. Choice A, *a chance to compete,* is something that numbers of off-highway-vehicle users enjoy. However, the paragraph's second sentence states that "While *some* participants *are interested* only in *competition . . . , the majority prefer more casual touring and sight-seeing.*" This means that some are interested in a chance to compete, but *most* are not. Therefore, you can rule out Choice A. Choice C, *inexpensive urban transportation,* is not supported by the passage, which stresses the usefulness of off-highway vehicles in hunting, fishing, camping, and other non-urban activities. Therefore, you can rule out Choice C. While off-highway vehicle use can result in property destruction, most off-highway-vehicle users are not out there looking for *opportunities for property destruction.* Therefore, you can rule out Choice D. Only Choice B is left. For the majority of users (those people who prefer more casual touring and outdoor activities to the joys of competition), "off-highway vehicles are popular because they allow them *great mobility in the out-of-doors.*" Choice B is the correct answer.

3. Answer D.   Soil erosion

The last paragraph of the passage mentions the problems in using off-highway vehicles. Read through it again to find out which problem most concerns conservationists. The next-to-last sentence of the passage states plainly that they "are most concerned with the harm that unrestricted off-highway vehicle use may cause through soil erosion...." Clearly, Choice D (soil erosion) is the correct answer.

In answering this sort of question, you may find it helpful to make a quick *guess* about the correct answer and then to skim back over the passage just to test out whether your guess was accurate. From just a quick glance at the four answer choices, you could probably guess that a conservationist would most likely fear soil erosion as a possible problem. Thus, you could immediately scan the passage, looking for the words "soil erosion," and, on locating the phrase, read through that part of the passage quickly to confirm your guess.

4. Answer D. Trespass on private property

The same strategy mentioned above for question 3 works well here also: guess which of the four answer choices is most likely to concern property owners, and then check back in the third paragraph to see if your guess was right. A property owner is likely to be concerned about someone's trespassing on his or her property, so Choice D is a good guess. The third sentence of the paragraph discussing the problems of off-highway vehicle use says "Property owners are sensitive to trespass." That means they can get pretty touchy when someone intrudes on their land. The wording isn't exactly the same here as it is in the question, but the meaning's very close: you can assume your guess is correct. (Besides, Choices B and C are mentioned as concerns of conservationists and land management officials, not of property owners, so you can rule them out. What's more, Choice A makes no sense in the context, so you can rule it out as well.)

5. Answer D. Restrictions placed on off-highway vehicle use

This question asks you to reason a little bit beyond what is actually said in the passage. The passage's concluding paragraph deals with the problems of off-highway vehicle use. The second sentence of this paragraph says that "There has been a good deal of public protest and opposition to uncontrolled use of these vehicles." Then, after describing some of the protests, the paragraph concludes with the statement that "All of these interests call for some limitation of the use of off-highway vehicles." What you need to do at this point is to think things through. If the problems caused by off-highway vehicle use continue, what is likely to occur? The protests and opposition are likely to continue, and even to increase. As a result of this growing opposition, there will likely be some limitation of off-highway vehicle use. Thus, Choice D is a likely result if the problems continue.

Check the other answers to see whether any of them is a likely *result* of continued problems. Choice A, *an expansion of off-highway vehicle use,* actually might be a cause of continued or intensified problems, not a result of them. You can eliminate Choice A. Continuing problems should lead to an increase of protest, not a lessening of complaints. You can eliminate Choice B. Continuing problems caused by off-highway vehicles in general wouldn't be likely to lead to an increase in numbers of one particular kind of recreational vehicle. You can eliminate Choice C. Only Choice D is left; it is the correct answer.

6. Answer C. 3:4

The ratio of two numbers is a comparison of the two reduced to lowest terms. In this case, the sale price is 1/4 (25%) off the list price, so it is easy to see that it compares to the full price as 3/4 to 1. Multipliying by 4, 3/4:1 becomes 3:4.

7. Answer B. 99 gallons

First you must find the area of the garden in square feet. Multiplying the length by the width, you get 120 square feet. Then multiply by the number of quarts required per square foot (3.3 quarts for each).

$$
\begin{array}{r}
120 \\
\underline{3.3} \\
36\ 0 \\
\underline{360\quad} \\
396.0
\end{array}
$$

To convert 396 quarts to gallons, you must remember that a gallon is 4 quarts. 396/4 = 99.

8. Answer A. 10 inches

Look for the lowest point on the graph; it isn't necessary to be absolutely certain which point is lowest, if there are several at about the same height. When there are a lot of points, it may help to cover most of the graph with a piece of paper (for example, your answer sheet) and move it down parallel to the x-axis until only one point or a very few points are visible. There are three points below all the others, with one in the late '40s (about 1947) being almost exactly on the 10-inch line.

9. Answer B. 20 inches

The average rainfall is in the center of the range of yearly rainfall numbers. For every year with more rainfall, there must be one or more other years that "balance" it on the other side. So, to find the average on a graph, look for a level that has about as many points above it as below it. A piece of paper helps in this question, as it did for the previous one. Setting it at the 15-inch level, you will see a large majority of the point lying above 15. At 20 inches, it looks like about half of the points are covered (but try the other answers before being too quick to jump at this one.) At the 25-inch-level, there are no more than 9 or 10 points above the sheet of paper, and at 30 inches only two. The graph does center on 20 inches.

10. Answer B. 15

Count the number of points that are below the 15-inch line on the graph. If you're not sure whether a point is exactly on the line or below it, count it anyway, and check whether that makes a difference in the answer you would choose. In this case, there are thirteen points that are definitely below the line, one that probably is below it (1939) and a couple that are hard to tell exactly (1956 and 1984). The answer *must* be more than 10 (Choice A), and it cannot be as high as 20 (Choice C). The only reasonable choice is 15.

11. Answer B. Coarse

The word "refined" means polished or cultivated. Its opposite therefore is "coarse" or crude and unrefined.

12. Answer C. Unwell

To be "under the weather" is to feel sick or ailing. Its synonym therefore is "unwell" or sickly.

13. Answer B. 1/4

The rent slice of the pie, in the upper right, has a right angle at the center—just what you get if you cut a pie in quarters.

14. Answer D.   Other

Since the video for Diana's mother's birthday has nothing to do with Rent, Food, Car, Clothing, or Utilities, it must fall under the category of Other.

15. Answer A. $50.00

The Clothing budget is only one part of the upper left quadrant of the pie chart (Utilities, Clothing, and Other together make up about 1/4 of the budget). These are all about the same size pie slices, so each is about 1/3 of 1/4 of the whole budget. $1/3 \times 1/4 = 1/12$, which is smaller than 1/10. Therefore, Diana must have budgeted 10% or less of her $500 income for clothing. $50 might be a little too large, but it is fairly close. The other answers are larger, so the answer must be A. (The guess that Clothing is exactly 1/3 of the one quadrant may be a bit off; however, the question is not asking for precise dollar amounts, just an approximation.)

16. Answer C.   Spendthrift

To be spendthrift is to be extravagant and wasteful with one's money. Bountiful or abundant generosity is good. Liberal or openhanded generosity is good. Unselfish generosity clearly is good. However, spendthrift or improvident generosity is excessive. The word has strong negative connotations.

17. Answer D.   There is no change needed; the sentence is correct as written.

The use of the capital letter "A" in the name of the United States Military Academy is correct. There is no need for a comma or any other punctuation mark between the words "school" and "that." There is no need for an apostrophe or any other punctuation mark before or after the ending "s" in "officers."

18. Answer D.   A thesaurus

A thesaurus is a dictionary of synonyms and antonyms.

19. Answer D.   2, 1, 4, 3

The paragraph makes the most sense read in the following order:
(2) The invention of television has caused Americans to lose interest in reading. (1) In the early days of television, few programs were available and people still had time to read. (4) As television became more and more widespread, however, more hours of programming were available each day. (3) In consequence, people who were attracted to the new medium found themselves with less time in which to read.

20. Answer B.   Sentence B is correctly punctuated.

Sentence A is incorrectly punctuated: the title "Mrs." must end with a period. Sentence C is incorrectly punctuated: there should be a comma between the words "basketball" and "he." Sentence D is incorrectly punctuated: there should be no comma in the sentence.

21. Answer C.   2/5

A quarter has the same value as five nickels, so two nickels = 2/5 of a quarter in value. Alternatively, you can figure in cents: a quarter is 25¢, and two nickels are 10¢, making the two nickels 10/25 of a quarter. Reduce that fraction to the lowest terms for the answer.

22. Answer B. 20%

Although 24 neighbors joined the association, six did not. That makes a total of 30 neighbors altogether. The question asks for the percentage of those who did not join, so you need the percentage equivalent of the fraction 6/30. This fraction reduces to 1/5, which you may remember is 20%. (If you don't remember that percentage, just do the division; that is also easier if you use the fraction reduced to lowest terms:

$$5 \overline{)\,1.00}^{\,0.20}$$

23. Answer D. (x/3 + 5) years

You need to write an expression for the *son's* age in five years, given the information presented in the questions. Since it is the son's age that is asked for, start by writing an expression for the son's age now. We are told that the man's age (x) is three times the son's age now. Using y for the son's age, that statement becomes: $x = 3y$, or dividing by 3 to get y:

y = the son's age now = $x/3$.

In five years, the son will be $y + 5 = x/3 + 5$.

24. Answer D. A cube 1 foot on a side

You do not need to remember formulas for the volume of a sphere or a cone to answer this question. What you need is to imagine the figures, or make a sketch of them on paper. Both the cone and the sphere will fit inside the cube (each is 1 foot at the longest in height, width, and depth, the same as the cube); but the sphere and the cone reach their longest value at only one point in each dimension. (You could carve either the cone or the sphere out of a 1-foot cube of wood; doing that would remove volume from the cube to get to the other figure.)

A picture doesn't help for comparing the rectangular solid with the cube, as that is larger in one dimension than the cube, but smaller in another. Here, you do have to remember that the volume of a rectangular solid is width × depth × height. The solid in A has a volume of $11 \times 13 \times 12$ in^3, and the cube has volume $12 \times 12 \times 12$ in^3. The last dimension is the same in both, so it "cancels out" in deciding which solid has the larger volume; you just need to calculate that $11 \times 13 = 143$ and $12 \times 12 = 144$. The cube is larger than solid A as well as the other figures.

25. Answer C. Giant Economy Size

Each size is twice as big as the one before (a gallon is four quarts, and therefore a half-gallon is two quarts.) If each size *cost* twice as much as the smaller one, all sizes would cost the same per quart. But in fact each size is *less* than twice as much. Each of the two quarts of the half-gallon is cheaper than the one-quart size. And each two quarts (half-gallon) in the gallon is cheaper than the two quarts of the intermediate size. The cheapest per quart is the gallon size.

26. Answer C. Soapy water

With this and later passages, we will assume that you have read over the passage to get a general idea of its meaning and to have a sense of where in the passage to look for specific details to answer the individual questions. You can usually get a good idea of the contents of a paragraph by reading just its first sentence (generally the "topic sentence" of the paragraph), so your first skimming of the passage doesn't have to be complete or take a lot of time.

The very first sentence of the passage explains what "gray water" is: water left over after showers or baths or in washing machines. Such water is soapy and a bit dirty. Question 6 asks you for an example of gray water. The possible choices are:

    A. Carbonated water. NOT gray water. It is not something left over after washing. It is what you drink as sparkling water or seltzer.

    B. Rain water. NOT gray water. Rain water, in fact, is usually quite clean.

    C. Soapy water. This is the type of water left after showering or washing. Clearly, Choice C is an example of gray water.

    D. Tap water. NOT gray water. This is the water that comes out of the tap *before* you wash.

27. Answer A. Drinking

Use the process of elimination to begin answering this question. The second paragraph of the passage says that gray water "can be used on your plants." Therefore, Choice B, *irrigating fields,* IS a good use for gray water, as is Choice D, *watering house plants.* You can eliminate Choices B and D. Choices A and C (*drinking* and *rinsing sidewalks*) are not mentioned in the passage, so you have to think a bit to see which one would be an appropriate use for gray water and which one would not. There is no obvious reason why you couldn't use slightly soapy water to rinse your sidewalks. There are several reasons why you probably shouldn't drink the stuff. (At the very least, it would taste bad; at worst, the cleaning agents in the water might do you some real harm.) Clearly, the best answer is Choice A: *drinking* would not be a good use for gray water.

28. Answer A. Contains borax soap

To answer this question, you should scan the passage looking for three key words: "irrigation," "chlorine," and "borax soap." You may remember seeing them in the second paragraph; you may even remember what the passage has to say about them. Even if you don't remember what the passage says, you can catch it on a second detailed reading as you check out each answer choice.

The second paragraph recommends that gray water be used for irrigation, but gives three points to remember. Point 2 is: "If the rinse water contains borax soap, do not use it for irrigation." Point 3 is: "If chlorine bleach is in the rinse water, you can use it for irrigation" as long as you are careful to pour it on different spots each day. Thus, chlorine is all right to use (if you take some precautions); borax is not. The correct answer is Choice A.

29. Answer D. Pollute the water system

You can find what the health department wishes or requires in the second list of three points given in the passage. This list is introduced in the passage by the sentence "Plumbing and health codes also have a few requirements." Point 2 states that "There must not be any way for gray water to contaminate the water system." This suggests that Choice D is correct. To double-check, look at the other answers and see how they agree or disagree with the contents of the passage.

    A. be used for irrigation. This is exactly what the passage suggests *should* be done with gray water, and nothing in the list of plumbing and health code requirements says you should *not* do this.

    B. be carried outdoors in buckets. This is the method Point 1 suggests you use to satisfy the plumbing and health requirements: "Use buckets or trash pails to carry it outdoors."

    C. contain detergent or soap. Gray water by definition is used water that contains soap or detergent. It makes no sense for the health department to wish gray water not to contain these substances.

The only possible answer is Choice D. It is the correct answer.

30. Answer D. Use a garden hose siphon or buckets

The passage specifically states "You may not allow the gray water to flow onto your neighbor's property." Thus, Choice A is incorrect. Similarly, the passage warns the reader not to "pump used water into the sprinkler system." Choice B is incorrect. The passage also cautions the reader, "Don't rearrange your plumbing to lead the gray water outside." Choice C is incorrect. However, the passage does suggest the helpfulness of garden hose siphons to get gray water outside the house and recommends the use of buckets or trash pails. The correct answer is D.

31. Answer C. 40 mph

The man's average speed is the total distance divided by the total time it took (speed is the rate, which is distance over time). In this case, the man drove 50 miles at one rate, and then 150 miles at another rate. But his total distance was 200 miles, and the total time was $2 + 3 = 5$ hours, so that his average rate of travel was 200 miles/5 hours = 200/5 mph = 40 mph.

32. Answer C. 23

Find the change from each number to the next one. In this case, the difference is always 3 (such a sequence is called an arithmetic sequence). To find the eighth number in the sequence, it is simplest to just continue for a few terms and then count the positions:

1st	2nd	3rd	4th	5th	6th	7th	8th	9th ...
2	5	8	11	14	17	20	23	26 ...

33. Answer C. 52 yards

Since the angle between Rosebud and San Simeon is 30°, and that between 23rd and San Simeon is 90°, the other angle must be 60°. The 23rd Street side of the triangle is half of a side of an equilateral triangle, so it is 30 yards long. If x stands for the San Simeon side, then the Pythagorean formula gives $x^2 + 30^2 = 60^2$, or $x^2 = 3600 - 900 = 2700$. You can eliminate Choices A and D without any arithmetic; the San Simeon side of the triangle has to be shorter than Rosebud (the hypoteneuse) and longer than the 23rd Street side, because it is opposite a larger angle. The choice is between B and C, and you can check by squaring them that 52 yards ($52 \times 52 = 2704$) is closer than 50 yards ($50 \times 50 = 2500$).

You could also find the answer by remembering that a 30–60 right triangle has its sides in the ratio of $1:\sqrt{3}:2$, and that $\sqrt{3}$ is approximately 1.73; therefore, the San Simeon side is about $1.73 \times 30 = 51.9$ yards.

34. Answer C. 80¢

Algebraic solution:

Let c be the original price per pound (the number you are asked to figure out), and let n be the original number of pounds that you could buy for $8. You can write this initial condition as

$c \times n = \$8 = 800¢$ (n pounds at c per pound costs n times c)

The price drops 30¢ a pound (and so, it becomes $c - 30$, if we take c in cents), and the same $8 or 800 cents buys ($n + 6$) pounds. That is the same as

$(c - 30) \times (n + 6) = 800¢ = c \times n$

Simplify the left side: $(c - 30) \times n = cn - 30n$, and $(c - 30) \times 6 = 6c - 180$. Putting these together you get

$cn - 30n + 6c - 180 = cn$ or (canceling the cn) $6c - 30n = 180$

But what can you do now? Don't forget the original equation: $c \times n = 800\cancel{c}$. You can use this to replace either c or n in the last equation. Since we want to find c, use $n = 800/c$ to write

$$6c - 30 \times 800/c = 180$$

Multiply by c to get

$$6c^2 - 24,000 = 180c \qquad \text{or} \qquad 6c^2 - 180c = 24,000$$

Divide by 6:

$$c^2 - 30c = 4,000 \qquad \text{or} \qquad c^2 - 30c - 4,000 = 0$$

At this point, you can use the quadratic formula, or try to factor this to solve for c.

$$c^2 - 30c - 4,000 = (c - 80)(c + 50) = 0.$$

From this, c must either be 80¢ or –50¢ (which is not realistically possible); so $c = 80$¢.

Checking the given answers:

Doing all the above is a significant amount of work. Is there an easier way? Yes, in fact. Work "backwards" from the choices, to find one that meets the terms of the problem.

Choice A. If the original price is 50¢ per pound, then for $8 you can buy 16 pounds (800¢/50¢). If the price drops 30¢ per pound, the cost is 20¢ per pound, and $8 buys 800¢/20¢ = 40 pounds. That is 40 – 16 = 24 pounds more than before, not 6 as the question states.

Choice B. If the original price is 60¢ per pound, $8 buys 800/60 = 80/6 = $13\frac{2}{3}$ pounds, and a drop of 30¢ buys 800/30 – twice as much, i.e., $13\frac{2}{3}$ pounds more, not six pounds more.

Choice C. If the original price is 80¢ per pound, $8 buys 800/80 = 10 pounds, and a drop of 30¢ buys 800/(80 – 30) = 800/50 = 80/5 = 16 pounds, six pounds more than before, just what the question requires.

Choice D. If the original price is $1 per pound, $8 buys 8 pounds, and a price of $1 – 30¢ = 70¢ buys 800/70 = 80/7 = $11\frac{3}{7}$ pounds, not six pounds more than the original price.

This is a case in which you are better off testing each answer than in solving the problem, unless you happen to be a whiz at algebra.

35. Answer B. $8,000

The man who owns one-third of the business gets $20,000 as his share of the profits. His partners must share the other two-thirds of the profits, and this two-thirds must be twice as much as his one-third; that is, they must divide 2 × $20,000 = $40,000. There are five other partners, each with an equal part of this amount. They must each receive $40,000/5 = $8,000.

36. Answer C. The end of the previous fiscal year

In paragraph two you read that the budget battle protests have been going on since the new fiscal year began on July 1. The state's fiscal or financial year runs from July 1 of one calendar year to June 30 of the next. Up until June 30, the end of the previous fiscal year, the state had been able to pay its bills following the guidelines established in last year's budget. Thus, the correct answer is C.

37. Answer B. Nursery schools

From the accounts of the protesters, it is obvious that handicapped persons, retired teachers, and people out of work feel adversely affected by the budget deadlock: they are not receiving their checks, and they are suffering. Nursing *homes* are also suffering because they are not receiving their payments for the Medi-Cal services they perform for the elderly. However, nursing homes are *not* nursery schools. You have no particular grounds to assume that the deadlock has affected nursery schools. The best answer is Choice B.

38. Answer B.   Statements I and III only

Use the process of elimination to answer this question. Putting together the information contained in paragraphs two and seven, you can easily infer that California has been budgetless since July 1. Thus, Statement 1 is true, and you can eliminate Choice C. Curt Pringle, however, is named in paragraph six as Republican Assembly leader; he is not a senator but is instead an assemblyman. Therefore, Statement II is false, and you can immediately eliminate Choices A and D. The correct answer must be Choice B.

39. Answer D.   All of the statements

Again, use the process of elimination to choose the correct answer. A close reading of the first two paragraphs reveals that, although 300,000 checks have been delayed, only hundreds of protesters have engaged in picketing. Therefore, Statement I is false, and you can eliminate Choice C. Similarly, paragraphs four and five make it clear that Democratic Assembly Speaker Bustamente is highly unlikely to support *any* Republican on the tax issue. Therefore, Statement II is false, and you can eliminate Choice B. Finally, paragraph eight indicates that the Democrats are holding off from voting for a Democrat-fashioned budget. Thus, Statement III is also false, and you can eliminate Choice A. Only Choice D is left; it is the correct answer.

40. Answer D.   Deadlock

When things are at an impasse, nothing can pass. Thus, an impasse is a deadlock or stalemate.

41. Answer B.   757 square feet

The figure is composed of a rectangle 20 feet wide by 30 feet high, and a half-circle on top of it. The half circle has a diameter of 20 feet (the same as the width of the rectangle); so its radius is 10 feet. A complete circle of this radius has area $\pi r^2 = 100 \pi = 314.16$ square feet. A half-circle is therefore $314 \div 2 = 157$, to the nearest square foot. Adding this to the area of the rectangle ($20 \times 30 = 600$ square feet) gives answer B.

42. Answer C.   1

Both A and B are negative (less than zero), so the product will be positive. To estimate the magnitude of $A \times B$, notice that B is less than 1, so that multiplying by it will "shrink" the product in comparison to A. The magnitude of B is roughly 1/2, and that of A is a bit less than 2; their product will be close to $1/2 \times 2$; that is, $A \times B$ is approximately 1.

43. Answer A.   1982

Compare the white bars for New York with the black bars for California. You must look for the year, or years, when the white bar is higher than the black bar. Only 1982, Choice A, can be correct.

44. Answer C. The number of citizens naturalized increased and then decreased.

For this question, you can ignore the white New York bars. All the choices deal with the increase or decrease of naturalizations in California. The black bars increase in height to 1986 and then get lower. You can immediately rule out Choices A and B, which say that the increase or decrease were continuous. The numbers on the scale to the left of the graph show that the higher bars stand for more naturalized citizens (over 100,000 in 1986; fewer in other years.) So only Choice C states what is actually visible in the chart.

45. Answer D. 400,000

You need to add the approximate values for the naturalizations in each year to get the total. Choice A can be ruled out right away, as naturalizations in 1986 alone were more than 100,000 and adding other years can only increase that. You can add the numbers in any order you like, but it may be simplest to start with the largest bars and go down from there: in 1987 there were about 80,000; in 1985 about 70,000; in 1988 maybe a bit less than 70,000. Adding just these years gives 100,000 + 80,000 + 70,000 + 70,000 = 320,000. This is already more than any answer except D, and if you go on to add in 40,000 for 1984 and about 30,000 for 1982 and 1983 you come out to a bit more than 400,000. Choice D must be the correct answer.

46. Answer A. "street" in line 1

In line 1, the word "street" should be capitalized. When you are referring to a specific geographical location, you should capitalize the names of nations, states, continents, oceans, lakes, rivers, mountains, cities, and streets. "I ran along Webster Street" is correct. You are referring to a specific street *by name*. "I ran along the Street," however, is incorrect.

47. Answer A. hard-working

Choice A contains an error in hyphenation: the word should not be hyphenated. It should be *hardworking*.

48. Answer A. Sentence 1

As it stands, sentence 1 is a run-on sentence. It consists of two independent sentences that have been run together without proper punctuation between them to separate them and without a capital letter starting the second sentence. Rewrite sentence 1 as follows: I would very much like to work at your cafe. Please consider me for any openings you have.

49. Answer A. 160

An alarm once every three minutes is a rate of 60/3 = 20 alarms per hour. In eight hours, this gives 8 × 20 = 160 alarms.

50. Answer D. You should consult your physician

Choices A, B, and C all fail to correct the very common error of the dangling modifier. Ask yourself who or what is going to start an exercise program. The answer is, of course, *you*. Before *you* start an exercise program, *you* should consult your physician.

Do not let an introductory or concluding phrase dangle with no word or group of words to modify.

51. Answer A. 5

The change is $10.00 − $9.53 = $0.47. He will get the smallest number of coins possible if the clerk uses the largest denomination coin available at each step of making the change:

47¢	largest coin less than this is a quarter	47¢ − 25¢ = 22¢
22¢	largest usable coin is a dime	22¢ − 10¢ = 12¢
12¢	largest usable coin is a dime	12¢ − 10¢ = 2¢
2¢	largest usable coin is a penny	2¢ − 1¢ = 1¢
1¢	largest usable coin is a penny	1¢ − 1¢ = done.

52. Answer B. −1

The slope of a line is the ratio of change in the vertical (y) direction to change in the horizontal (x) direction. In this case, y is decreasing while x increases; therefore, the slope will be a negative number (there is a negative change in y as x changes positively). To decide between Choices A and B, you need to estimate how fast y is changing with respect to a change in x. A slope of −2 would mean that as x goes some distance to the right, y would go down *twice* as much, but a look at the line shows that it is always about as far away from the origin in y as it is in x. The y coordinates change at about the same rate as the x coordinates do; hence the magnitude of the slope is about 1, and since we know that it is negative (sloping down), the correct answer is Choice B, −1.

53. Answer B. $207

The man bought merchandise priced at $200 + $30 (the suit plus the slacks) and received a 10% discount, so 1/10 of $230 was subtracted from the total bill. He paid $230 − $23 = $207.

54. Answer C. Atlanta

To get a team's winning percentage, you need to divide the games won over the total. In this case, all teams have played 18 games. For a percentage .333 (the same as 33.3%), the team must have won less than half (50%) of their games. If you remember that 33 1/3% = 1/3, you know that you are looking for the team that won 1/3 of 18 = 6 games. But even if you do not notice that, you can eliminate Choices A and B without doing any division, just by noticing that they won more than they lost.

55. Answer C. $83,400

To make a profit of 20%, the man must add 20% to the total amount he spent on the condo; that is, he must add 20% of ($63,000 + $2,500 + $4,000) = $69,500. 20% is the same as 0.2, so you can multiply $69,500 by 0.2.

$69,500
× .2
$13,900.0

(You can also do this in your head by noticing that 20% = 2 × 10%, and 10% × 69,500 = 6,950.) The price at which the man must sell the condo to get the 20% profit is

$69,500
$13,900
$83,400

56. Answer C. Brought

The missing word must be in the past tense. The simple past tense of the irregular verb *bring* is *brought:* I brought, you brought, he brought, she brought, it brought, we brought, they brought.

57. Answer B. Happy

The missing word must be an adjective. Helen's score made her parents *happy*. Choice D, *happier,* the comparative form of the adjective *happy,* could work if the sentence read this way: Helen's good score on the proficiency test made her parents *happier than* Bob's low score on the test made his parents.

58. Answer A. Food

The correct order of the four terms, starting with the most GENERAL or encompassing and ending with the most SPECIFIC or particular is: food, fruit, melon, cantaloupe. A cantaloupe is a specific kind of melon. A melon is a specific kind of fruit. Fruit is one kind of food.

59. Answer C. Ranch house

The correct order of the four terms, starting with the most SPECIFIC or particular and ending with the most GENERAL or encompassing is: ranch house, house, dwelling place, building. A ranch house is a specific kind of house. A house is a specific kind of dwelling place. (Other examples of dwelling places are tents and caves.) A dwelling place is a specific kind of building.

60. Answer C. The common anaconda, a member of the boa family, which may reach 20 feet in length as an adult, is the largest snake in the Western Hemisphere.

Note the relative brevity of this answer choice. Two words shorter than the three original sentences, it retains all the ideas of the originals while combining them into a complex whole.

61. Answer D. $14

Write down expressions for the information given in the problem. Since you are looking for the amount of money Al started with, use that as the unknown to solve for. The first condition is that Al starts with x and Jay with $x - \$5$. Each one spends \$4 on lunch; afterward, Al has $x - \$4$ and Jay has $(x - \$5) - \$4 = x - \$9$. Finally, you can relate these two expressions in an equation, since the amount Al has after lunch is twice what Jay has:

$$
\begin{aligned}
x - 4 &= 2\,(x - 9) && \text{now simplify the right side} \\
x - 4 &= 2x - 18 && \text{add 18 to both sides} \\
x + 14 &= 2x && \text{and subtract } x \\
14 &= x
\end{aligned}
$$

62. Answer A. 5 hours and 6 minutes

The man drives 15 miles in the city at 25 miles per hour, and the rest of the trip (240 – 15 = 225 miles) on the freeway at 50 miles per hour. Since distance = rate × time, you can get the time he spent at each of these rates as time = distance / time. The freeway time is 225/50 hours. Instead of dividing this out directly, reduce the fraction by dividing numerator and denominator by 5 to get 45/10 = 4.5 hours. The city time is 15/25, which reduces to 3/5. You don't actually have to calculate the minutes to get the answer in this case. 3/5 hours is more than half an hour (that would be 2.5/5!), so that the two sections of the man's trip take 4½ plus something over one half hour, and the answer must be over 5 hours. Only Choice A satisfies this requirement.

ALWAYS delay doing calculations until you are sure you need the exact answer; many times you will be able to decide the correct answer to a question without doing any hard work.

63. Answer A. 15

Write each statement in terms of the number you want to determine, the daughter's current age (x). The first statement is that Mrs. Brown is $x + 20$ years old. The next statement is about five years ago, and so you can write expressions for their ages at that time:

	Mrs. Brown	daughter
ages now	$x + 20$	x
5 years ago	$x + 20 - 5$	$x - 5$

and the statment is that Mrs. Brown's age was three times that of her daughter:

$$x + 15 = 3\,(x - 5)$$
$$x + 15 = 3x - 15$$
$$x + 30 = 3x$$
$$30 = 2x$$

and therefore $x = 15$.

64. Answer D. 1850 square feet

Amy has the ceiling and four walls to paint. The ceiling is 25 feet by 30 feet, with area $25 \times 30 = 750$ square feet. The two longer walls are 30 feet long by 10 feet high, adding $2 \times 30 \times 10 = 600$ square feet. Finally, the two shorter walls are 25 feet by 10 feet. The total area is

$$25' \times 30' + 2 \times 30' \times 10' + 2 \times 25' \times 10' = 750 + 600 + 500 \text{ square feet}$$
$$= 1850 \text{ square feet}$$

65. Answer B. 85°

The sum of the angles of the triangle must be 180° (this is one of the geometrical facts you need to memorize). The two angles you know, from the statement of the question, are 55° and 40°. The remaining angle is $180 - (55 + 40) = 180 - 95 = 85°$.

66. Answer C. 4

The fabric will shrink 25%; that is, it will lose 1/4 of its original length. The man needs to have 3 yards left after shrinkage. Using x to stand for the amount he needs, the problem can be restated as

$x - x/4 = 3$. This equation simplifies to $\dfrac{3x}{4} = 3$.

Divide both sides of the equation by 3 and multiply by 4, to get $x = 4$.

67. Answer B. The condemned man

The "He" in line 1 is also the "He" in line 6 who curses his luck. He is the man condemned to death.

68. Answer C. Divisions of an hour

Think of quarter hours. Every quarter hour, the steeple tells the people of the town the time: one stroke for 15 minutes past the hour, two strokes for half-past, three strokes for three-quarters-past, four strokes for the hour's close.

69. Answer D. Cannot escape his fate

The condemned man is waiting to be executed. He curses his luck because he has been captured and condemned to death. There is no way out for him. He cannot escape his fate.

70. Answer C. The nature of his crime

Although we know a great deal about the condemned man, we do not know what crime he committed that led him to his fate. Murder? Treason? The poem gives us no clue. We do have information about his emotions: he "cursed his luck." He resents his fate. Therefore, Choice A is incorrect. We also have information about the manner of his execution: he is "noosed." There is a noose around his neck; he is going to be hanged. Therefore, Choice B is incorrect. We definitely have information about the setting: the market place, with the clock tower overlooking the gallows. Therefore, Choice D is incorrect. Only Choice C is left. It is the correct choice.

71. Answer C. The percentage of the French population under 20 decreased and then increased, while the percentage between the ages of 20 and 64 first increased and then decreased.

Looking at the graph, you see the top line (labeled "percentage age 20 to 64") going up from about 55% to about 60% and then dropping back down; the lower line (labeled "percentage under 20") first drops and then from 1946 to 1966 it rises. Comparing these lines to the choices given we find:

- A. Choice A is not correct for the part of the graph from 1946 to 1966 (the percentage under 20 increases and the 20 to 64 part decreases, exactly the opposite of the statement in A).
- B. Choice B is incorrect since the 20 to 64 percentage also changed during this period.
- C. Choice C is correct; that is just how we described the graph above.
- D. Choice D is incorrect; the graph gives percentages for people under 20, and for people from 20 to 64. Subtracting those percentages from 100% gives the percentage of people 65 and over in the French population during the years covered by the graph.

72. Answer D. 1851

The "percentage under 20" line begins high, drops lower, and then rises again. To decide where it is highest, compare the 1851 value with the 1966 value by laying a pencil or a piece of paper on the graph, level with the bottom axis. Since the percentage drops after 1851, the only possibility for a higher percentage is at the 1966 end, after the percentage has had some time to rise again. But you will see that the 1851 value is still higher (about 38% or 39%) than the 1966 value (about 35%).

73. Answer C. 55%

The line labeled "percentage age 20 to 64" starts out (in 1851) at the level of the 55% tick mark on the y axis of the graph. Therefore, about 55% of the French population in 1851 was between the ages of 20 and 64.

74. Answer A. 7%

There is no line on the graph for people age 65 and over, but you can figure out the percentage in this group since the whole population (100%) must be made up of the people under 20, the people between 20 and 64, and the people 65 and over. The percentage between 20 and 64 was 55% in 1851 (see the previous question). Likewise, the percentage under 20 was about 38%. (You don't have to be exact about these numbers, as long as you are fairly close; the choices are far enough apart that being off by one or two percentage points in estimating the values shouldn't matter.) After adding 55% and 38%, you get 93% for the combined percentage of the population that is 64 or under; therefore, the population 65 and over is 100% − 93% = 7%.

75. Answer C. The percentage of the French population aged 65 and over increased steadily from about 7% to about 12% of the total population.

To answer this question, with statements about the history of the French population age 65 or over, you may need to repeat for other dates the kind of reasoning used for the last question. The choices are for a decreasing (Choice A), unchanging (Choice B), or increasing percentage of the 65 and over segment of the population. Choice D (that we can't determine this from the graph) is wrong from the start, since question 74 shows how we can go about finding out what happened to this age group during the period covered by the graph. The first thing to do is to compare the end of the graph to its start; if that doesn't give us enough information, we can look at points in the middle as well.

In 1966, about 54% of the population is in the 20–64 age group, and about 34% in the under-20 age group. Together, these are 54 + 34 = 88%, leaving 12% for the part of the French population aged 65 and over. This is distinctly larger than the 7% in 1851, so it is clear that Choices A (that the over-64 population decreased) and B (that it remained the same) are wrong, and Choice C (increase from 7% to 12%) is likely correct. (To be absolutely certain, you could check intermediate dates to see that they have percentages between 7% and 12%; this is unnecessary here, since you have already eliminated the other choices.)

76. Answer B. In the year 1931, the percentage of the French population under 20 was lower than it was in 1946.

Look at each of the answers, and mark any that could be false. It is likely (with a question phrased this way) that there will be only one obviously false statement.

A. In 1851, the percentage under 20 was about 38%; this is clearly TRUE from the graph.
B. In 1931, the percentage under 20 was lower than it was in 1946. TRUE. The values are not too far apart, but the graph goes down from 1931 to 1946, so the percentage under 20 in 1931 must have been higher.
C. In 1931, the percentage under 20 was higher than in 1966. FALSE. This is just the reverse of B.
D. After 1946, the portion under 20 grew as a result of the post-World War II baby boom. You can't tell from the graph whether the reason given (the baby boom) is correct, but it is TRUE that the under-20 fraction grew after 1946; the low point of the under-20 line is 1946 at about 30%, and in 1956 and 1966, the values on this line are greater.

77. Answer B. Distinguish

To alienate someone is to estrange that person, setting him or her at a distance: Junior was so nasty to his big sister that he totally alienated her. Choice A is incorrect. To realize something is to understand or achieve it: Bob realized he could pass the test; Alice realized her ambition of going to college. Choice C is incorrect. To shun someone is to avoid or reject that person: Because the judge warned him to keep away from bad influences, William shunned many of his former friends. Choice D is incorrect. To distinguish something, however, is to recognize it as different from something else: Although some people say all babies look alike, I could always distinguish my grandson from the other infants in the nursery. He had a birthmark that set him apart or distinguished him from the other babies. Choice B is correct.

78. Answer C. Novice

A performer can be an entertainer; he or she can also be someone who accomplishes or achieves something: As a tennis player, Steffi Graf is a great performer; she outperforms her competition regularly. Choice A is incorrect. A visionary is a dreamer or prophet: Predicting that someday every American home would have a computer, Steve Jobs was a visionary. Choice B is incorrect. A referee is a judge or umpire: Deciding the challenger was too punch-drunk to fight any longer, the referee ended the bout. Choice D is incorrect. A novice, however, by definition is new to an activity. Choice C is correct.

79. Answer D. Resolute

An enthusiastic person is eager and earnest about something, really into it, so to speak: Justin is an enthusiastic Boy Scout who eagerly involves himself in scouting activities. Choice A is incorrect. Something evenhanded is impartial and fair, as in "evenhanded justice." Choice B is incorrect. A poised person is dignified and self-assured: No minor bickering around the office disturbed Joyce, who remained cool and poised. Choice C is incorrect. Resolute, however, by definition, means strongly determined: Betty was resolute in her determination to succeed in school; nothing could shake her purpose. Choice D is correct.

80. Answer D. $712

She is paid every two weeks and works 40 hours per week. Her gross wages are figured for 80 hours:

$$\begin{array}{r} \$8.90 \\ \times\ 80 \\ \hline \$712.00 \end{array}$$

81. Answer C. $3.91

The total bill is $10.20 and they leave a 15% tip:

$$\begin{array}{r} \$10.20 \\ \times .15 \\ \hline 51\ 00 \\ 102\ 0 \\ \hline \$1.53 \end{array}$$

Each woman's share is 1/3 of $10.20 (= $3.40) plus her 1/3 share of the tip (1/3 of 1.53 = 0.51); $3.40 + $0.51 = $3.91, Choice C.

82. Answer B. Second quarter

We need to find the quarter in which the man had the highest income, since this is the quarter used to set his unemployment benefit. Go through the list and compare each quarter with the next, crossing it out if it is lower. After going through the full list, only the second quarter is not crossed out.

First quarter   ~~$2,500~~   Cross out because lower than second quarter.
Second quarter $4,750
Third quarter   ~~$3,600~~   Cross out because lower than second quarter.
Fourth quarter   ~~$4,360~~   Cross out because lower than second quarter.

83. Answer C. 12

The answer is found in the statement of the previous question. The base period is 12 months long. It is divided into three-month quarters, which determine the amount of the unemployment benefit, but the base period by itself is 12 months.

84. Answer B. $3,600

The "third quarter of his base period" is the third stretch of 3-month periods recorded in the table. The income listed in this line of the table is $3,600.

85. Answer D. 48

A gallon is four quarts. The woman made 12 gallons of preserves and needs 12 × 4 quart jars = 48.

86. Answer B. 91

A yard is 36 inches (a bit less than a meter, which is 39.36 inches). 100 yards is therefore 3600 inches, and it must be less than 100 meters. This rules out Choices C and D. Choice A is also impossible, since 100 yards would equal 50 meters only if a meter were equal to two yards. In fact, the conversion given (1 meter = 39.36 inches) means that 1 meter is a bit less than 1.1 yards (a meter would be exactly 1.1 yards if it were 36 + 3.6 = 39.6 inches). 100 meters is about 110 yards; 100 yards has to be *less* than 100 meters.

87. Answer B. 9

In the four earlier stages, the number of coins added each time was 1, 3, 5 and 7; the number increased by two each time. Therefore, nine coins are needed at the fifth stage. You can also see this by looking at the overall pattern of the figure, which is a square of coins at each stage, with N by N coins at the Nth stage, so the fifth repetition will have a total of 25 coins, 9 more than the 16 coins shown in the diagram.

88. Answer B. Commercial rabbit raisers

The title of this passage tells you that its subject is systems of breeding, in this instance, systems of breeding or raising rabbits. While the opening paragraph *does* refer to genetic concepts, it does so only to emphasize the usefulness of these ideas to breeders. The passage is a summary of information a breeder or commercial rabbit raiser needs, not a summary of information a professional geneticist would need.

89. Answer D. Parts of cells

The opening paragraph describes chromosomes as "very small threadlike bodies found in every cell of the body." They are therefore parts of cells. (Note that the definition of this technical term immediately follows the first use of the term, set off from the term itself by a comma. This technique, known as apposition, is very common in texts, so that if you come across an unfamiliar technical term in a passage, you should take a close look at the words immediately following the new term to see if they define it.) You can also come up with the answer by ruling out the other answer choices. Chromosomes are not genes; they are locations for genes. Therefore, Choice A is incorrect. Chromosomes are not species (classes of animals); therefore, Choice B is incorrect. Chromosomes are certainly not types of rabbits; therefore, Choice C is incorrect. The correct answer must be Choice D.

90. Answer B. Statements I and II only

Once again, apply the process of elimination to answer this question. The opening sentence states that "(i)n planning a breeding program for rabbits, you first need to understand the concept of the *gene pool*." In other words, breeders need genetic information to plan their breeding programs." Therefore, Statement I is correct. You can cross out Choice C. The paragraph goes on to describe the gene pool as a "group of many, perhaps thousands, of hereditary units, commonly referred to as genes." Although there are 22 chromosome pairs in each rabbit, the gene pool itself consists of all the genes of all the rabbits who make up the breed. Therefore, Statement II is false. You can cross out both Choices A and D. The correct answer must be Choice B. To check your reasoning, examine Statement III. The passage's concluding sentence states that the ability to adapt "makes for survival and is the mechanism by which species have evolved." Statement III is indeed true, and the correct answer is, as you suspected, Choice B.

91. Answer D. Even nature makes mistakes.

Look at the sentence immediately following "But even nature slips." What does it discuss? Lost species, species that failed to survive because they could not cope with a change in circumstances. Malformed offspring, infant creatures that fail to survive because they are born with serious flaws. These are examples of nature's failures as a breeder: although nature is still the most successful breeder, even nature cannot claim complete success, for "even nature makes mistakes."

92. Answer B. 3/4

Slope is "rise over run"—vertical change divided by horizontal change. In this case, the line goes through the points (1,0) on the x-axis and (5,3) at the highest point shown on the graph. So it changes 3 units in the vertical direction (from 0 to 3), while changing 4 units horizontally (from 1 to 5). The slope is therefore 3 divided by 4, Choice B.

93. Answer B. $56.48

Only $8 out of the total purchases of $56 is taxable; the tax on this $8 is $8 \times .06 = \$0.48$. Add this to the purchase amount to get his total bill, $56 + $0.48 = $56.48.

94. Answer B. The underlined word is spelled incorrectly.

The sentence should read: "I was deeply *affected* (moved or influenced) by the news of his death." To *effect* something is to bring it about or cause it. To *affect* someone or something is to influence or change or emotionally touch that person or thing.

95. Answer B. The underlined word is spelled incorrectly.

Do you remember the old spelling rule I before E *except* after C? Here, the letters I and E follow the letter C. The sentence should read: "Please save all your receipts so that we can reimburse you."

96. Answer D. Europe

The bars on the graph go from 0 on the left to 3.0% on the right. As you scan down the regions on the graph, you should notice that the bars for Europe are shorter (always less than 1.0%) than any others. Even the longest bar for Europe (for 1960–1970) is shorter than the shortest bars of Northern America or the Soviet Union.

97. Answer A. Africa

The growth rates for 1970–1980 are given by the middle bars for each region. Consider each of the choices in turn:

A. Africa   1970–1980 growth rate is about $2^3/_4$%.
B. Asia   1970–1980 growth rate is a bit more than 2%.
C. Latin America   1970–1980 growth rate is about $2^1/_3$%.
D. Oceania   1970–1980 growth rate is about $1^1/_2$%.

The largest growth rate among these was Africa's $2^3/_4$%.

98. Answer A. Soviet Union

To look for the smallest change in growth rate from the seventies to the eighties, compare the bottom bar with the middle bar just above it in each region. Latin America, Northern America, and Europe all decreased by a larger, more noticeable amount than the Soviet Union did.

99. Answer B. Growth rates have decreased everywhere since the sixties.

Check each of the choices to see whether the graph supports it.

A. Population is increasing in all regions. TRUE. Since the growth rate is positive (all bars extend to the right from the zero y-axis), population is growing in each region.
B. Growth rates have decreased everywhere. FALSE. The growth rate for Africa increased from the sixties to the seventies and again from the seventies to the eighties.

Since B is contradicted by the graph, you don't need to look at any of the other choices to pick B as the "unsupported conclusion." (If you do check C and D, you will see that they are true.)

100. Answer D. 5

During the seventies, the growth rate in Africa was more than $2^1/_2$% (maybe as much as 2.7%), and the growth rate of Europe was about 1/2%. Since $\frac{2.5}{0.5} = \frac{25}{5} = 5$, the best choice is Choice D.

CHAPTER 6
Model Test B

ANSWER SHEET

Part One: Essay

Use the space allowed following the test question to write your answers to each of the essay questions.

Part Two: Short-Answer Questions

1. Ⓐ Ⓑ Ⓒ Ⓓ
2. Ⓐ Ⓑ Ⓒ Ⓓ
3. Ⓐ Ⓑ Ⓒ Ⓓ
4. Ⓐ Ⓑ Ⓒ Ⓓ
5. Ⓐ Ⓑ Ⓒ Ⓓ
6. Ⓐ Ⓑ Ⓒ Ⓓ
7. Ⓐ Ⓑ Ⓒ Ⓓ
8. Ⓐ Ⓑ Ⓒ Ⓓ
9. Ⓐ Ⓑ Ⓒ Ⓓ
10. Ⓐ Ⓑ Ⓒ Ⓓ
11. Ⓐ Ⓑ Ⓒ Ⓓ
12. Ⓐ Ⓑ Ⓒ Ⓓ
13. Ⓐ Ⓑ Ⓒ Ⓓ
14. Ⓐ Ⓑ Ⓒ Ⓓ
15. Ⓐ Ⓑ Ⓒ Ⓓ
16. Ⓐ Ⓑ Ⓒ Ⓓ
17. Ⓐ Ⓑ Ⓒ Ⓓ
18. Ⓐ Ⓑ Ⓒ Ⓓ
19. Ⓐ Ⓑ Ⓒ Ⓓ
20. Ⓐ Ⓑ Ⓒ Ⓓ
21. Ⓐ Ⓑ Ⓒ Ⓓ
22. Ⓐ Ⓑ Ⓒ Ⓓ
23. Ⓐ Ⓑ Ⓒ Ⓓ
24. Ⓐ Ⓑ Ⓒ Ⓓ
25. Ⓐ Ⓑ Ⓒ Ⓓ

26. Ⓐ Ⓑ Ⓒ Ⓓ
27. Ⓐ Ⓑ Ⓒ Ⓓ
28. Ⓐ Ⓑ Ⓒ Ⓓ
29. Ⓐ Ⓑ Ⓒ Ⓓ
30. Ⓐ Ⓑ Ⓒ Ⓓ
31. Ⓐ Ⓑ Ⓒ Ⓓ
32. Ⓐ Ⓑ Ⓒ Ⓓ
33. Ⓐ Ⓑ Ⓒ Ⓓ
34. Ⓐ Ⓑ Ⓒ Ⓓ
35. Ⓐ Ⓑ Ⓒ Ⓓ
36. Ⓐ Ⓑ Ⓒ Ⓓ
37. Ⓐ Ⓑ Ⓒ Ⓓ
38. Ⓐ Ⓑ Ⓒ Ⓓ
39. Ⓐ Ⓑ Ⓒ Ⓓ
40. Ⓐ Ⓑ Ⓒ Ⓓ
41. Ⓐ Ⓑ Ⓒ Ⓓ
42. Ⓐ Ⓑ Ⓒ Ⓓ
43. Ⓐ Ⓑ Ⓒ Ⓓ
44. Ⓐ Ⓑ Ⓒ Ⓓ
45. Ⓐ Ⓑ Ⓒ Ⓓ
46. Ⓐ Ⓑ Ⓒ Ⓓ
47. Ⓐ Ⓑ Ⓒ Ⓓ
48. Ⓐ Ⓑ Ⓒ Ⓓ
49. Ⓐ Ⓑ Ⓒ Ⓓ
50. Ⓐ Ⓑ Ⓒ Ⓓ

51. Ⓐ Ⓑ Ⓒ Ⓓ
52. Ⓐ Ⓑ Ⓒ Ⓓ
53. Ⓐ Ⓑ Ⓒ Ⓓ
54. Ⓐ Ⓑ Ⓒ Ⓓ
55. Ⓐ Ⓑ Ⓒ Ⓓ
56. Ⓐ Ⓑ Ⓒ Ⓓ
57. Ⓐ Ⓑ Ⓒ Ⓓ
58. Ⓐ Ⓑ Ⓒ Ⓓ
59. Ⓐ Ⓑ Ⓒ Ⓓ
60. Ⓐ Ⓑ Ⓒ Ⓓ
61. Ⓐ Ⓑ Ⓒ Ⓓ
62. Ⓐ Ⓑ Ⓒ Ⓓ
63. Ⓐ Ⓑ Ⓒ Ⓓ
64. Ⓐ Ⓑ Ⓒ Ⓓ
65. Ⓐ Ⓑ Ⓒ Ⓓ
66. Ⓐ Ⓑ Ⓒ Ⓓ
67. Ⓐ Ⓑ Ⓒ Ⓓ
68. Ⓐ Ⓑ Ⓒ Ⓓ
69. Ⓐ Ⓑ Ⓒ Ⓓ
70. Ⓐ Ⓑ Ⓒ Ⓓ
71. Ⓐ Ⓑ Ⓒ Ⓓ
72. Ⓐ Ⓑ Ⓒ Ⓓ
73. Ⓐ Ⓑ Ⓒ Ⓓ
74. Ⓐ Ⓑ Ⓒ Ⓓ
75. Ⓐ Ⓑ Ⓒ Ⓓ

76. Ⓐ Ⓑ Ⓒ Ⓓ
77. Ⓐ Ⓑ Ⓒ Ⓓ
78. Ⓐ Ⓑ Ⓒ Ⓓ
79. Ⓐ Ⓑ Ⓒ Ⓓ
80. Ⓐ Ⓑ Ⓒ Ⓓ
81. Ⓐ Ⓑ Ⓒ Ⓓ
82. Ⓐ Ⓑ Ⓒ Ⓓ
83. Ⓐ Ⓑ Ⓒ Ⓓ
84. Ⓐ Ⓑ Ⓒ Ⓓ
85. Ⓐ Ⓑ Ⓒ Ⓓ
86. Ⓐ Ⓑ Ⓒ Ⓓ
87. Ⓐ Ⓑ Ⓒ Ⓓ
88. Ⓐ Ⓑ Ⓒ Ⓓ
89. Ⓐ Ⓑ Ⓒ Ⓓ
90. Ⓐ Ⓑ Ⓒ Ⓓ
91. Ⓐ Ⓑ Ⓒ Ⓓ
92. Ⓐ Ⓑ Ⓒ Ⓓ
93. Ⓐ Ⓑ Ⓒ Ⓓ
94. Ⓐ Ⓑ Ⓒ Ⓓ
95. Ⓐ Ⓑ Ⓒ Ⓓ
96. Ⓐ Ⓑ Ⓒ Ⓓ
97. Ⓐ Ⓑ Ⓒ Ⓓ
98. Ⓐ Ⓑ Ⓒ Ⓓ
99. Ⓐ Ⓑ Ⓒ Ⓓ
100. Ⓐ Ⓑ Ⓒ Ⓓ

MODEL TEST B

Part One: Essay

30 MINUTES

Directions: The following two essay questions are designed to test your knowledge of written English. Read each question carefully, and then select one as your essay topic. You have 30 minutes to write a short essay on the topic you choose.

ESSAY TOPICS

Topic A

What was the best gift you ever received? Describe the gift (it does not need to be an expensive one). Who gave you the gift, and under what circumstances was it given to you? What made this gift special to you? Title your essay "Favorite Gift."

Topic B

For many, reading is an exciting experience. For others, it is frustrating and even boring. Tell the story of your life as a reader. What were your earliest experiences with reading? What was your favorite book as a child? What role does reading play in your life today? Title your essay "Reading Autobiography."

_____

_____

_____

_____

_____

_____

_____

_____

_____

_____

_____

Part Two: Short-Answer Questions   2 HOURS, 30 MINUTES

The kinds of questions used on this part of the test are varied. Be sure you read the directions carefully before beginning to answer the questions that follow.

Directions: Refer to the following passage to answer the next five questions. You are to choose the *one* best answer, marked A, B, C, or D, to each question. Answer all questions on the basis of what is *stated* or *implied* in the passage.

The Pacific Ocean forms the western border of San Diego County. This 76-mile coastline is characterized by long stretches of open sandy beaches interrupted by rocky headlands. In many areas the beaches and headlands are backed by precipitous cliffs several hundred feet high.

There is also a series of lagoons and bays extending along the entire coastline. Included in this series are a number of small marshy estuaries fed by intermittent streams, intertidal lagoons of moderate size, and two large bays. The estuaries and lagoons are valuable mainly as wildlife habitat, while Mission and San Diego Bays are of major significance for recreation and commerce.

Mission Bay is the result of a reclamation project by the city of San Diego. About 5,000 acres of marshland were dredged and filled to produce a modern recreation complex. Mission Bay now provides extensive water surfaces for boating and fishing, and the adjacent shoreline is highly developed for recreational purposes.

San Diego Bay is the district's largest natural harbor, the site of a major naval base, a busy center of commerce, and an important recreational complex. Local government has taken a positive stance on water pollution and has prohibited the dumping of municipal and industrial sewage into the bay. Direct dumping of sewage from naval vessels is being phased out, and pleasure craft will soon be required to have sewage holding tanks. These measures have resulted in a marked improvement in the water quality of the bay, and, as a result, all types of water-associated recreation are increasing.

1. Which of the following does NOT characterize the San Diego coastline?
    A. rocky headlands
    B. sandy beaches
    C. steep cliffs
    D. tropical rainforests

2. The major value of San Diego County's lagoons today is their use as
    A. commercial harbors.
    B. sewage disposal areas.
    C. sites for naval bases.
    D. wildlife habitat.

3. How does Mission Bay differ from San Diego Bay?
    A. Mission Bay has been set aside as a wildlife refuge.
    B. Mission Bay has less commercial importance than San Diego Bay does.
    C. Mission Bay has suffered from the dumping of industrial and municipal sewage.
    D. Mission Bay has been developed as a major naval base.

4. According to the third paragraph, local government took a positive stance on water pollution by

A. encouraging its existence.
B. increasing its extent.
C. banning actions that caused it.
D. prohibiting water-associated recreation.

5. Water pollution regulations concerning San Diego Bay have led to a(an)

A. increase in naval vessels.
B. increase in sewage dumping.
C. increase in its recreational use.
D. decrease of pleasure craft.

---

6. A man weighs 230 pounds. How many pounds must he gain in order to weigh 1/8 of a ton?

A. 10 pounds
B. 20 pounds
C. 70 pounds
D. He must lose 30 pounds.

7. A man buys a condo for $62,500. He pays $400 for grading, $950 for rewiring, and $650 for painting and plastering. If he sells the condo for $65,000, how much profit does he make?

A. $500   B. $1,500   C. $1,550   D. $2,500

Refer to the following table to answer the next three questions.

PIETRO'S PIZZERIA				
	SMALL	**MEDIUM**	**LARGE**	**GIANT**
Single Topping	$2.50	$3.90	$4.90	$5.40
Two Toppings	$2.80	$4.20	$5.20	$5.70
Three or More Toppings	$3.30	$4.70	$5.70	$6.20
Soft Drinks, Small 30¢, Large 50¢				
All Pizzas Come with Tomato Sauce and Mozzarella Cheese ------------------- Anchovies Optional at No Extra Cost				

8. Karl comes to the pizza parlor with $3.10. He buys a single pizza and a small soft drink. After paying for the pizza and soft drink, he has no money left. What sort of pizza did he buy?

A. a small pizza with a single topping
B. a small pizza with a single topping and anchovies
C. a small pizza with two toppings and anchovies
D. a medium pizza with a single topping

9. Kathy orders a large pizza with two toppings, two large orange sodas, and one small lemon-lime soda. She does not want any anchovies on the pizza. How much will her order cost?

A. $6.70   B. $6.50   C. $6.30   D. $5.20

10. The pizza parlor gives a 20% discount on all pizzas to birthday parties. They do not give birthday parties any discount on soft drinks. A man orders two giant pizzas with two toppings for a birthday party. He orders six small soft drinks as well. How much is he charged for the two pizzas?

   A. $13.20   B. $11.40   C. $10.92   D. $9.12

---

11. The word "straightforward" means the OPPOSITE of

   A. inconsiderate.
   B. indirect.
   C. unlikely.
   D. uneven.

12. The word "melancholy" means the SAME as

   A. gloomy.
   B. malignant.
   C. tentative.
   D. uninterested.

Refer to the following graph to answer the next three questions.

EFFECTS OF INFLATION ON INCOME

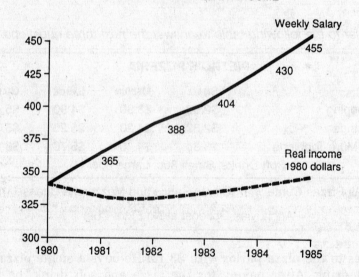

13. Which of the following statements about key entry operators' salaries in 1980 is true?

   A. Weekly salary and real income both rose.
   B. Weekly salary rose but real income fell.
   C. Weekly salary fell but real income rose.
   D. Weekly salary and real income both fell.

14. In which year were the key entry operators receiving the greatest real income as measured in 1989 dollars?

   A. 1985   B. 1984   C. 1983   D. 1982

15. In which year did the key entry operators' real income return to the same value it had in 1980?

   A. 1982   B. 1983   C. 1984   D. 1985

---

16. Which of the following conveys the most POSITIVE or favorable meaning in describing a person's attitude toward money?

   A. thrifty
   B. grasping
   C. miserly
   D. stingy

17. There may be an error in capitalization or punctuation in the following sentence.

Mark Twain's experiences as a navigator_on the Missouri and Mississippi
         A   B
rivers provided him with material for several books.
C

   A. Underlined part A needs to be changed to make the sentence correct.
   B. Underlined part B needs to be changed to make the sentence correct.
   C. Underlined part C needs to be changed to make the sentence correct.
   D. There is no change needed; the sentence is correct as written.

18. To find an article about a particular mammal, you would consult

   A. an almanac.
   B. an atlas.
   C. an encyclopedia.
   D. a thesaurus.

19. The following paragraph may not be in a logical sequence. Read the sentences and select the best order for them.

(1) One of the earliest Europeans to behold this natural spectacle was a French priest, Father Louis Hennepin. (2) They were the territory's first inhabitants some 2,000 years ago. (3) The first people to gaze upon Niagara Falls were ancestors of the Seneca Indians. (4) According to historical accounts, upon seeing the mighty waterfall Hennepin fell to his knees in prayer, saying of the awesome phenomenon that the universe did not hold its equal.

   A. Correct as is
   B. 3, 1, 4, 2
   C. 3, 2, 1, 4
   D. 2, 1, 4, 3

20. Which of the following sentences is CORRECTLY punctuated?

   A. Many scientists have thought that life could not exist on Mars; but the most recent satellite photographs indicate the contrary.
   B. The Mexican War was triggered by a border dispute in 1846; it came to a close with America's occupation of Mexico City in 1848.
   C. Although Henry Kissinger was born in Europe he was eligible to become this country's secretary of state.
   D. The game was easily won by the Packers, this was in part due to the Patriots' poor morale.

21. A triangle has one angle of 55° and one of 40°. How many degrees is the third angle?

    A. 75°   B. 85°   C. 90°   D. 95°

22. What is the next number, *N*, in this sequence?

    8   6   10   4   12   2   *N*?
    A. 0   B. 10   C. 14   D. 16

23. A woman is 62 years old. Her daughter is 29 years old. In how many years will the mother be exactly twice as old as her daughter?

    A. 3   B. 4   C. 5   D. 6

24. How many miles apart are the cities of Philipstown and De Witt, shown on the map below as 3/4 inch apart? The scale of miles on the map is 1 inch = 100 miles.

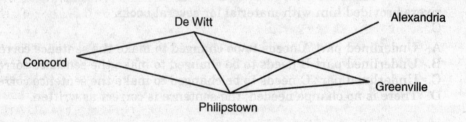

    A. 3/4 mile   B. 30 miles   C. 75 miles   D. 750 miles

25. Tom promises to meet his wife at 4:45 P.M. on the corner of Hollywood and Vine. She arrives there at 4:38 P.M. and waits for 35 minutes before growing discouraged and leaving. At what time does she leave?

    A. 4:45 P.M.   B. 4:58 P.M.   C. 5:03 P.M.   D. 5:13 P.M.

Directions: Refer to the following passage to answer the next five questions. You are to choose the *one* best answer, marked A, B, C, or D, to each question. Answer all questions on the basis of what is *stated* or *implied* in the passage.

THE SENATE

The Committee Structure

Senate committees are established by the Rules Committee early in each legislative session. Since it is impossible to discuss at length the merits and demerits of even a few bills on the Senate floor, committees play the crucial role of assuring that each detail of proposed legislation is given a thorough hearing. The committee members then vote upon each bill, determining whether or not it should be sent to the floor for final consideration by the whole Senate. Committee hearings are open to the public and to the press. All votes and other actions taken in committees are recorded and published.

Senators must spend most of their time in committee study. They devote long, irregular hours, often working nights and holidays, hearing witnesses and debating, from general policy to the finest details of punctuation, those bills assigned to their committees.

Committee membership is determined basically by the interests of the individual senators. Although no one senator can be expert in all fields, the majority of them, through training or inclination, are highly conversant in certain areas. All effort is made to see that each senator is assigned the committees of his or her choice.

Rules and Regulations

To insure decorum, fairness, and order in their deliberations, the members of the Senate are bound by Article IV of the Constitution of California. They further govern themselves by adopting Standing Rules (covering the details of daily procedure) and Joint Rules (covering procedures for transactions between Senate and Assembly).

A senator who wants to speak must raise the microphone at his or her desk. The presiding officer will ask, "Senator Doe, for what purpose do you rise?" The senator may then proceed to speak on the matter under consideration, usually speaking for as long as he or she wishes. Ordinarily, no record is kept of debates or speeches made on the Senate floor.

When all members who are interested in the bill have given their arguments, pro and con, the bill's author asks for a vote, and the roll is called. Should the bill fail to receive the votes necessary for passage and a number of members are absent from their seats, a Call of the Senate may be moved. At that time the sergeant at arms is directed to lock the chamber doors and bring in all absentee members. On their arrival, the Call of the Senate is lifted and the roll completed.

26. According to this article, state senators spend most of their time
    A. in committee work.
    B. in the Senate chamber.
    C. in their offices.
    D. in their home districts.

27. Senators are assigned to committees
    A. by the sergeant at arms.
    B. according to their own expressed interests.
    C. despite their expertise in different fields.
    D. at the request of the governor.

28. Which of the following reasons explains why the Senate establishes committees?
    A. to permit senators to vote on bills in secret before they come before the whole Senate
    B. to allow certain bills to be passed without a majority vote
    C. to allow a detailed discussion of the good and bad points of bills coming before the Senate
    D. to give senators privacy as they practice public speaking

29. The word "covering" in the fourth paragraph most likely means
    A. protecting.
    B. hiding.
    C. journeying over.
    D. dealing with.

30. What is the most likely reason for a senator to move a Call of the Senate?
    A. The senator wishes it to be held in a different location.
    B. The senator hopes to prevent the absentee members from returning.
    C. The senator is looking for additional votes to enable the bill to pass.
    D. The senator was locked out of the Senate chamber when the vote was taken.

---

31. Smart's latex paint can cover 400 square feet of wall surface per gallon. Al needs to paint a wall that measures 59 feet by 15 feet, with two circular holes in the wall, each one 4 feet in diameter. He needs to do two coats of paint. Approximately how many gallons of paint will he need to do this job?
    A. 2.2 gallons   B. 4.1 gallons   C. 4.3 gallons   D. 4.4 gallons

32. A man drove 75 miles in three hours and then 100 miles in two hours. What was his average speed for the whole period?
    A. 25 mph   B. 35 mph   C. 50 mph   D. 175 mph

33. A grocery store has OJ frozen orange juice in three sizes: the 6-ounce size, on sale at $0.63 a can; the 12-ounce size, on sale at $1.29 a can; and the 16-ounce size, selling at its regular price of $1.79 a can. What size of OJ frozen orange juice should a person buy to get the greatest quantity of orange juice for the least amount of money?
    A. 6-ounce size   C. 16-ounce size
    B. 12-ounce size   D. All cost the same per ounce.

34. What percent of the figure below is shaded?

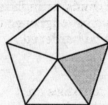

    A. 2%   B. 20%   C. 40%   D. 50%

35. A librarian is asked to catalog 72 books. If he can catalog six books an hour, and his assistant can catalog three books an hour, how many days will it take them to catalog the books, if they both spend three hours a day at this task?

    A. two days   B. two and one-half days   C. three days   D. four days

---

Directions: Refer to the article below to answer the next five questions. You are to choose the *one* best answer, marked A, B, C, or D, to each question. Answer all questions on the basis of what is *stated* or *implied* in the article.

MINIGARDENS FOR VEGETABLES

Containers

To start a minigarden of vegetables, you will need a container large enough to hold each plant when it is fully grown. You can use plastic or clay pots, an old pail, a plastic bucket, a bushel basket, a wire basket, or a wooden box. Most any container is satisfactory, from tiny pots for your kitchen windowsill to large wooden boxes for your patio.

The size and number of the containers can vary with the space you have and the number of plants you want to grow. Six-inch pots are satisfactory for chives. Radishes, onions, and a variety of tomato (Tiny Tim) will do well in ten-inch pots. For the average patio, five-gallon plastic cans are suitable. They are easy to handle and provide enough space for the larger vegetable plants.

Light

Vegetable plants grow better in full sunlight than in the shade. Some vegetables need more sun than others. Leafy vegetables (lettuce, cabbage, mustard greens) can stand more shade than root vegetables (beets, radishes, turnips). Root vegetables can stand more shade than vegetable fruit plants (cucumbers, peppers, tomatoes), which do very poorly in the shade. Plant your vegetable fruit plants where they will get the most sun, and your leafy vegetables and root vegetables in the shadier areas.

Starting Plants Indoors

You can give some plants a jump on the growing season by starting them indoors on windowsills that have plenty of sunlight. Then, after the weather gets warmer, you can transplant them into larger containers and move them outdoors.

Hardening

Plants should be gradually "hardened," or toughened, for two weeks before being moved outdoors. This is done by withholding water and lowering the temperature. Hardening slows down the plants' rate of growth to prepare them to withstand such conditions as chilling, drying winds, or high temperatures.

Lettuce, cabbage, and many other plants can be toughened to withstand frosts; others, such as tomatoes and peppers, cannot be hardened.

36.   Which of the following statements are TRUE?

   I. Lettuce does better in shade than tomatoes do.
  II. Plants started indoors need some toughening time before you move them outdoors.
 III. Radishes grow well in six-inch pots.

   A.   Statements I and II only
   B.   Statements I and III only
   C.   Statements II and III only
   D.   All of the statements

37.   You toughen a seedling

   A.   by putting it in a cooler environment.
   B.   by putting it in a six-inch pot.
   C.   by watering it thoroughly.
   D.   by increasing its rate of growth.

38.   To "give some plants a jump on the growing season" is to

   A.   shake off the effects of transplanting them.
   B.   get them off to an early start.
   C.   skip a necessary stage in their growth.
   D.   keep them in the shade.

39. Which of the following statements are FALSE?

    I. Some plants do well if you start them indoors.

    II. Green peppers can be hardened by withholding water.

    III. Root plants need more sun than vegetable fruit plants do.

    A. Statements I and II only

    B. Statements I and III only

    C. Statements II and III only

    D. All of the statements

40. Who is the most likely intended audience for the article?

    A. An experienced farmer

    B. A botany student

    C. A novice gardener

    D. An authority on gardening

---

41. In the figure below, the line BC is perpendicular to both AB and CD. What is the shortest possible distance from A to D?

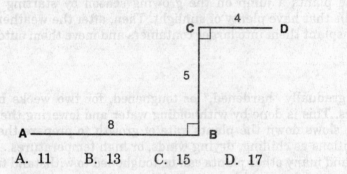

    A. 11   B. 13   C. 15   D. 17

42. Three men had an average age of 36. The oldest was 39, while the youngest was 32. How old was the third man?

    A. 33   B. 34   C. 36   D. 37

Refer to the chart below to answer the next three questions.

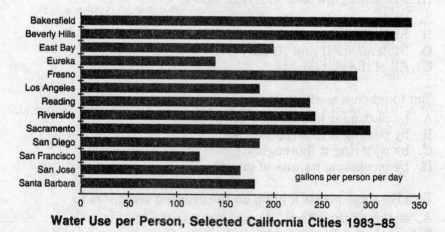

Water Use per Person, Selected California Cities 1983–85

43. Water use per person in Santa Barbara was about what fraction of the use in Bakersfield?

    A. 1/2   B. 1/3   C. 1/4   D. 1/5

44. Which of the following cities had lower water use per person than Los Angeles?

    A. Eureka   B. Fresno   C. Reading   D. Riverside

45. How many of the cities listed had water usage of 200 or more gallons per person per day?

    A. 5   B. 7   C. 9   D. 11

Refer to the letter below in answering the three questions that follow.

1930 Glencoe Way
Los Angeles CA 90068
January 23, 1997

Dear Ann Landers,

    (1) I met a boy at the mall last week; and I do not know whether I should go out with him. (2) He is very goodlooking and has nice manners. (3) All my friends say they like him; they think he likes me, too. (4) They say I should go out with him, but I just am not sure.

    (5) The trouble is, although we are both hispanics, this boy is actually an illegal alien. (6) He was born in Colombia, not in the United States. (7) I asked him how he managed to get into this country. (8) He said that many people go to Puerto Rico and then fly to New York. (9) Since Puerto Ricans are Americans, no one asks passengers from Puerto Rico for identification papers.

    (10) I am a law-abiding citizen. (11) Do you think it is right for me to go out with someone who is in this country illegally?

Yours truly,

Carmen Diaz

46. Which of the following words contains an error in capitalization?

    A. "Way" in the first line
    B. "mall" in sentence 1
    C. "hispanics" in sentence 5
    D. "citizen" in sentence 10

47. Which of the following terms contains an error in hyphenation?

    A. goodlooking
    B. illegal alien
    C. identification papers
    D. law-abiding

48. Which of the following sentences contains an error in punctuation?

    A. Sentence 1
    B. Sentence 3
    C. Sentence 5
    D. Sentence 11

---

49. A company estimates its income for next year will be $160,000. They have $40,000 in fixed expenses. After they subtract their fixed expenses from their income, the remainder of the income provides them with enough money to cover their variable expenses plus an estimated profit of 10%. What is their estimated profit in dollars?

    A. $40,000   B. $12,000   C. $1,600   D. $1,200

50. <u>If the Confederate Army would have carried the day at Gettysburg,</u> the history of America during the past century would have been profoundly altered.

    The sentence would be better if the underlined part were written as:

    A. If the Confederate Army would have carried the day at Gettysburg,
    B. Had the Confederate Army carried the day at Gettysburg,
    C. The Confederate Army having carried the day at Gettysburg,
    D. If the Confederate Army will carry the day at Gettysburg,

51. Two cars are heading south on Highway 5, one at 65 miles per hour, the other at 50 miles per hour. The car traveling at 50 miles per hour is 48 miles ahead of the faster car. In how many hours will the faster car catch up with the slower car?

    A. 4⅘ hours   B. 3½ hours   C. 3⅕ hours   D. 2⅘ hours

52. What is the product of the slope of line *B* and the slope of line *A*?

    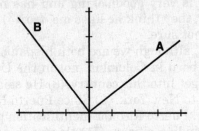

    A. –3   B. –1   C. 3/4   D. 3

53. A man has a choice of buying a camera for cash at $38 or of paying $10 down and four monthly payments of $8 each. How much will he save if he pays cash?

    A. $10   B. $8   C. $6   D. $4

54. Thom has a cylindrical barrel 4 feet across and 5 feet high. About how many cubic feet of water will the barrel hold?

    A. 30 cubic feet   C. 50 cubic feet
    B. 40 cubic feet   D. 60 cubic feet

55. A carpenter has to cut a stick one meter long into two pieces. He wants to have one piece four times as long as the other. How long will the shorter piece be?

    A. 16⅔ cm.   B. 20 cm.   C. 20 in.   D. 33⅓ cm.

Complete the following sentences with the correct form of the missing word.

56. Although they are twins, Susie is _____ than Sarah.
    A. pretty   C. prettiest
    B. prettier   D. prettily

57. As soon as the sun _____, Johnny was awake and ready to climb out of his crib.
    A. rises   C. rise
    B. risen   D. rose

58. Which of the following terms is the most GENERAL?

A. bikini   C. bathing suit

B. swimwear   D. garment

59. Which of the following terms is the most SPECIFIC?

A. gemstone   C. mineral

B. stone   D. diamond

60. (1) The Marine Mammal Protection Act was passed in 1972. (2) Its purpose was to prevent exploitation of dolphins and related aquatic mammals. (3) Later, it was amended in 1988 and in 1992.

Which answer below most effectively combines the above three sentences?

A. The Marine Mammal Protection Act was passed in 1972 in order to prevent exploitation of dolphins and related aquatic mammals, but later it was amended in 1988 and 1992.

B. The Marine Mammal Protection Act of 1972, later amended in 1988 and 1992, was passed to prevent exploitation of dolphins and related aquatic mammals.

C. The exploitation of dolphins and related aquatic mammals was prevented by the Marine Mammal Protection Act, which was passed in 1972, it was amended in 1988 and 1992.

D. The Marine Mammal Protection Act, passing in 1972, was amended in 1988 and 1992 to prevent exploitation of dolphins and related aquatic animals.

Refer to the following graph to answer the next three questions.

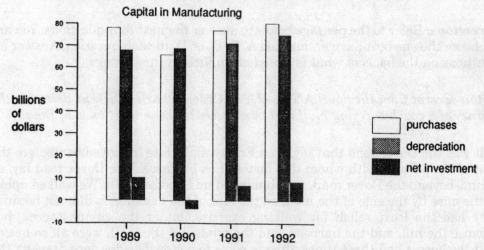

Capital in Manufacturing

61. In which year were manufacturing capital purchases highest?

A. 1989   B. 1990   C. 1991   D. 1992

62. The net investment in manufacturing capital is the amount spent on new capital investments (purchases) minus the depreciation on existing capital. Which year had negative net investment?

A. 1989   B. 1990   C. 1991   D. 1992

63. In which year did manufacturers spend about $10 billion more on purchases than they lost in depreciation?

A. 1989   B. 1990   C. 1991   D. 1992

64. A highway was built in Kern County at a cost of $132,000. The costs were borne by the county, the state, and the federal governments. The state paid twice as much as the county, and the federal government paid four times as much as the state. How much did the county pay?

A. $11,000   B. $12,000   C. $13,200   D. $18,500

Refer to the following notice to answer the next two questions.

FUN-FLICKS VIDEOTAPE RENTAL

non members:	
$3.50 overnight rental	$5 weekend (Friday–Monday)
members:	
$2 overnight	$4 weekend
Memberships are $20, including 5 free overnight rentals	

65. Emily Wallace is considering joining the Fun-Flicks videotape rental club. How many videotapes must she check out in order for the membership plan to save her money?

A. 5   B. 6   C. 7   D. 8

66. If she joins, what is the greatest number of videotapes Emily can get for a total expenditure of $35?

A. 10   B. 11   C. 12   D. 13

Directions: Refer to the passage below to answer the next four questions. You are to choose the *one* best answer, marked A, B, C, or D, to each question. Answer all questions on the basis of what is *stated* or *implied* in the passage.

In this excerpt from the novel A Tale of Two Cities, *Charles Dickens describes the journey of a coach carrying mail and passengers to the seaport town of Dover.*

It was the Dover road that lay, on a Friday night late in November, before the first of the persons with whom this history has business. The Dover road lay, as to him, beyond the Dover mail, as it lumbered up Shooter's Hill. We walked uphill in the mire by the side of the mail, as the rest of the passengers did; not because they had the least relish for walking exercise, under the circumstances, but because the hill, and the harness, and the mud, and the mail, were all so heavy, that the horses had three times already come to a stop, besides once drawing the coach across the road, with the mutinous intent of taking it back to Blackheath.

With drooping heads and tremulous tails, the horses mashed their way through thick mud, floundering and stumbling between whiles as if they were falling to pieces at the larger joints. As often as the driver rested them and brought them to a stand, with a wary "Wo-ho! so-ho then!" the near leader violently shook his head and everything upon it—like an unusually emphatic horse, denying that the coach could be got up the hill. Whenever the leader made this rattle, the passenger started, as a nervous passenger might, and was disturbed in mind.

67. It can be inferred that the passengers are walking because

    A. they need fresh air and exercise.
    B. they are afraid of the horses.
    C. their trip is over.
    D. the coach cannot carry them uphill.

68. In the first paragraph, the word "relish" most nearly means

    A. spice.
    B. liking.
    C. ability.
    D. need.

69. In the second paragraph, the phrase "brought them to a stand" most nearly means

    A. led them to a booth.
    B. made them get up after a fall.
    C. caused them to come to a halt.
    D. carried them to their station.

70. The "near leader" (second paragraph) is

    A. the driver.
    B. one of the horses.
    C. one of the passengers.
    D. a mentally disturbed person.

---

71. What is the eighth number in the sequence of numbers below?

    1 3 6 10 15 21 . . .

    A. 25   B. 28   C. 32   D. 36

72. What part of a two-dollar bill is a quarter?

    A. 1/4   B. 1/8   C. 1/12   D. 2/25

Refer to the following graph to answer the next four questions.

Birth and Death Rates: 1960 to 1985
Rate per 1,000 population

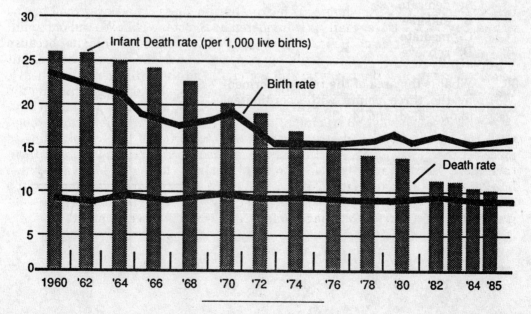

73. Which of the following statements about birth and death rates in the United States is NOT true?

    A. The infant death rate decreased steadily from 1960 to 1985.
    B. Births exceeded deaths by at least 5 per thousand for the period shown.
    C. The birth rate decreased steadily from 1960 to 1985.
    D. The death rate in 1985 was less than it had been in 1960.

74. In 1968, the population of the United States was about 200 million people. Approximately how many Americans died in 1968?

    A. 1 million   B. 2 million   C. 5 million   D. 10 million

75. The infant death rate in 1985 was about what percent of the rate in 1960?

    A. 20%   B. 30%   C. 40%   D. 50%

76. From 1960 to 1975, the birth rate decreased every year EXCEPT

    A. 1966   B. 1968   C. 1970   D. 1972

---

77. Find the answer choice that matches the following definition.

    Definition: persistence of effort; steady application to a task

    A. diligence
    B. habit
    C. monotony
    D. willfulness

78. Find the answer choice that matches the following definition.

    Definition: lacking a definite plan or purpose; by chance

    A. detached
    B. impractical
    C. random
    D. untidy

79. Find the answer choice that matches the following definition.

    Definition: express support or approval publicly

    A. dedicate
    B. endorse
    C. mediate
    D. retrieve

80. What is the area of the triangle formed by the three points with coordinates (2,5), (−2,−3) and (4,−3)?

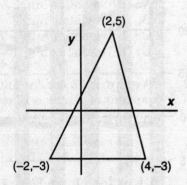

    A. 12   B. 24   C. 36   D. 48

81. An aluminum mine gets a yield of 1¼ pounds of metal for each ton of ore. How many tons must be processed to produce 200 pounds of the metal?

A. 125 tons   B. 160 tons   C. 250 tons   D. 320 tons

82. Four cups of grated cheese weigh one pound. How many ounces does one cup weigh?

A. 1 ounce   B. 2 ounces   C. 4 ounces   D. 8 ounces

83. The debate team at Johnny's high school went from 25 in his first year to 30 in his second year. What was the percentage increase the second year?

A. 2%   B. 5%   C. 10%   D. 20%

Refer to the following table to answer the next two questions.

RAINFALL				
Precipitation data, 4 P.M. Monday for selected California Stations				
CITY	LAST 24 HOURS	SEASON TO DATE	NORMAL TO DATE	SEASONAL NORM
Oakland	0	5.43	6.98	18.69
San Jose	0	2.33	4.84	13.65
Fresno	0	1.68	3.32	10.24
Los Angeles	0	.24	4.49	14.05
(Season: July 1 to June 30)				

84. Which city NORMALLY has had the least amount of rainfall by this date in the season?

A. Oakland   B. San Jose   C. Fresno   D. Los Angeles

85. What percentage of its normal rainfall for the year has Oakland had so far this season?

A. 5%   B. 29%   C. 48%   D. 78%

86. A man buys a pair of shoes for thirty-three dollars and forty-five cents. He pays for them with two twenty dollar bills. What change will he probably be given back?

A. 1 five-dollar bill, 2 one-dollar bills, 2 quarters, and 1 nickel
B. 1 five-dollar bill, 2 one-dollar bills, 1 quarter, and 2 dimes
C. 1 five-dollar bill, 1 one-dollar bill, 2 quarters, and 1 nickel
D. 1 five-dollar bill, 1 one-dollar bill, 1 quarter, and 2 dimes

87. A quart is 32 ounces and a liter is approximately 30.3 ounces. About what percent of a liter is one quart?

A. 90%   B. 95%   C. 105%   D. 110%

Directions: Refer to the following descriptions to answer the next four questions. You are to choose the *one* best answer, marked A, B, C, or D, to each question. Answer all questions on the basis of what is *stated* or *implied* in the descriptions.

RATINGS: COAST GUARD JOB DESCRIPTIONS

YEOMAN—The Coast Guard's effective administration depends on the efficient performance of a highly trained clerical staff. The Yeoman fills that need. He prepares records and keeps the Coast Guard's vast amount of letters, messages, and reports flowing smoothly.

Qualifications: Yeomen need qualifications similar to those of secretaries, stenographers, and typists in private industry. Yeomen should be above average in general learning ability, should possess a degree of manual dexterity, and must be able to work harmoniously with others in an office organization. Courses in English and in business subjects such as typewriting and filing are very useful.

MARINE SCIENCE TECHNICIAN—The Marine Science Technician observes, collects, analyzes, and disseminates meteorological and oceanographic observations. He makes visual and instrumental weather and oceanographic observations, and he conducts routine chemical analysis. His analysis and interpretation of weather and sea conditions furnishes advice used in search-and-rescue operations.

Qualifications: Marine Science Technicians should be above average in general learning ability and should have an aptitude for mathematics. School courses in algebra, trigonometry, chemistry, physics, and typing are very helpful.

PORT SECURITYMAN—The Port Securityman supervises and controls the safe handling, transportation, and storage of explosives and other dangerous cargoes. He is well versed in the regulations and equipment responsible for the security of vessels, harbors, and waterfront facilities. He is also an expert in the field of fire prevention and extinguishment.

Qualifications: Port Securitymen should be average or above average in general learning ability and should have normal hearing and vision. School courses in practical mathematics, chemistry, and English are helpful.

88. Which of the following school courses would be useful for BOTH a Marine Science Technician and a Port Securityman?
   A. Algebra
   B. Chemistry
   C. English
   D. Typing

89. Which of the following is NOT part of the job of a Marine Science Technician?
   A. Analyzing sea conditions
   B. Collecting meteorological observations
   C. Handling explosives
   D. Interpreting the weather

90. Which of the following civilian jobs is LEAST related to the work of a Port Securityman?
   A. Clerk
   B. Fireman
   C. Security guard
   D. Warehouseman

91. What special ability would be MOST useful to a Yeoman?
A. Better than normal hearing   C. Manual dexterity
B. Better than normal vision   D. Mathematical aptitude

92. Jody has a circular flower bed in her back yard, with a diameter of 4 feet. If she doubles the diameter of the flower bed, how many square feet will she ADD to the flower bed?
A. 4π square feet   C. 12π square feet
B. 8π square feet   D. 24π square feet

93. A grocer bought 10 crates of oranges for $90. One crate arrived spoiled and unsuitable for sale. What should he charge per crate to make a profit of 20% on his total cost?
A. $3.00   B. $10.80   C. $12.00   D. $18.00

94. At a barn-raising party, <u>neighbors</u> from farms far and near would gather to erect a new barn for their friends.
A. The underlined word is spelled correctly.
B. The underlined word is spelled incorrectly.

95. On Memorial Day, politicians make speeches in <u>rememberance</u> of those who died for their country.
A. The underlined word is spelled correctly.
B. The underlined word is spelled incorrectly.

Refer to the charts below to answer the next three questions.

Racial Composition in California Public Schools, 1988

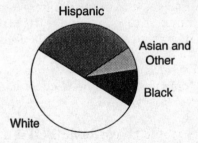

California average

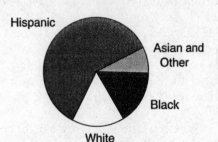

Los Angeles

96. Which group had the largest fraction of the students in Los Angeles schools in 1988?
A. White   B. Black   C. Asian and Other   D. Hispanic

97. Which group averaged the smallest fraction of students in all California schools in 1988?
A. White   B. Black   C. Asian and Other   D. Hispanic

98. How did the proportion of Hispanic students in the average California school in 1988 compare with that in Los Angeles?
A. It was about 1/4 as big.   C. It was about the same size.
B. It was about 1/2 as big.   D. It was about twice as big.

99. It takes a crew of four painters 15 hours to prepare an apartment for painting. How many hours would it take a crew of six?

A. 7½ hours   B. 8 hours   C. 10 hours   D. 12 hours

100. A man pays $1600 a year for medical insurance. At the end of five years he is ill and hospitalized. The insurance company reimburses him $19,200, covering all but $500 of his expenses for the hospital. How much money has he saved by carrying medical insurance?

A. $19,200   C. $10,700

B. $17,100   D. He has saved no money at all.

ANSWER KEY   TEST B

Part One: Essay

There are no "correct" answers to this part.

Part Two: Short-Answer Questions

1. D	21. B	41. B	61. D	81. B
2. D	22. C	42. D	62. B	82. C
3. B	23. B	43. A	63. A	83. D
4. C	24. C	44. A	64. B	84. C
5. C	25. D	45. B	65. C	85. B
6. B	26. A	46. C	66. C	86. C
7. A	27. B	47. A	67. D	87. C
8. C	28. C	48. A	68. B	88. B
9. B	29. D	49. B	69. C	89. C
10. D	30. C	50. B	70. B	90. A
11. B	31. C	51. C	71. D	91. C
12. A	32. B	52. B	72. B	92. C
13. B	33. A	53. D	73. C	93. C
14. A	34. B	54. D	74. B	94. A
15. C	35. C	55. B	75. C	95. B
16. A	36. A	56. B	76. C	96. D
17. C	37. A	57. D	77. A	97. C
18. C	38. B	58. D	78. C	98. B
19. C	39. C	59. D	79. B	99. C
20. B	40. C	60. B	80. B	100. C

ANSWER EXPLANATIONS   TEST B

Part Two: Short-Answer Questions

Before attempting to answer any of the questions, you should read through the passage quickly, in order to get a good general idea of what is said and where to look in the passage for more details. In others words, don't try to remember lots of specific details during this first reading; instead, try to remember where in the passage the author makes *major points*. This passage consists of four paragraphs; you need to have a general idea what each of these paragraphs says about the coastline of San Diego County. Each paragraph discusses a particular aspect of the coastline.

Paragraph 1:   Land forms of the coastline (beaches, headlands, cliffs)
Paragraph 2:   Coastal waters (bays, lagoons, estuaries)
Paragraph 3:   Mission Bay
Paragraph 4:   San Diego Bay

Now go on to answer the questions.

1. Answer D. Tropical rainforests

Question 1 asks which of its four possible answers is *not* found on the coast of San Diego Country: rocky headlands, sandy beaches, steep cliffs, or tropical rainforests. From your quick overview of the passage, you know you can find the answer to this question in paragraph 1. Use the process of elimination here. Are there rocky headlands along the coastline? Yes—the stretches of open beaches are "interrupted by rocky headlands." Cross out Choice A. Are there sandy beaches? Certainly there are. Cross out Choice B. Are there steep cliffs? Paragraph 1's final sentence mentions "precipitous cliffs several hundred feet high." That sounds steep. Cross out Choice C. Only Choice D is left. There are no tropical rainforests along San Diego County's coast.

2. Answer D. Wildlife habitat

Which paragraph in the passage discusses lagoons? Paragraph 2. Read this paragraph over again looking for anything that explains why the lagoons are valuable. The last sentence of the paragraph begins, "The estuaries and lagoons are valuable mainly as wildlife habitat." Clearly, the correct answer is *wildlife habitat*, Choice D.

3. Answer B. Mission Bay has less commercial importance than San Diego Bay does.

Since its shoreline is highly developed for recreational purposes, Mission Bay clearly has not been set aside as a wildlife refuge. Therefore, Choice A is incorrect. Though San Diego Bay has had to be protected from the dumping of industrial and municipal sewage, nothing in the passage suggests that Mission Bay has suffered from such pollution. Choice C is incorrect. Not Mission Bay, but San Diego Bay, is the site of a major naval base. Choice D is incorrect. While Mission Bay is highly developed for recreation, it is not, as San Diego is, a busy center of commerce. Thus, it has less commercial importance than San Diego Bay does. Choice B is correct.

4. Answer C. Banning actions that caused it

Since water pollution is bad, the way you do something positive about it is to get rid of it. San Diego has "prohibited the dumping of municipal and industrial sewage into the bay." Thus, the government has banned actions that caused water pollution.

5. Answer C. An increase in its recreational use

This final question on the passage concerns San Diego Bay. To answer it, turn to paragraph 4. The middle sentences of this paragraph discuss what water pollution regulations have been enacted; these mostly concern limiting the dumping of sewage by the city, by industry, and by naval and private boats. The paragraph's concluding sentence discusses what effects these regulations have had: there has been "a marked improvement in the water quality," and "all types of water-associated recreation are increasing." Compare this statement with the answer choices given. The correct answer is Choice C: the recreational use of San Diego Bay has grown as its pollution has lessened.

6.   Answer B.   20 pounds

A ton is 2,000 pounds. Figure out how much 1/8 of a ton is by dividing 2,000 by 8, and then subtract the man's current weight to see how much he has to gain to weigh 1/8 ton.

$$\begin{array}{r} 250 \\ 8\overline{)2000} \\ 16 \\ \hline 40 \end{array}$$

Subtracting 230 from 250 gives 20 pounds to gain.

7. Answer A. $500

Add together all the man's costs and then subtract this from the selling price of $65,000 to find his profit:

$62,500	for the original cost of the condo
$ 400	for grading
$ 950	for wiring
$ 650	for painting and plastering
$64,500	

The selling price was $65,000; therefore the man's profit was $65,000 − $64,500 = $500.

8. Answer C. A small pizza with two toppings and anchovies

Karl bought a small soft drink and a pizza for a total of $3.10 (since he used up all the money he came in with). The soft drink cost 30¢, so he spent $3.10 − $0.30 = $2.80 on the pizza. Looking through the price list, you will see that the only pizza he could have bought would be a small pizza with two toppings. Choices A, B, and D all say single topping, so they cannot be right. Choice C is possible since it is a small pizza with two toppings—the anchovies don't add anything to the price, according to the last line on the sign. Choice C must be the correct answer.

9. Answer B. $6.50

Add the items of the bill:

$5.20	for a large pizza, 2 toppings
$1.00	for two large sodas (50¢ each)
$0.30	for one small soda
$6.50	

10. Answer D. $9.12

The question only asks for the cost of the pizzas, so you can ignore the soft drinks. The two giant pizzas with two toppings would ordinarily cost 2 × $5.70 = $11.40, but with a 20% discount, we can subtract 20% (= 1/5 or 0.20) of this amount:

$$\begin{array}{r} \$11.40 \\ \times\ 0.2 \\ \hline \$2.280 \end{array}$$

$11.40 − $2.28 = $9.12.

11. Answer B.   Indirect

The word "straightforward" means direct or candid. Its opposite therefore is "indirect" or devious and roundabout.

12. Answer A.   Gloomy

To be "melancholy" is to feel sad or despondent. Its synonym therefore is "gloomy."

13. Answer B.   Weekly salary rose but real income fell.

In 1980, the salary paid to the key entry operators rose from $340 a week to $365 a week at the start of 1981, and the real income fell to a value of about $330 in constant 1980 dollars. That is, weekly salary rose and real income fell, which is just what Choice B says.

14. Answer A.   1985

For the choices given, covering the years 1982 to 1985, the graph of real income (the dashed line) is steadily rising, reaching its highest point at the end, in 1985.

15. Answer C.   1984

To compare later dates with the value of real income in 1980, lay a pencil or piece of paper on the graph at the level of the 1980 starting value and level with the horizontal axis of the graph, and follow this out until the graph of real income (the dashed line) meets or rises above it again. From that point, look down to the scale on the horizontal axis (for instance, by rotating the pencil 90°). The 1980 value is reached again in 1984.

16. Answer A.   Thrifty

To be thrifty is to be careful about one's money. A grasping or greedy attitude toward money is bad. A miserly or closefisted attitude toward money is bad. A stingy or mean attitude toward money is bad. However, a thrifty or prudent attitude toward money is wise. The word has positive connotations.

17. Answer C.   Underlined part "C" needs to be changed to make the sentence correct.

The use of the apostrophe in the name of Mark Twain is correct. There is no need for a comma or any other punctuation mark between the words "navigator" and "on." However, the word "rivers" must be capitalized here: the sentence refers not to rivers in general but to two specific rivers, the Missouri River and the Mississippi River.

18. Answer C.   An encyclopedia

An encyclopedia is a book containing articles (usually alphabetically arranged) on all branches of knowledge, or, sometimes, on a particular field. Thus, you could find an article on dogs, for example, in the general *Encyclopædia Britannica* or in the specialized *Animal Life Encyclopedia*.

19. Answer C.   3, 2, 1, 4

The paragraph makes the most sense read in the following order:
(3) The first people to gaze upon Niagara Falls were ancestors of the Seneca Indians. (2) They were the territory's first inhabitants some 2,000 years ago. (1) One of the earliest Europeans to behold this natural spectacle was a French priest, Father Louis Hennepin. (4) According to historical accounts, upon seeing the mighty waterfall Hennepin fell to his knees in prayer, saying of the awesome phenomenon that the universe did not hold its equal.

20. Answer B. Sentence B is correctly punctuated.

Sentence A is incorrectly punctuated: there should be a comma in place of the semicolon. Sentence C is incorrectly punctuated: there should be a comma between the words "Europe" and "he." Sentence D is incorrectly punctuated: either there should be a semicolon in place of the comma in the sentence, or there should be a period following "Packers" and "this" should be capitalized.

21. Answer B. 85°

The sum of the angles of the triangle must be 180°; the two known angles have 55 + 40 = 95 degrees. The third angle must have 180 − 95 = 85 degrees.

22. Answer C. 14

Find the change from each number to the next in the sequence:

from 8 to 6	subtract 2	−2
from 6 to 10	add 4	+4
from 10 to 4	subtract 6	−6
from 4 to 12	add 8	+8
from 12 to 2	subtract 10	−10

To follow this pattern, the next number should add 12, to give 2 + 12 = 14.

23. Answer B. 4

In an unknown number of years ("x"), the mother's age will be twice the daughter's. The mother is now 62 and the daughter 29. Add x years to each and make an equation:

$$62 + x = 2(29 + x); \qquad 62 + x = 58 + 2x$$

Subtracting x from both sides, and then 58, gives $x = 4$.

24. Answer C. 75 miles

The towns are 3/4 inches apart on the map, and 1 inch stands for 100 miles; therefore the towns are really 3/4 × 100 miles = 75 miles apart.

25. Answer D. 5:13 P.M.

Tom's wife arrives at 4:38; 35 minutes later is 4:38 + 35 = 4 P.M. + (38 + 35) minutes. And since 38 + 35 = 73 minutes, or 1 hour and 13 minutes, the time she leaves is 4 P.M. + 1 hour + 13 minutes = 5 P.M. + 13 minutes = 5:13 P.M.

26. Answer A. In committee work

The second paragraph of the article describes the work of senators in committee. Its opening sentence states "Senators must spend most of their time in committee study." This is Choice A; the other choices (the Senate chamber, their offices, and their home districts) are not mentioned as places where senators spend the bulk of their time.

27. Answer B. According to their own expressed interests

According to the opening paragraph, "committees are established by the Rules Committee early in each legislative session." Therefore, you would expect that the Rules Committee assigned senators to their committees. However, the Rules Committee is not mentioned in any of the answer choices given. Scan the passage further to find other references to committees and their structure. The opening sentence of paragraph 3 states that "Committee membership is determined basically by the interests of the individual senators." The rest of this paragraph confirms that senators usually choose the committees on which they serve because they are experts in a particular area or are especially interested in it.

28. **Answer C. To allow a detailed discussion of the good and bad points of bills coming before the Senate**

Check each of the answer choices against the text of the article.

A. To permit senators to vote on bills in secret before they come before the whole Senate. FALSE. The article says that all votes taken in committee are published. Committee votes are not secret.

B. To allow certain bills to be passed without a majority vote. FALSE. All bills have to be passed by the full Senate and require a majority or a two-thirds vote.

D. To give senators privacy as they practice public speaking. FALSE. Committee hearings are open to the public and the press; they offer no privacy. Whether or not the senators need privacy to practice public speaking, this is not a reason mentioned for the formation of committees.

Only Choice C is left. It is the correct answer. The first paragraph of the article states that committees assure "that each detail of proposed legislation is given a thorough hearing."

29. **Answer D. Dealing with**

If rules cover certain procedures, they include these procedures and deal with them.

30. **Answer C. The senator is looking for additional votes to enable the bill to pass.**

The second sentence of the concluding paragraph states that, should a bill "fail to receive the votes necessary for passage, and a number of members are absent from their seats, a Call of the Senate may be moved." What happens when a senator moves a Call of the Senate? The sergeant at arms rounds up the absentees and brings them back to the locked chamber where they must either vote or abstain when the roll is called. Why does the senator want to force them to vote? The senator hopes that their additional votes will be enough to enable the bill to pass. (If the senator wanted the bill to fail, he or she could have left things alone and not moved a Call of the Senate; after all, the bill had already failed to get the number of votes necessary for it to be passed.)

31. **Answer C. 4.3 gallons**

Al must get enough paint to cover the area of the wall twice over. The area is that of a rectangle 59 feet by 15 feet *minus* the area of the two circular holes. The holes are 4 feet in diameter, so each has a radius of 2 feet. The area of each circular hole is πr^2 or, in this case, $\pi \times 2 \times 2 = 4\pi$ square feet. Each circle has an area of about $4 \times 3.14 \ldots$ square feet, or roughly $12\frac{1}{2}$ square feet. The two circles together take about 25 square feet from the total area of the rectangle. That is $59 \times 15 = 885$ square feet (notice that it is easier to calculate this as $60 \times 15 = 900$ *minus* 15 than to use brute force to do the multiplication). Subtracting the circle area of 25 square feet, the wall has 860 square feet to be painted. Two coats require 1720 square feet of coverage, and each gallon covers 400 square feet. So the final answer is the result of dividing 1720 square feet by 400:

$$
\begin{array}{r}
4.3 \\
400\overline{)1720.00} \\
\underline{1600} \\
120\,0
\end{array}
$$

32. Answer B. 35 mph

The average speed for the whole trip is the total distance divided by the total time. The two parts took three hours and two hours respectively, and covered 75 + 100 miles. Therefore, the average speed was 175 miles per five hours, which reduces (divide both numbers by 5) to 35 miles per one hour.

33. Answer A. 6-ounce size

Figure the unit price (that is, the price per ounce) for each size. The smallest unit price is the best buy. You need to do this for all three cases, or at least for the 6-ounce and 16-ounce sizes. The 12-ounce size can be compared as a ratio to the 6-ounce size—if it costs less than twice as much, it is a better buy; if it costs more than twice as much, it is not as good; and if it costs exactly twice as much, it is the same unit price. But the 12-ounce size is selling for $1.29 and the 6-ounce size for $0.63. Twice the cost of the 6-ounce size would be $1.26, so the 12-ounce size is more expensive per ounce, as you can see quickly without doing any division. (Incidentally, this also rules out Choice D, as it shows that the different sizes do not all cost the same per ounce.) In the end, you have to actually compute cost per ounce for the 6-ounce and 16-ounce sizes, in order to see which is cheaper:

$$6)\overline{63} \quad 10\tfrac{3}{6} \qquad 16)\overline{179} \quad 1\,1\tfrac{3}{16}$$

$$\frac{6}{3} \qquad \frac{16}{19}$$

The six-ounce size is less than 11¢ per ounce, the 16-ounce size more; the best buy is the 6-ounce size.

34. Answer B. 20%

The figure (a pentagon, and apparently a regular one with all the sides equal) has five equal parts. The shaded part is 1/5 of the whole figure. In percentage terms, 1/5 is 100% / 5 = 20%.

35. Answer C. Three days

You can answer this question by figuring out the combined rate of work of the librarian and his assistant (he does six books an hour, the assistant does two; together they can catalog eight books an hour). Since there are 72 books to catalog, the total number of hours they will spend is 72/8 = nine hours. Each of them spends three hours a day, so the nine hours will take nine days / three hours-per-day = three days to complete.

36. Answer A. Statements I and II only

Use the process of elimination to answer this question. In the paragraph on "Light," it is stated that leafy vegetables, such as lettuce, can stand more shade than root vegetables, and that root vegetables in turn can stand more shade than vegetable fruit plants, such as tomatoes. Thus, it logically follows that lettuce does better in shade than tomatoes do. Statement I is true. Therefore, you can eliminate Choice C. Likewise, the opening sentence of the section on "Hardening" asserts that "Plants should be gradually 'hardened,' or toughened, for two weeks before being moved outdoors." If indoor plants *should* be hardened or toughened for two weeks, clearly they need this toughening time. Statement II is true. Therefore, you can eliminate Choice B. The second paragraph, however, states that although chives do well in six-inch pots, radishes flourish in ten-inch pots. Statement III is false. Therefore, you can eliminate Choice D. Only Choice A is left. It is the correct answer.

37. Answer A.   By putting it in a cooler environment

In the next-to-last paragraph you are advised to harden your seedlings "by withholding water and lowering the temperature." One way to lower the temperature of a plant is to put the plant in a cooler environment.

38. Answer B.   Get them off to an early start

Think of what happens when you get a jump on your competition—you get a head start. Similarly, when you give plants a jump on the growing season, you get them to start growing earlier than normal: you get them off to an early start.

39. Answer C.   Statements II and III only

To answer this question, you discover which statements are false by eliminating those statements that you can prove to be true. The paragraph entitled "Starting Plants Indoors" states that you "can give some plants a jump on the growing season by starting them indoors." Thus, it is true that some plants do well if you start them indoors. Statement I clearly is NOT false; it is true. You immediately can eliminate Choices A, B, and D; the only possible answer is Choice C.

40.   Answer C.   A novice gardener

Neither an experienced farmer nor an authority on gardening would need such basic information on growing vegetables. Choices A and D are incorrect. Students of botany would have more interest in plants as scientific specimens than in plants as garden crops. Choice B is incorrect. Remember, the title of the passage is "Minigardens for Vegetables." It is intended for an audience of novice or beginner gardeners.

41. Answer B.   13

The shortest distance from A to D is along the straight line between them. This is the hypotenuse of a right triangle. (Extend AB to the right and draw a line parallel to BC to complete a rectangle.) Since the horizontal leg AE is 12, and the vertical leg ED is 5, this is a 5-12-13 right triangle, and the distance AD = 13. You can use the Pythagorean Theorem if you don't remember about 5-12-13 right triangles.

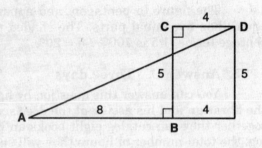

$$AD = \sqrt{(12 \times 12 + 5 \times 5)} = \sqrt{(144 + 25)} = \sqrt{169} = 13$$

42. Answer D.   37

The average age is the sum of the men's ages divided by 3. This can be stated in an equation with the unknown age a of the third man:

$$\frac{(32 + 39 + a)}{3} = 36$$

Simplify this in stages to find a: $(32+39) + a = (3 \times 36) = 108$; $a = 108 - 71 = 37$.

43. Answer A.   1/2

Compare the usage for Bakersfield (the top bar of the chart) with Santa Barbara (the bottom bar). The top bar extends nearly to the value of 350 gallons per person per day on the horizontal scale. The bar for Santa Barbara lies between 150 and 200. Half of 350 would be 175, which is a reasonable guess for Santa Barbara. All the other choices would be too small (for example, 1/3 of 350 ≈ 127).

44. Answer A. Eureka

Move a pencil or piece of paper to touch the Los Angeles bar on the right, and look to see which of the cities named as choices has a bar that doesn't reach as far as your marker. This is fairly easy since all the cities named are near L.A. in the chart. You will see that only Eureka has a bar that ends to the left (signifying lower water use than in L.A.).

45. Answer B. 7

A piece of paper helps with this question, as with the previous one. Place the paper so that its bottom edge is along the scale and its right edge is at the 200 mark. Then count the number of bars that go past the right edge of the paper. You should count six bars that extend past the paper, and also see that the bar for the East Bay reaches the paper (if you shift it slightly to the left, you'll see the end of the East Bay bar), making a total of seven cities with water usage of 200 or more.

46. Answer C. "hispanics" in sentence 5

The word "hispanics" should be capitalized. When you are referring to a specific ethnic or national group, you should capitalize its name. Think of African-American, or French.

47. Answer A. goodlooking

Choice A contains an error in hyphenation: this word should be hyphenated. It should be *good-looking*.

48. Answer A. Sentence 1

As it stands, sentence 1 is incorrect. When two independent clauses in a compound sentence are joined by a coordinating conjunction (in this case, by *and*), you should place a comma between the clauses immediately before the conjunction. Rewrite sentence 1 as follows: I met a boy at the mall last week, and I do not know whether I should go out with him.

49. Answer B. $12,000

Subtract the $40,000 in fixed expenses from the total income of $160,000; this leaves the company with $120,000. The 10% profit mentioned is figured from this value of income (the problem states that after they subtract their fixed expenses, the remaining amount leaves them with an estimated profit of 10%). The question asks for the dollar amount of this profit, and 10% of $120,000 = $120,000/10 = $12,000.

50. Answer B. Had the Confederate Army carried the day at Gettysburg,

Choices A, C, and D all fail to correct the problem with the form of the verb. Choice A is incorrect: do not use *would have* as a substitute for *had*. Choice C is incorrect: the present perfect form of the participle (*having carried*) is used to indicate action that has taken place prior to the action of the main verb. Choice D is incorrect: the Battle of Gettysburg took place in the past, not in the future. The correct sentence reads as follows: Had the Confederate Army carried the day at Gettysburg, the history of America during the past century would have been profoundly altered.

51. Answer C. $3^1/_5$ hours

The slower car is 48 miles ahead of the faster car. The faster car is going 65 mph and the slower one 50 mph; that is, the faster car is gaining on the slower one at (65 − 50) = 15 mph. If x stands for the number of hours needed to overtake the slower car, the *distance* to be covered is 48 miles and the *rate* is 15. Since *distance = rate × time*, 48 = 15x, and x = 48/15 = 16/5 = 3⅕ hours.

52. Answer B. –1

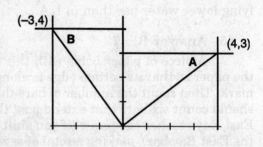

Find the two slopes and then calculate their product. The slope of a line is its *rise* (vertical change) divided by the *run* (horizontal change). To figure this for the two lines shown, try to find convenient points on the lines by using a piece of paper or a pencil to match points on the line with the tick marks on the x and y axes. Line A rises from the origin a vertical distance of 3 units in a horizontal change of 4 units; the slope of A = 3/4. Line B drops 4 units in moving right 3 units; its slope is negative, –4/3. The product of the two slopes is 3/4 × –4/3 = –12/12 = –1.

53. Answer D. $4

The cash price is $38; if the man paid $10 down and four installments of $8, he would have to pay a total of $10 + 4 × $8 = $10 + $32 = $42. The difference in price is $42 – $38 = $4, which is how much the man saves by paying cash.

54. Answer D. 60 cubic feet

You need to *estimate* the volume of the cylinder; the exact value involves π, and all choices are suspiciously round numbers, so you need only use an approximate value for π, say 3.1 or 3.14. The volume of the cylinder is its circular area times its height, $V = \pi r^2 h$. The radius of the cylinder is 2 feet (the question states that the barrel is "4 feet across," so its diameter is 4 feet), and it is 5 feet high. $V = \pi(2 \times 2)5 = 20\pi \approx 20 \times 3.14 \approx 63$. This is closer to Choice D than to any of the other choices.

55. Answer B. 20 cm.

If the shorter piece has length x, the longer has length 4x, and the total length is $x + 4x = 5x$ = 1 meter = 100 cm. Therefore, x = 100 cm. / 5 = 20 cm.

56. Answer B. Prettier

The missing word must be an adjective: it is used to describe a person. However, in this case it is used to compare one person with another. Thus, the adjective "pretty" must be in its comparative form: "Susie is *prettier* than Sarah."

57. Answer D. Rose

The missing word must be in the past tense. The simple past tense of the irregular verb *rise* is *rose*: I rose, you rose, he rose, she rose, it rose, we rose, they rose.

58. Answer D. Garment

The correct order of the four terms, starting with the most GENERAL or encompassing and ending with the most SPECIFIC or particular is: garment, swimwear, bathing suit, bikini. A bikini is a specific kind of bathing suit. A bathing suit is a specific kind of swimwear. Swimwear is one kind of garment.

59. Answer D. Diamond

The correct order of the four terms, starting with the most SPECIFIC or particular and ending with the most GENERAL or encompassing is: diamond, gemstone, stone, mineral. A diamond is a specific kind of gemstone. A gemstone is a specific kind of stone. Stone is a specific kind of mineral.

60. Answer B. The Marine Mammal Protection Act of 1972, later amended in 1988 and 1992, was passed to prevent exploitation of dolphins and related aquatic mammals.

Note the relative brevity of this answer choice. Six words shorter than the three original sentences, it retains all the ideas of the originals while combining them into a complex whole.

61. Answer D. 1992

Purchases are shown by the white bars (the bars furthest left in each group). It should be clear that 1990 purchases were less than 1989 and 1991 purchases less than 1992. You need to check whether 1992 purchases were higher or lower than 1989. Put a pencil or piece of paper along the top of the 1989 bar, keeping it level with the bottom of the graph. You will see that the 1992 bar is higher. (The 1989 bar comes to just below the 80 billion tick mark at the top of the scale, while the 1992 bar is a bit above that mark.)

62. Answer B. 1990

Note that all the bars stretch between 0 and another value so that the length of the bar is a measure of the purchases, depreciation or net investment. The only year in which the black net investment bar goes below 0 is 1990. You can check this by seeing that 1990 is the only year in which the depreciation bar (the gray middle bar of each group) is taller than the bar for purchases.

63. Answer A. 1989

When purchases are $10 billion more than depreciation, the net investment is (positive) $10 billion. In the graph, the difference between the left bar (purchases, in white) and the middle bar (depreciation, in gray) is the black net investment bar on the right. Look for a black bar that just reaches the $10 tick mark on the vertical scale of the graph. The only possibility is 1989.

64. Answer B. $12,000

Write the facts given in the question as equations. If you let c, s, and f stand for the county, state, and federal shares in the total cost, you get

$c + s + f = \$132,000 \qquad s = 2c \qquad f = 4s = 8c$

Rewriting the total cost entirely in terms of c (the unknown you need for the answer) gives

$c + 2c + 8c = 11c = \$132,000 \qquad c = \$132,000 / 11 = \$12,000$

65. Answer C. Seven

Compare the prices for videotape rental with and without the membership fee:

	with membership	without
A. five videos	$20 (membership fee)	5 × $3.50 = $17.50
B. six videos	$20 + $2	6 × $3.50 = $21
C. seven videos	$20 + 2 × $2 = $24	7 × $3.50 = $24.50

As soon as Emily rents seven videotapes, the membership is cheaper.

66. Answer C.   12

After five videotapes for the free rentals with the membership fee, Emily has $35 − $20 = $15 left and can rent a video for each $2 of this. She can't rent half a tape, so the answer is the whole number of times 2 goes into $15 (that is, seven) plus the original five for a total of 12.

67. Answer D.   The coach cannot carry them uphill.

The passengers were walking because pulling a fully loaded coach uphill through the mud had been too much for the horses. Note that the horses had already come to a stop three times because of the difficulties involved.

68. Answer B.   Liking

The passengers do not have the least liking or *relish* for tramping through the mud; in fact, they don't like it at all!

69. Answer C.   Caused them to come to a halt

Look at the words immediately preceding "brought them to a stand" in the sentence. The "driver rested them" (the horses). How did he rest them? He pulled back on the reins and made them stand still for a little while. In other words, he "caused them to come to a halt."

70. Answer B.   One of the horses

When horses or other draft animals are hitched together, the ones on the driver's left are on the near side; the ones to his right are on the off side. Thus, the near leader that shakes "his head and everything upon it" is the leading horse on the driver's left. As evidence, look at the phrase "everything upon it." The passengers and the driver may be wearing hats, but a hat is just one thing. A draft horse in full harness has all sorts of things hooked up around his head—blinkers, cheek straps, bit, reins. That's what the horse shakes when he tosses his head.

71. Answer D.   36

To figure out the pattern in the numbers given, look at the difference at each step:

$$3 - 1 = 2$$
$$6 - 3 = 3$$
$$10 - 6 = 4$$
$$15 - 10 = 5$$
$$21 - 15 = 6$$

The difference increases by one at each step. The next number in the sequence will be the seventh, and it will be 21 + 7 = 28. The question asks for the *eighth* number, which will be 28 + 8 = 36.

72. Answer B.   1/8

A quarter is 1/4 of *one* dollar, and one dollar is 1/2 of $2. So a quarter is 1/4 of 1/2 of $2; that is, $\frac{1}{4} \times \frac{1}{2} = \frac{1}{8}$.

73. Answer C.   The birth rate decreased steadily from 1960 to 1985.

Check each of the statements, looking for one that you can confirm to be false by looking at the graph:

A. The infant death rate decreased steadily. TRUE. The infant death rate is shown by the gray bars on the graph, and each one is lower than the one before it (to its left).

B. Births exceeded deaths by at least five per thousand for the period shown. TRUE. The line labeled "Birth rate" is always above the 15 per 1,000 line on the graph, while the line labeled "Death rate" is always below or just at the 10 per 1,000 line. The gap between them is always at least five (per 1,000).

C. The birth rate decreased steadily from 1960 to 1985. FALSE. The birth rate line drops from 1960 to 1967, then rises to 1970. The decrease does not continue all the way to 1985.

D. The death rate in 1985 was less than it had been in 1960. Probably TRUE, but hard to tell from the thick lines on the graph—in 1960, the line is close to 10 per 1,000 and in 1985 maybe just a little bit lower than that.

In any case, C is obviously false, and must be the correct choice for this question.

74. Answer B.   2 million

The death rate in 1968 was very close to 10 deaths per thousand, or about 1% (10/1000 = 1/100). Since the population was about 200 million, the number of deaths that year had to be about 1% of 200 million, or

$$\frac{1}{100} \times 200\,\text{million} = 2\,\text{million}.$$

75. Answer C.   40%

In 1960 the infant death rate (given by the gray bar) was about 26 per thousand, and in 1985 it had decreased to about 10 to 11 per thousand. You can make a close guess about the percentage by rounding these numbers to 25 and 10; then the 1985 value is about 10/25 = 2/5 of the 1960 value, and 2/5 = 40%. If you use 26 for the 1960 value and carry out the long division, you can stop as soon as you see that the answer is closer to 40% than to any other of the choices. Be careful to use the gray bars (the infant death rate) and not the lower line, which is the overall death rate.

76. Answer C.   1970

Look on the graph of birth rates for a year between 1960 and 1975 where the curve rises to show a higher birth rate. The bump in the graph occurs at 1970.

77. Answer A.   Diligence

Habit is a customary practice, a regularly followed pattern of behavior: Smoking cigarettes is a bad habit. Choice B is incorrect. Monotony is the boredom that comes from following routine: Doing the same old thing day after day, Martha quickly became fed up with the monotony of her job. Choice C is incorrect. Willfulness is stubbornness in following one's own wishes: The disobedient boy's mother scolded him for his willfulness. Choice D is incorrect. Diligent people stick to what they are doing: He's being diligent and industrious in applying himself to his work. Choice A is correct.

78. Answer C.   Random

Detached means not connected; it can also mean impartial and objective. Sue lives in a detached house, not a condo. As a marriage counselor, Marie tries to remain a detached observer. Choice A is incorrect. Impractical means unrealistic, possibly even useless: Bill constantly came up with ideas for impractical gadgets that never work. Choice B is incorrect. Untidy means not neat: Pigpen's bedroom is not just untidy; it's a total mess. Choice D is incorrect. Random, however, by definition means unplanned or accidental; think of a random sampling. Choice C is correct.

79. Answer B.   Endorse

To dedicate is to devote wholly to a purpose or to set apart: Martin Luther King, Jr., dedicated his life to the cause of civil rights. We dedicate this hall to his memory. Choice A is incorrect. To mediate is to arbitrate or negotiate or intervene: Both labor and management agreed to have an arbitrator mediate their dispute. Choice C is incorrect. To retrieve is to fetch or recover something, to get it back: I threw sticks for my dog to retrieve. Choice D is incorrect. To endorse someone or something, however, by definition is to express support of it. Choice B is correct.

80. Answer B.   24

The area of a triangle is 1/2 (base × height). In this figure, the base is along the line $y = -3$ from $x = -2$ to $x = 4$, and the height is 8 [5 units from the vertex at (2,5) down to the x-axis and 3 more to reach the base]. Therefore, the area is $1/2(6 \times 8) = 48/2 = 24$.

81. Answer B.   160 tons

One ton produces 5/4 pounds of aluminum. Use a proportion equation to find out how many tons, T, are needed for 200 pounds:

$$T : 200 \ = 1 : 5/4$$

T must be the same multiple of 1 ton that 200 pounds is of 5/4 pounds; that is, $T = 200 \div (5/4)$. Dividing by 5/4 is the same as multiplying by 4/5. $T = 200 \times (4/5) = (200 \times 4)/5 = 800/5 = 160$.

82. Answer C.   4 ounces

You have to remember that 1 pound = 16 ounces. With that, the answer is simple; 4 cups of the cheese are 16 ounces, so 1 cup is $1/4 \times 16$ ounces = 4 ounces.

83. Answer D.   20%

The percentage increase is the change (five students more in the second year) divided by the original number of students (25). This is $5/25 = 1/5 = 2/10 = 20/100$ or 20%.

84. Answer C.   Fresno

The column labeled "Normal to Date" gives the amount of rainfall that the cities normally have by this date of the season. The largest value is for Oakland (nearly 7 inches) and the lowest value is the 3.32 inches for Fresno.

85. Answer B.   29%

Oakland has had 5.43 inches of rain in the season so far. The amount of rain it normally gets for the year is the 18.89 inches in the last column of the table—the "season" is the whole year from one July 1st to the next June 30th. Be careful to use this seasonal norm in answering the question ("What percentage of its normal rainfall for the year has Oakland had so far this season?"). That percentage is 5.43/18.89, but before doing a laborious long division, make a rough estimate of the percentage and compare it to the choices given. The easy numbers near 5.43 and 18.89 would be 5/20 (1/4 = 25%) or 6/18 (1/3 = 33%). 6/18 will actually be a bit large, since the numerator 6 is larger than 5.43 *and* the denominator 18 is smaller than 18.89. Either estimate is good enough to eliminate all the choices except B.

86. Answer C. 1 five-dollar bill, 1 one-dollar bill, 2 quarters, and 1 nickel

The man paid $33.45 for the shoes; his change from $40 (the two $20 bills) must come to $40.00 − $33.45 = $6.55. All the answers have 1 five-dollar bill. Taking account of that, there is $6.55 − $5 = $1.55 left to make change for. You can now rule out Choices A and B, which have 2 one-dollar bills—these would give more than $7 in change, which is too much. Choices C and D have a single one-dollar bill; the man needs a further $0.55 in change. Choice C has 2 quarters and 1 nickel (which add up to 2 × 25¢ + 5¢ = 55¢, just what is expected); in contrast, Choice D has 1 quarter and 2 dimes, for a total of 25¢ + 2 × 10¢ = 45¢ in coins. Only Choice C gives the correct change.

87. Answer C. 105%

A quart is 32 ounces and a liter is ~30.3; therefore a quart is a fraction 32/30.3 of a liter. You can see immediately that the percentage has to be greater than 100%. You can either do the long division, to find that 32/30.3 = 1.056, or you can test Choices C and D for which one is closer to giving 32 ounces. 110% of 30.3 means 30.3 + 3.03, so Choice D is more than an ounce too big. But 105% adds exactly half as much (1.51 ounces) to the 30.3; that comes out about 31.8 ounces, close to 32 (and *much* closer than Choice D).

88. Answer B. Chemistry

Notice that the three job descriptions all follow the same form: they begin with a general statement of the nature of the job, go on to give the qualifications for filling the job, and finally conclude with a sentence that lists the courses that it would be useful for someone to have as qualifications for the job. Therefore, when you encounter this question asking which course would be useful for *both* Marine Science Technicians and Port Securitymen, you know just where to look for the answer: go to the last sentence of each job description and compare the two course lists given there. For Marine Science Technician the courses suggested are algebra, trigonometry, chemistry, physics, and typing. For Port Securityman the courses suggested are practical mathematics, chemistry, and English. The only course common to both lists is chemistry. Choice B must be the correct answer.

89. Answer C. Handling explosives

Check each of the four answer choices by looking through the first part of the job description for a Marine Science Technician. Remember, you are looking for something that is NOT a part of the science tech's job. Therefore, if an answer choice is a task the science tech would do, you can eliminate that choice.

A. Analyzing sea conditions. This task is listed in the Marine Science Technician's job description. The last sentence of the description begins "His analysis of weather and sea conditions furnishes advice..." You can cross out Choice A.

B. Collecting meteorological observations. This task appears in the second sentence of the job description: "He makes visual and instrumental weather and oceanographic observations..." You can cross out Choice B.

C. Handling explosives. This is not part of the job description for a Marine Science Technician. (In fact, it is listed in the Port Securityman's job description.) As soon as you come to this answer choice, you know that you have found the task that is NOT part of the technician's job. This is the correct answer to the question.

90. Answer A. Clerk

This question requires you to compare the job description for a Port Securityman with what you know of other (civilian) jobs. If aspects of the civilian job resemble aspects of the Port Securityman's work, you can rule out that answer choice. First look at the Port Securityman's job description. What does he do? He is an expert in *fire prevention and extinguishment*: his job is like a fireman's; you can eliminate Choice B. He is knowledgeable ("well-versed") in the regulations and equipment for *safeguarding* vessels, harbors, and waterfront facilities: his job is like a security guard's; you can eliminate Choice C. He deals with the *storage* and transportation of dangerous cargoes: his job is like a warehouseman's; you can eliminate Choice D. Only Choice A, clerk, is left. A Port Securityman is not someone who specializes in filing and similar office work. The least related civilian job clearly is that of a clerk.

91. Answer C. Manual dexterity

The special abilities useful for a Yeoman are found in the "Qualifications" section of the job description. The second sentence of this section states that "Yeomen should be above average in general learning ability, should possess a degree of manual dexterity, and must be able to work harmoniously with others." The correct answer, therefore, must be one of three qualities: above-average learning ability, manual dexterity, and cooperativeness. ("Plays well with others" is the elementary school report card rating.) Only one of these three positive qualities appears among the answer choices: Choice C, manual dexterity. It is the correct answer.

92. Answer C. 12π square feet

The original flower bed has a diameter of 4 feet and hence a radius of 2 feet. Its area is

$$A = \pi r^2 = \pi(2 \times 2) = 4\pi.$$

If the diameter is doubled, the radius is doubled, to 4 feet. The new circle has area $\pi(4 \times 4) = 16\pi$. However, the question asks how many square feet Jody will add to the flower bed, and so the answer is the difference of the two areas, $16\pi - 4\pi = 12\pi$.

93. Answer C. $12.00

To make a 20% profit on his cost of $90, the grocer must receive 20% = 2/10 of $90 = $18 in addition to the cost. The total sales must be $108. Since one crate is spoiled, each crate must be sold for 1/9 of $108, which is $12.

94. Answer A. The underlined word is spelled correctly.

Do you remember the old spelling rule I before E *except* after C, or when sounded like A, as in "neighbor" and "weigh"?

95. Answer B. The underlined word is spelled incorrectly.

The sentence should read: "On Memorial Day, politicians make speeches in <u>remembrance</u> of those who died for their country."

96. Answer D. Hispanic

The question concerns only the Los Angeles schools, so you can ignore the pie chart on the left. Look for the largest slice of the pie in the chart on the right. The medium gray shaded Hispanic portion is obviously more than half, so all the other segments must be smaller.

97. Answer C.   Asian and Other

This question is a mirror image of the last one; here you need to look in the pie chart on the left (for California average) for the smallest slice of the pie. White is obviously the largest slice, followed by Hispanic and then Black; this leaves Asian and Other as the smallest slice.

98. Answer B.   It was about 1/2 as big.

This question requires you to compare the two pie charts, specfically to compare the size of the gray Hispanic slices in the two pies. In the California average, the Hispanic pieces is less than half, while in Los Angeles it is more than half. So you can rule out Choices C and D right away. It remains to be seen whether the gray slice on the left is half or quarter the size of the one on the right. Try drawing a line cutting the Los Angeles slice in two equal parts, and divide one of these again into two (to get a quarter of the original slice). Because the Los Angeles slice takes up a bit more than half the right-hand pie, half of it will take up a bit more than a quarter, which is just what you see in the left-hand pie.

99. Answer C.   10 hours

It takes four painters 15 hours to do the job. Thus, the job requires 4×15 "painter-hours." Any other combination of workers and times must add up to the same 60 painter-hours to get the job done. For a crew of six painters, this means 60 painter-hours $\div$ 6 painters = 10 hours.

100. Answer C. $10,700

In five years' time the man has paid a total of $5 \times \$1,600 = \$8,000$ to the medical insurance company. They have paid $\$19,200 - 500 = \$18,700$ towards his hospital bill. He has saved the difference, $\$18,700 - \$8,000 = \$10,700$.

LOOKING FOR STUDY STRATEGIES THAT WORK? HAVE WE GOT SECRETS FOR YOU!

Study Tactics

$8.95, Canada *$11.95*
(0-8120-2590-3)
An easy-to-follow plan for sound study habits. Included are pointers for improving writing skills, increasing reading speed, reviewing for exams and taking them, developing good working habits, and much more.

Student Success Secrets, 4th Edition

$8.95, Canada *$11.95*
(0-8120-9488-3)

These sure-fire strategies can increase every student's test scores and raise their grades. Advice covers methods for forming good study habits, retaining information from reading, and taking useful class-room notes. There are also tips to help students do their best when taking exams.

B's & A's in 30 Days

$8.95, Canada *$11.95*
(0-8120-9582-0)
Here's a sure-fire student success system for better grades, less stress, and greater self confidence. The book is divided into thirty short enter-taining, instructive chapters—one for each day of the program. Students will learn how to set goals they can reach, study better in less time, take better classroom notes, and more. Amusing cartoon illustrations keep the mood appropriately light.

You Can Succeed! The Ultimate Study Guide for Students

$5.95, Canada *$7.95*
(0-8120-2084-7)

Encourages students to make a personal pact with themselves for setting goals and achieving them. Topics covered range from lack of motivation and success habits to word power and how to take tests. This handy guide will help students raise their grades and develop good study and working habits that will be of great help throughout their academic life.

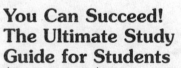

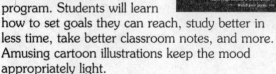

Barron's Educational Series, Inc.
250 Wireless Boulevard
Hauppauge, New York 11788

In Canada:
Georgetown Book Warehouse
34 Armstrong Avenue • Georgetown, Ontario L7G 4R9

Prices subject to change without notice. Books may be purchased at your bookstore, or by mail from Barron's. Enclose check or money order for total amount plus sales tax where applicable and 18% for postage and handling (minimum charge $5.95).
All books are paperback editions.

Visit our website at: barronseduc.com

(#9) R 6/00

MAXIMIZE YOUR MATH SKILLS!

BARRON'S EASY WAY SERIES

Specially structured to maximize learning with a minimum of time and effort, these books promote fast skill building through lively cartoons and other fun features.

ALGEBRA THE EASY WAY
Revised Third Edition
Douglas Downing, Ph.D.
In this one-of-a-kind algebra text, all the fundamentals are covered in a delightfully illustrated adventure story. Equations, exponents, polynomials, and more are explained. 320 pp. (0-8120-9393-3) $12.95, Can. $16.95

CALCULUS THE EASY WAY
Revised Third Edition
Douglas Downing, Ph.D.
Here, a journey through a fantasy land leads to calculus mastery. All principles are taught in an easy-to-follow adventure tale. Included are numerous exercises, diagrams, and cartoons which aid comprehension. 228 pp. (0-8120-9141-8) $12.95, Can. $16.95

GEOMETRY THE EASY WAY
Revised Third Edition
Lawrence Leff
While other geometry books simply summarize basic principles, this book focuses on the "why" of geometry: why you should approach a problem a certain way, and why the method works. Each chapter concludes with review exercises, 288 pp. (0-7641-0110-2) $12.95, Can. $16.95

TRIGONOMETRY THE EASY WAY
Revised Second Edition
Douglas Downing, Ph.D.
In this adventure story, the inhabitants of a faraway kingdom use trigonometry to solve their problems. Covered is all the material studied in high school or first-year college classes. Practice exercises, explained answers and illustrations enhance understanding. 288 pp. (0-8120-4389-8) $13.95, Can. $18.95

FM: FUNDAMENTALS OF MATHEMATICS
Cecilia Cullen and Eileen Petruzillo, editors
Volume 1 (0-8120-2501-6)—
Formulas; Introduction to Algebra; Metric Measurement; Geometry; Managing Money; Probability and Statistics. 384 pp. $19.95, Can. $24.95

BARRON'S MATHEMATICS STUDY DICTIONARY
Frank Tapson, with consulting author, Robert A. Atkins
A valuable homework helper and classroom supplement for middle school and high school students. Presented here are more than 1,000 math definitions, along with worked-out examples. Illustrative charts and diagrams cover everything from geometry to statistics to charting vectors. 128 pp., (0-7641-0303-2) $9.95, Not Available in Canada

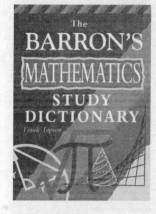

ESSENTIAL MATH
Second Edition
Edward Williams and Robert A. Atkins
Basic math principles everyone should know are made easy by being put into the context of real-life situations. Games and puzzles help make math interesting. Practice exercises appear at the end of every chapter. 384 pp., (0-8120-1337-9) $13.95, Can. $19.50